THE PETROLOGY OF
ARCHAEOLOGICAL ARTEFACTS

The petrology of archaeological artefacts

Edited by

D. R. C. KEMPE

and

ANTHONY P. HARVEY

CLARENDON PRESS · OXFORD
1983

Oxford University Press, Walton Street, Oxford OX2 6DP
London   Glasgow   New York   Toronto
Delhi   Bombay   Calcutta   Madras   Karachi
Kuala Lumpur   Singapore   Hong Kong   Tokyo
Nairobi   Dar es Salaam   Cape Town
Melbourne   Wellington
and associate companies in
Beirut   Berlin   Ibadan   Mexico City

Published in the United States by
Oxford University Press, New York

British Library Cataloguing in Publication Data

The Petrology of archaeological artefacts.
1. Petrology 2. Archaeology
I. Kempe, D. R. C.   II. Harvey, Anthony P.
552'.002493   QE431.2

ISBN 0-19-854418-9

Library of Congress Cataloging in Publication Data

Main entry under title:

The Petrology of archaeological artefacts.

Bibliography: p.
Includes index.
1. Petrology in archaeology – Addresses, essays, lectures.
I. Kempe, D. R. C. (David Ronald Charles), 1927–0000.
II. Harvey, Anthony, P.
CC79. P4P47 1982   930.1   82-7976
ISBN 0-19-854418-9   AACR2

Typeset by Oxford Verbatim Limited
and Printed in Great Britain
by The Thetford Press Limited, Thetford, Norfolk

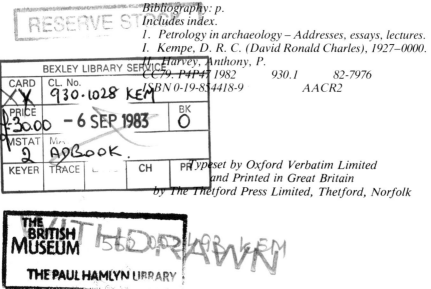

Foreword

There is nothing new in the relationship between geology and archaeology, for ever since William Buckland excavated Kirkland Cave and investigated the 'Red Lady' (a young male, in fact) of Paviland, about 160 years ago, geologists have intruded into the domains of the archaeologist. This is wholly appropriate, for where a site that is being studied by excavation antedates any written record, there is only one way in which it may be investigated. The archaeologist follows the traditional method of the geologist tackling a stratigraphical problem. He or she applies the basic law propounded by William Smith about 170 years ago, the *Law of Superposition*. The archaeologist will talk of having established a stratigraphy and when he says that Layer A is 'sealed' by Layer B he means exactly the same as the geologist who states that Layer B rests disconformably on A. A post-hole cut into an occupation level bears a similar relationship to relative time as does an igneous plug bursting through stratified sediments. Archaeological field-work is now painstaking and methodical and bears little relation to the hurried trench or central shaft cut into a burial mound, the relative success of which was judged by the variety and value of the funerary goods discovered.

The development of the scientific method in excavation, and in the recording of its results, is as nothing to the revolution which has taken place in the follow-up to those excavations. The archaeologist may now seek the help of the geologist, mineralogist, zoologist, botanist, soil scientist, chemist, physicist, astronomer, or civil engineer. The isotopes of carbon, or the decay chains of radioactive uranium or potassium, or even the changes in the amino-acids of organisms may be harnessed in order to put dates to the discoveries. A piece of wood showing annual growth-rings may be placed in time by the dendrochronologist who may also be able to tell a little about the climate of the period from it. The facts of this research may be stored in a computerized data bank and retrieved in a variety of selections and arrangements, for future analysis.

Environmental archaeology is a new and rapidly growing subject. By using such of the many disciplines that can help in a particular case study, it seeks to reconstruct the mode of life of the people and to assess the environment in which they lived. There is a growing body of young archaeologists not only trained in their main subject but able personally to apply one or several of the assisting disciplines which have been mentioned above, to the refinement of the conclusions and the testing of their theories. In brief, Archaeology, or should one say Prehistoric Archaeology, is now a science, rather than an art.

It is the tremendous progress of archaeology towards scientific techniques and methods which justifies this book, dealing only with the application of one of the serving disciplines, the branch of geology known as petrology. Admittedly petrology in this case is interpreted widely. For more than 30 years I have been investigating the petrology of stone artefacts, mainly axes, adzes, and perforated axes or hammers, with an occasional flirtation with a quern or a grindstone, a hone, building stone, Roman tesserae, and even sometimes a Victorian fake antique. The impulses behind this work have always been the desire to assess the efficiency of the tool for the purpose of use, the problems of its manufacture, where it was made, and how it was dispersed from its point of origin. All these things and many more are discussed and elaborated in this book, and I am greatly impressed, after reading the manuscript, by the depth of research that has gone into finding examples of the application of petrological techniques from all over the world. This book has enlarged my vision and dispelled my ignorance about so many things. I am sure it will have a similar effect on the young student and the older person rich in experience, upon the professional and the amateur enthusiast.

F. W. Shotton, Professor Emeritus
Department of Geology
The University
Birmingham

Preface

As editors we would like to thank all the contributors for their tolerance. Any review of this nature depends on ready access to a good library and it is therefore a pleasure to record our thanks to the staff of the Department of Library Services at the British Museum (Natural History) and to the library staff of the Institute of Archaeology, University of London. We also thank the many members of the staff of the Department of Mineralogy, British Museum (Natural History) for discussion and help and in particular we owe a great debt of gratitude to Dr A. C. Bishop, Keeper of Mineralogy, for his constant encouragement throughout the project, his friendly and knowledgeable assistance so freely and willingly given, and for critically reading the chapters emanting from his Department.

F. A. Hassan (*American Antiquity* **44**, 267–70 (1979)) has recorded that petrological studies can yield much of value in the elucidation of manufacturing techniques, source areas of archaeological raw materials, and the spatial range of site catchment areas. Hence, such studies are of considerable value and importance to archaeologists and geologists with an archaeological interest, to all of whom, both professional and amateur, this book is dedicated in the hope that it will provide both a foundation and stimulus to the petrological study of archaeological artefacts.

For explanation of geological terms, the reader is recommended to the *Glossary of geology*, 2nd edition, edited by Robert L. Bates and Julia A. Jackson, and published in 1980 by the American Geological Institute, Falls Church, Va.

London 1981   D.R.C.K. and A.P.H.

Contents

Contributors

E. Youngblood Anthony, Department of Geosciences, University of
    Arizona, Tucson, Arizona.

Don Brothwell, Institute of Archaeology, University of London,
    31–34 Gordon Square, London.

J. R. Cann, Department of Geology, The University, Newcastle upon Tyne.

W. A. Cummins, Department of Geology, The University, University Park,
    Nottingham.

B. J. Fredriksson, Department of Mineral Sciences, Smithsonian
    Institution, Washington DC.

K. Fredriksson, Department of Mineral Sciences, Smithsonian Institution,
    Washington DC.

Anthony P. Harvey, Department of Library Services, British Museum
    (Natural History), Cromwell Road, London.

M. P. Jones, Department of Mineral Resources Engineering, Royal School
    of Mines, Imperial College of Science and Technology, London.

D. R. C. Kempe, Department of Mineralogy, British Museum (Natural
    History), Cromwell Road, London.

D. T. Moore, Department of Mineralogy, British Museum (Natural
    History), Cromwell Road, London.

F. W. Shotton, Department of Geology, The University, Birmingham.

J. A. Templeman, Institute of Geological Sciences, Exhibition Road,
    London.

D. F. Williams, DOE Ceramic Project, Department of Archaeology, The
    University, Southampton.

A. R. Woolley, Department of Mineralogy, British Museum (Natural
    History), Cromwell Road, London.

Introduction

The editors

Each year the international earth science magazine *Geotimes* provides a review of significant work and developments in the preceding year in the major areas of geology. In the review of 1976 a new category was added: 'Archaeological Geology' (Rapp 1977). In the same year there were moves to establish an archaeological geology division of the Geological Society of America and Davidson and Shackley produced their volume entitled *Geoarchaeology*.

However, the application of the natural sciences to archaeology is not a new development. As Don Brothwell states in the first chapter of this book: 'Geology has a long history of association with archaeology, especially where they share common ground in environmental and palaeontological studies of the Pleistocene'. A recent example of such co-operation is provided by Butzer (1965). The application of petrology (the branch of geology dealing with the origin, occurrence, structure, and history of rocks (Bates and Jackson 1980)) and petrological techniques to archaeology have not received the same attention although it is appreciated that they can be of considerable value in establishing the provenance of artefacts and hence in elucidating exchange mechanisms, as well as providing geographical and chronological evidence of man's activities.

Textbooks devoted to artefacts generally ignore the value of petrological studies and often the geological content of archaeological monographs and papers, especially as regards the identification of rocks and minerals, and the use of correct terminology, has not been of the highest standard. However Evans, as early as 1897, did often identify rocks types and more recently Hodges (1964) has attempted to show the value of petrological work.

Since the war many texts have examined the value of the natural sciences, or parts of them, to archaeology. A major contribution to the field is *Science and archaeology* edited by Brothwell and Higgs (1963).

Many texts briefly examine the role of petrology and archaeology (Aitken 1961; Allibone 1970; Beck 1974; Berger 1970; Biek 1963; Brill 1971; Carter 1978; Drews 1978; Goffer 1980; Pyddoke 1963; Tite 1972) whilst Rosenfeld (1965) has attempted the only work of a similar nature to this volume, though he was concerned mainly with the macroscopic description of rocks and minerals. Compilations concerned with dating, especially in the treatment of obsidian hydration (e.g. Fleming 1976; Michels 1973), also impinge on some of the papers in this volume. The middle to late 1970s have thus witnessed the advent of geoarchaeology as a discipline in its own right (Davidson and Shackley 1976; Rapp 1975, 1977; Shackley 1977). Shackley (1979) has provided a succint review of the field and proposed a model for earth science application to archaeology (Fig. 0.1).

The use of petrological techniques in archaeology is not new, however, for, as Shotton and Hendry (1979) state in their review of this developing field, the 'earliest appraisals were made by visual inspection and possibly the first was the recognition by Sir William Dugdale in 1656 that a chipped and polished stone axe from Oldbury in north Warwickshire which he figured and described, was made of flint which did not occur 'in this part of the Countrie, nor within XI miles from hence'. In 1968 Shotton provided a review of prehistoric man's use of stone in Britain, whilst other accounts of

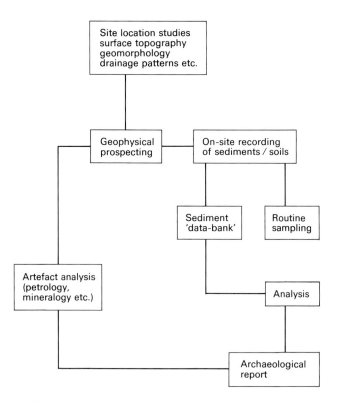

Fig. 0.1. Geoarchaeology – a model for earth science applications in archaeology.
(After Shackley 1979.)

the value of petrology are those by Gordus, Fink, Hill, Purdy, and Wilcox (1967); Jope (1953); North (1938); Štelcl and Malina (1975); and Wallis (1955). We believe, however, that this is the first review volume to be devoted solely to the contribution of petrology to archaeology. It is not concerned with either the artistic or practical uses of artefacts or with the discussion of the philosophy, technology, and history behind the development of man's use of stone, which rightly fall within the domain of the archaeologist. The following chapters are intended to provide a comprehensive review of the current state of knowledge of the petrology of archaeological artefacts.

The first chapter by Brothwell provides a review of the entire field, while the two following chapters, on techniques and raw materials, are intended to be reference sources for the sections which follow. However, where a particular technique, for example dating by obsidian hydration, is intimately linked to and described in a particular chapter it has been dealt with only generally in Chapter 2. The remaining chapters review particular topics.

Those covering a broad range, for example building and sculptural stones, necessarily reflect the depth of interest by petrologists in certain materials, e.g. marbles and soapstones.

References

Aitken, M. J. (1961). *Physics and archaeology*. Interscience, New York. 2nd edn 1974. Clarendon Press, Oxford.

Allibone, T. E. (1970). *The impact of the natural sciences on archaeology*. Oxford University Press.

Bates, R. L. and Jackson, J. A. (ed.) (1980). *Glossary of geology*. 2nd edn. American Geological Institute, Falls Church, Va.

Beck, C.W. (ed.) (1974). Archaeological chemistry. *Advances in Chemistry* **138**, 1–254.

Berger, R. (ed.) (1970). *Scientific methods in medieval archaeology*. University of California Press. (*UCLA Center for Medieval and Renaissance Studies Contributions IV*.)

Biek, L. (1963). *Archaeology and the microscope*. Lutterworth Press, London.

Brill, R. H. (ed.) (1971). *Science and archaeology*. MIT Press, Cambridge, Mass.

Brothwell, D. and Higgs, E. (ed.) (1963). *Science and archaeology*. Thames and Hudson, London. (2nd edn 1969.)

Butzer, K. W. (1965). *Environment and archaeology. An introduction to Pleistocene geography*. Methuen, London.

Carter, G. F. (ed.) (1978). Archaeological chemistry II. *Advances in Chemistry* **171**, 1–389.

Davidson, D. A. and Shackley, M. L. (ed.) (1976). *Geoarchaeology*. Duckworth, London.

Drews, G. (1978). Archäometrie – ein interdisziplinäres Arbeitsgebiet. *Fortschritte der Mineralogie* **55**, 197–238.

Dugdale, W. (1656). *The antiquities of Warwickshire*. Thomas Warren, London.

Evans, J. (1897). *The ancient stone implements, weapons and ornaments of Great Britain*. 2nd edn rev. Longman, Green, London.

Fleming, S. (1976). *Dating in archaeology*. Dent, London.

Goffer, Z. (1980). *Archaeological chemistry: a source book on the applications of chemistry in archaeology*. Wiley, New York.

Gordus, A. A., Fink, W. C., Hill, M. E., Purdy, J. C., and Wilcox, T. R. (1967). Identification of the geologic origins of archaeological artifacts. *Archaeometry* **10**, 87–96.

Hodges, H. (1964). *Artifacts. An introduction to early materials and technology*. Baker, London.

Jope, E. M. (1953). History, archaeology and petrology. *Advancement of Science* **9**, 432–5.

Michels, J. W. (1973). *Dating methods in archaeology*. Seminar Press, New York.

North, T. J. (1938). Geology for archaeologists. *Archaeological Journal* **94**, 73–115.

Pyddoke, E. (ed.) (1963). *The scientist and archaeology*. Phoenix House, London.

Rapp, G. (1975). The archaeological field staff: the geologist. *Journal of Field Archaeology* **2**, 229–37.

—— (1977). Archaeological geology. *Geotimes* **22**, 16.

Rosenfeld, A. (1965). *The inorganic raw materials of antiquity*. Weidenfeld and Nicholson, London.

Shackley, M. (1977). *Rocks and man*. Allen and Unwin, London.

—— (1979). Geoarchaeology. Polemic on a progressive relationship. *Naturwissenschaften* **66**, 429–32.

Shotton, F. W. (1968). Prehistoric man's use of stone in Britain. *Proceedings of the Geologists' Association* **79**, 477–91.

—— Hendry, G. L. (1979). The developing field of petrology in archaeology. *Journal of Archaeological Science* **6**, 75–84.

Štelcl, J. and Malina, J. (1975). Základy petroarchéologie. Universita J. E. Purkine v. Brrie.

Tite, M. S. (1972). *Methods of physical examination in archaeology*. Seminar Press, New York.

Wallis, F. S. (1955). Petrology as an aid to prehistoric and medieval archaeology. *Endeavour* **14**, 146–51.

1. Petrology and archaeology: an introduction

Don Brothwell

It may well be that in another hundred years most of archaeology will be conducted in a precise scientific manner, but until then it seems necessary to demonstrate the importance of scientific work within archaeology which is derived from, or influenced by, other fields of science. Geology has a long history of association with archaeology, especially where they share common ground in environmental and palaeontological studies of the Pleistocene. However, petrological work is only now being appreciated for the breadth and wealth of information it can provide to archaeologists.

Admittedly, Stukeley studied the rocks of Stonehenge as early as 1740 (Shotton 1969) and the nineteenth century saw increasing effort put into the proper identification of rocks used for artefacts. The amount and character of this work seems to permit the creation of a new term 'geoarchaeology', to indicate the scope of this aspect of archaeology (Davidson and Shackley 1976; Shackley 1979). Hassan (1979) considers that geoarchaeology encompasses:
1. Locating archaeological sites.
2. Evaluating the geomorphic landscape for site catchment activities and site location.
3. Studying regional stratigraphic and microstratigraphic materials for relative dating and recognition of lateral and vertical distribution of activity areas.
4. Analysing sediments for the elucidation of site-forming processes and quantification of microarchaeological remains.
5. Analysing palaeoenvironments.
6. Studying artefacts to determine manufacturing practices, procurement range, trade, and exchange networks.
7. Modelling cultural/environmental interactions.
8. Conserving archaeological resources.
9. Geochronology.
Clearly there is much to geoarchaeology beyond petrological studies, but this chapter provides an introductory review of the range of information specifically on rocks and minerals which have relevance to archaeology, whether prehistoric or more recent cultures. It is not the intention, therefore, to give comprehensive mention of all the rock varieties utilized by

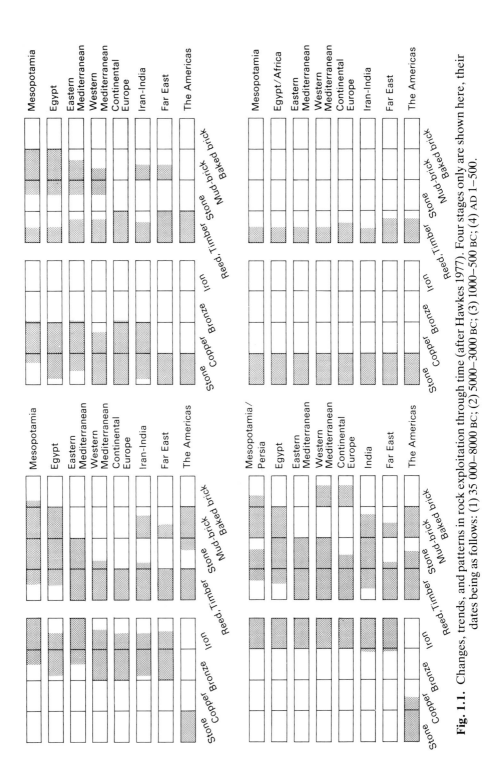

Fig. 1.1. Changes, trends, and patterns in rock exploitation through time (after Hawkes 1977). Four stages only are shown here, their dates being as follows: (1) 35 000–8000 BC; (2) 5000–3000 BC; (3) 1000–500 BC; (4) AD 1–500.

earlier peoples – an enormous range anyway – but to select examples to demonstrate the versatility of man in his exploitation of geological resources. It is also relevant to look for possible trends which may have occurred in the exploitation of rock resources at different times and in different parts of the world (Fig. 1.1).

The use of stone by pre-metal or Stone Age cultures

On present evidence, it is very difficult to establish when tool-making began in the hominids. There is growing information on the early occurence of stone tools, but to what extent might wood and bone have been used prior to the discovery of the non-perishable and texturally strong nature of stone for implements? Isaac (1978) has discussed these 'first geologists', and demonstrates that by about 1.5 million years ago stone tool production was occurring near a number of hominid sites. Clark (1970) and others had previously indicated that in the early Oldowan and later Acheulian culture phases, a wide variety of rocks were used, including limestone, chert, and quartzite. Other African Stone Age sites further demonstrated the use of diabase, indurated shale, ferricrete, sandstone, flint, dolerite, jasper, silcrete, chalcedony, and obsidian. One or two of these rocks, such as limestone and sandstone, are surprising in the list and tools from them seem unlikely to have remained functional for long. Choice of materials is clearly a recurring theme, and it is certainly not always clear why particular rocks were used when better alternatives seem to have been available. At times, this may have been a result of mis-identification by the user. For example, some Palaeo-Indian groups in South America (Lanning 1970) were using not only chert, quartzite, obsidian, basalt, felsite, and welded tuff, but also a silicified limestone – a rock which probably was not quickly distinguishable from some other limestones.

In a later Stone Age site from the Kafue of southern Africa, Gabel (1965) established that most of the raw material was local, except for imported chalcedony and sandstone. Quartz and quartzite pebbles were frequently used, and Gabel notes a 'significant differential in the proportion of quartz and quartzite represented by the percussion-flaked artefacts on the one hand and the cores, flakes and blades on the other' (p. 49). This suggested to him that this hunting community attempted to select better quality, more easily worked, stones for their tools. In the case of about thirty hammerstones, quartzite and gneiss were used; while querns were basalt and quartzite, and thirty-eight hand rubbers were mainly of quartzite, basalt, diorite, and gneiss, with one sandstone specimen.

Moving through time to the Neolithic of Britain, the evidence of rock use in the Windmill Hill and Avebury area of Wiltshire is illuminating (Smith 1965). As might be expected in an area where flint is easy to find, over 2800 tools were made of this siliceous material. It is interesting to note that the

	K/Ca	Ti/Ca	Fe/Sr	Rb/Sr	Y/Sr	Zr/Sr	Mahalanobis' distance from Nijosan group
Ikegami 1–3	2·0	−0·5	−1·1	0·1	3·7	−0·3	19·3
Ikegami 1–4	0·1	0·4	−1·7	0·6	0·2	0·4	4·8
Ikegami 4–2	2·1	−0·3	−2·6	−1·7	−0·5	−0·9	24·0
Ikegami 4–2′	3·9	−1·3	−3·9	−1·7	−0·2	0·2	71·6
Ikegami 5–1	0·8	−1·9	−2·0	0·1	−0·1	2·2	34·8
Ikegami 6–1	−1·8	−1·3	−3·0	0·2	−0·5	4·0	48·2
Uryudo 1	−1·5	−1·5	−0·8	−0·5	0·1	−1·3	8·2
Uryudo 2	−0·1	0·2	−1·8	−2·2	−0·4	−0·6	13·1
Uryudo 3	−1·2	−0·3	−0·7	3·1	0·0	−0·6	14·9
Tano 1	−2·4	−2·2	1·1	3·7	−0·1	1·0	22·7
Tano 2	−1·2	−0·7	0·6	−0·9	1·2	−1·3	11·4
Tano 3	−1·6	−1·2	−1·7	0·6	−0·4	0·2	8·5
Kaminoshima 1	−0·5	−0·2	−0·9	3·0	−0·4	−0·5	13·6
Mukonosho 1	0·1	0·7	−0·1	2·7	−0·3	1·7	8·8
Kutsube 1	−1·4	−0·4	−0·9	−0·2	2·2	−1·7	19·0
Kamo 1	24·4	−1·2	0·6	8·0	3·8	16·2	1480

Fig. 1.2. Map of western Japan showing the location of geological sources of sanukite (o), and archaeological sites with implement samples. Below is shown part of the element analysis (normalized deviations of peak ratios) of implements from one area, as well as D² values showing noticeable variation (After Higashimura and Warashina 1975.)

finding of various implements which were foreign to the Cretaceous geology of the area provided the initial impetus for the initiation and work of the Sub-Committee on the Petrological Identification of Stone Axes (SW Group). On the basis of their petrology, implements were identified from Cornwall, Westmorland, Great Langdale, and possibly Wales. Other objects were also made of dolerite, rhyolite, slate, tonalite, tuffs, schists, and quartzite from other areas. Most of this material was derived from beds within a 48 km radius. Sedimentary rocks included flint, chert, limestone, a variety of sandstones, ferruginous grit, and sarsen. Rather surprisingly,

Chalk was also used, perhaps because it was easily carved, the objects found including cups, figurines, phalli, and symbolic axes. The excavator concludes that such easily carved material 'afforded an opportunity for the expression of artistic impulses and symbolism otherwise scarcely represented in the surviving remains of neolithic cultures' in southern England.

Although the petrological identification of particular types of stone tool has received extensive study in Britain (Clough and Cummins 1979), it should be noted that similar revealing work is now being undertaken in relation to very different peoples and cultures. In the case of sanukite tools excavated in Japan (Higashimura and Warashina 1975), geochemical analyses and the application of multivariate statistics to these results have proved a useful way of establishing the locality origins of these tools (Fig. 1.2). The stone choice and perceptiveness of early Maori peoples is demonstrated in the recent study of side-hafted adzes from New Zealand (Moore, Keyes, and Orchiston 1979). This type of adze is essentially a canoe-building tool, and it was demonstrated from the study that argillites and basalt were particularly favoured (Fig. 1.3) for this type of regular cutting work.

Rock use in more recent cultures

With the evolution of more advanced cultures, including those using metals, there seems likely to have been varying adjustments in the use of stone. But stone tools were still used in a variety of ways, and ornamentation increased in association with the increasing construction of larger stone buildings and urban developments. Referring to the trends outlined in Fig. 1.1, concern is now with the technological stages 3 and 4.

Examples of the general use of stone in advanced societies are the 386 objects (statues, vases, sarcophagi, stelae) listed and displayed in the Egyptian collection in Cairo at the turn of the century (Maspero 1903). Although the petrological divisions are not as precise as they could be, it is clear from the relative frequencies of the rocks (Fig. 1.4) that even excluding building stones, a variety were still in use. In particular limestone and 'granite' were favoured, and it is impressive that large highly polished statues and monuments were made of igneous rock by such cultures, without advanced machinery for quarrying and preparing the stone (Fig. 1.5). Far less variety is seen in the rocks used in the tombs, sculptures, and other materials described from Roman York, for instance (Royal Commission on Historical Monuments 1962). About 70 per cent of the objects were gritstone, 20 per cent limestone, and the rest were Magnesian Limestone and occasionally sandstone and marble. From Maiden Castle in Dorset (Wheeler 1943) there were numerous stone objects of Roman and Iron Age date. There were 208 loom weights, surprisingly of Chalk, and 94 objects of Kimmeridge Shale. The stone for 63 querns was mainly of local origin,

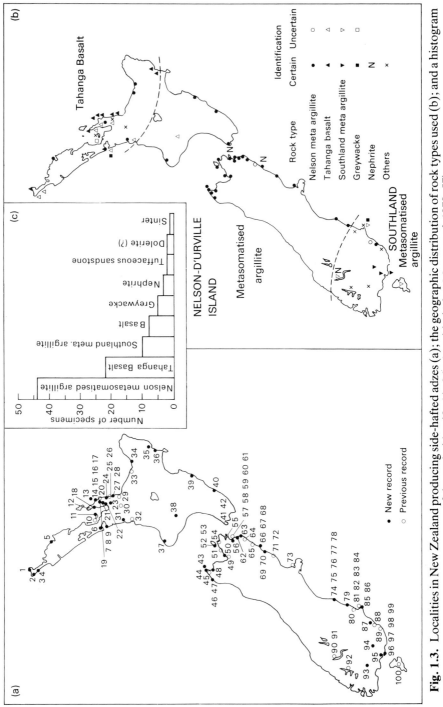

Fig. 1.3. Localities in New Zealand producing side-hafted adzes (a); the geographic distribution of rock types used (b); and a histogram of the rocks identified in 96 adzes (c). (After Moore *et al.* 1979: 57)

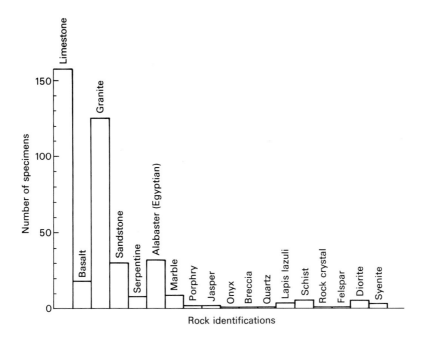

Fig. 1.4. Rocks used by early Egyptian societies, as evidenced by objects listed in Cairo Museum in 1903.

including sarsen, silicified conglomerate, chert, limestone (16 cases!), sandstone/gritstone, and dolomitic conglomerate. In view of the long history of stone use for grinding corn, it is very surprising that quite a number of the querns were of limestone. These would certainly have added plenty of unintentional calcium to the diet but presumably they would have needed regular replacement. Alternatively they may have been less abrasive on the teeth, and thus before accusing this early community of not being perceptive as to the qualities of stone best fitted for querns, it might well be questioned as to whether limestone might not even have been preferred by some?

The apparent inappropriate use of materials can be raised again in relation to the manufacture of stone lamps by the earlier inhabitants of Kodiak Island, Alaska (Heizer 1956). Assembling all types of lamp together (500–1750 AD), the distribution is as follows:

Diorite	Granite	Sandstone	Basalt	Andesite	Soapstone	Diabase
43	56	20	4	3	1	3

Other materials used included slate (as knives, flensing, and ulo blades), limestone or marble (for pendants/beads), and gypsum (labrets), as well as

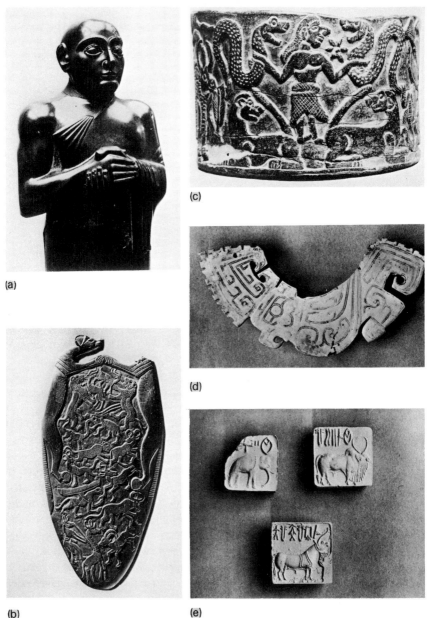

Fig. 1.5. Examples of worked stone objects. (a) Sumerian portrait in diorite, 2100 BC; (b) slate palette from Heirakonpolis, Egypt, c. 2900 BC; (c) Sumerian steatite bowl, c. 2700 BC; (d) Chinese jade ornament of the Shang Dynasty; (e) Steatite seals from Mohenjodaro. (a), (c), (d), and (e) are courtesy of the British Museum; (b) is courtesy of the Ashmolean Museum, Oxford.

jet or black cannel coal (labrets) and lignite (beads/pendants). The easiest materials to work for lamps would have been limestone, slate, soapstone, and sandstone (excluding the carbonaceous rocks), yet granite and diorite were preferred. The possibility of heat damage may have excluded the use of slate, but why not use the other materials? Frost damage is another factor which is relevant in evaluating materials, and possibly fragility is important if objects must be packed or simply regularly moved. Durability combined with heat resistance might then have been the critical selective factors in this case.

The evaluation of the 'worth' of a material to an early society may be difficult to assess from the standpoint of the latter part of the twentieth century. For example, shale and lignite might now be rated as materials of limited 'worth' in material culture terms, and yet they were used in a variety of ways. Prehistoric shale beads have been found in a number of contexts in Wiltshire (Smith 1965; Smith and Simpson 1966). Over a hundred lignite beads were found in a Wessex grave in Hampshire (Ashbee 1967). Considerable use of shale objects was made in Roman times in Dorset (Calkin 1955; 1973). Shale armlet production appears to have been a significant Romano-British industry in the Isle of Purbeck area, perhaps with its origins in the Iron Age. This appears to have been the equivalent of the jet armlets which were 'popular' among Hallstatt peoples of the continent. Armlets of Kimmeridge shale were transported (some would say 'traded') as far away as Leicester, Corbridge, and Penmaenmaur. This shale was also used in Roman furniture (Liversidge 1955), as exemplified by finds of table tops (Silchester) and table legs (from over eight sites).

Rocks and minerals of special value

Rock use was probably established early in the hominids, and was certainly widespread by the emergence of *Homo erectus* (c. 1500 000–400 000 years ago). As societies advanced into the later prehistoric phases that eventually gave rise to urban complexes, rocks became of value in the production of a wide variety of material objects in different early societies. Even with the use of naturally occurring metals, or the extraction of others, non-metallic stone tools and other equipment were still to be found, and of course rocks were important alternatives to wood in the construction of buildings. Early peoples were at least to some extent aware not only of the technological qualities of rocks – their value for quern stones, lamps, or figurines – but also of their value as actual or potential scarcity items, or at least to be prized for particular qualities. The beautifully worked jet necklaces in the stone cists at Balcalk and Mountstuart House (Anderson 1886; Munro 1897) could not have been common items. In the Shetland Isles, communities from the Neolithic to the Norse period were aware of the unusual and uncommon commodity, steatite, and made robust vessels and beads from it (Wainwright 1962). At the site of Kayatha in central India, steatite was similarly valued, and in one pot there were 40 000 microbeads of this material, dated to c. 2000–1800 BC (Ansari and Dhavalikar 1971). Yet again, one can find its use by Amerindian communities, as exemplified by the pipes, incised jars and sea mammal carvings from sites in California (Fig. 1.6).

Numerous minerals could be listed in the same way. Lapis lazuli, valued in jewellery-making throughout the Ancient East, is derived from only a few deposits and yet has a considerable distribution. Sarianidi (1971) has discussed the spread of lapis lazuli objects from just one of the source areas in Badakshan and it can be seen that considerable distances have been covered in the transportation of this mineral by man (Fig. 1.7). Some of the objects date back to the second half of the fourth millenium BC (see also Jones p. 347 in this volume).

From the New World, there is the example of the special use of the clay mineral attapulgite by the Maya of Mesoamerica. It would seem that the durable pigment Maya Blue, used in decorating pottery, murals, and other art work, is composed of a mixture of this uncommon mineral and blue indigo dye. Evidence of this has been found in the Yucatán, the Petén, highland Guatemala, and central Mexico (Arnold and Bohor 1975) and is

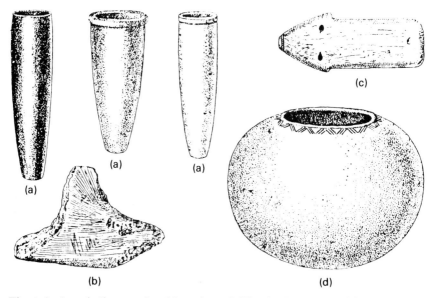

Fig. 1.6. Amerindian steatite objects from California. Objects are: (a) pipes; (b) is a killer whale (?); (c) may be another sea mammal; (d) is a jar with incised decoration. (After Martin, Quimby, and Collier 1967.)

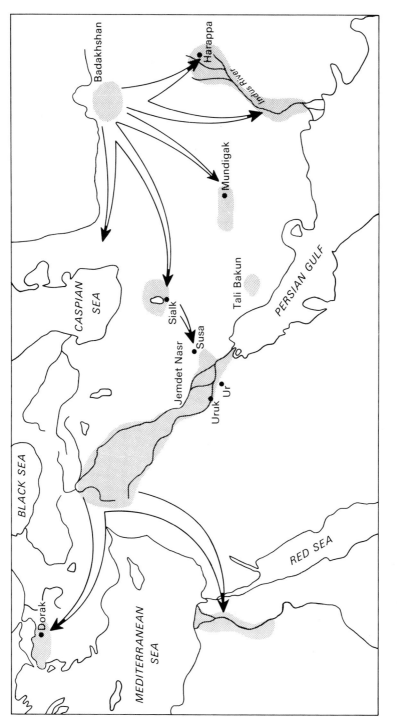

Fig. 1.7. Map showing the possible routes for the spread of lapis lazuli in the Ancient East. (After Sariandi 1971.)

especially associated with Classic and Post-Classic times (AD 300–1500). It is interesting that sources of the material were not known in the Mayan area until comparatively recently, but now a number of deposits have been located. One of these, at the village of Sacalum, is thought to have been worked extensively in antiquity (Fig. 1.8). Ethnohistoric evidence suggests that this 'white earth' (locally called *sak lu'um*) was not only used in the production of Maya Blue, but was also regarded as having a medicinal value.

A very different pigment, and one which may well have been a serious health hazard, was the mercury ore, cinnabar. In his study of the Hohokam peoples of Arizona, Haury (1976) suggests that these Amerindians used this mercury compound as body paint, following the exploitation of the Dome Rock cinnabar deposits in northern Yuma County.

The evaporites have tended to be used in very different ways. Gypsum was exploited and used as a form of cement by the early Indus valley people at Mohenjodaro (Prakashi and Rawat 1965). Gypsum packing was used by the Romans as coffin 'fillings' and appears to have assisted in the preservation not only of the skeleton, but of body hair as well. Salt has a universal taste appeal, and could well have been used in at least a casual way since Palaeolithic times. It probably began to assume an economic importance (Fig. 1.9) by the Neolithic (Nenquin 1961) and by European Iron Age times, Hallstatt and other centres of rock salt mining were evidence of its status as a valued mineral (although this does not mean that it was a generally used condiment). In China, salt first became of economic value, under state monopoly, in the seventh century BC (Chiang 1975). Although much of the salt was derived from the sea, inland exploitation accounted for 7 per cent of the national total.

Perhaps it would be more appropriate to conclude this section by briefly

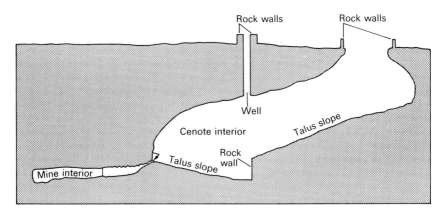

Fig. 1.8. Cross-section of the attapulgite 'mine' (extending from a cenote) at Saculum, Yucatan. (After Arnold and Bohor 1975.)

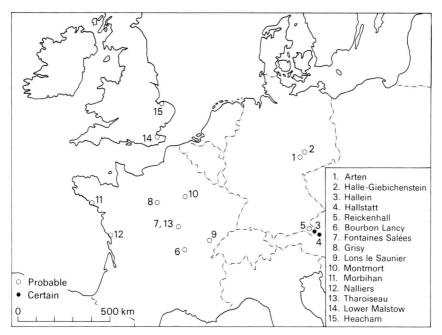

Fig. 1.9. Neolithic sites which may be linked with early salt exploitation in Europe. (After Nenquin 1961.)

considering the most precious of all minerals, the diamond. Unlike some minerals used in jewellery, it appears only to have been recognized for its special properties and valued as a rare stone by about the fourth century BC. Initially it was from India that the exportation of diamonds began, and the stones found their way to Babylon, Mesopotamia, Syria, Israel, Egypt, and Ceylon. Some idea of the 'diamond routes' established by the third century BC is shown in Fig. 1.10. In more recent Indian cultures, large diamonds were indicators of rank. Pliny the Elder was aware of the extreme hardness of diamonds, and since Roman times a considerable folk mythology has grown up around this stone. Diamonds in the Roman World were also prized for their magical powers. A splendid example of the 'middle man' in early commerce is to be seen in the re-exportation of diamonds from Rome to China, the stones being set in iron holders as a tool for cutting jade and drilling pearls (Bruton 1978).

The nature of quarrying and mining

Quarrying and mining were stimulated in response to demands by members of the local community for rock or as a result of the material acquiring a

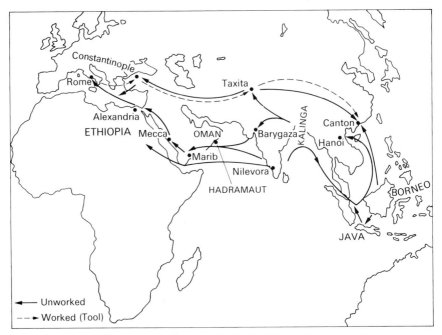

Fig. 1.10. Tentative reconstruction of early diamond routes. First to third century BC. (After Bruton 1978.)

trade or exchange value. It would be out of place here to discuss in detail the purely technological factors related to the extraction of the geological deposits, but a brief mention is needed in order to indicate the extent and antiquity of such operations. Forbes (1966) has reviewed this field extensively, giving a wealth of information on such a diversity of topics as the mining of flint at Grimes Graves, the stone quarries of Ancient Egypt, and the shaft and tunnel complex related to the finding of copper ore at Salzburg.

Summers (1969), in a little-known work on ancient mining in Rhodesia and adjacent areas, makes a new contribution to the study of ore exploitation in one area in one particular period. These generally Iron Age sites represent native ('Mashona') workings, and are quite extensive. The 'mines' were the result of working fruitful localities for nodules of malachite (with chalcocite), and at lower depths also bornite. Gold was found (by the seventh century AD) and by the second century AD the occurrence of iron slag demonstrates the growing importance of this metal. Trans-Zambezi trade in copper had developed by the seventh century AD.

From the Greek and Roman world there is a wealth of evidence of quarrying and mining, discussed most recently by Healy (1978) and Hopper (1979). The extraction of mineral resources from the earth was of great importance in the economy of early Greece. Precious metals were widely searched for, and eventually the use of iron ore was widespread. Marble was recognized for its monumental and ornamental qualities and was quarried extensively. Emery abrasives were employed in marble working. About 490 BC the Pentelic marble quarries were opened near Athens. Previously, this source had been little exploited, but it now permitted a reduction in imported marble and the eventual rebuilding of the Parthenon (Morris 1974). Both for Greece and Rome, the evidence of the search for gold, silver, copper, lead, mercury, marble, and other materials is derived from literary references, the objects of their material culture, and from ancient mining sites themselves, where spoil heaps can at times still be identified. A considerable number of the sites exploited by the Romans had already been worked for a long time by the Greeks and Phoenicians. An idea of the number and geographical extent of these mining areas which were in use in Classical times is shown in Healy's (1978) maps (Figs. 1.11 and 1.12).

A very different example of mining is to be seen in the ancient clay 'mine' at Yo'K'at in the Yucatan, Mexico (Arnold and Bohor 1977). Between AD 800–1000, clay at this site was dug for the purpose of pottery making. Surprisingly, although raw materials like obsidian are quite well studied, clay sources are often not so well defined, although it is clearly important at times to know the sources of clay in order to be able to evaluate the way in which local pottery has travelled or been traded (see Chapter 10).

As regards Mayan needs for monumental and building stone, Graham and Williams (1971) show that the situation was not altogether simple. In the Maya lowlands there are massive limestone deposits which have clearly been used in building, and quarries are sometimes near to the actual sites. Sandstone and grey slate are occasional alternative materials. Also, from the Copan and Quirigua areas, the local ignimbrites and sandstones were quarried (ignimbrite being preferred to the local limestone). The monument at Ichpaatun, now identified as probably of phyllonite, is likely to have been constructed from rock which had been rafted to the site along the coast.

In the case of the classic Maya of Tikal, Guatemala, Haviland (1974) discussed the possibility that there were occupational specializations at this centre, in stoneworking and monument carving, and indeed he suggests that perhaps these special occupations were confined to a specific family within a lineage.

Building materials

Obviously, the sort of material which is suitable for monuments is also going to be of equal value in some aspects of general building construction. From Neolithic times onwards, human communities have been gaining knowledge about the jointing, durability, weight-bearing strength, and hardness of a

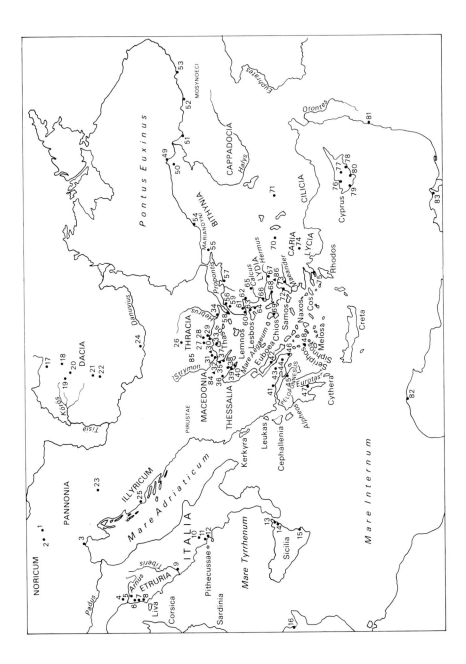

Fig. 1.11. Early mining areas and sites in the central and eastern Mediterranean area. (After Healy 1978.)

1. Hallstatt
2. Mitterberg
3. Aquileia
4. Luca
5. Volterra
6. Campiglia Marittima
7. Bottino
8. Populonia
9. Roma
10. Capua
11. Neapolis
12. Pompeii
13. Alì
14. Nizza
15. Syracusae
16. Carthago
17. Baia Mare
18. Körösbanya
19. Vicus Pirustarum (Verespatak)
20. Ruda
21. Alsó Telek
22. Sarmizegethusa, Ulpia Traiana
23. Siscia
24. Corabia
25. Salonae
26. Philippopolis
27. Crenides, Philippi
28. Scapte Hyle
29. Madenokhorio
30. Abdera
31. Amphipolis
32. Eion
33. Thasos
34. Aenus
35. Stratonike
36. Therma
37. Stageira
38. Olynthus
39. Potidaea, Cassandra
40. Mende
41. Delphi
42. Chalcis
43. Thebae
44. Athenae
45. Corinthus and Pentaskoufi
46. Laurion
47. Sparta
48. H. Sosti
49. Sinope
50. Pompeiupolis
51. Amisus
52. Cerasus
53. Trapezus
54. Heraclea
55. Nicomedia
56. Lampsacus
57. Cyzicus
58. Abydus
59. Cremaste
60. Assus
61. (?) Andeira
62. Cisthene
63. Methymna
64. Mytilene
65. Pergamum
66. Phocaea
67. Sardes
68. Smyrna
69. Chios
70. Apamea
71. Iconium (Konya)
72. Ephesus
73. Magnesia
74. Cibyra
75. Rhodes
76. Soli
77. Tamassus
78. Citium
79. Paphos
80. Amathus
81. Byblus
82. Cyrene
83. Alexandria
84. Mt Dysoron
85. Mt Pangaeus

Fig. 1.12. Early mining areas and sites in Britain, France, Spain, and the western Mediterranean area. (After Healy 1978.)

1. Inchtuthil
2. Leadhills
3. Borcovicium (Housesteads)
4. Corstopitum (Corbridge)
5. Pateley Bridge
6. Eboracum (York)
7. Amlwych
8. Gt Orme
9. Pentre
10. Deva (Chester)
11. Alderley Edge
12. Lindum (Lincoln)
13. Shrewsbury
14. Dolaucothi
15. Corby
16. Ariconium
17. Lydney
18. Isca (Caerleon)
19. Venta Silurum (Caerwent)
20. Gt Chesterford
21. Aquae Sulis (Bath)
22. Verulamium (St. Albans)
23. Camulodunum (Colchester)
24. Calleva Atrebatum (Silchester)
25. Londinium
26. Chun Castle
27. Isca Dumnoniorum (Exeter)
28. Regnum (Chichester)
29. Ictis (St. Michael's Mt)
30. Vetera Castra
31. Colonia Agrippina (Cologne)
32. Saalburg
33. Augusta Trevorum (Trier)
34. Josselin
35. Lutetia (Paris)
36. Penestin
37. Melle
38. Avaricum
39. Bibracte
40. Mediolanum
41. Vaulry
42. Montebras
43. Lugdunum (Lyons)
44. L'Argentière
45. Victimulae
46. Tolosa (Toulouse)
47. Nemausus (Nîmes)
48. Ampus
49. Arelate (Arles)
50. Aquae Sextiae (Aix)
51. Narbo
52. Massalia (Marseilles)
53. Forum Iulii (Fréjus)
54. Brigantium
55. Salabe
56. Lucus Augusti
57. Pontevedra
58. Montefurado
59. Las Medulas
60. Legio vii Gemina (León)
61. Asturica Augusta (Astorga)
62. Minho
63. Rio Duerna
64. Zamora
65. Osca
66. Bilbilis
67. Tarraco (Tarragona)
68. Toletum (Toledo)
69. Emerita Augusta
70. Saguntum
71. Sisapo (Almaden)
72. Aljustrel
73. Minas de Mouras
74. Sto Domingos
75. Tharsis
76. Sotiel Coronada
77. Sta Rosa
78. Rio Tinto
79. Ilipa
80. Posadas
81. Corduba
82. Linares
83. Castulo
84. Hemeroscopeium, Dianium
85. Huelva
86. Lucentum (Alicante)
87. Gades (Cadiz)
88. Malaca
89. Mazzarón
90. Carthago Nova (Cartagena)
91. Neapolis
92. Flumini Maggiore
93. Iglesias

wide variety of materials. Some of the late prehistoric monuments in the Orkney islands, such as the structures at Skara Brae, the tomb at Maeshowe, and the various brochs, bear witness to the wide selection of better quality Old Red Sandstone. In contrast to these, the Old Red Sandstone used in construction of the Norse cathedral of St Magnus in Kirkwall is clearly inferior material, as indicated by the serious weathering which has taken place on some parts of the external surface.

Jope (1953) has pointed out that, in contrast to detailed work on the petrology of stone axes, there has been far less systematic work on the nature of building materials: marble has perhaps received more attention than most rocks. He notes the use of granite in fifteenth and sixteenth century churches in Devon and Cornwall, which must be derived from five outcrops. No doubt using modern geochemical analyses these five granites could be positively identified. In the case of roofing material, Jope and Dunning (1954) review the use of blue slate in medieval England, and show that the collection of precise geological information on roofing material can provide further evidence of early trade. In the case of the blue slate, it 'competed' well with local flagstone beds (of limestone and sandstone) and gave a much lighter roofing cover, as it split more thinly. Although the history of slate roofing extends back to Roman times, medieval transportation systems allowed a much better flow of the commodity and indeed, in 1436, we know that no fewer than 100 000 Devon slates were shipped from Southampton to Mont St Michel.

The study of trade from rocks

Mention has already been made of the economic relevance of petrological studies on artefacts. The movement and distribution of man-made stone objects beyond the source area or areas indicates that humans found a need in taking the material elsewhere. This could simply have been the result of people carrying personal objects with them during periods of travel, whether on personal visits or to invade new territory. However, as Bradley (1971) indicates, various alternative possibilities and explanations have been suggested. Artefact movement can involve less direct cultural contact or population movement. The objects could be domestic products or output from specialist workshops. The distribution of artefacts can indicate the demarcation of a cultural zone, but seems as likely to be the result of economic transactions. Moreover, the spatial distribution of rock objects might also be related to the opportunities for trade existing in particular areas. Additionally, in the case of large rock objects, carrying or trading distance may well be related to weight of object. Jope's (1964) study of late Saxon building materials in central and southern England gives examples of products from a number of separate quarries, but there is evidence that the distributions 'respect' each other, as if by some unwritten trade convention, although the full reasons are likely to be more complex (see Chapter 4).

Various authors have considered man-made stone objects with a view to evaluating the cultural factors behind the distributions, as well as possible identification and analytical problems. Nandris (1975) reviews the history of studies on obsidian in southeast Europe, and casts doubt on some of the claims for this rock. However, he notes that obsidian occurs as a redistributed natural resource as early as the Aurignacian period. In the western Mediterranean, Longworth and Warren (1979) found four main sources of obsidian available to prehistoric groups, basing their work on the analyses of obsidian samples by Mössbauer spectroscopy (see Chapter 7).

Jade was a material which was clearly prized in cultures of both Europe and eastern Asia; in the case of central America, it was prized more highly than gold. Jade objects were used and traded extensively in early China, from the Shang dynasty through to the eighteenth century AD (Laufer 1974). The jade funeral suits of over 2000 pieces worn by Princess Ton Wan and Prince Lie Shang (late second century BC) testify to the importance of this material. Jade was also used for axes, chisels, knives, tables, rings, buckles, sword guards, amulets, coins, seals, girdle pendants, ornaments, buttons, pins, and earrings. By the late Chou and Han periods (300 BC – AD 200) large jade objects were being employed in ceremonial events (Watson 1966) (see Chapter 8).

Both obsidian and jade objects, as well as salt and other items, were the concern of Mayan merchants (Sabloff and Rathje 1975), and indeed they were to be called the Phoenicians of the New World. Mayan craftsmanship in working jade (Digby 1972) was in no way inferior to the workmanship seen in early China. Similar techniques to those employed in the Chinese funeral suits were used in the Maya jade masks composed of several segments and exemplified by a Classic Period specimen from Palenque (Bernal 1968). But, of course, jade and obsidian were by no means the only rocks of trade value in the early Americas. The Hopewell people of North America were able to obtain large sheets of mica and produced from them somewhat bizarre silhouettes of figures, hands, and claws (Fig. 1.13) (Bushnell 1967; Martin, Quimby, and Collier 1967). Of the early Tropical Forest Cultures of South America, the people of Huayurco in the valley of the Marañón, Peru, were clearly engaged in some form of trade with coastal Peru. At Huayurco, a quantity of fragmentary and unfinished stone bowls seem to indicate that this was a manufacturing centre and, moreover, similar bowls have been found in a range of late Preceramic and Initial Period sites (Lathrap 1970).

A final example of the way in which geological resources can provide knowledge of trading activities might be given in relation to a very different material – amber. Fossil resin has always been a scarce resource, and thus trading in this 'northern gold' is not surprising. An important source of

European amber has been the Baltic area, and by the the fourth century BC the Greek navigator Pytheas and later Pliny the Elder record expeditions north to collect supplies. Trade routes south probably varied at first, but eventually became more established. As Malinowski (1974) indicates, there were probably two main routes by Iron Age times – first, the 'Jutland track', running along the Elbe and Moldan rivers to the Danube; then a second, or 'Sambian track', from the Sambian Peninsula and estuary of Vistula towards the northeastern shore of the Adriatic and the eastern Alps. There is still a need to substantiate this view with archaeological finds of the kind made at the Polish settlement site of Komorowo, which could have been an important community in the amber trade. Studies of geological resources used by earlier societies can greatly assist at times in the evaluation of trading complexes, and of the extent of the distribution of some materials.

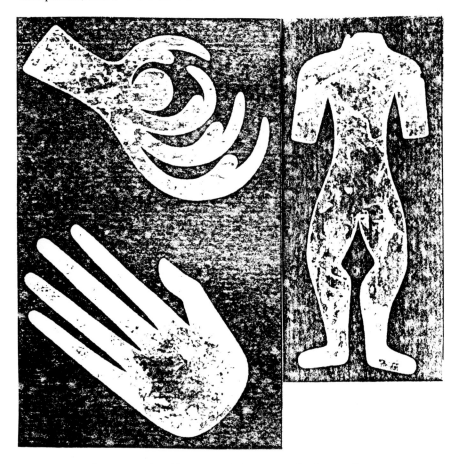

Fig. 1.13. Mica silhouettes of the Hopewell culture, USA.

Rock as medicine

This brief introductory review of rocks in relation to the study of earlier societies has demonstrated the use of stone for a variety of tools and ritual objects, of its use as a building material, and of the relevance of petrological identification to a full consideration of the development of trade and trading routes. It would seem useful to conclude with a reference to the question of rock exploitation in relation to medicine. Mention has already been made of the materials which can be detrimental to the communities using them (e.g., the use of cinnabar as a body paint by the Hohokam (p. 12) (Haury 1976)). On the other hand, the use of mercury compounds by some early Arab societies may have assisted in the control of treponemal disease, and this 'Saracen ointment' was taken back north by the Crusaders from the Holy Land in order to treat so-called 'leprosy' (Hudson 1958). The well-organized exploitation and use of lead in Romano-British times provided not only pipes, cisterns, and pewter tableware (Tylecote 1964), but also varying degrees of lead poisoning.

In contrast to these detrimental possibilities, some minerals were used for what Shackley (1977) calls 'quasi-medicinal purposes . . . in the pharmacopaeia of several civilizations'. Alum was one such substance, and although perhaps mainly used in tanning, dyeing, and glass making, it appears to have acquired some medical use, especially for the treatment of diseases of the head, ears, and eyes, according to Assyrian cuneiform texts. Egypt not only quarried alum for home use (even as late as the fifteenth century AD) but also exported it to Mesopotamia. Natron was another material dug in early Egypt, and although mainly used in glass and glaze production and mummification, it was also considered to have purifying powers. Sulphur also was used in Egypt, particularly in the treatment of skin disease (Sigerist 1951).

The list could be increased considerably, but it is sufficient to indicate yet again the inventiveness of earlier peoples in exploiting rocks and minerals in many divergent avenues of their lives.

References

Anderson, J. (1886). *Scotland in pagan times. The Bronze and Stone Ages*. Douglas, Edinburgh.
Ansari, Z. D. and Dhavalikar, M. K. (1971). New light on the prehistoric cultures of central India. *World Archaeology* **2**, 337–46.
Arnold, D. E. and Bohor, B. F. (1975). Attapulgite and Maya Blue. An ancient mine comes to light. *Archaeology* **28**, 23–9.
—— —— (1977). An ancient clay mine at Yo'K'at, Yucatan. *American Antiquity* **42**, 575–82.
Ashbee, P. (1967). The Wessex grave. *Proceedings of the Hampshire Field Club and Archaeological Society* **27**, 7–14.

Bernal, I. (1968). *The Mexican National Museum of Anthropology*. Thames and Hudson, London.

Bradley, R. (1971). Trade competition and artefact distribution. *World Archaeology* **2**, 347–52.

Bruton, E. (1978). *Diamonds*. N.A.G. Press, London.

Bushnell, G. H. S. (1967). *Ancient arts of the Americas*. Thames and Hudson, London.

Calkin, J. B. (1955). Kimmeridge coal money. The Romano-British shale armlet industry. *Proceedings. Dorset Natural History and Archaeological Society* **75**, 45–71.

—— (1973). Kimmeridge shale objects from Colliton Park, Dorchester. *Proceedings. Dorset Natural History and Archaeological Society* **94**, 44–8.

Chiang, T-C. (1975). The salt industry in Ming China. *Geographical Review* **65**, 93–106.

Clark, J. D. (1970). *The prehistory of Africa*. Thames and Hudson, London.

Clough, T. H. McK. and Cummins, W. A. (1979). Stone axe studies. Archaeological, petrological, experimental and ethnographic. *Research Reports Council for British Archaeology* **23**, viii + 137 pp.

Davidson, D. A. and Shackley, M. L. (ed.) (1976). *Geoarchaeology: earth science and the past*. Duckworth, London.

Digby, A. (1972). *Maya jades*. British Museum, London.

Forbes, R. J. (1966). Ancient geology: ancient mining and quarrying; ancient mining techniques. *Studies in Ancient Technology* **7**, 259pp.

Gabel, C. (1965). *Stone Age hunters of the Kafue. The Gwisho A Site*. Boston University Press.

Graham, J. A. and Williams, H. (1971). Two unusual Maya stelae. *Contributions of the University of California Archaeological Research Faculty* **13**, 161–6.

Hassan, F. A. (1979). Geoarchaeology: the geologist and archaeology. *American Antiquity* **44**, 267–70.

Haury, E. (1976). *The Hohokam, desert farmers and craftsmen. Excavations at Snaketown 1964–1965*. University of Arizona Press, Tucson.

Haviland, W. A. (1974). Occupational specialization at Tikal, Guatemala; stoneworking-monument carving. *American Antiquity* **39**, 494–6.

Hawkes, J. (1977). *The atlas of early man*. Macmillan, London.

Healy, J. F. (1978). *Mining and metallurgy in the Greek and Roman world*. Thames and Hudson, London.

Heizer, R. F. (1956). Archaeology of the Uyak site Kodiak Island, Alaska. *Anthropological Records University of California* **17**, 1–199.

Higashimura, T. and Warashina, T. (1975). Sourcing of sanukite stone implements by X-ray fluorescence analysis. *Journal of Archaeological Science* **2**, 169–78.

Hopper, R. J. (1979). *Trade and industry in classical Greece*. Thames and Hudson, London.

Hudson, E. H. (1958). *Non-venereal syphilis, a sociological and medical study of Bejel*. Livingstone, London.

Isaac, G. L. (1978). The first geologists – the archaeology of the original rock breakers. *Geological background to fossil man. Recent research in the Gregory Rift Valley, East Africa*. In W. W. Bishop (ed.). Scottish Academic Press, Edinburgh, 139–47.

Jope, E. M. (1953). History, archaeology and petrology. *Advancement of Science* **9**, 432–5.

—— (1964). The Saxon building-stone industry in southern and midland England. *Medieval Archaeology* **8**, 91–118.

—— Dunning, G. C. (1954). The use of blue slate for roofing in medieval England. *Antiquaries Journal* **34**, 209–17.

Lanning, E. (1970). Pleistocene man in South America. *World Archaeology* **2**, 90–111.

Lathrap, D. W. (1970). *The Upper Amazon*. Thames and Hudson, London.

Laufer, B. (1974). *Jade. A study in Chinese archaeology and religion*. Dover, New York.

Liversidge, J. (1955). *Furniture in Roman Britain*. Tiranti, London.

Longworth, G. and Warren, S. E. (1979). The application of Mössbauer spectroscopy to the characterization of western Mediterranean obsidian. *Journal of Archaeological Science* **6**, 1–15.

Malinowski, T. (1974). An amber trading-post in early Iron Age Poland. *Archaeology* **27**, 195–200.

Martin, P. S., Quimby, G. I., and Collier, D. (1967). *Indians before Columbus*. University of Chicago Press.

Maspero, G. (1903). *Guide to the Cairo Museum*. Printing Office of the French Institute of Oriental Archaeology, Cairo.

Moore, P. R., Keyes, I. W., and Orchiston, D. W. (1979). New records and an analysis of the side-hafted adze from New Zealand. *New Zealand Journal of Archaeology* **1**, 53–84.

Morris, A. E. J. (1974). *History of urban form*. Wiley, New York.

Munro, R. (1897). *Prehistoric problems*. Blackwood, Edinburgh.

Nandris, J. (1975). A re-consideration of the south-east European sources of archaeological obsidian. *Bulletin of the Institute of Archaeology. University of London* **12**, 71–94.

Nenquin, J. (1961). *Salt. A study in economic prehistory*. Brugge.

Prakashi, S. and Rawat, N. S. (1965). *Chemical study of some Indian archaeological antiquities*. Asia Publishing House, Bombay.

Royal Commission on Historical Monuments. (1962). *Eburacum, Roman York*. Vol. 1. London.

Sabloff, J. A. and Rathje, W. L. (1975). The rise of a Maya merchant class. *Scientific American* **233** (4), 72–82.

Sarianidi, V. I. (1971). The lapis lazuli route in the Ancient East. *Archaeology* **24**, 12–15.

Shackley, M. (1977). *Rocks and man*. Allen and Unwin, London.

—— (1979). Geoarchaeology. Polemic on a progressive relationship. *Naturwissenschaften* **66**, 429–32.

Shotton, F. W. (1969). Petrological examination. In: D. Brothwell and E. Higgs (ed.): *Science in archaeology*. 2nd edn. Thames and Hudson, London, 571–7.

Sigerist, H. E. (1951). *A history of medicine*. Oxford University Press.

Smith, I. F. (1965). *Windmill Hill and Avebury: excavations by Alexander Keiller 1925–1939*. Clarendon Press, Oxford.

—— Simpson, D. D. A. (1966). Excavation of a round barrow on Overton Hill, north Wiltshire. *Proceedings of the Prehistoric Society* **32**, 122–55.

Summers, R. (1969). Ancient mining in Rhodesia and adjacent areas. *Museum Memoir National Museums of Rhodesia* **3**, xv, 236pp.

Tylecote, R. F. (1964). Roman lead working in Britain. *British Journal for the History of Science* **2**, 25–43.

Wainwright, F. T. (1962). *The Northern Isles*. Nelson, London.

Watson, W. (1966). *Early civilization in China*. Thames and Hudson, London.

Wheeler, R. E. M. (1943). Maiden Castle Dorset. *Report of the Research Committee of the Society of Antiquaries* **12**, xx + 399pp.

2. Techniques

D. R. C. Kempe and J. A. Templeman

Today a wide variety of physical and chemical techniques exist which can assist the archaeologist in establishing the nature and provenance of his artefacts. They range from simple physical tests, which require little or no special equipment and give results easily interpreted by the layman, to complex and esoteric methods, which often need elaborate apparatus and considerable experience to obtain and interpret meaningful results (cf. Hall 1964; Tite 1972; Meschel 1978).

It is the purpose of this chapter to review the current analytical methods without going into technical details. Emphasis is placed on their availability, suitability for different analytical purposes, and their non-destructive or destructive nature. In the latter case, the minimum quantity of sample required is stated whenever possible. Key references are given for most of the techniques, and it is hoped that this short account will assist the archaeologist or geologist to select the most appropriate methods for the examination of his artefacts and specimens, and the solution of his problem (Table 2.1).

Physical properties of rocks and minerals

1. Hardness, density, and refractive index

These are perhaps the three most basic physical properties which can be measured on a crystalline object.

Hardness is a property of the individual mineral grains within a specimen; an average hardness can be calculated for a rock, but care must be taken to ensure that this is meaningful.

The simplest method for determining hardness is the comparative method based upon Mohs' scale of hardness. Mohs' scale ranks ten minerals in increasing order of hardness, and assigns to these arbitrary hardness values from 1 to 10; the ten minerals are, in increasing order of hardness: talc, gypsum, calcite, fluorite, apatite, feldspar, quartz, topaz, corundum, and diamond. The hardness of a mineral on Mohs' scale is found by determining which of the minerals will scratch, or are scratched by, the specimen; this value is, however, only a qualitative guide to hardness, since the test only

Table 2.1. Flow chart of available analytical methods

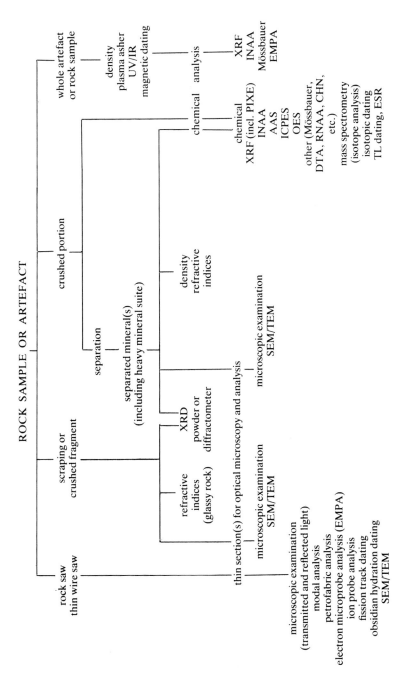

assigns a mineral to its ranking in the hardness scale rather than providing an absolute value. Thus, a mineral of Mohs' hardness 8 (equivalent to topaz) cannot be said to be twice as hard as one of hardness 4 (equivalent to fluorite). As a rough guide for use in the field, quartz is common and scratches glass; a knife will just scratch feldspar, and will easily scratch calcite; and a finger nail will just scratch gypsum and will easily scratch talc, the mineral name for the main constituent of steatite and soapstone.

A quantitative *micro-indentation hardness* test can be performed if facilities are available for reflected light microscopy (Bowie and Simpson 1977); a pointed probe is dropped on to the mineral surface under precisely controlled conditions, and the size of the pit produced is measured. This micro-indentation test is an extremely accurate method of hardness determination.

An interesting study of the durability under abrasion of various rock types was conducted by Abbott and Peterson (1978), who investigated the resistance of clasts from Cretaceous and Eocene conglomerates from the San Diego area of California. Their conclusions reflect the hardness of the component minerals; from most to least resistant were clasts of: chert, quartzite, rhyolite, metabreccia, obsidian, metasandstone, gneiss, granodiorite, gabbro, basalt, marble, and schist. Clearly, however, as well as mineral hardness, the texture of a rock such as schist was a governing factor.

Density and specific gravity. A simple method for determining the density (D, in g cm^{-3}) or specific gravity (Muller 1977b) can be used to give an indication of rock type. Certainly, comparison with a rock of known source will establish whether to continue the examination or whether to begin again. In very general terms, the quartz-rich rocks are less dense than the basic rocks – those rich in ferromagnesian minerals – and there will be little point in attempting comparison of samples which have widely differing densities.

To determine density, take a graduated measuring cylinder sufficiently full of distilled water to cover the rock chip, read the level, and carefully lower in a previously weighed chip of rock, using a length of cotton. Note the new level on the cylinder, subtract the original reading, and divide this difference into the weight of sample. The result gives the density. The method is based on the fact that one cm^3 of pure water weighs one gram; the displacement of the rock chip represents its volume. With large specimens, a similar method is used, requiring greater ingenuity; so long as the displacement can be measured and the weight is known, the density can be determined. With minerals, much greater precision is required, but the value of the method is much more limited; an X-ray identification is as quick and more precise.

Specific gravity (S.G. or sp. gr.) is a ratio, involving no units. It is determined by weighing the rock or mineral chip in air (W^1) and, again using a length of cotton, in distilled water (W^2). The ratio $W^1/(W^1 - W^2)$ gives S.G.; it is related to density, according to Archimedes' principle, and the numerical values are virtually identical.

Refractve index. The refractive index of a mineral grain or fragment, determined in oils of known refractive index, is not often likely to be useful in artefact petrology. However, the R.I. of flint, chert, obsidian, pumice, and sanukite (glassy andesite), or any similar glassy material used for tools and other artefacts, may well be of value, perhaps in association with trace element composition, in discriminating between materials from different sources. Unlike minerals, which may have up to three refractive indices, these glassy rocks have only one, which is very easy to determine. A sample of the mineral or rock is crushed, and a few grains placed on a microscope slide. A drop of R.I. liquid is added, and it is then simple (Kerr 1977) to determine which has the greater refractive index, mineral or liquid; by repeating this process, using a liquid with a R.I. nearer to that of the grain, as determined by the Becke line, a point will be reached when the grains and liquid are indistinguishable – at this point the refractive indices of liquid and sample are approximately equal. Fornaseri, Malpieri, and Tolomeo (1975) used refractive indices, in conjunction with chemical composition and heavy mineral content, in an attempt to determine the source of artefact pumice collected from sites near Morphou Bay, on the north coast of Cyprus. The data correspond with those from samples of pumice from Santorini (Thera), Kos, and Yali, so establishing these islands as the probable sources of the artefact material.

2. Heavy mineral analysis

Some sedimentary rocks, principally sandstones, greywackes, and lime-stones, and their metamorphic equivalents such as schists and marbles, are widely distributed and their identification as such is of little help in establishing provenance. However, they may contain rare accessory minerals or a characteristic suite of heavy (high density) minerals. These can be separated (Muller 1977a) by crushing the rock, using various types of jaw crusher, cone grinder, pestle and mortar, or other device, and separating the heavy minerals. Separation is carried out on a sieved fraction of, ideally, -120 to $+200$ mesh (125 to 75 μm) in size, allowing for the grain size of the rock, using heavy liquids or a magnetic separator. Four heavy liquids are commonly used: bromoform ($CHBr_3$; S.G. 2.89), tetrabromoethane ($C_2H_2Br_4$; 2.95), methylene iodide (CH_2I; 3.32), and Clerici's solution (a solution of thallium organic salts; 4.33). The first three may be diluted with acetone or other organic solvents, whilst Clerici's solution is soluble in hot water. All these liquids present a health hazard, especially Clerici's solution which is extremely toxic, and they should all be used, with suitable protective clothing, in a fume cupboard. The method of separation consists of adjusting the specific gravity of the liquid by dilution until it is just below that of the heavy mineral fraction; the sample is then stirred into the liquid, and either left for the 'heavy' fraction to sink under gravity or, if a quick separation is required, spun down in a centrifuge. The 'heavy' and 'light' fractions can then be removed, washed, dried, and examined microscopically. Magnetic separators, such as Frantz or Cook, separate minerals according to their relative magnetic susceptibility. They are often used as a final separation technique on the heavy fraction from the liquids; they are not essential, however, unless the different heavy minerals need to be separated from one another. In certain cases – notably the micas, chlorites, and other sheet silicates – the superpanning technique, a refinement of that used by the precious metal prospectors and employing a mechanized panner (Muller 1977a) can also be used.

The heavy fraction can then be mounted in balsam or resin on a glass slide and examined in the same way as thin sections or scrapings; it may well make it possible to differentiate between otherwise similar rocks and if the mineral assemblages can be matched with those from known sources, will establish provenance. This method is particularly favoured in the study of ceramic material; it is also useful for sculptural sandstones and schists and sometimes for marbles. The same separation techniques, but requiring a very pure sample, often achieved by hand picking, are used if one of the separated minerals is to be analysed. Typical heavy mineral assemblages will include some of the following: olivine, pyroxenes, amphiboles, epidotes, tourmaline, apatite, sphene, zircon, garnet, staurolite, andalusite, kyanite, sillimanite, iron oxides, etc.

3. Thin-section microscopy

The time-honoured method of examining rocks and minerals and ceramic materials remains the thin section and the polarizing microscope (Kerr 1977; Muir 1977). First used about 130 years ago, it enables the petrologist to study the texture and mineralogy of a rock, and thus identify it, and to ascertain the optical properties of its minerals. The method is available in virtually all geological laboratories; it is also used by lapidarists for examining minerals and by metallurgists for metals and alloys. Thus, it is recommended to all archaeologists and petrologists as a starting point for artefact study, yielding the basic information – the nature of the material studied – on which to build a plan for more detailed examination.

Using a rock saw, a thin slice of the material is cut, say 1–2 mm thick; one side is polished on a series of laps, using progressively finer grades of carborundum (silicon carbide), and the slice is then fixed to a glass slide with Canada balsam or epoxy resin. If material is abundant, aim for a section 2.5 × 2 cm; if scarce, a square of 2–3 mm is often quite adequate. In the case of soft or friable rocks, or ceramic materials, a small chip is first impregnated in araldite or other epoxy resin, or thermoplastic cement such as lakeside 70, and the block is sliced. If the section is to be taken from a valuable artefact, a sliver less than 1 mm thick can be cut using a *thin wire saw* (e.g. Lastec saw) (Bishop and Woolley 1973; Burleigh and Seeley 1975), which employs a thin wire impregnated with diamond or armoured with carborundum dust. The slot left by the saw can be filled with putty and painted, leaving little trace. Further, the wire saw, unlike the diamond wheel, generates very little heat and thus imparts no thermal effects on the sample. The mounted slice is then ground down on the same laps, using graded carborundum as before, to a thickness of 30 μm and covered with a thin cover glass. This is a standard thickness, used to give polarizing colours of known orders, on which comparative study can be carried out using a polarizing microscope. The theory and method are fully described by, for example, Kerr (1977). The thin sections can also be used for electron microprobe analysis (q.v.), after removal of the cover glasses and further polishing.

In some cases, even a thin sliver or chip of the rock is unobtainable: the artefact is too small, delicate, or valuable, or a general ruling precludes breaking off such a fragment. It may still be possible to take a scraping, using a steel blade or similar tool: the powder can then be mounted in balsam or resin and covered, or placed in R.I. liquid, and examined in the same way. The grains will not be of standard thickness but a skilled petrographer can nevertheless identify the minerals and give an indication of the rock type.

The *modal analysis* of a thin section using a point counter is a widespread petrographical technique, but will only rarely be of value in the study of artefacts. A counter is used to record the number of points for each of the constituent minerals, brought under the central cross wires of the microscope by an automatic stage activated to move over a grid system. The percentage content by volume of each mineral in the rock can then be calculated. More sophisticated electronic methods are now available, generally referred to as *automatic image analysis* (Jones 1977). *Petrofabric analysis* determines the orientation of the mineral grains in a thin section, from which the structural elements – planes, lineations, folding – of a rock can often be determined. Examples of the use of this technique in the study of marbles are given in Chapter 4.

Acetate peels can sometimes be used as a rapid method of obtaining some of the textural information normally derived from thin sections. Limestones and other carbonate rocks are particularly suitable but chert, chalcedony, and jasper have also been treated in this way. The usual method is to etch the rock by applying hydrofluoric acid to a cut and polished surface of the artefact. A peel using clear cellulose acetate film can then be taken. Many of the textural features, fossil remains, colour bandings, etc., will be recorded on the peel (Young and Syms 1980).

The *reflected light microscope* (Bowie and Simpson 1977), also used for the determination of micro-indentation hardness, is employed primarily for the petrographic study of opaque minerals, and for determining reflectance (the degree to which opaque minerals reflect light of known wavelength). It is also used in the study of metallic alloys and eutectic mixtures. This form of microscopy, as opposed to transmitted light microscopy, is relatively specialised and would have only limited application in archaeological investigations, perhaps mainly in the field of native metals (see Chapter 10).

4. X-ray diffraction (XRD)

A detailed study of a mineral may be made using X-ray diffraction (XRD) (Zussman 1977). The wavelength of X-rays is shorter than, but of the same order of magnitude as, the distance between the planes of atoms in crystals. Hence, X-rays will be diffracted by the array of atoms in the structure in a manner analogous to that of light by a diffraction grating. The well known Bragg law ($n\lambda = 2d \sin \theta$) relates the wavelength of X-rays, the spacing between atomic layers in the crystal, and the angle of diffraction of the X-rays. Using this expression, since the wavelength is known and the diffraction angle measurable, the interlayer spacing and hence the characteristic lattice constants for the mineral can be calculated.

The most commonly used method in XRD is that of *powder photography*. A sample of pure mineral is very finely ground (to less than 240 mesh), mixed with a suitable adhesive (Durofix or Cow Gum), and rolled into a ball or spindle less than 0.3 mm in diameter. In such a finely powdered specimen there will be grains in all conceivable orientations, and since each grain will diffract X-rays at several angles to the main beam, a conical fan of secondary X-radiation will be produced. A strip of photographic film placed around the sample will record these fans of X-rays as a series of concentric lines. The arrangement of lines on the film is characteristic of a mineral (or group of minerals), and can be used to identify it. A mixture of minerals will show lines characteristic of all the minerals present (Fig. 2.1).

In a *diffractometer*, instead of recording the reflections photographically, a scintillation counter connected to a chart recorder is used. The detector scans the sample through a range of diffraction angles, each reflection resulting in a peak on the chart. Standard tables for the identification of minerals by their peak positions and relative intensities exist, and thus mixtures of minerals can be separately identified, and in some cases semi-quantitative modal analyses of the mixture can be made. This method can therefore be used for crushed rock samples (Fig. 2.1), or minerals separated from the rock; it is probably most useful in the case of rare accessory minerals, or approximate rock identifications when only scrapings are available. X-ray generators with cameras and/or diffractometers are available in most geology and physics laboratories. A powder mount requires only 2–5 mg of material; a diffractometer 'smear' mount, on a glass slide, at least 20 mg.

5. *Differential thermal analysis (DTA)*

DTA (Neumann 1977) is the most commonly used of several thermal techniques, and can be useful in the identification of several groups of

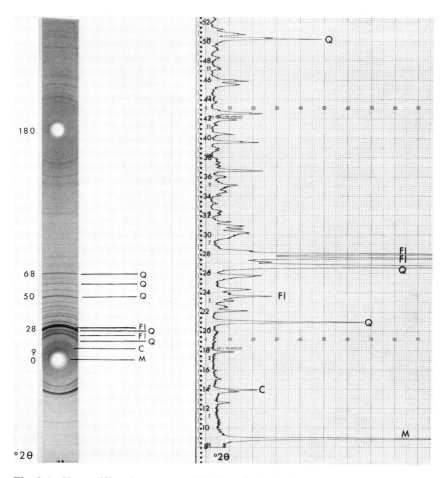

Fig. 2.1. X-ray diffraction patterns (Cu *Kα* radiation) of a granite, containing quartz, feldspar, mica, and a little clay. The mixture could also represent a micaceous feldspathic sandstone or a quartz-mica schist. Left, powder photograph. Right, diffractometer trace. The three strongest lines of quartz (Q) and feldspar (Fl) are labelled, plus (on the film) two further quartz lines; also the strongest mica (M) and clay (kaolinite) (C) lines. Note that the diffractometer trace (8°–52° 2θ) corresponds with only a small part of the film.

minerals, especially the clays and micas; for example, different curves can often be obtained for samples of the same mineral from different sources. In artefact petrology, however, it is far less widely used than thermoluminescence (described under Dating methods), probably because a considerable amount of skill is necessary to interpret the charts. The technique records the heat absorbed or emitted by a mineral when it is heated under carefully controlled conditions. This absorption or emission occurs because minerals sometimes undergo various physical changes and chemical reactions. The instrument records the change in temperature (relative to an inert reference material such as γ-Al_2O_3) against the temperature at which the change occurs. Powdered samples of less than 0.1 g are required, but the technique is not commonly employed in artefact petrology.

Thermogravimetric analysis (TGA) is a related technique in which the weight changes on heating or cooling are recorded as a function of time.

6. Infrared spectroscopy (IR)

The nature of the bonds between atoms in a mineral (Farmer 1974; Estep-Barnes 1977) allows them to absorb infrared radiation. If the amount of radiation absorbed at each wavelength is measured, the spectrum so obtained can be used as a rapid means of mineral identification; it has been used for amber. Very small amounts of finely ground sample (less than 5 mg) are required, and it is relatively simple to produce a good spectrum, although considerable experience is necessary in interpreting the spectra. It is not a very widely used technique, except for amber (Beck, Adams, Southard, and Fellows 1971; Savkevich 1981).

Infrared photography can be valuable in detecting patterns that have become faded or erased. Aerial thermal IR photography is widely used for detecting prehistoric settlement patterns and other archaeological sites, and in geology for photographing sandbanks and similar underwater configurations.

7. Laser Raman spectroscopy (LRS)

This technique, based upon the discovery of the Raman effect in 1928 (Woodward 1967; Griffith 1974), is often discussed together with infrared spectroscopy, since both methods are used to investigate the bonding forces between atoms, but employing different principles.

Laser Raman and infrared spectroscopy are complementary techniques and should, where possible, be used together. LRS is most useful for investigating those parts of the spectrum where IR is unsuitable, for investigating liquids, and for single-crystal work; it also has the advantage that spectra are somewhat easier for the untrained eye to interpret.

8. Ultraviolet fluorescence (UV)

Ultraviolet fluorescence has been used to distinguish between marbles from different sources. Calcite is one of several minerals which fluoresce in long wave (i.e. > 300 nanometres) UV light and although of strictly limited application, Renfrew and Peacey (1968) used it successfully to separate marbles from Rhodes – which fluoresced salmon pink – from others which showed a violet colour. Other fluorescent minerals include aragonite, gypsum (alabaster), fluorite, and several zinc minerals. Marks that have become faded or erased, such as quarry and sculptor's marks on marble and alabaster, often show up visually under long wave UV; short wave is not appropriate and can be dangerous. Some wavelengths can cause chemical breakdown reactions to take place, and marks can become permanently visible again in ordinary light.

9. Electron microscopy (EM)

Many universities and research institutions now have a central electron microscope unit. EM (McConnell 1977; Grundy and Jones 1976) can be used to examine mineral particles in very great detail, given the resolution obtainable by a beam of accelerated electrons produced by a heated tungsten filament and focussed by an electromagnetic field. Two main methods are available: scanning electron microscopy (Grundy and Jones 1976), with magnifications up to 50 000 ×, and transmission electron microscopy (McConnell 1977), with magnifications up to 250 000 ×. For comparison, an optical microscope can only achieve magnifications up to about 1000 × as its resolution is limited by the wavelength of light. In a scanning electron microscope, the image is formed by back-scattering of electrons from the specimen surface, which has previously been made conductive by coating with gold or carbon. This technique is most suitable for studying the different morphologies and microtextures of, for example, calcite grains in marble. Transmission electron microscopy can be used to study features of the atomic arrangement in minerals, since the wavelength of the electrons is less than the size of an atom. Very thin specimens are required; sufficiently small crystals can be produced by grinding or a small area may be thinned by ion-beam etching.

When fitted with an energy dispersive attachment, either type of electron microscope can be used as a *microprobe* (q.v.) for the semi-quantitative analysis of the mineral under examination.

10. Mössbauer spectroscopy

Nuclear gamma resonance spectroscopy, or Mössbauer spectroscopy (Gibb 1976), is the only method other than those involving wet or classical chemistry for determining the Fe_2O_3/FeO ratio of a rock or mineral.

Although chemical methods are normally used for FeO determination, Mössbauer should be mentioned.

This somewhat esoteric technique is based upon the Mössbauer effect – certain isotopes will produce γ-rays by a process known as 'recoil-free emission', and these may be absorbed strongly by certain sensitive atoms ('resonant absorption'). The resonant absorption spectra obtained can be used, among other things, to determine valency states and examine the local chemical environment of atoms; Mössbauer-sensitive atoms include Fe, Ni, Zn, and Al.

The technique has been used by Longworth and Warren (1979) for distinguishing between Mediterranean obsidian sources, using the ferric/ferrous ratio and other parameters; the method requires 0.3 g of powdered sample, or small whole artefacts can be used.

Dating methods

1. Thermoluminescence (TL)

Thermoluminescence (TL) is probably the most widely used technique for dating inorganic archaeological material. At first, it was used almost exclusively for ceramic fragments but it is now also employed on rocks and minerals. A huge volume of literature has grown up around it; the more general accounts describing the method and its applications include Aitken (1974, 1977); Fleming (1976, 1979); Meschel (1978); Michels (1973); and Seeley (1975).

The method depends upon the fact that when crystalline material (rock or mineral) is heated to around 500 °C, light is emitted in addition to the normal incandescence at that temperature. The light represents a release of metastable energy stored in the material in the form of electrons trapped in imperfections. These electrons become excited (ionized) by radiation from radioactive isotopes such as trace impurities of U, Th, and ^{40}K, and the light-glow (TL) or energy release results from the fact that, on heating, the electrons return to their normal configuration. The amount of glow is related to the concentration of the radioactive elements but also to the time elapsed since the previous heating, which was the occasion on which the ceramic pottery was fired, at a temperature probably in excess of 750 °C. This firing would in turn have 'cleared' natural radiation damage acquired through geological time and turned the 'clock' back to zero. Thus, the time interval between the 'firing' heating and the 'ageing' heating is the age of the ceramic or material from which a stone artefact was made; in the case of the latter, if the rock was an igneous variety, the 'firing' was the occasion when the material crystallized from a magma or very hot solid rock. The method is accurate to $\pm$ 10 per cent over a range of 100 to 50 000 years before the present.

TL was used extensively for dating ceramics because quartz, feldspar, and calcite were already present in or were added to the clay to give improved strength and 'breathing' capacity. In addition, uranium-rich minerals, such as zircon and apatite, may be present. It was also later realized that many artefacts made from siliceous rocks or minerals (flint, chert, jasper, chalcedony, silicified limestone, tuff, glassy basalt and, especially, obsidian) may well have been heated ('burnt', 'fired', or 'annealed') by the toolmaker to give improved flaking or 'knapping' qualities. For this purpose the temperature had to exceed 380 °C and probably approached 500 °C, resetting the rock's time clock and perhaps enabling the same technique to be applied as in the case of ceramics; in fact, it has already been used for flint (Rowlett, Mandeville, and Zeller 1974). It must be added, however, that a controversy has existed over whether or not the tool raw material was in fact heated; it is now generally accepted that at least some material was subjected to this treatment. In the case of artefact material heated only to about 300 °C, however, well below the temperature (500 °C) at which gross structural changes occur, it is useful to have a method which positively identifies unheated flint and similar material. TL will to some extent do this with flint, chert, and similar materials (Rowlett et al. 1974; Melcher and Zimmerman 1977). TL can also sometimes be used on burnt stones once used for cooking, as in the case of Orcadian Old Red Sandstone; basalt and other lavas overlying artefact-bearing strata; and calcite from stalactites, stalagmites, and other cave formations (Wintle 1980).

Electron spin resonance spectroscopy (ESR), a technique also sometimes called electron paramagnetic resonance and allied to TL, is able to provide a signal (the C-signal) to identify positively those flint fragments which had received heat treatment. The method is also useful for tools older than 10 000 years, which may have acquired sufficient thermoluminescence for its TL value to approach the saturation value for the unheated geological material (Robins, Seeley, McNeil, and Symons 1978; Garrison, Rowlett, Cowan, and Holroyd 1981). ESR – which measures trapped electron energy by direct measurement of microwave absorption in a strong magnetic field – has been used instead of TL as a dating technique on, for example, cave stalagmites (Ikeya 1978) and ceramics (Maurer, Williams, and Riley 1981).

The TL glow curve is now also used as a technique for establishing the *source* of obsidian (Huntley and Bailey 1978), other tool material, and limestones and marbles. The natural TL glow curve may well be characteristic; the presence of zircons, for example, will help to distinguish it. The method is useful when used in conjunction with colour variation and other features, in cases where XRF or other chemical data are in doubt; it does not *replace* chemical analytical techniques, however. In the case of the work on Greek marble fragments, which have only a single peak in their glow curves, Afordakos, Alexoponlos, and Miliotis (1974) used artificial

(ATL) and mixed thermoluminescence (MTL) on samples after erasing the natural curves (NTL) by heating – for ATL only – and then subjecting both groups – ATL and MTL – to X-rays, to induce electron capture, and to further heat treatment. A total of five parameters can thus be obtained – three temperatures and two intensity ratios – which are considerably more diagnostic than NTL alone. The application of this technique is discussed in Chapter 4. Artificial TL has also been induced in obsidian when attempting to establish its source by this method (Leach and Fankhauser 1978). In a purely geological context, TL has been tried, but not extensively applied, on fluorite as well as dolomite, aragonite, and calcite from a variety of source rocks; reliable results, however, are few and far between. Thermoluminescence measurements require a finely ground sample of at least 10 g.

2. Archaeomagnetic dating

The direction and intensity of the Earth's magnetic field vary with time (Aitken 1974; Fleming 1976; Michels 1973). Clays, as used in ceramics, and in the construction of hearths, ovens, and kilns, and also clay soils, all contain iron oxides which assume the direction and proportional intensity of the magnetic field which surrounds them when they are heated to about 700 °C; this magnetism is called 'thermoremanent' (TRM). If the magnetic secular variation curve is known for the archaeological period to which the clay sample belongs, its date can be established from the direction of remanent magnetization. Conversely, if the sample age is known from other methods, the remanent magnetization information provides valuable geophysical data. VRM and CRM (viscous and chemical remanent magnetism) are some of the other magnetic components which may be present and for which corrections may be needed; natural remanent magnetism (NRM) is the total natural magnetism in the untreated samples. It is, of course, essential that the precise orientation of a sample be known, if it is to be measured magnetically.

3. Fission track dating

Many minerals, especially zircon, and natural glasses, such as obsidian, contain very small quantities of uranium (Fleischer, Price, and Walker 1975; Fleming 1976; Michels 1973). Most uranium atoms decay by alpha particle emission but a very few decay by spontaneous fission. Fission decay produces narrow 'damage tracks' in the mineral, the density or frequency of which, counted under the microscope in an etched thin section, depends not only upon uranium content but also on age; since U-content can be measured, the age can be calculated. In the case of man-made glass, the age of the artefact is taken from the time of manufacture; in petrological artefact analysis, the value of the technique is greatest in the case of obsidian, as a geological age marker for the artefacts or remains accompanying it. Such a lava was erupted in Olduvai Gorge, Tanzania, establishing the age of the artefact bed. Also, in the case of obsidian, heating or annealing the natural glass to improve its flaking qualities resets the clock to zero, as in the case of thermoluminescence. Thus, obsidian known to have been heated intentionally, or even unintentionally when caught up in pottery clay, will give an archaeological age corresponding with its time of manufacture. Fission track analysis has been used by Durrani, Khan, Taj, and Renfrew (1971) as a method of establishing the source of obsidian – as well as determining its U and Th content – by comparison of its fission track frequency with those of known source rocks. Natural radioactivity has also been used for characterizing obsidian.

4. Isotopic dating

Best known of the radioactive decay methods of dating in archaeology is that of ^{14}C (Aitken 1974; Fleming 1976; Michels 1973). A small proportion of the total carbon in the Earth's outer layers (atmosphere, hydrosphere, and lithosphere) is radioactive, produced by the reaction between neutrons emanating from cosmic rays and atoms of ^{14}N. This ^{14}C, forming a fixed proportion of the total homogenized mass of carbon at the Earth's surface, enters all living things throughout their lifetime. At death, no further carbon enters the 'body' and the radioactive ^{14}C amassed therein decays at a fixed rate equivalent to a 'half life' (i.e. half of the total of the ^{14}C isotope present) of 5568 ± 30 years. Since the proportion of ^{14}C to non-radioactive ^{12}C and ^{13}C is known, the proportion of ^{14}C remaining in the body relative to the total amount of carbon will indicate the time during which decay has taken place, which is the time since death and thus effectively the age of the organism. Determination by the β-counting method, using a liquid scintillation counter, requires about 5 g of carbon from charcoal, wood, peat, or demineralized bone, etc., and will give an age up to about 40 000 years (occasionally 70 000), the limit of the method. Mass spectrometry, using an accelerator, requires as little as 1–5 mg (Reeves and Brooks 1978). An associated but controversial method is *amino acid racemization*, giving the relative ages of mollusc shells based on their diagenetic changes. For petrological artefacts, the ^{14}C method, like *dendrochronology* (the study of unique patterns of annual growth rings in trees), has only an associational value, although dateable organic material is sometimes caught up in pottery.

Another well known and much used method is K/Ar dating. In this case ^{40}Ar, formed by the decay of radioactive ^{40}K, can be measured, using mass spectrometry. Since the proportion of ^{40}K to ^{39}K and ^{41}K is known, the amount of ^{40}K in a potassium-bearing rock or mineral as a proportion of the total amount of potassium is an indicator of the age since the rock or mineral was formed by an igneous or metamorphic process. The half-life of ^{40}K is 1250 million years, enabling the method to extend from say 30 000–100 000 years up to 4500 million years. A related technique involves artificially induced $^{40}Ar/^{39}Ar$ transitions.

The $^{87}Rb/^{87}Sr$ method is only suitable for very old rocks but the ^{238}U, ^{235}U, and ^{232}Th decay series, yielding ^{206}Pb, ^{207}Pb, and ^{208}Pb, respectively, has many archaeological applications. As with ^{14}C, however, the dates are generally associational only in the case of petrological artefacts. Schwarcz, Blackwell, Boldberg, and Marks (1979) describe a useful $^{230}Th/^{234}U$ method (part of the ^{238}U decay series) for dating travertine, in the absence of lavas suitable for K/Ar dating, provided that the travertine is impermeable and free of detritus. The method extends the range of the U/Th techniques considerably, and gives good ages ($\pm$ 5–10 per cent) from 5000 to 400 000 years.

A technique for measuring the fluorine picked up from groundwater by 'chipped lithic' materials has been used for dating artefacts of trachyte, phonolite, dacite, arkose, ortho- and metaquartzite, and hornfels (Taylor 1975). A proton-induced nuclear resonant reaction, in which gamma rays are produced, gives ^{19}F profiles. The γ-rays are counted and for a given depth of burial are proportional to fluorine content and thus to age.

Reviewing radioactive dating methods, Hedges (1979) covers several other decay-based techniques, whilst Stuiver (1978) reviewed ^{14}C dating and its correlation with magnetic and other techniques.

5. Obsidian hydration dating

Although obsidian contains up to some 1 per cent of magmatic water, it will absorb water from its surroundings whenever a freshly fractured surface is exposed (Fleming 1976; Friedman and Trembour 1978; Michels 1973). Thus a newly manufactured artefact will begin to form a hydrated surface layer from the moment it is made. The rate of growth of the hydrated rind depends on such factors as the temperature and the humidity of the environment, and the chemical composition of the obsidian (in particular its water content). The growth of the rind is expected to follow the diffusion law: $x = kt^{1/2}$, where x is the thickness of the rind in micrometres, t is time elapsed, and k is the diffusion coefficient, which depends on the complex factors outlined above.

Because of these complex factors, the method should be calibrated for each source of obsidian and each environment, using flakes for which t can be determined by ^{14}C or other method. Since there is some controversy about the applicability of the diffusion equation in its simple form, a range of calibration of different ages is usually necessary. Rim thicknesses can be measured on thin sections of obsidian using a petrological microscope. Once the method has been calibrated to provide a time-scale within a site area or region, and for a given time-span, artefacts within that area can be compared rapidly and simply. Introduction of obsidian from outside can be noted; gaps in artefact manufacture revealed; and stratigraphic correlation within the site area carried out: hydration thickness of course increases downwards.

Very generally, the first micrometre of rim takes a few hundred years to grow, and the upper limit is usually taken as about 50 micrometres, corresponding to about 0.5 million years, after which the rim tends to break up and spall off.

Extension of the technique to basaltic glass has revealed that this less acidic material hydrates more rapidly and at a predictable rate: 12 micrometres per 1000 years. The material has been in very little use for artefacts; otherwise it would be a more valuable variant of the rim hydration dating method.

A full discussion of obsidian hydration dating is given in Chapter 7.

Chemical composition

This section (cf. Goffer 1980) includes a few methods which, strictly, are physical; they are included here in order to keep all the determinative methods of chemical composition together. The destructive methods require preparation of a powdered sample. For this (cf. Reeves and Brooks 1978), the crushing technique given for heavy mineral analysis is used, except that all the material is crushed and sieved to, ideally, less than 200 mesh (75 μm) in size. The degree of heterogeneity of the rock governs the size of bulk sample requiring to be crushed in order to give a representative sample. For a coarse-grained rock such as granite, some 2 kg of rock might be needed; for a homogeneous, non-porphyritic (aphyric) or non-porphyroblastic rock, 100 g should suffice, although in practice a small chip is often all that is available.

References are given for most techniques but there are a few general sources which should be mentioned. Meschel (1978) includes a useful bibliography of papers concerned with general or specific analytical techniques; Reeves and Brooks (1978) cover most aspects of trace element analysis; Stross (1960) and Shotton and Hendry (1979) include accounts both of methods and specific applications; and other applications are given in this book (e.g. Chapter 4).

1. Classical or 'wet' analysis

Despite the introduction of instrumental methods, there is still a place for wet chemical methods in the analysis of rocks, minerals, and ceramic materials.

The basic technique (Maxwell 1968) is that of gravimetric analysis, by which a fused sample is dissolved and successive oxides precipitated in acid or alkali solution, filtered, dried, and weighed. Included in 'wet' methods are the flame photometer for the determination of the alkali oxides – sodium and potassium – and the colorimetric technique for a variety of other elements (Si, Ti, Al, Fe (total as Fe_2O_3), Mn, and P). True classical methods are often retained for the determination of FeO (by titration, for subtraction from total Fe_2O_3), H_2O^+, H_2O^-, and CO_2. A complete analysis using wet chemical techniques requires a minimum sample of 1 g. The methods are widely available and are perhaps the most reliable for the major and minor element oxides.

2. Optical emission spectroscopy (OES)

Optical emission spectroscopy is a well tried, but now largely superseded technique (Ahrens and Taylor 1961). A sample of the rock or mineral is powdered and mixed with graphite; the mixture is then inserted into a carbon arc and vaporized. The light emitted at specific wavelengths characteristic of each element is diffracted and then recorded on a photographic plate. The densities of the lines produced are compared with standards using a densitometer.

Although the method is reasonably rapid, it has declined in use in recent years; its main drawbacks are the differential volatilization of some elements, and the low accuracy of the method, generally resulting in only semi-quantitative results. Nevertheless, it covers a wide range of elements, is widely available in geology and chemistry laboratories, and has been extensively used. More modern refinements of the OES technique are claimed to produce highly accurate results. A sample of 0.05 g or less is required for an analysis embracing all major and minor and most trace elements; it cannot, of course, determine the Fe_2O_3/FeO ratio, water, or carbon dioxide.

A similar technique, employing a *laser* beam, can vaporize a minute sample from an unprepared area of the rock or artefact surface, only a few μm in diameter. The method is thus virtually non-destructive but is available only in a very few laboratories.

3. Atomic absorption spectroscopy (AAS)

In atomic absorption spectroscopy (Maxwell 1968; McLaughlin 1977), as with flame photometry, a solution of the sample is sprayed into a flame, causing the compounds present in the solution to dissociate into their constituent atoms. Monochromatic light of the characteristic wavelength for the element to be determined is shone through the flame, and the atoms of the element will absorb this light. The total amount of light absorbed is measured and, by comparison with standards, concentrations can be calculated. Each element usually needs a different lamp to produce its characteristic radiation, unless multi-element lamps are used, so that simultaneous multi-element determinations are not usually feasible.

The method has become increasingly widely used. It requires ideally 1 g of sample for a complete analysis, although 0.2–0.4 g will normally suffice. It cannot, again, determine Fe_2O_3/FeO ratio, water, or carbon dioxide, but is amongst the best techniques for the determination of major, minor, and many trace elements (rare earths excepted).

Recent research has been directed towards finding ways of removing interferences and improving sensitivity. One recent development concerns the fitting of an ICP (inductively coupled plasma) attachment to an AAS spectrometer; although this can improve performance dramatically, it has been felt by some that it is preferable to use a specially designed ICP spectrometer (see below) whenever possible.

4. Inductively coupled plasma emission spectrometry (ICPES)

This relatively new method (Boumans 1979; Walsh 1980; Walsh and Howie 1980) is only available in a limited number of geological and chemical laboratories but is rapidly becoming more widespread. Once the sample is in solution, it is very rapid – 2–3 minutes for a complete analysis – and requires only a small amount of material: 0.03 g. The method uses the ionization of a gas (argon) by radio frequency excitation to produce a plasma, into which a solution of the sample is sprayed. The excited atoms in the solution then emit light, which can be measured. It is claimed that this method produces a linear calibration of emission with concentration over very large concentration ranges (10 p.p.m. to over 10 per cent), and greater freedom from interferences than AAS or OES. Preparation of a suitably stable solution of the sample requires care and skill. The method is proving ideal for major, minor, and trace elements, with the exception of FeO, H_2O^+, H_2O^-, and CO_2, but is less suitable than AAS or XRF for K_2O and than XRF for P_2O_5. SiO_2 is accurate to ± 1 per cent. Complete analysis requires, ideally, three 10 mg solutions, one for the major and minor elements, one for trace elements, and one for rare earths.

Another technique using plasma – *plasma ashing* – has proved a useful low-temperature technique for cleaning marble and other rock and mineral artefact surfaces preparatory to sampling or direct determination of, for example, composition or isotope ratios. The method does not contaminate or damage the inorganic material or alter its composition or isotopic values; it merely removes organic grime and other surface contaminants.

5. X-ray fluorescence spectrometry (XRF)

X-ray emission spectrography (Maxwell 1968; Norrish and Chappell 1977) is now widely used with manual or automated systems. The powdered sample, which can either be fused into a glass disc or pressed into a pellet, is irradiated with primary X-rays (or γ-rays) which cause the excitation of the orbital electrons of the atoms of the elements in the sample, causing them to emit secondary or fluorescent X-rays with wavelengths characteristic of each element.

Analyser crystals, such as LiF (lithium fluoride) are used to disperse the secondary X-rays into a spectrum, and their intensity or energy is measured by a suitable detector, usually a gas-filled proportional counter or scintillation detector. This method, known as WDS (wavelength dispersive spectrometry), can only be used to determine one element per counter at a time, and is therefore rather slow; several methods have been tried to get round this problem, including multi-spectrometer arrangements and computer control of spectrometers. A more rapid, but often less accurate, method employs solid state semiconductor detectors, usually made of silicon or germanium doped with lithium; these can be used to count over a wide range of X-ray energies simultaneously, thus giving XRF the capability to perform simultaneous multi-element analyses. This method is known as EDS (energy dispersive spectrometry), and is tending to challenge WDS more and more as advances are made in the design and construction of detectors and their associated electronics. In both these methods, the rate of emission of secondary X-rays is proportional to concentration and, by comparison with standards, can be converted into a measurement of the amount of that element present.

The WDS method is now precise for most major, minor, and many trace elements, including the rare earths. It is unreliable for elements of low atomic number (sodium and below, lithium being an important element that cannot be determined) and will not determine the Fe_2O_3/FeO ratio, water, or CO_2. Ideally, 1 g is required, but 0.4 g will suffice. Most geological and chemical laboratories now have XRF. The method is non-destructive, but since the sample is normally powdered, this is no advantage in the case of artefacts. However, small complete artefacts, such as axe heads, can be measured semi-quantitatively provided a flat surface is present. Use of the *milliprobe* attachment (Banks and Hall 1963) enables the X-ray tube to be 'stopped down' and focused on a small area for analysis.

Proton-excited XRF (proton PIXE or proton-induced X-ray emission), using protons rather than X-ray photons to excite the specimen, is very much more sensitive than XRF and uses much less material (a few milligrams). However, the high cost of the instrument means that it is only available in a very few centres. It has been used by Nielson, Hill, Mangelson, and Nelson (1976) and Nelson, Nielson, Mangelson, Hill, and Matheny (1977) for trace element analysis of Mexican obsidians.

A related technique – *X-ray photoelectron spectroscopy* – provides another non-destructive method for analysing powder or small whole artefacts (Lambert and McLaughlin 1976). Also, *proton-inelastic scattering* has been used for obsidian analysis (Coote, Whitehead, and McCallum 1972).

6. Instrumental neutron activation analysis (INAA)

If a rock or mineral sample is irradiated in a reactor by a prolonged and intense neutron bombardment, certain elements will undergo nuclear reactions to produce radioactive isotopes (Gordus 1970; Goles 1977; Widemann 1980).

The number of gamma photons produced as the isotopes decay is proportional to concentration, and can be counted by using solid-state Ge/Li or Si/li detectors. The characteristic γ-ray energies for each isotope are well known, and sample concentrations may be found by comparison of sample peak heights with those of suitable standards irradiated in the same batch. Elements suitable for determination by INAA include the rare earths, Mn, Sc, Ta, Th, Na, Fe, Hf, U, and certain other major elements – some, such as Mg, Al, Ti, and V, produce isotopes with short half-lives (less than 10 minutes) which require special techniques.

Advantages of the method include small sample size (less than 0.1 g), and very good accuracy and precision with low detection limits. Small whole artefacts can be irradiated, providing probably the best non-destructive, as well as specific, analytical method available. The main disadvantage with this method is the need for a reactor or particle acceleration facility for irradiation, but if measurement of the rare earth elements is necessary, this is probably one of the best methods to use. Irradiation facilities are often available at Atomic Energy Establishments and university reactor centres, which may also run a complete INAA service.

The detection limits can be improved by using *radiochemical separation* to isolate the elements of interest. This requires specialized laboratory facilities, and is not as widely used as INAA, but may be necessary if very low levels of the REE are encountered; facilities for RNAA may also be available at the centres mentioned above.

7. Electron microprobe analysis (EMPA)

The electron microprobe (Reed 1975; Smith 1976; Long 1977), of which several models are now available, has become the most popular method of mineral analysis. Its main advantage lies in its ability to provide quantitative analyses of single crystals without destroying their relationship to the texture of the host rock. Apart from being more rapid than chemical analysis of separated minerals, it obviates the laborious separation process already described. Provided they are sufficiently small and can be mounted, whole artefacts can be analysed. Normally, however, a polished thin section is prepared, left without cover glass, coated with carbon, and scanned by a focused electron beam. The beam can be trained on areas as small as 10 μm square, so that small grains and zones within grains can be analysed. The electron beam causes the mineral to emit secondary X-rays, which can be separated and measured in exactly the same way as for XRF. The same two methods of counting – wavelength dispersive and energy dispersive spectrometry – are used and excellent results can be obtained for the major, minor, and most trace elements present in minerals, with the same limitations as for XRF (FeO, water, CO_2). Microprobes are no longer a rarity but their use in artefact petrology is probably restricted; the most likely use is perhaps for chemically and mineralogically homogeneous rocks like obsidian and the flint–chert–jasper group, which in this context can be treated like minerals.

A refinement of the microprobe – the *ion probe* – employs a beam of ions rather than electrons to excite the sample. The impact of the ions on the sample dislodges ions and ionized fragments from the surface of the sample, which can be used to form a spectrum, as in conventional electron-beam or X-ray instruments. The method is still largely in the experimental stage since, although it is very sensitive, there are problems in interpreting the spectra; this is because even a simple silicate structure can give rise to many different types of ion fragments, which can lead to a spectrum containing several dozen peaks.

Cathodoluminescence, a related technique, is the visual observation of the luminescence generated by the electron beams; it will reveal the distribution patterns of trace element impurities in a mineral grain and thus 'fingerprint' it. The method has hardly been used in artefact petrology but its value in sandstone petrology (Zinkernagel 1978) in distinguishing three luminescence types of quartz – 'violet', brown, and non-luminescing – could perhaps lead to an archaeological application.

8. Other chemical methods

The *CHN analyser* (Din and Jones 1978) is used to determine the content of carbon, hydrogen (usually from water), and nitrogen in a sample. The powdered material is burnt in oxygen, releasing C, H, and N as carbon dioxide, water, and oxides of nitrogen. These oxides are then reduced to their respective elements, and their concentrations measured by thermal conductivity methods; a powdered sample weighing about 25 mg is required. This method is much more rapid than classical gravimetric methods, although with such a small sample, great care must be taken to avoid even the slightest trace of organic contamination.

Chromatography embraces a variety of techniques in which substances absorbed in a fractionating column can be released selectively and measured using a variety of detectors. The method is used for the analysis of amber, resins, oils, and other organic materials.

Neither of these methods is likely to be of widespread use in artefact petrology; analysis of water and amber are the most likely applications.

Isotope studies

Mass spectrometry is a technique for determining the concentrations in a specimen of the different isotopes of an element. Positively charged streams of ions can be separated into a mass spectrum by means of suitably disposed magnetic fields. In addition to measuring radioactive isotopes for age determination techniques, mass spectrometry is used for the measurement of *stable isotopes* such as those of carbon, oxygen, sulphur, and deuterium. Carbon and oxygen isotope abundances vary in certain rocks, such as marble and limestone, in accordance with certain physiochemical laws related to their mode of formation – as biogenic sediment, chemical precipitate, and so on. The isotope ratios $^{13}C/^{12}C$ and $^{18}O/^{16}O$ vary by 1 to 2 per cent in marbles from different areas. The differences between these ratios and a suitable standard (e.g. Standard Mean Ocean Water, SMOW; or PDB) can be plotted against each other; they reveal characteristic isotope fields for many of the classic Mediterranean marbles (see Chapter 4). The oxygen isotopes of *Spondylus* shells used as ornaments have been used to deduce Neolithic trade and travel routes in southern Europe (Shackleton and Renfrew 1970). The measurements can be carried out on 0.01 g samples. Oxygen isotope studies have also been carried out on East African chert (Stiles *et al.* 1974).

A further technique, in which the *strontium isotope ratio* ($^{87}Sr/^{86}Sr$) is determined, can also be used to distinguish between gypsum (alabaster), marble, and obsidian from different sources. In the case of gypsum, the method depends on the fact that the present-day strontium isotopic composition of gypsum is essentially identical to that of the sea water from which it was deposited.

Interpretation of results

Of the various chemical and analytical methods briefly described here, XRF, AAS, and INAA have become by far the most popular. The reasons are straightforward; the methods are commonly available, they have low detection limits and high precision, they are rapid, and they require relatively small amounts of material. The early favourite, OES, has largely been abandoned in favour of more modern methods, although it can still yield good results in certain cases. It is probable that ICPES will become another favourite as it gains acceptance and becomes more widespread. In all cases, the classical 'wet' methods are used in addition when required, especially for the determination of FeO to enable the Fe_2O_3/FeO ratio to be established.

The analytical methods covered in this chapter fall naturally into two groups – those which provide a quantitative, numerical result, and those which give qualitative results such as spectra. Where a method gives the latter type of result, it is often best to obtain expert assistance in interpreting the data, as it is very easy to reach erroneous conclusions; this is especially true of thermal analysis, X-ray diffractograms, and Mössbauer and infrared spectrometry. When, however, a method gives numerical output, there are many ways in which the data can be treated; for example, it is customary to select a relatively small number of trace elements, perhaps, but not necessarily, in conjunction with major and minor element analysis, when attempting to match an artefact composition with that of a possible source. The number may be as low as two – say Ti and Zr – or three – say Sr, Zr, and Rb or Ba, Zr, and Sr. The pairs are plotted on two axis plots, the groups of three on triangular diagrams, the concentrations (in p.p.m.) being divided by, say, 100 for Ti and two for Sr in order to bring the points plotted into the central region of the triangle. If the points fall into clearly defined fields, and that of the artefact matches that of a source, a high degree of probability exists that the true source has been established; it by no means establishes this fact, however, although a wide disparity between artefact and source almost certainly indicates the latter not to have been the place of origin of the artefact. Remember, too, the possible presence of *unknown* sources. Since *ratios* are so important, the use of log abundances is valuable, since it changes a log normal frequency distribution to a normal distribution. Care should be taken to avoid placing too much credence on insufficient evidence. If the plot shows a wide scatter but some degree of correspondence between artefact and source samples, there are various statistical methods which can be applied to determine the degree of probability of a match. Standard deviations should always be tabled in such cases, and discriminant, multivariate, principal component, or factor analysis applied (Reeves and Brooks 1978). An excellent and eminently readable guide to the use of statistics in this field has been written by Davis (1973).

Bieber, Brooks, Harbottle, and Sayre (1976) applied multivariate techniques to INAA data on Aegean ceramics; the same group (Weigand, Harbottle, and Sayre 1977) used them for turquoise artefacts and sources in Mesoamerica and the south-western USA. Weigand *et al.* again used INAA on 15 to 20 elements and applied cluster analysis in a dendrogram study, with which they distinguished mines in Mexico, New Mexico, and south-western USA as potential sources of some of the tens of thousands of artefacts used by the Toltecs of Chaco Canyon, Teotihuacan, in the central valley of Mexico, and the later Aztecs. A 'provenience postulate', to reveal differences between sources that are greater than the differences between samples from a single source, was developed; it excluded the Mexican and south-western US mines, pointing strongly to a source in New Mexico, perhaps Cerrillos, for a group of 80 or so artefacts at least, and possibly for others.

A popular technique for comparing the origins of samples is to use rare earth element patterns. This usually takes the form of a plot of atomic number from lanthanum ($Z = 57$) to lutecium ($Z = 71$), against log concentration normalized to (divided by) the average concentration of each rare earth in chondritic meteorites, regarded as the most 'primitive' or undifferentiated material known. The resulting pattern usually indicates, as well as variation in absolute concentrations, enrichment of depletion in the light or heavy rare earths, as well as anomalous 'highs' or 'lows', particularly for europium.

Correspondence of REE patterns between different specimens is an indication as to whether the artefacts derive from a common source, and can be matched to one or more known sources. Similar plotting methods are used for the stable isotopes. If $\delta^{18}O$ and $\delta^{13}C$ are plotted (see Chapter 4), 'isotope fields' may result which point strongly to a match or the lack of it. In the case of strontium isotopes, a plot of, say, Sr against Rb concentration will serve similarly, taken alongside the grouping of the values for the $^{87}Sr/^{86}Sr$ ratios.

Acknowledgements

The authors would like to thank P. Henderson for critically reading the manuscript, and M. J. Aitken, J. E. Chisholm, V. K. Din, J. G. Francis, and B. R. Young for technical help and advice.

References

Abbott, P. L. and Peterson, G. L. (1978). Effects of abrasion durability on conglomerate clast populations: examples from Cretaceous and Eocene conglomerates of the San Diego area, California. *Journal of Sedimentary Petrology* **48**, 31–42.

Afordakos, G., Alexopoulos, K., and Miliotis, D. (1974). Using artificial thermoluminescence to reassemble statues from fragments. *Nature* **250**, 47–8.

Ahrens, L. H. and Taylor, S. R. (1961). *Spectrochemical analysis*, 2nd edn. Pergamon, London.

Aitken, M. J. (1974). *Physics and archaeology*, 2nd edn. Oxford University Press.

—— (1977). Thermoluminescence and the archaeologist. *Antiquity* **51**, 11–19.

Banks, M. and Hall, E. T. (1963). X-ray fluorescent analysis in archaeology: the 'milliprobe'. *Archaeometry* **6**, 31–6.

Beck, C. W., Adams, A. B., Southard, G. C. and Fellows, C. (1971). Determination of the origin of Greek amber artifacts by computer-classification of infrared spectra. In: R. H. Brill (ed.): *Science and archaeology*. MIT Press, Cambridge, Mass., 235–40.

Bieber, A. M., Jr, Brooks, D. W., Harbottle, G., and Sayre, E. V. (1976). Application of multivariate techniques to analytical data on Aegean ceramics. *Archaeometry* **18**, 59–74.

Bishop, A. C. and Woolley, A. R. (1973). A new technique for cutting archaeological material. *Antiquity* **47**, 302–3.

Boumans, P. W. J. M. (1979). Inductively coupled plasma-atomic emission spectroscopy: its present and future position in analytical chemistry. *Fresenius Zeitschrift für analytische Chemie* **299**, 337–61.

Bowie, S. H. U. and Simpson, P. R. (1977). Microscopy: reflected light. In: J. Zussman: *Physical methods in determinative mineralogy*. 2nd edn. Academic Press, London, 109–65.

Burleigh, R. and Seeley, M. A. (1975). Use of a wire saw for slicing certain sample materials for thermoluminescent dating. *Archaeometry* **17**, 116–19.

Coote, G. F., Whitehead, N. E., and McCallum, G. J. (1972). A rapid method of obsidian characterization by inelastic scattering of protons. *Journal of Radioanalytical Chemistry* **12**, 491–6.

Davis J. C. (1973). *Statistics and data analysis in geology.* Wiley, New York.

Din, V. K. and Jones, G. C. (1978). The determination of total carbon and combined water in silicates using a C, H, N elemental analyser. *Chemical Geology* **23**, 347–52.

Durrani, S. A., Khan, H. A., Taj, M., and Renfrew, C. (1971). Obsidian source identification by fission track analysis. *Nature* **233**, 242–5.

Estep-Barnes, P. A. (1977). Infrared spectroscopy. In: J. Zussman: *Physical methods in determinative mineralogy.* 2nd edn. Academic Press, London, 529–603.

Farmer, V. C. (ed.) (1974). *The infrared spectra of minerals.* Mineralogical Society, London. (Monograph no. 4.)

Fleischer, R. L., Price, P. B. and Walker, R. M. (1975). *Nuclear tracks in solids.* University of California Press, Berkeley.

Fleming, S. (1976). *Dating in archaeology: a guide to scientific techniques.* Dent, London.

—— (1979). *Thermoluminescence techniques in archaeology.* Clarendon Press, Oxford.

Fornaseri, M., Malpieri, L., and Tolomeo, L. (1975). Provenance of pumice in the north coast of Cyprus. *Archaeometry* **17**, 112–16.

Friedman, I. and Trembour, F. W. (1978). Obsidian: the dating stone. *American Scientist* **66**, 44–51.

Garrison, E. G., Rowlett, R. M., Cowan, D. L., and Holroyd, L. V. (1981). ESR dating of ancient flints. *Nature* **290**, 44–5.

Gibb, T. C. (1976). *Principles of Mössbauer spectroscopy.* Chapman & Hall, London.

Goffer, Z. (1980). *Archaeological chemistry: a sourcebook on the applications of chemistry to archaeology.* Wiley, Chichester.

Goles, G. G. (1977). Instrumental methods of neutron activation analysis. In: J. Zussman: *Physical methods in determinative mineralogy.* 2nd edn. Academic Press, London, 343–69.

Gordus, A. A. (1970). Neutron activation analysis of archaeological artefacts. *Philosophical Transactions of the Royal Society A* **269**, 165–74.

Griffith, W. P. (1974). Raman spectroscopy of minerals. In: V. C. Farmer (ed.) *The infrared spectra of minerals,* Mineralogical Society, London. (Monograph no. 4.)

Grundy, P. J. and Jones, G. A. (1976). *Electron microscopy in the study of materials.* Edward Arnold, London. (The structures and properties of solids 7.)

Hall, E. T. (1964). Archaeometry – the physical sciences applied to archaeology. *Journal of the Royal Institute of Chemistry* **88**, 146–8.

Hedges, R. E. M. (1979). Radioisotope clocks in archaeology. *Nature* **281**, 19–24.

Huntley, D. J. and Bailey, D. C. (1978). Obsidian source identification by thermoluminescence. *Archaeometry* **20**, 159–70.

Ikeya, M. (1978). Electron spin resonance as a method of dating. *Archaeometry* **20**, 147–58.

Jones, M. P. (1977). Automatic image analysis. In: J. Zussman: *Physical methods in determinative mineralogy.* 2nd edn. Academic Press, London, 167–99.

Kerr, P. F. (1977). *Optical mineralogy.* 4th edn. McGraw-Hill, New York.

Lambert, J. B. and McLaughlin, C. D. (1976). X-ray photoelectron spectroscopy: a new analytical method for the examination of archaeological artifacts. *Archaeometry* **18**, 169–80.

Leach, B. F. and Fankhauser, B. (1978). The characterization of New Zealand obsidian sources by use of thermoluminescence. *Journal of the Royal Society of New Zealand* **8**, 331–42.

Long, J. V. P. (1977). Electron probe microanalysis. In: J. Zussman: *Physical methods in determinative mineralogy*. 2nd edn. Academic Press, London, 273–341.

Longworth, G. and Warren, S. E. (1979). The application of Mössbauer spectroscopy to the characterization of western Mediterranean obsidian. *Journal of Archaeological Science* **6**, 179–93.

Maurer, C., Williams, S., and Riley, T. (1981). ESR dating of archaeological ceramics: a progress report. *MASCA Journal* **1**, 202–4.

Maxwell, J. A. (1968). *Rock and mineral analysis*. Interscience Publishers, Wiley, New York.

McConnell, J. D. C. (1977). Electron microscopy and electron diffraction. In: J. Zussman: *Physical methods in determinative mineralogy*. 2nd edn. Academic Press, London, 475–527.

McLaughlin, R. J. W. (1977). Atomic absorption spectroscopy. In: J. Zussman: *Physical methods in determinative mineralogy*. 2nd edn. Academic Press, London, 371–89.

Melcher, C. L. and Zimmerman, D. W. (1977). Thermoluminescent determination of prehistoric heat treatment of chert artifacts. *Science* **197**, 1359–62.

Meschel, S. V. (1978). Chemistry and archaeology: a creative bond. In: G. F. Carter (ed.): Archaeological chemistry Volume II. *Advances in Chemistry Series* **171**, 3–24.

Michels, J. W. (1973). *Dating methods in archaeology*. Seminar Press, New York.

Muir, I. D. (1977). Microscopy: transmitted light. In: J. Zussman: *Physical methods in determinative mineralogy*. 2nd edn. Academic Press, London, 35–108.

Muller, L. D. (1977a). Mineral separation. In: J. Zussman: *Physical methods in determinative mineralogy*. 2nd edn. Academic Press, London, 1–34.

—— (1977b). Density determination. In: J. Zussman: *Physical methods in determinative mineralogy*. 2nd edn. Academic Press, London, 663–75.

Nelson, F. W., Nielson, K. K., Mangelson, N. F., Hill, M. W., and Matheny, R. T. (1977). Preliminary studies of the trace element composition of obsidian artifacts from northern Campeche, Mexico. *American Antiquity* **42**, 209–25.

Neumann, B. S. (1977). Thermal techniques. In: J. Zussman: *Physical methods in determinative mineralogy*. 2nd edn. Academic Press, London, 605–62.

Nielson, K. K., Hill, M. W., Mangelson, N. F., and Nelson, F. W. (1976). Elemental analysis of obsidian artifacts by proton particle-induced X-ray emission. *Analytical Chemistry* **48**, 1947–50.

Norrish, K. and Chappell, B. W. (1977). X-ray fluorescence spectrometry. In: J. Zussman: *Physical methods in determinative mineralogy*. 2nd edn. Academic Press, London, 201–72.

Reed, S. J. B. (1975). *Electron microprobe analysis*. Cambridge University Press.

Reeves, R. D. and Brooks, R. R. (1978). *Trace element analysis of geological materials*. Interscience Publishers, Wiley, New York.

Renfrew, C. and Peacey, J. S. (1968). Aegean marble; a petrological study. *Annual of the British School at Athens* **63**, 45–66.

Robins, G. V., Seeley, N. J., McNeil, D. A. C., and Symons, M. R. C. (1978). Identification of ancient heat treatment in flint artefacts by ESR spectroscopy. *Nature* **276**, 703–4.

Rowlett, R. M., Mandeville, M. D., and Zeller, E. J. (1974). The interpretation and dating of humanly worked siliceous materials by thermoluminescent analysis. *Proceedings of the Prehistoric Society* **40**, 37–44.

Savkevich, S. S. (1981). Physical methods used to determine the geological origin of amber and other fossil resins; some critical remarks. *Physics and Chemistry of Minerals* **7**, 1–4.

Schwarcz, H. P., Blackwell, B., Goldberg, P., and Marks, A. E. (1979). Uranium series dating of travertine from archaeological sites, Nahal Zin, Israel. *Nature* **277**, 558–60.

Seeley, M.-A. (1975). Thermoluminescent dating in its application to archaeology. Review. *Journal of Archaeological Science* **2**, 17–43.

Shackleton, N. J. and Renfrew, C. (1970). Neolithic trade routes re-aligned by oxygen isotope analyses. *Nature* **228**, 1062–5.

Shotton, F. W. and Hendry, G. L. (1979). The developing field of petrology in archaeology. *Journal of Archaeological Science* **6**, 75–84.

Smith, D. G. W. (ed.) (1976). *Microbeam techniques.* Co-op Press, Edmonton, (Mineralogical Association of Canada Short Course Handbook vol. 1.)

Stiles, D. N., Hay, R. L. and O'Neil, J. R. (1974). The MNK chert factory site, Olduvai Gorge, Tanzania. *World Archaeology* **5**, 285–308.

Stross, F. H. (1960). Authentification of antique stone objects by physical and chemical methods. *Analytical Chemistry* **32** (3), 17A–36A.

Stuiver, M. (1978). Radiocarbon timescale tested against magnetic and other dating methods. *Nature* **273**, 271–4.

Taylor, R. E. (1975). Fluorine diffusion: a new dating method for chipped lithic materials. *World Archaeology* **7**, 125–35.

Tite, M. S. (1972). *Methods of physical examination in archaeology.* Seminar Press, New York.

Walsh, J. N. (1980). The simultaneous determination of the major, minor and trace constituents of silicate rocks using inductively coupled plasma spectrometry. *Spectrochimica Acta* **35B**, 107–111.

—— Howie, R. A. (1980). An evaluation of the performance of an inductively coupled plasma source spectrometer for the determination of the major and the trace constituents of silicate rocks and minerals. *Mineralogical Magazine* **43**, 967–74.

Weigand, P. C., Harbottle, G., and Sayre, E. V. (1977). Turquoise sources and source analysis: Mesoamerica and the southwestern U.S.A. *In* T. K. Earle and J. E. Ericson (ed.) *Exchange systems in prehistory*, Academic Press, London, 15–34.

Widemann, F. (1980). Neutron activation analysis for provenance studies of archaeological artefacts. *Journal of Radioanalytical Chemistry* **55**, 271–81.

Wintle, A. G. (1980). Thermoluminescence dating: a review of recent applications to non-pottery materials. *Archaeometry* **22**, 113–22.

Woodward, L. A. (1967). General introduction. In: H. A. Szymanski (ed.): *Raman spectroscopy, theory and practice.* Plenum Press, New York, 1–43.

Young, H. R. and Syms, E. L. (1980). The use of acetate peels in lithic analysis. *Archaeometry* **22**, 205–8.

Zinkernagel, U. (1978). Cathodoluminescence of quartz and its application to sandstone petrology. *Contributions to Sedimentology* **8**, iv + 69.

Zussman, J. (1977). X-ray diffraction. In: J. Zussman: *Physical methods in determinative mineraology.* 2nd edn. Academic Press, London, 392–473.

3. Raw materials and miscellaneous uses of stone

D. R. C. Kempe

Raw materials

All stone artefacts consist of minerals or rocks; those made of synthetic or artificial materials – slags, bricks, tiles, concretes, cements, plasters, and composition blocks – cannot be called 'stone' although they derive almost entirely from natural rock and mineral material. A mineral is a naturally occurring inorganic substance, of fixed composition or having a composition falling within strictly defined limits, and with an ordered atomic arrangement. As almost always in nature, there are a few exceptions and amber, jet, lignite, cannel coal, all the bituminous materials, and the calcite and aragonite which form pearl are organic in origin; nevertheless, the definition given above is generally valid. Rocks consist of aggregates of grains of one or more minerals. Common rock types contain, say, from one to four essential minerals, with up to perhaps six or more 'minor' or accessory minerals in addition. There are also rare cases of the use of meteoric material as artefacts (Khan 1938; Rickard 1941) but these are not considered here.

Minerals are usually classified into groups based on their chemical composition. Thus there are elements and alloys; oxides and hydroxides; carbonates; sulphates, nitrates, borates, and phosphates; chlorides and other halides; sulphides; and silicates, together with other lesser groups. Only a few are treated in this book; they include some of the native precious metals (gold, silver, platinum, palladium), native copper and iron; the gem minerals diamond; corundum (ruby and sapphire); beryl (emerald and aquamarine); chrysoberyl (alexandrite); topaz, garnet, zircon, labradorite and green feldspar, olivine (peridot), tourmaline, quartz (amethyst, citrine, cairngorm, rock crystal), and the chalcedony group (jasper, agate, chrysoprase, onyx, sardonyx, carnelian, and sard) as well as opal; and the decorative sculptural minerals (jadeite and nephrite, turquoise, lapis lazuli (lazurite), soapstone or steatite (talc), alabaster (gypsum), fluorite, and malachite). Many of these are discussed where appropriate in chapters 4, 8, and 10. Further information on minerals – their chemical composition, physical and crystallographic properties, occurrence, and uses – can be found in many books: Read (1970) and Dana and Ford (1955) are particularly to be recommended, but for coloured illustrations the more popular works are required. One of these that is particularly valuable for its colour photographs of hand specimens of rocks is Hamilton, Woolley, and Bishop (1974).

Rocks are of course more complex. They also can be classified according to their mineralogical and chemical composition but first need to be divided into three major groups: the igneous, sedimentary, and metamorphic rocks. Examples of the more common rocks from these three groups are illustrated in later pages by photomicrographs, representative chemical analyses, and typical specific gravities.

The igneous rocks, formed of solidified ('frozen') magma which was generated by the melting of pre-existing rocks in the Earth's crust or mantle, largely by radiogenic heat, include the huge granite masses (batholiths) and the basaltic and other lavas. In Table 3.1 a simple classification of the principal igneous rock types is given. Horizontal division reflects a chemical change from 'acid' to 'basic', represented mainly in a decrease in silica and an increase in the percentage of coloured (Fe-Mg) minerals from left to

Table 3.1. Common igneous rocks

	$\longleftarrow$ SiO_2 $\longrightarrow$ Na_2O, K_2O $\longrightarrow$ CaO, MgO, FeO $\longrightarrow$ mafic (Fe–Mg) minerals $\longrightarrow$				
chemical type	acid	intermediate		basic	ultrabasic
fine-grained, extrusive, volanic lavas	rhyolite OBSIDIAN pitchstone	trachyte	andesite	BASALT	PICRITE (also coarser-grained)
intermediate-grained, 'hypabyssal', dykes, sills, and small masses	microgranite[1] FELSITE PORPHYRY	microsyenite	microdiorite	DOLERITE (diabase[2]) (epidiorite[3], greenschist, or greenstone)	most lamprophyres (e.g. kersantite[1])
coarse-grained, plutonic, 'abyssal', batholiths and major intrusions	GRANITE	syenite LARVIKITE[1]	DIORITE tonalite	gabbro	peridotite and pyroxenite (SOAPSTONE or STEATITE and SERPENTINE[3])

CAPITALS indicate common artefact material.
[1] Specific examples given in Chapter 4.
[2] Alternative name in USA and elsewhere; also often used in early literature synonomously with dolerite.
[3] Metamorphic equivalent.

right. The vertical division is into three groups. The volcanic rocks, principally the fine-grained extrusive lavas, cooled rapidly on reaching the surface: they include the glassy rocks such as obsidian (see Chapter 7). The medium-grained, 'hypabyssal' rocks were intruded as dykes, sills, and small masses to within a short distance of the Earth's surface and were thus more slowly cooled. Finally, the coarse-grained, plutonic, 'abyssal' rocks formed the huge batholithic intrusions, as of granite, often in mountain ranges. In each case, large crystals (called phenocrysts) can occur in rocks of generally finer grain; this texture is called porphyritic. There are of course many gradations of chemical and mineralogical composition, and of the form of the intrusions; this scheme is highly simplified and greater detail should be sought in, for example, Hatch, Wells, and Wells (1972) or Williams, Turner, and Gilbert (1954).

There are also the pyroclastic rocks: these comprise mixed volcanic ash and rock and crystal debris, as well as sedimentary material, in a continuous gradational series, depending on their environment, from aerial to submarine, and distance from the volcanic source. They are included here within the igneous rocks but are sometimes treated as sediments. They include the tuffs and welded tuffs or ignimbrites; artefact examples are the Easter Island volcanic tuff of which the majority of the statues are carved, and the Group VI Neolithic axe material of England.

The sedimentary rocks (Table 3.2) are those deposited mainly by water or wind action. The water-laid rocks are mainly marine but there are also lacustrine, fluvial, and glacial deposits. Wind-laid (aeolian) rocks are almost entirely lithified or indurated sandstones and siltstones but the water-laid sediments include limestones, sandstones, and the finer-grained siltstones, shales, and mudstones, and the coarse-grained conglomerates (with rounded pebbles) and breccias (with angular fragments). Of the three most important groups – limestones, sandstones, and shales – the first two form the majority of building stones and much of the sculptural material.

Limestones, including dolomites, form in a wide range of marine and some fresh-water environments, and consist principally of the calcareous

Table 3.2. The most common sedimentary and metamorphic rocks

Sedimentary ⟶ Metamorphic		
LIMESTONE	MARBLE	
SANDSTONE	QUARTZITE	
GREYWACKE ⎱	⎧hornfels⎫	⎧schist
SHALE, argillite ⎰	⎨phyllite ⎬	⎨gneiss
	⎩SLATE ⎭	⎩granulite

CAPITALS indicate common artefact material.

shells and skeletal debris of marine animals, with some chemically precipitated inorganic calcite and secondary dolomite. Their composition varies
from pure $CaCO_3$ to highly impure types where dolomitic, siliceous, and
other impurities occur. Their textures are also highly variable, ranging from
fine-grained homogeneous rocks, such as chalk, to banded, fossil-bearing
types; some of the latter are mistakenly named 'marble' (see below).

The sandstones also vary; the desert, aeolian types are usually red in
colour, often contain a significant proportion of feldspar, and are usually
cemented by secondary silica. The marine sandstones generally formed in
relatively shallow water, are white to grey in colour, and highly variable in
texture and mineral content, the greywackes containing, as well as quartz,
the highest percentage of feldspar, clay, mica, and other mineral grains.
Three matrix types commonly occur: silica, calcite, and clay or mica. Greywacke is a rock commonly used for honestones; 'brownstone' is a popular
building sandstone in the north-eastern United States. The chemical composition of sandstones thus also varies widely, from pure silica rocks to those
with a high content of other oxides.

The third common type of sedimentary rock, shale and argillite, is
deposited principally in deep water or in estuarine muds, is very fine-grained,
and has a composition varying even more widely. These argillaceous rocks
have been used relatively rarely in artefact manufacture, although clays
have been put to a wide variety of uses.

Minor sedimentary rock types important in artefact petrology are the
calcareous rocks, travertine and tufa, and the secondary siliceous rocks, flint
and chert. Travertine and tufa are deposited chemically by hot springs and in
lakes and rivers; the travertine of Tivoli, Italy, well known as a building
stone, is an example deriving from a lake bed once fed with volcanic water.
Flint and chert, including jasper, have been used the world over as material
for axes, scrapers, adzes, blades, and other tools, and flint had a limited use
as a building stone. The black varieties sometimes have a superficial
resemblance to obsidian. The residual tropical weathering products – laterite and bauxite – and the surface desiccation or duricrust rocks – calcrete,
silcrete, and ferricrete – have also been put to restricted use as building
stone. For detailed descriptions of all sedimentary rocks, including evaporites and other minor groups not mentioned here, and a discussion of their
origin, refer to Pettijohn (1975) or Greensmith, Match, and Rastall (1978).

The third major group – the metamorphic rocks (Table 3.2) – contains the
products of members of the first two groups after alteration and recrystallization at high temperatures and pressures. Such changes were caused by
regional earth movements, as crustal plates moved and collided with each
other throughout geological time, or more rarely by local earth movements,
and by the thermal effects of igneous intrusions on the surrounding country
rocks. By far the best known as an artefact material is marble: metamor-

phosed limestone and dolomite. This category includes the classical building and sculptural stones of the Mediterranean region, where it is limestone metamorphosed by the events of the Alpine and earlier orogenies, responsible for the Alps and related mountain chains. Decorative banded or fossiliferous limestones – such as the Forest 'Marble' or Purbeck 'Marble' – are not true marbles: they have been so called by quarrymen, masons, and sculptors because they would take and retain a high polish, and the misnomers have remained. The use of trace element and isotope analysis to 'fingerprint' particular marbles is discussed in Chapter 4.

With the further exception of quartzite – metamorphosed sandstone – the metamorphic rocks are relatively unimportant as artefact material, although metamorphosed ultrabasic rocks – serpentinite and steatite or soapstone – were popular sculptural stones, and metamorphosed dolerite or diabase, called greenschist or epidiorite, were used almost as often for artefacts as the original igneous rock. Together with marble, the thinly banded schists and the coarsely banded gneisses and granulites are widely distributed metamorphic rocks.

The highly cleaved slate and phyllite, produced by dynamic (compressive) metamorphism and used widely as a roofing material, and hornfels – also usually argillaceous sediment (shale), hardened by thermal metamorphism – are other widely distributed metamorphic rock types. By analogy with the igneous rocks, metamorphic rocks containing large crystals – porphyroblasts – are said to have a porphyroblastic texture. Most of these rocks, in fact, derive from the metamorphism of shales and similar sediments; more or less homogeneous rocks, such as sandstone or limestone, convert to quartzite or marble which are similar in most respects to their progenitors, whilst igneous rocks similarly tend to show relatively little indication of metamorphism. Recommended texts on metamorphic rocks are Harker (1950) and Williams *et al.* (1954).

Rocks

In the following pages, 'typical' or 'representative' analyses and specific gravities are given. To attempt to give accurate ranges would be virtually impossible and suggest, unjustifiably, precise limits. The values given here must therefore be regarded purely as what they are: indications. Data are taken from sources cited in the text and from Guppy and Sabine (1956).

Minerals: Q   quartz   M   white or dark mica
AF   alkali feldspar   A   amphibole
PF   plagioclase feldspar   P   pyroxene
F   feldspathoid   O   olivine.

In addition, all rocks contain some accessories, in widely variable amounts; they are not given here. Photomicrographs, all × 18, are in plane polarized light. Some (e.g. flint) have the light cut down.

Granite

Typical analysis

SiO_2	71.69
TiO_2	0.33
Al_2O_3	14.03
Fe_2O_3	0.57
FeO	1.93
MnO	–
MgO	0.66
CaO	1.49
Na_2O	3.03
K_2O	4.59
H_2O	1.76
P_2O_5	–
Others	0.29
Total	100.37

Typical specific gravity: 2.63

Typical main minerals: Q, AF, PF, M

Fig. 3.1. Granite (the Sphinx, Giza, Egypt).

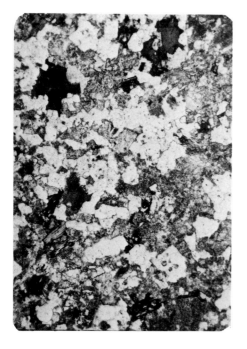

Fig. 3.2. Fine-grained granite (Cornwall).

Rhyolite and Obsidian

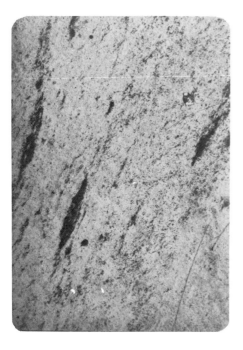

Typical analysis

SiO_2	76.78
TiO_2	0.08
Al_2O_3	12.09
Fe_2O_3	0.56
FeO	0.81
MnO	–
MgO	0.10
CaO	0.57
Na_2O	3.79
K_2O	4.93
H_2O	0.20
P_2O_5	–
Others	0.38
Total	100.29

Typical specific gravity: 2.52

Typical main minerals: Q, AF, M, glass

Fig. 3.3. Obsidian (Lipari Islands, Italy).

Fig. 3.4. Rhyolite (Stonehenge rhyolite, from the Preselau Hills).

Syenite

Typical analysis

SiO_2	65.40
TiO_2	0.71
Al_2O_3	16.99
Fe_2O_3	1.40
FeO	1.83
MnO	0.12
MgO	0.54
CaO	0.86
Na_2O	6.48
K_2O	5.20
H_2O^+	0.22
H_2O^-	0.08
P_2O_5	0.17
Total	100.00 (recalculated)

Typical specific gravity: 2.58

Typical main minerals: AF, Q or F, A, P

Fig. 3.5. Larvikite, Norway.

Fig. 3.6. Riebeckite microgranite (Ailsa Craig).

Fig. 3.7. Porphyry.

Fig. 3.8. Felsite or granophyre (English Group VII axe material, from Graig Lwyd, North Wales).

Trachyte

Typical analysis

SiO₂	64.5
TiO₂	0.8
Al₂O₃	17.2
Fe₂O₃	2.4
FeO	2.1
MnO	–
MgO	0.3
CaO	1.4
Na₂O	6.3
K₂O	5.0
H₂O	–
P₂O₅	–
Total	100.0 (recalculated anhydrous)

Typical specific gravity: 2.58
Typical main minerals: AF, Q
　　　　　　　　　or F, M, A, P

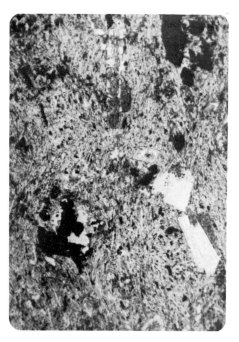

Fig. 3.9. Trachyte (Solfatara, Naples, Italy).

Diorite

Typical analysis

SiO₂	59.67
TiO₂	0.77
Al₂O₃	16.68
Fe₂O₃	2.93
FeO	4.09
MnO	–
MgO	3.62
CaO	6.22
Na₂O	3.50
K₂O	2.13
Others	0.39
Total	100.00 (recalculated anhydrous)

Typical specific gravity: 2.79
Typical main minerals: PF, A, P

Fig. 3.10. Diorite (from an Egyptian sphinx).

Andesite

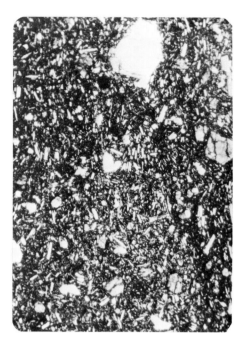

Typical analysis

SiO₂	58.17
TiO₂	0.80
Al₂O₃	17.26
Fe₂O₃	3.07
FeO	4.17
MnO	–
MgO	3.23
CaO	6.93
Na₂O	3.21
K₂O	1.61
H₂O	1.24
P₂O₅	0.20
Total	99.89

Typical specific gravity: 2.72
Typical main minerals: PF, A, P

Fig. 3.11. Andesite.

Gabbro

Typical analysis

SiO₂	48.01
TiO₂	1.51
Al₂O₃	19.11
Fe₂O₃	1.20
FeO	8.44
MnO	–
MgO	7.72
CaO	10.33
Na₂O	2.34
K₂O	0.17
H₂O	0.60
P₂O₅	–
Others	0.82
Total	100.25

Typical specific gravity: 2.85
Typical main minerals: PF, O, P

Fig. 3.12. Gabbro.

Dolerite

Typical analysis

SiO_2	54.11
TiO_2	3.37
Al_2O_3	11.65
Fe_2O_3	2.76
FeO	7.02
MnO	0.21
MgO	5.30
CaO	8.77
Na_2O	2.63
K_2O	1.75
H_2O^+	0.81
H_2O^-	0.68
P_2O_5	0.58
Others	0.33
Total	99.97

Typical specific gravity: 2.87
Typical main minerals: PF, P

Fig. 3.13. Dolerite

Fig. 3.14. Dolerite (Stonehenge spotted 'diabase', from the Preselau Hills).

Basalt

Typical analysis

SiO$_2$	45.4
TiO$_2$	3.0
Al$_2$O$_3$	14.7
Fe$_2$O$_3$	4.1
FeO	9.2
MnO	0.2
MgO	7.8
CaO	10.5
Na$_2$O	3.0
K$_2$O	1.0
H$_2$O	–
P$_2$O$_5$	0.4
Total	99.3

Typical specific gravity: 2.80
Typical main minerals: PF, O, P

Fig. 3.15. Alkali olivine basalt (Easter Island statue).

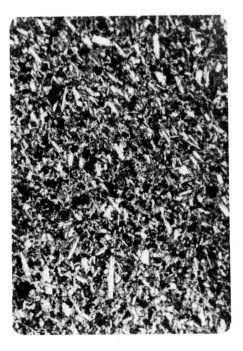

Typical analysis

SiO$_2$	49.78
TiO$_2$	0.68
Al$_2$O$_3$	15.69
Fe$_2$O$_3$	2.73
FeO	9.20
MnO	0.35
MgO	7.79
CaO	11.93
Na$_2$O	1.21
K$_2$O	0.29
H$_2$O	–
P$_2$O$_5$	0.07
Others	0.29
Total	100.01

Typical specific gravity: 2.85
Typical main minerals: PF, P

Fig. 3.16. Tholeiitic basalt.

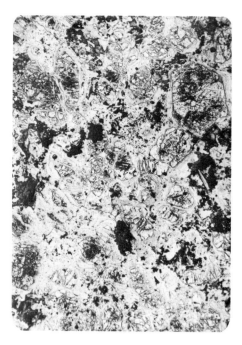

Serpentinite

Typical analysis

SiO₂	40.12
TiO₂	–
Al₂O₃	0.98
Fe₂O₃	6.52
FeO	1.21
MnO	0.52
MgO	35.78
CaO	0.12
Na₂O	0.24
K₂O	0.08
H₂O⁺	12.17
H₂O⁻	1.69
P₂O₅	0.10
CO₂	0.15
Others	0.44
Total	100.12

Typical specific gravity: 2.65
Typical main minerals: serpentine,
O

Fig. 3.17. Serpentinite (Lizard, Cornwall).

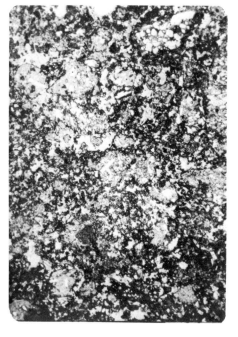

Tuff

Analysis of the Easter Island tuff
(see Chapter 4)

SiO₂	45.52
TiO₂	2.40
Al₂O₃	14.32
Fe₂O₃	6.92
FeO	5.14
MnO	0.20
MgO	2.98
CaO	5.88
Na₂O	2.89
K₂O	1.34
H₂O⁺	4.81
H₂O⁻	7.22
P₂O₅	0.27
CO₂	0.30
Total	100.19

Fig. 3.18. Rano Roraka tachylyte tuff, Easter Island.

Fig. 3.19. Tuff (English Group VI axe material, from the Great Langdale area, in the Lake District)

Limestone

Typical analysis

SiO_2	5.19
TiO_2	0.06
Al_2O_3	0.81
Fe_2O_3 } FeO }	0.54
MnO	0.05
MgO	7.90
CaO	42.61
Na_2O	0.05
K_2O	0.33
H_2O^+	0.56
H_2O^-	0.21
P_2O_5	0.04
CO_2	41.58
Others	0.16
Total	100.09

Typical specific gravity: 2.70

Typical main mineral: calcite

Fig. 3.20. Fossiliferous Carboniferous Limestone.

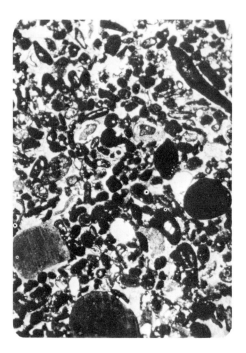

Fig. 3.21. Fossiliferous oolitic limestone.

Fig. 3.22. Silty limestone (or calcareous siltstone; Roman tessera, Dorset).

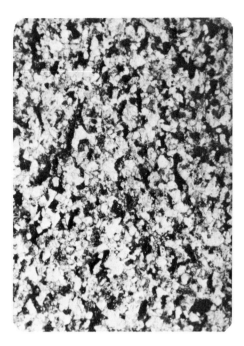

Greywacke

Typical analysis

SiO_2	66.7
TiO_2	0.6
Al_2O_3	13.5
Fe_2O_3	1.6
FeO	3.5
MnO	0.1
MgO	2.1
CaO	2.5
Na_2O	2.9
K_2O	2.0
H_2O^+	2.4
H_2O^-	0.6
P_2O_5	0.2
CO_2	1.2
Others	0.5
Total	100.4

Typical specific gravity: 2.70

Typical main minerals: Q, AF, PF, M, clays

Fig. 3.23. Greywacke (Coal Measures Pennant Grit; honestone material).

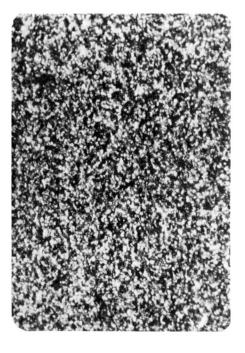

Fig. 3.24. Sandstone (Old Red Sandstone, Pembrokeshire; the Altar Stone at Stonehenge).

Shale

Typical analysis

SiO_2	58.10
TiO_2	0.65
Al_2O_3	15.40
Fe_2O_3	4.02
FeO	2.45
MnO	–
MgO	2.44
CaO	3.11
Na_2O	1.30
K_2O	3.24
H_2O	5.00
P_2O_5	0.17
CO_2	2.63
Others	0.64
C_{org}	0.80
Total	99.95

Typical main minerals: Q, AF, PF, M, clays

Minor sedimentary rocks

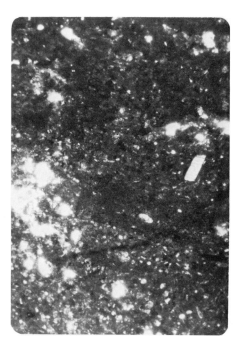

Fig. 3.25. Travertine, Italy

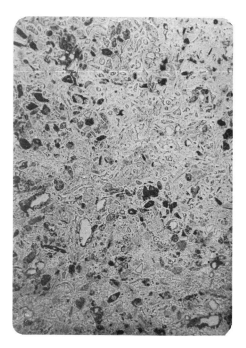

Fig. 3.26. Flint, England.

Fig. 3.27. Sarsen stone (Reading Beds, southern England; Stonehenge).

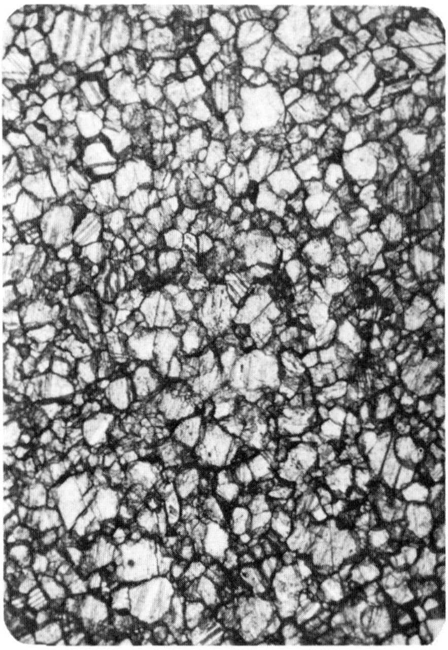

Fig. 3.28. Fine-grained marble (Paros, Greece).

Fig. 3.29. Porphyroblastic marble (Mount Pentelikon, Greece).

Fig. 3.30. Red marble (rosso antico), Laconia, Greece (from a tomb in Mycenae).

Fig. 3.31. Coarse-grained marble (Carrara, Italy).

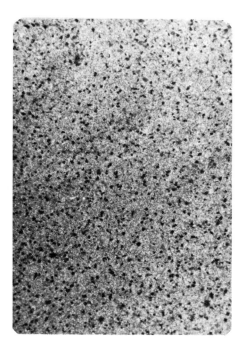

Slate

Typical analysis

SiO_2	58.41
TiO_2	1.00
Al_2O_3	20.25
Fe_2O_3	0.63
FeO	8.05
MnO	0.07
MgO	2.02
CaO	0.41
Na_2O	0.68
K_2O	2.50
H_2O^+	4.87
H_2O^-	0.46
P_2O_5	0.23
Others	0.04
C_{org}	0.39
Total	100.01

Typical specific gravity: 2.77

Typical main minerals: Q, AF, PF, M, clays

Fig. 3.32. Slate (Delabole, Cornwall).

Schist

Analysis of the Gandhara schist, Pakistan (see Chapter 4)

SiO_2	56.9
TiO_2	1.26
Al_2O_3	25.0
Fe_2O_3	2.73
FeO	3.28
MnO	0.13
MgO	0.86
CaO	0.28
Na_2O	1.40
K_2O	2.58
H_2O^+	4.89
P_2O_5	0.06
CO_2	0.49
Others	0.25
C_{org}	0.33
Total	100.44

Fig. 3.33. Gandhara bluish grey chloritoid-mica schist, NW Pakistan.

Fig. 3.34. Epidiorite (metamorphosed dolerite; English Group I
axe material, from Cornwall).

Other metamorphic rocks

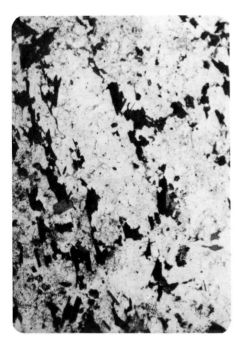

Fig. 3.35. Biotite gneiss.

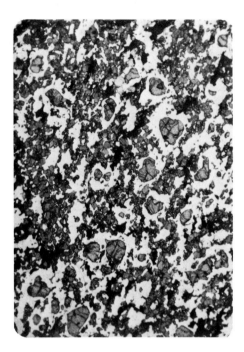

Fig. 3.36. Granulite.

Miscellaneous uses of stone

The principal uses to which man has put rocks and minerals are discussed in the following chapters. There are a few applications which are not referred to later, however, and which deserve a passing mention.

In addition to building, the geotechnical uses include ballast for ships, foundations for dams and bridges, the permanent ways and early sleepers for railways, and road metal. Almost any hard rock will suffice for these purposes but for roads and railways there is a strong preference for graded chips of limestone, basalt, andesite, and even fine-grained granite. In other words, fine- and even-grained rocks, in abundant supply, that will withstand pressure. Friable rocks, such as some sandstones, are not suitable; nor is a rock with a planar structure, such as slate, schist, or gneiss. A large category of rock use embraces the natural materials used in the manufacture of synthetic products, all of which are beyond the scope of this book; see, for example, Firman and Firman (1967) for a discussion of the sources of the materials used in mediaeval bricks and Lucas (1962) for ancient Egyptian bricks. Ornamental uses include painted plaster, stucco, faïence, clay for moulds, terra cotta, and the whole range of ceramics (Chapter 11); also glass, glazes, and pigments. In terra cotta, or baked earth, the manufactured product perhaps comes closest to the original. Terra cotta has been moulded, carved, or hand sculpted into such masterpieces as the 6000 soldiers, horses, and chariots of Xian, representing the battle array of the first Emperor of China, and the little human and animal figurines of the Indus Valley peoples.

Coal and limestone are used for fuel and for the preparation of quick-lime, whilst a multitude of marbles and ornamental stones are employed for table tops, ashtrays, paperweights, and other ornaments. As well as for carving, gypsum was used as cement and as a coffin 'filling'. Lithographic limestone, especially the Solnhofen stone from the Upper Jurassic of Bavaria, has been widely used for engraving (Twyman 1972). Verging on the sculptural is the use of the rare rocks riebeckite microgranite from Ailsa Craig, a tiny island off Ayrshire, south-west Scotland, and the alkaline gabbro essexite, from Crawfordjohn, Lanarkshire, for the manufacture of curling stones. Rock was frequently used for cannon balls; some recovered from the Dardanelles were of granite whilst those of the *Mary Rose*, a Tudor battleship in Henry VIII's fleet, sunk off Portsmouth, were of limestone. A thin-section study of this material showed it to be fossiliferous and slightly recrystallized, perhaps of Mesozoic age. Stone shot recovered from another wrecked ship has also been examined; a Cretaceous foraminiferal limestone from the Pyrenees could be identified, strongly suggesting that the ship had a Spanish or possibly French origin (C. G. Adams and A. C. Bishop, pers. comm. 1979).

Forensic study has enabled police forces to identify rocks and minerals – the latter commonly in cases of theft – used in crime. One example of a forensic investigation leading to the publication of a petrological account of some oolitic rocks in central Tanzania was given by Harpum. The Kidugallo oolitic limestone from a quarry near the central railway was examined in order to compare it with samples of rock used in a criminal action, with a view to establishing the source of the latter; the comparison was successful. The writer then went on to publish his data for purposes of petrological research (Harpum 1961). Cadogan, Harrison, and Strong (1972) examined volcanic glass shards from a Late Minoan I site in Crete in an attempt to determine whether a fifteenth century eruption of ash from the volcano Thera (Santorini), and associated tsunamis, could have caused the enig-matic destruction of a number of Minoan sites, as suggested by Marinatos (1939). The results were inconclusive; volcanic material was found in a Late Minoan IB destruction level in Crete which could be ascribed to Thera, but it did not prove that an eruption of Thera at this time caused the destruction. It is more probable that ash from Thera was blown over Crete in Late Minoan IA time and that the area was abandoned. Cadogan and Harrison (1978) now conclude that it did not cause the destruction; furthermore, a 3 cm^3 fragment of pumice with a refractive index matching that of the erupted glass shards has been found which could only have been transported by man (see also, e.g., Pichler and Schiering 1977). This controversy has been briefly but well reviewed by Keller (1980).

Two enigmatic 'uses' of rock are the vitrified forts of Scotland and elsewhere (Chapter 5) and the 'cramp' from the Stones of Stenness, Orkney (Fleet 1975–6). Cramp seems to have been soil or fine silt, with a small amount of quartz sand, which was heated until the silt fused. The volatiles were in solution at high temperatures, as happens with pumice, and similarly were released when the rock cooled. How the heating occurred is not known; the preferred explanation is that the 'cramp' was caught up in seaweed which was being burned, presumably for some domestic use.

Rocks and minerals have long appealed to man's mythical or superstitious sense, as Pliny and Agricola amply testify. The Hertfordshire 'pudding stone' conglomerate, a rock of the same age as the Wiltshire sarsens, has been used to ward off evil visitations. Another recently described attribution concerns aetites or the eagle-stone (Bromehead 1947). Any hollow stone with a smaller stone or sand within it, providing a rattle, earned this title: there are even male and female varieties. In fact, a nodule of pyrite, ironstone, agate, flint, or a septarian nodule provides the explanation, but this example is typical of the place rocks and minerals have so often held in man's imagination.

Acknowledgement

The author is very grateful to A. R. Woolley for critically reviewing the manuscript.

References

Bromehead, C. N. (1947). Aetites or the Eagle-stone. *Antiquity* **21**, 16–22.

Cadogan, G. and Harrison, R. K. (1978). Evidence of tephra in soil samples from Pyrgos, Crete. *In: Thera and the Aegean World I.* Thera and the Aegean World, London, 235–55.

—— —— Strong, G. E. (1972). Volcanic glass shards in Late Minoan I Crete. *Antiquity* **46**, 310–13.

Dana, E. S. and Ford, W. E. (1955). *A textbook of mineralogy.* 4th edn. Wiley, New York.

Firman, R. J. and Firman, P. E. (1967). A geological approach to the study of medieval bricks. *Mercian Geologist* **2**, 229–318.

Fleet, A. J. (1975–6). Appendix 7 – 'Cramp' from the Stones of Stenness, Orkney. In: J. N. Graham Ritchie: The Stones of Stenness, Orkney. *Proceedings of the Society of Antiquaries of Scotland* **107**, 46–8.

Greensmith, J. T., Hatch, F. H., and Rastall, R. H. (1978). *The petrology of the sedimentary rocks.* Murby, London.

Guppy, E. M. and Sabine, P. A.(1956). *Chemical analyses of igneous rocks, metamorphic rocks and minerals 1931–1954.* H.M.S.O., London. (*Memoirs of the Geological Survey of Great Britain.*)

Hamilton, W. R., Woolley, A. R., and Bishop, A. C. (1974). *The Hamlyn guide to minerals, rocks and fossils.* Hamlyn, London.

Harker, A. (1950). *Metamorphism.* 3rd edn. Methuen, London.

Harpum, J. R. (1961). A note on the petrology of the Kidugallo oolitic limestone. *Records of the Geological Survey of Tanganyika* **9**, 50–3.

Hatch, F. H., Wells, A. K., and Wells, M. K. (1972). *Petrology of the igneous rocks.* 13th edn. Murby, London.

Keller, J. (1980). Did the Santorini eruption destroy the Minoan world? *Nature* **287**, 779.

Khan, M. A. R. (1938). On the meteoritic origin of the Black Stone of the Ka'bah. *Popular Astronomy* **47** (7), 1–5.

Lucas, A. [Revised Harris, J. R.] (1962). *Ancient Egyptian materials and industries.* 4th edn. Edward Arnold, London.

Marinatos, S. (1939). The volcanic destruction of Minoan Crete. *Antiquity* **13**, 425–39.

Marshall, D. N. (1976–7). Carved stone balls. *Proceedings of the Society of Antiquaries of Scotland* **108**, 40–72. [This paper describes the stone balls, of which some 390 are known; 385 come from Scotland, including some from Skara Brae, Orkney. Resembling tennis balls in size, their use is unknown, but was probably ceremonial or religious; they date from *c.* 2000 BC].

Pettijohn, F. A. (1975). *Sedimentary rocks.* 3rd edn. Harper Row, New York.

Pichler, H. and Schiering, W. (1977). The Thera eruption and Late Minoan – 1B destructions Crete. *Nature* **267**, 819–22.

Read, H. H. (1970). *Rutley's elements of mineralogy.* 26th edn. Murby, London.

Rickard, T. A. (1941). The use of meteoritic iron. *Journal of the Royal Anthropological Institute* **71**, 55–65.

Twyman, M. (1972). Lithographic stone and the printing trade in the nineteenth century. *Journal of the Printing Historical Society* **8**, 1–41.

Williams, H., Turner, F. J., and Gilbert, C. M. 1954. *Petrography: an introduction to the study of rocks in thin sections.* Freeman, San Francisco.

4. The petrology of building and sculptural stones

D. R. C. Kempe

Building Stones

Probably no aspect of man's use of rock has resulted in a greater body of geological literature than that of building stone (see Hull 1872; Howe 1910; Davey 1961). Many books have been devoted to the provenance and use of rocks for this purpose, together with the techniques of quarrying and construction. In this chapter a more limited approach is adopted; its aim is to discuss the rock types both available and used in some countries for various building purposes: the rock types themselves are described in an earlier chapter. The building stones included here are not restricted to those used by ancient societies, since this would involve an arbitrary and unnecessary limitation; rocks used up to the present are included but, where possible, their recent adoption is noted. Until relatively recently, the question of provenance of building stones rarely arose; because of the problems of transport, man tended to use local stone rather than attempt large-scale, long-distance haulage of massive blocks of rock. Indeed two simple rules govern the choice of stone: ease of working, largely governed by sedimentary bedding, igneous jointing, and metamorphic foliation (splitting planes); and local availability in sufficiently large quantities.

However, in both prehistoric and historic times there are instances of man labouring to transport a particular type of rock over considerable distances. Examples of such activity are described in other sections of this chapter as, for example, Stonehenge.

Early man lived in caves, thus in a sense utilizing natural material for building purposes; indeed, there are instances where this is still the case. He sometimes adorned or protected his home with paintings and engravings of animals and human figures. One of the earliest examples of the use of stone as a building material comes from the excavations in Olduvai Gorge, northern Tanzania, where there is evidence of loose boulders being used to construct simple shelters. The quarrying of rock *in situ* for building purposes perhaps began with the Egyptians who, like their successors the world over, preferred to use the two most common 'hard' sedimentary rocks – limestone and sandstone. Igneous rocks – especially granite, with the lesser use of basalt –

were also employed, together with other hard rocks such as schist, gneiss, and quartzite, and the softer marble, serpentine, and gypsum. The adoption around the 1930s of the cladding style of building – the use of stone slabs to face steel or reinforced concrete structures – gradually replaced the use of solid blocks of stone in building.

The importance of limestone, sandstone, and granite in building generally is such that all the other rock types utilized add up to only a small fraction of the total volume of stone used, selection usually being governed by local abundance, ornamental value, or even, perhaps, myth or superstition. Often rocks of similar type from different formations, or of a completely different type, are used intentionally in a single building, especially now that so much building stone is imported into, for example, the United Kingdom (cf. Robinson and Bishop 1980). Not always are the distinctions between rocks in the former category particularly obvious.

Sandstone

Sometimes called siliceous freestone, sandstone (if free of carbonate cement) is corrosion-resistant when compared with limestones, dolomites, and marbles, since it is insoluble in the sulphuric and other acids commonly present in industrially polluted atmospheres. Nevertheless, if the quartz grains are held together only loosely by a weak cement, sandstone can be highly vulnerable to physical weathering.

In Britain and Ireland sandstones from three geological systems – the Devonian, Carboniferous, and Triassic – have been extensively used for building. These include two highly ornamental red sandstone formations – the Devonian Old Red Sandstone and the Triassic New Red Sandstone – both of which have been used widely, especially in the areas near their outcrops. Sandstones of Carboniferous age, from the Yoredale series, Millstone Grit, and Coal Measures (including the type known as ganister), have the same pattern of use; for example, the local abundance of sandstone in the Midland Valley of Scotland is shown in its extensive use in Edinburgh, Glasgow, and elsewhere. However, Millstone Grit has been much used for grinding and milling wheels and in the construction of industrial as well as the more usual buildings. There are many examples of the use of the Carboniferous sandstones in London, and many of the paving stones are of the Upper Carboniferous 'York Stone' flagstones which are highly resistant to corrosion since the cement of the groundmass is equally as durable as the quartz grains, and diagenesis has resulted in an interlocking texture. In general, however, sandstone is little used in London compared with limestone (Elsden and Howe 1923). Jurassic and Cretaceous sandstones have found local use in, for example, Yorkshire and south-east England. Thin flaggy sandstones, from various geological horizons from the Cambrian to the Cretaceous, have been used for roofing tiles since Roman times.

An early example of the transport of rock is the Mesolithic site at Farnham, Surrey, where the 'chipping' floors were constructed of sandstone, siltstone, and amphibolite from Devon and Cornwall (Rankine 1949).

In Europe, sandstones of Devonian, Triassic (e.g. Bunter), and Jurassic age are used in building. In France, for example, particular use has been made in Paris of the well-known Tertiary Grès de Fontainebleau, and sandstone has been much used in Germany, Switzerland, and even Italy, especially in Florence and Pisa. In Switzerland, a study of the heavy mineral and carbonate content of a sandstone relief on Sursee Town Hall has shown that it matches sandstone from the Bruchmatt quarry, near Luzern, suggesting the latter as the source of the carved rock (Gautschi and Quervain 1978; Quervain 1979).

In Egypt sandstone plays a major part in building and sculpture but always in second place to Nummulitic Limestone. In use since the middle of the 18th Dynasty (Lucas 1962), sandstone served principally for foundations, pavements, pillars, architraves, roofs, and walls. Occurring along the Nile valley from Esna to Aswan, it was quarried mainly at Silsila and used by the Meroe in the construction of the pyramids in the south of Egypt and in Nubia, northern Sudan; the Nubians also used sandstone slabs for house building. The colossal statues of the 19th Dynasty at the temple of Rameses II at Abu Simbel are carved out of the sandstone cliff and most of the temples of Upper Egypt are of this material, although some are of limestone.

The two huge ancient statues at Thebes – the Colossi of Memnon – are carved from single monolithic blocks, weighing some 720 tonnes, of medium- to coarse-grained ferruginous quartzose sandstone (quartzite). The northern statue was partly toppled by an earthquake. The Roman emperor Septimius Severus, just before the turn of the third century, attempted a reconstruction, also using quartzite. There has long been discussion as to which of the six possible quartzite quarries in Egypt provided the stone. Heizer, Stross, Hester, Albee, Perlman, Asaro, and Bowman (1973) analysed 63 quarry and 41 artefact samples by neutron activation analysis. The results showed that strong correlation in iron, cobalt, and europium contents exists between stone from the original statues and their related artefacts, and material from the Gebel el Ahmar quarry near Cairo, 1125 km to the north. The geochemical evidence is supported by thin-section petrographic studies which, on the presence of, for example, chert and rare tourmaline, strengthened the suggestion that the original stone came from Cairo. The rock used in the reconstruction appears to have come from Edfu, near Thebes.

Around Carthage, in present day Tunisia, the Phoenicians also made use of sandstone. In Ethiopia, the early Christian rock-churches at Lalibela were carved out of the sandstone rock faces or cliffs; Petra, Jordan, is carved out of the local Nubian pinkish calcareous sandstone; and in Israel and Palestine sandstone was among the rocks most commonly used for building. Superb examples of cliff carving in sandstone are the two huge statues of Buddha at Bamiyan, in Afghanistan. Further east, in northern India, the red and mottled sandstones of the Vindhyan series were much favoured, particularly at the great artistic centre of Mathura, from the last centuries BC onwards. The Mughal emperor Akbar made use of this stone for the Fatehpur Sikri palace and for the forts at Agra and Allahabad. His successor, Shah Jahan, incorporated it into the mainly marble Taj Mahal, and used it for the Jama Masjid and the Lal Kila or Red Fort in Delhi; Aurangzeb built the palace at Benares of Vindhyan sandstone. In more recent times, the same stone was used for buildings and bridges in major cities, including Lutyens' New Delhi, for which it was quarried from Dhaulpur, 240 km to the south. Sandstone was used all over the sub-continent including the deep red to grey sandstones from Rajputana and varieties from Bengal. In the south, at Aihole and elsewhere, the elaborately carved Jain and other temples were excavated out of the reddish yellow sandstones of the region. In Cambodia, the temple of Angkor Wat contains much sandstone, as well as bauxite.

The Mayan and other peoples of the American continent have made considerable use of sandstone; the Indians of Chaeo Canyon in New Mexico built with it, and the Incas of Peru handled blocks weighing up to 100 tonnes. In historic times, sandstones from early Proterozoic rocks, and also the Potsdam and Quebec formations, have yielded material suitable for many public buildings in Canada. In the United States the dark red-brown Triassic Brownstones of Connecticut have been much used for building, including the Smithsonian Institution in Washington D.C., and in New York, New Jersey, and Pennsylvania. Use has been made for pavements and other purposes of the Devonian-Mississippian Euclid 'bluestone' sandstone; the rock is quarried in Cleveland, Ohio, and used in many parts of north-eastern America.

Limestone

Taken together with its metamorphic equivalent, marble, limestone, including dolomite, probably accounts for more than half of all the rock used for building (Hull 1872; Burnham 1883). These rocks suffer more than most from deterioration due to pollution, especially as a result of the generation of sulphuric acid from rainwater combining with SO_2 and SO_3 fumes in the atmosphere.

The study of conservation is beyond the scope of this book but the interested reader is referred to the publications of del Fà C. Manganelli, S. Vanucci, and their co-workers, especially those published as proceedings by the University of Florence after, for example, the International Symposia on conservation and the deterioration of building stones held in 1975 in

Bologna, 1976 in Athens, 1977 in La Rochelle, and 1978 in Paris. In Britain, work in this field is published in *Studies in Conservation*, and *The Conservator* (both at: 6 Buckingham Street, London WC2N 6BA, U.K.). An interesting note on the weathering of the Great Pyramid at Giza (Emery 1960) lists the limestone types used in its construction: grey, hard, and dense; grey and soft; grey and shaly; and yellow, limy, shaly sandstone. All have different weathering patterns but Emery concludes that the Pyramid should last another 100 000 years! Pellerin (1980) discusses *la pétrophysique*, the study of porosity and permeability in decaying limestone buildings.

In Britain the principal limestone formations are the Carboniferous Limestone, the Permian Magnesian Limestone, and the oolitic limestones and freestones of Jurassic age. Other minor stones, like the Lower Jurassic Lias limestone, were used locally. There are three other limestones in Britain which, because of their patterned appearance resulting from the fossil shells or tests of invertebrate animals of which they largely consist, are regarded by masons and sculptors as marbles. For this reason the Devonian limestone of south-west England, the Jurassic Purbeck Marble, and the Cretaceous Sussex Marble are treated in the next section.

Three main formations in Britain have been utilized extensively both in their areas of outcrop and also in major public buildings in the capital and elsewhere. Thus, Carboniferous Limestone was used in building Durham Cathedral and many major buildings in Bristol and elsewhere. The yellowish Magnesian Limestone, which outcrops in the north-east of England, is the least well known of the major British limestones. The upper part is too flaggy to be much used but the lower was employed for domestic and other buildings near to its outcrop; it was also used in London in the Houses of Parliament and the flying butresses of Westminster Abbey, and in Germany to build Koningsburg Castle.

The Jurassic oolitic limestones – the Inferior Oolite and the overlying Great (Bath) Oolite – form a scarp running NE–SW across England, from Yorkshire to Dorset. It is in the western half of the country, especially in the Cotswolds, that these superb mellow stones – first used by the Saxons for building (Jope 1964) – are seen at their best. The Inferior Oolite includes some well known local varieties, such as the Mendip Doulting stone, the Ham Hill stone from Yeovil, and the Clipsham stone or Lincolnshire Limestone. The stratigraphically higher Great Oolite and Bath Stone was quarried extensively by the Romans at Bloomfield Crescent, south of Bath. This stone has been used extensively for local building and also in towns such as Oxford (Arkell 1947), while Jope (1948–9) discussed the supply of limestone for medieval buildings, and in another study Waterman (1970) describes an interesting example of the use of 'foreign' limestone in medieval buildings. Between 1175 and 1400, Jurassic oolitic limestones from

Dundry Hill, Somerset, were taken to south-eastern Ireland, between Drogheda, north of Dublin, and Kinsale, south of Cork, for the construction of monasteries and castles. Other oolitic limestones from Doulting and Bath, and Caen stone from France, were also used in this region.

One of the world's most famous limestones is the Jurassic Portland stone quarried apparently limitlessly from Portland Bill, near Weymouth, Dorset. The classic freestone, introduced to London in 1619 by Inigo Jones, has been in use since the mid-seventeenth century for many public buildings (Elsden and Howe 1923), although it is less suitable than the oolitic limestones for delicate Gothic style chiselling and embellishment. London abounds with examples of the use of Portland stone, including St Paul's Cathedral, while much of Dublin is also built of it, as is the United Nations building in New York. A local variant, the Chilmark siliceous limestone of Wiltshire, was used for Salisbury Cathedral and elsewhere locally for building. Much earlier, as noted by Jope (1953), the Saxons and Normans were using the local Portland Beds in the clay lands north-east of Oxford.

Chalk is too soft for major building work and is also highly vulnerable to chemical attack, but it was used by the Romans at Faversham, in Sussex, and more recently in cottage building. Flint nodules occurring in the Chalk were also used by the Romans in conjunction with lime mortar, in their buildings in East Anglia. Below the Chalk, a sandy limestone in the Lower Greensand, the Kentish Ragstone, was also employed by the Romans at Faversham and, though too hard for fine work, for many walls in London. Williams (1971) gives a good account of first century AD Roman public buildings employing these stones, together with the Tertiary Bembridge Limestone, Bracklesham Beds ferruginous sandstone, and the Jurassic Ham Hill stone. A short but valuable account of the quarries from which Roman and medieval building stones were taken is given by Wood (1963, p. 127–8).

On the continent of Europe, one of the two other classic limestones of the world occurs in France and Belgium: the Jurassic Caen stone, the equivalent of the Great Oolite of Britain. The most famous locality, Calvados in Normandy, yields a stone regarded as the equivalent in building terms of Carrara marble in sculpture. Made use of by the Romans at Faversham, it also forms much of Canterbury Cathedral and Westminster Abbey and was used by Inigo Jones in the old St Paul's. France also has Tertiary limestones from the Paris Basin, which were used for many Parisian buildings, as well as the cathedrals of Amiens and Rouen. Further south, Tertiary limestones were utilized in Bordeaux, Montpellier, and Marseilles. Germany and Holland have the Triassic Muschelkalk, whilst limestone has also been used in Denmark, Sweden, Russia, Switzerland, and Austria. In Spain, much of Madrid is built of siliceous dolomite – a magnesian limestone – and in Italy Nummulitic Limestone has been used in many cities, such as Verona, Padua, and Venice, although the stone is called marble.

The early Maltese temples were of limestone, including stalactitic travertine, and in Greece the Cretan labyrinth was probably built in Tertiary limestone, also used by the Trojans for buildings and stelae, and by the Phoenicians in Carthage. Investigations are currently in progress to determine the source of the limestones used for the buildings at Knossos, in Crete, using fossil assemblages as well as petrological techniques (C. J. Lister, pers. comm. 1980). The Greeks made considerable use of limestone for early buildings; after turning their main attention to marble they still employed limestone, for example, for the Roman Greek Sanctuary of Isis, on the Athenian Acropolis, which is of rough Acropolis limestone and re-used marble, embellished with Attic marble for stylobate, capitals, and columns (Walker 1979a). Similarly, Burford (1969), in an excellent account of the technology and logistics of an ancient building operation recounts how, for the Temple at Epidauros, the local grey and coarse-grained limestones were used for the foundations, steps, and pavements; imported Corinthian fine-grained golden limestone ('Poros') for the main fabric; imported dark grey or black limestone from Argos for the tholos; and Pentelic and some Parian marble for the sculpture.

Included with limestone must be the variety known as travertine. Perhaps the best known example occurs near Tivoli, in Italy, where water highly charged with volcanic CO_2 has resulted in a massive deposit of the stone in the bed of a former lake. Soft when fresh and during cutting, it hardens on exposure and formed the principal building stone for general use in both ancient and modern Rome. The Etruscans and pre-Roman Italians made great use of travertine and the similar tufa, as well as limestone, tuff, and concrete, for public and domestic buildings; the major edifices and temples were decorated with painted stucco and terracotta revetments (Boëthius and Ward-Perkins 1970). The Ampitheatrum Flavium – the Colosseum – was built of travertine in the first century AD: in the fifteenth and sixteenth centuries it was quarried for the Palace of St Mark, Venice; the Farnese Palace; St Peter's in Rome; Bernini's colonnades; and many other famous buildings. It was also transported to New York for Pennsylvania railway station. A less superior variety occurs in Naples, also of volcanic origin and deposited over the former sea bed, which was much used in Pompeii and Paestum. Travertine was also used in Turkey.

The last of the classic limestones – the Tertiary Nummulitic – runs from the French Pyrenees through the Alps and the Apennines into Greece and Turkey; it continues through the Carpathians into Asia minor and central Asia, through Afghanistan, Pakistan, India, and Burma, to Indonesia. It is in Egypt, however, that use of this famous stone reached its peak (Lucas 1962). It was used in the 1st Dynasty but the first complete building was the 2nd Dynasty pit chamber of the tomb of King Khasekhemui. Turning to the pyramids, the 3rd Dynasty Step pyramid at Saqqara was built by King

Djoser of brownish limestone cased with white limestone; the 4th Dynasty (2600–2500 BC) Great Pyramid of Cheops at Giza and many others were constructed of large blocks of Nummulitic Limestone, quarried on the spot; the Great Sphinx was carved out of a huge block left over, the hollow in which it stands being the quarry. Many tombs were similarly built of *in situ* rock. From the 4th to the 12th Dynasties there was a break in pyramid building, after which the new pyramids were built principally of brick with stone facings; imported Nummulitic stone was probably used at Thebes (Luxor), where the local stone was in short supply and of poor quality (Davey 1961; Lucas 1962). From Egypt the chief building centre moved to the eastern Mediterranean, to the Minoan and Mycenaean civilizations.

Nummulitic Limestone was used for many of the principal buildings in Jordan, Palestine, and the Holy Land; for Báalbek in the Lebanon, and Aleppo (Haleb) in Syria, among other cities. Solomon's Temple and Palace were built of the local rose and yellow Jerusalem limestone ('Misseh'). Also used in this region were dolomite, calcareous sandstone, and Nubian Limestone; limestone was also used in Aden. The main building stone of India is sandstone, together with marble, but one of the most interesting uses of limestone occurs on the island of Elephanta, near Bombay, with its cavern once containing a huge elephant carved in stone. There are many Hindu temples carved in limestone, containing many sculptures and with ornate columns holding up the roof, and in southern India also the Billa Soorgum cavern in limestone. Jain temples built of limestone and marble are found in Gumarat and Mysore. Limestone has been used for building throughout China – where there are Buddhist cave temples – Japan, Australia, and the USA, where the Indiana limestone is the best known variety. The ancient Yucatan city of Aké, and other ancient Mayan buildings were constructed mostly of limestone. The people of the island of Socotra, off Aden, used limestone for building and paving, and those of the Pacific Cook Islands used coral limestone. The stone is less evenly distributed around the world than sandstone, however, and the English, French, and Egyptian formations remain the undisputed leaders.

Marble

Quite a different distribution pattern applies in the case of marble (Hull 1872; Burnham 1883). Here, the limestones of the northern Mediterranean coast, metamorphosed into marble in the Alpine orogeny, are best represented by the Italian Carrara and the classic Greek and Anatolian marbles. These are the rocks used throughout classical and later ages for sculpture and statuary, and as such have provided one of the main areas where petrology has been applied to the study of provenance.

England has no genuine marbles. However, as stated earlier, the appearance and properties of certain limestones have resulted in their treatment as 'marbles' for building and sculptural purposes. The myriad fossil shells contained in certain limestones – mainly corals in the Devonian and Carboniferous and gastropods in the later formations – have given the rocks a pattern when polished which allows them to compete with many genuine variegated marbles. All the so-called marbles – including the Cretaceous Sussex 'Marble' and the black Carboniferous Limestone of Derbyshire – have been used for building but it is the black and white Jurassic Purbeck stone which has been most extensively utilized both in building and sculpture. This stone was first used for building by the Romans, who probably quarried it from its chief outcrop at Peveril Point at the eastern end of the Isle of Purbeck, in Dorset (Beavis 1971). Dunning (1949) pointed out that the Romans used Purbeck stone principally because of its abundance and ease of working, as well as its appearance, and it is found at Roman sites from Chichester to Chester; at Colchester it is accompanied by imported Greek, Italian, and Algerian marbles of different colours (Shackley 1977).

A serpentine marble from the Mona complex of Anglesey, Wales; marble from the Isle of Man; from Iona, Skye, and Borolan in Sutherland, Scotland; and marble from Ireland have all had limited use. Of these, the black, grey, cream, and variegated varieties from Ireland are the best known, including the Connemara green marble.

In France there are many varieties of red, white, and green marbles, including the so-called 'onyx' marble, a banded variety resembling true onyx, a species of chalcedony with parallel bands. Another misnamed marble, the Belgian 'granite', is accompanied in that country by red, blue, and at Tournai, black types. Varieties occur in Norway, Sweden, Germany, Switzerland, Austria, Hungary, and Russia. In southern Europe, Spain has splendid public buildings of marble, though many are probably of stone imported from Italy; Portugal has a good pale red marble; and in Gibraltar stalagmitic and stalactitic 'marble' – actually tufa – is obtained from caverns. Other examples derive from Sicily and Corsica, while the famous Numidian marble came from Morocco, Algeria, and Tunisia to form decorative columns in Roman times in Rome, Carthage, and in other Roman provinces.

The requirement for 'classical' marbles (Fig. 4.1 and Table 4.1), was that the stones should be pure or nearly pure white, completely flawless and homogeneous, and capable of the most detailed sculpting. The accessibility of the quarries to the nearest port, and thus to sea transport, was also vital. The two most famous Greek varieties are Parian, the 'Lychnite' from the island of Paros, and Pentelic, from Mount Pentelikon, in Attica, both extolled by Ruskin (Herz 1955a; Martin 1965). Their use for sculpture from perhaps the seventh century BC, their petrology, and the problem of provenance are considered in a later section, but the use of classical marbles (except Parian)

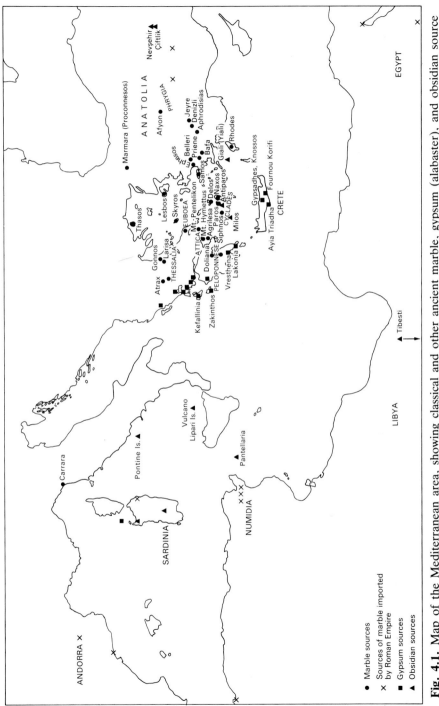
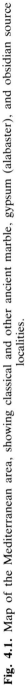

Fig. 4.1. Map of the Mediterranean area, showing classical and other ancient marble, gypsum (alabaster), and obsidian source localities.

Table 4.1. Mediterranean classical marbles

marble	geological features	Mg	Fe	Mn	Na	K (p.p.m.)	Ti	Sr	Si	Al	Ca/Sr ratio (range)	suggested origin	δ^{13}C $\quad\delta^{18}$O (typical values)
Carrara	white, with faint bluish tinge; coarse-grained; some grey		55–140	14–25		80–120	10–14	120–180	260–560	80–190	4.0–11.2	organic	−0.4 −0.9 (white); −1.6 −4.2 (grey)
Thessalia:													
Atrax	white; medium- to coarse-grained; twinned, equant grains	2800–5500	95–515	18–32				130–200				chemical ppt (some)	+3.6 −5.1
Kastrion	medium-grained; highly cleaved; preferred orientation	1200–16 000	150–470	40–140				120–170				organic	+2.6 −5.5
Tempi	very fine-grained; indicated by elongated, flattened, and bent crystals	1050–14 000	tr–700	5–66				160–225				organic	+2.2 −3.0
Gonnos	fine-grained; bent crystals	280–500	130–405	66–170								organic	+2.2 −2.3
Pentelikon	white; medium- to coarse-grained; porphyroblastic; translucent 15 mm; micaceous; patina and rusty weathering; flinty smell; some is blue-veined and fine-grained banded			100	60			360–625			10.4–14.0	organic	+2.8 −8.0
Hymettus	white or light grey, pink and bluish layers; fine- to medium-grained			35	80						7.9–10.9	organic	+2.3 −2.5
Paros	white; (fine- to) coarse-grained; translucent 35 mm; homogeneous; sulphurous smell when broken			3	23						7.8–12.2	chemical ppt	+4.7 −3.3
Naxos	white to grey; medium- to very coarse-grained			15	35						7.3–28.8	organic	+2.0 −6.0; +2.2 −9.1
Samos	white, with black veins; also grey-blue; coarse-grained; friable			30	35								
Marmara (Proconnessos)	white to blue, with grey or blackish veins; fine- to coarse-grained		80, 60	17,3	35	45	10	120, 160	55	100	8.2–17.7	chemical ppt (some)	+3.3 −1.3 (non-coloured)
Ephesos	white, or greyish to dark grey; medium- to coarse-grained		140–250	18–39		50–160	11–17	50–190	240–440	125–230	29.3–34.9	chemical ppt (some)	+4.5 −4.0; +0.3 −4.0
Phrygia													
Aphrodisias	white or dark grey; medium- to coarse-grained		20, 880	7,67		<1, 620	4, 75	60, 140	30, >1000	20, 690	8.7–17.1	organic	+1.6 −3.5 (non-coloured); +2.6 −1.3
Denizli	white or dark grey; medium-grained		310	40		125	13	220	340	160		organic	+1.4 −6.8
Afyon (Işçihissar)	white, or dark grey, violet (pavonazetto), or yellow; medium-grained		370, 520	44, 60	12	330, 590	44, 61	110, 50	650, 870	410, 590	21.9–34.6	organic	+1.5 −4.5

Data all from sources quoted in text.

in building is also, of course, legendary. During the 'Golden Age' of Athens, in the fifth century, the easily accessible and highly variable Pentelic marble was the principal building stone (Walker 1979b); it was augmented by a second Attic marble, the blue-grey rock from Mount Hymettus. Marbles from Skyros, Delos, Thasos, Samos, and Lesbos were used, amongst others; a red marble (rosso antico) from Laconia was also used for veneers. The Parthenon, on the Acropolis, was built of white Pentelic marble (Fig. 4.2), and in Rome, as well as in Roman Athens, a wide variety of Greek marbles were employed, such as in the Pentelic Arch of Titus.

In Italy, Carrara marble – metamorphosed Jurassic Apennine limestone – was first used some 500 or 600 years later. It was first quarried under Julius Caesar near the port of Luna in the first century BC. Since AD 100 it has been worked extensively at Carrara, Massa Serravezza, in the Bay of La Spezia. Both Julius Caesar and Augustus used it to replace the brick buildings of which Rome previously consisted. Tinged faintly blue the stone has been used for some statuary but far less widely than Greek marble. It was used for buildings and massive monuments such as the Column of Marcus Aurelius, arches, and temples. Other Italian marbles of note are the Siena and Verona varieties; the latter was used in Venice and in Vicenza. From Elba and Bardiglio come yellow, grey, black, red, and greenish varieties, and there are many others.

Fig. 4.2. The Parthenon, built of Pentelic marble, on its hill of Acropolis limestone, Athens.

The third group of classical marbles consists of those from the Anatolian region of Turkey (Asia Minor). Used widely by the Greeks and Romans, they include marble from the island of Marmara, in antiquity called Proconnesos. This was the commonest building marble in antiquity and was also used for sarcophagi and some statues. Next most widely used are the Phrygian or Docimion marbles, quarried from Aphrodisias to Afyon (Işçihissar). Afyon stone occurs in two varieties (Table 4.1): a white marble used for sarcophagi and portrait sculpture, perhaps with torsos of a cheaper stone, and the violet-streaked pavonazetto or peacock, employed for veneers, paving, and intricate sculpture (Monna and Pensabene 1977).

The Egyptian 'onyx' marble was used for monuments and decorations in Rome and Carthage and the breccia di verde was also used in Italy; generally, however, the country has very little white marble and relied mainly on imported material (Gnoli 1971; see also Fig. 4.1). In Iran, the tombs at Persepolis and Isfahan are made of local mountain marble and the palace of the Shah of Isfahan from Tabriz marble.

In India, extensive minor use has been made of marble quarried from Delhi, Gya, Syepore, Tinnevelly, Nerbudda, Rajputana, Madras, Assam, Durha in Bengal, Bellary, and Peshawar in north-west Pakistan. The Moghuls were undoubtedly the greatest builders in the sub-continent and marble was their favourite stone for temples, palaces, and statues. Shah Jahan used white marble for most of the Taj Mahal; Aurangzeb employed it for the Jama Masjid Mosque in Lahore, and Firuz for his mosque at Jumna. The Jains, similarly, were great users of this stone.

Marbles occur over most of the rest of the world: in Sri Lanka, Burma, Japan, Malaysia, Thailand, Indonesia, the Philippines, China – where the Great Hall of the People in Peking is of pink marble – Sudan, and South Africa. Australia has many marbles and New Zealand has some. In the new world, Canada has decorative marble but none of statuary quality; in the USA it is generally of poor quality but Mexico has another well-known banded 'onyx' marble.

Other metamorphic and sedimentary rocks

The other common metamorphic rocks – slate, phyllite, schist, gneiss, granulite, and quartzite – constitute a very large part of the Earth's continental crust; they form most of the very ancient 'shield' or 'cratonic' areas and have a geological importance which quite outweighs their value to man as raw material. Some of these rocks, however, were used locally as building material.

Serpentinite is of very localized occurrence but is highly prized as a decorative stone for facing buildings and for sculptural use. It occurs in Scotland, Ireland, Anglesey in Wales, and at the Lizard in Cornwall. The last of these is the best known in Britain, and has been much used in church decoration. Serpentinite was also used in France, Germany, Austria, Hungary, Spain, Greece (by the Minoans), Turkey, and Algeria, and is best known as a sculptural material in Egypt and Italy, where the 'verde' from Prato, Genoa, and nearby Pegli adorns many churches and mansions. Its use is also recorded in Russia, India, Japan, Australia, Canada, and the USA, particularly in the north-east. The related materials, steatite, soapstone, and – in China and Saxony – agalmatolite, are sculptural stones. Nevertheless, they have had limited use for mantels and floor tiles.

Slate, a highly cleaved metasediment, is best known as a roofing material as an alternative to tiles, and the most famous examples come from the British Isles. The Cornish Delabole Slates – metamorphosed Devonian sediments – are amongst the best known, but blue-green and other fine examples come from north Wales, from Llanberis and Ffestiniog; these meta-morphosed Cambrian and Ordovician sediments may have been traded round the coast from Portmadoc. An Ordovician green slate from the Lake District is formed from metamorphosed volcanic tuff from the Borrowdale Volcanics, and is also highly prized. The use of blue slate as a roofing material in England goes back to medieval times (Jope and Dunning 1954); it has also been used instead of lead for cisterns and, when highly polished, as an ornamental stone, as an alternative to marble. Thirty medieval sites in Sussex show the use of blue-grey slates, probably from the Devonian rocks of the South Hams area of Devon, north of Bolt Head and Start Point (Murray 1965). Stone from the Slate Islands, some 15 miles south-west of Oban, Scotland, was used from the seventeenth century to the 1960s, reaching its peak around 1900 (Tucker 1976). Slate is recorded as having been used from Ballachulish and elsewhere in Scotland and from Ireland, as well as Sweden, Norway, France, Germany, Austria, Italy, Egypt, Australia, Canada, the USA, and by the Mayans in Mexico.

Schist was employed in the Western Highlands of Scotland; for example calc-chlorite-albite schist was used for Castle Sween and Kilmory Chapel, Argyll, and for Oronsay Priory, and in similar areas where more conven-tional rocks were lacking. It was used in Norway, and in Egypt for obelisks, sarcophagi, and statues; chlorite schist and phyllite were employed for building and flooring at Akrotiri, Greece; schist was also used in the con-struction of the Buddhist monasteries of Gandhara at Takt i Bahi, Pakistan, and elsewhere.

Very little use in building of gneiss and the related rock granulite has been recorded. The alternate hard and soft layers in these rocks, together with lack of jointing, render them largely unsuitable for building and sculpting, a consideration also generally applicable to schist. Australia, Sri Lanka, and India are perhaps the best examples of countries using gneiss; some of the Indian cave temples contain sculpted gneiss, and at Polonnaruha, Sri Lanka, there are four Buddhas carved into a gneiss wall.

The Egyptians made limited use of quartzite from Gebel Ahmar for door threshholds and lining sepulchral chambers, as well as for sarcophagi and statues. Some use is also known of quartzite in India and Australia.

Anyolite, or 'Tanganyika artstone', is a metamorphosed anorthositic rock consisting of red ruby corundum and black amphibole set in a green matrix of chromian zoisite. This very decorative rock from the Narok-Longido area of northern Tanzania is much in demand abroad as an ornamental facing stone.

Of the minor sedimentary rocks, breccia can often be ornamental. Green varieties were used in Egypt for sarcophagi and statues, and also in Italy; Greece and Turkey made use of this material and also of conglomerate. Laterite was used in India, especially Orissa, for temples and houses. Soft when quarried, like some tufa it hardens on exposure and is highly durable; this is understandable since it is itself a weathering residue.

Granite

Granite is one of the noblest of building materials, with regular jointing patterns which help to offset its hardness by ease of working; however, its use is often governed largely by local abundance, obviating the need for transport. The Caledonian granites of Aberdeen are the most famous of all Scottish stones; others that have been used in building occur around Peterhead, Strontian, Galloway, and the islands of Mull and Arran. In Ireland, the rocks of Donegal, Galway, Wicklow, the Mourne Mountains, Newry, and Carlingford have also been employed. Wales lacks granite but England has some very fine stone. The Shap granite of Westmorland, Cumbria, with its pink and white feldspar phenocrysts, is well known as a 'finishing' stone, providing many fine facades. Other examples come from Lundy Island and the Channel Islands, but the best known southern English granites are the Hercynian rocks of Devon and Cornwall. These granites, including the tourmalinized varieties, are renowned as lower courses, plinths, columns, and facades in churches and public buildings throughout the United Kingdom, as well as in graveyards as tombstones and cemetery sculpture. Jope (1953) gives a detailed account of the use of the five main granites of the south-west in local church building in the fifteenth and sixteenth centuries, sometimes involving the transport by cart of blocks weighing over five tonnes for more than 30 km even when it could have been quarried locally.

In Europe, local granite has been used in France, from Normandy and Brittany; in Norway, Denmark, Sweden, Germany, Switzerland, Finland (including the rapakivi variety), and Russia, where it can be seen in Leningrad in the old St Petersburg palaces. Italy has a well known granite at Fariolo, near Baveno, used in Milan Cathedral, in Turin, and in a Roman basilica; other examples occur in Sardinia and Elba.

Egypt has one of the world's great granites, the 'rose syenite' from Syene, a red granite outcropping in upper Egypt between Aswan and the first cataract. This rock has been used since the 1st Dynasty for pavements in tombs; later it was employed as a lining material for chambers, tombs, sarcophagi, and passages, and as door frames in, for example, three of the large pyramids at Giza and in tombs and temples. Its use is known from pre-dynastic times for carving bowls and vases, during the dynasties for sarcophagi, and later for statues – for example, a huge king's head – and for obelisks and stelae. It was widely employed outside Egypt for monoliths, obelisks, sarcophagi, and statues. Aswan also has a grey granite, used extensively for building purposes in Egypt and abroad, and the Meroe of southern Egypt and northern Sudan used granite for pyramids and statues.

Granites have been quarried for building purposes in Turkey, Sinai (Egypt), Jordan, Saudi Arabia, Syria, and southern Africa – where it was employed in building the Acropolis of Zimbabwe; in India and Nepal granites occur, for example, in Trichinopoly and Nerbudda, where they were used for the lower storeys of Hindu temples and in cave temples, and for jambs and sills in Bihar and Bengal. Australia has red, grey, green, and variegated varieties; in north America, granites were at first neglected in Canada, where the quality is generally poor and the outcrops too far from the cities, whilst the United States has usable granites in the New England area, in Massachusetts, Rhode Island, Maine, Connecticut, and Dakota. The old city of Tonalá, in Mexico, was largely constructed of granite, and the rock was used by the Mayas in Guatemala and Honduras, and the Incas at Machu Pichu, in Peru.

Other igneous rocks

The use of igneous rocks for building purposes is, to say the least, confused by problems of nomenclature. Even in geological terms, many rocks have been variously and erroneously named in the past and these errors have often been perpetuated by quarrymen and others concerned with building. In archaeological circles also, this confusion has been further compounded by traditional usage; whereas geologists have attempted over the years to reduce, if not completely remove, the nomenclatural errors applied to igneous rocks, little correction has been made to the names of rocks used for statuary and other sculptural purposes. Thus, terms such as diorite, syenite, porphyry, trachyte, andesite, and basalt need to be regarded with caution; their application may lack scientific authenticity. This group of rocks tends to be most suitable for minor building purposes and for sculptural work and the distinction between the two functions becomes more than normally blurred. Further, the rocks considered here are of strictly local provenance; they are not widespread as are the common sedimentary rocks, sandstone and limestone, or even granite. Thus their use is governed, more than is the case with other rocks, by questions of availability.

There is one major exception to this generalization, in the case of basalt. This igneous rock is the most common of all lavas; its use, however, has been restricted to areas where other more suitable stones are not available. It is dull – black or dark grey – and hard, although liable to weather badly, and thus not an obvious choice for either large or small artefacts. But where it is abundant, and other rocks are lacking, considerable use has been made of basalt. It was used for paving and sarcophagi by the Greeks, Romans, and Egyptians, and for building in Turkey, Israel, Aden, Jordan, and Australia. The famous Buddhist rock-temples of western India, as at Ellora and Ajanta, in Hyderabad, are carved into the sides of hills of Deccan Trap – an amygdaloidal basaltic rock. Other obvious examples are in central and south America and in the oceanic islands, where prehistoric civilizations made considerable use of basalt for building and, especially, for the sculpting of major statues and megalithic monuments.

The medium-grained equivalent rock, dolerite (or diabase), has been widely used also but is often confused with basalt because of the ranges in grain size in both rock types. There are relatively few records, however, of the use of the coarse-grained basic rock, gabbro; exceptions are a rock from Sweden and the Rustenburg norite from the Bushveld complex of the Transvaal, South Africa.

Diorite (including tonalite) is a good example of nomenclatural uncertainty; for example, Hull's (1872) 'syenite' is probably diorite. In Britain, diorite occurs at Strontian and in other Caledonian plutonic masses in Scotland; a few examples occur in Wales, Ireland, and the Channel Islands; and in England there are the Mountsorrel and Charnwood Forest diorite and microdiorite of Leicester, both called 'granite' in the past. Few important instances are recorded of the use of these rocks for building purposes; those of Leicester are probably the best known. Sweden has a good diorite, and Egypt has recorded instances of statues, bowls, and vases carved of diorite. The rock was used for a 13th Dynasty sphinx, and for monuments in Iraq. Diorite is known from South Africa and Australia, and in Nova Scotia, Canada, as building material.

The fine-grained volcanic rock of intermediate composition – andesite – has undoubtedly been used for building purposes, but this lava may well have often been documented as 'basalt'. Andesite is recorded as one of several lavas used for building and paving at Akrotiri, Greece, and from Pergamon and Assos in Turkey; at Malinalco, Mexico, and at Olmec sites in Oaxaca, such as Mitla, porphyritic andesite was used to construct temples and other buildings.

Syenite has not often been recorded as a building stone, perhaps for the reasons already mentioned. One variety from Norway, known as larvikite, is famed as a facing stone because of the beautiful iridescent quality of the plagioclase feldspar (labradorite) of which it is largely composed. The medium-grained rocks, some of which are known variously as porphyry, porphyrite, felsite, and several other names have been widely used. Some of these are granitic in composition, others syenitic, but they are considered collectively here. Some of the best examples occur in Scotland (Ailsa Craig riebeckite microgranite), Cornwall ('elvans'), and in Sweden – used for sarcophagi and vases – Germany, Belgium, and France. In France, pavements made from porphyry from the Lessines quarry in south-west Belgium are well known, as is the porphyrite from Mons and examples from the Mediterranean. Sparta had a high quality porphyry, the dark green lapis lacedaemonius from Croceae. Other examples have been used from India, like the green felsite of Mysore, from Australia, and from the USA, but the country best known for rocks in this category is Egypt. The 'rosso antico' or red porphyry, found near the 1st cataract, has been used for sphinxes and statues in Egypt, and for sarcophagi and statues as well as building in Pompeii and other cities of the Roman empire; and in Florence of the Medicis and other Italian cities. The fine-grained, or volcanic, equivalent of syenite – trachyte – occurs in the Puys of the Massif Central of France and has been used for churches and bridges. Italy has abundant trachyte around Mount Vesuvius, near Naples; this pale grey lava has been much utilized for paving and bases, whenever a strong building stone was required. It was used by the Phoenicians in Carthage and also in Turkey. The Bowral trachyte of Sydney, Australia, is well known.

The volcanic pyroclastic rock known as tuff (also, sometimes, as agglomerate and ash) consists of fragments of rocks and minerals embedded in a matrix mainly of volcanic glass. In can be considered as an igneous rock and has been used as building material in the Massif Central of France, Turkey, Greece, and especially, in Italy, where it is known as 'peperino' and was also used for sculpture, especially in the second century BC. The first used variety was called 'monte verde,' a later one 'anio', and this rock was extensively employed near Naples in house building in Pompeii and Herculaneum. In Java, a Hindu temple, the Chandi of Gedog, is of hydrated tuff, and ignimbrite (welded tuff) was used at Mitla and other Olmec sites at Oaxaca, Mexico.

The fine-grained lamprophyric rock kersantite, and the following minerals, have been employed extensively in sculptural work; however, since they may appear also in buildings in a decorative capacity, they are listed here: malachite, a mineral which occurs in such massive form in the Urals of Russia that it has been used for fireplaces; alabaster, the massive form of the mineral gypsum, which has been used in England, Italy, and Egypt for tombs, sarcophagi, cinerary urns, and statues; quartz and the chalcedonic minerals; fluorite; lapis lazuli; turquoise; amazonite; the jades (jadeite and nephrite); charoite; catlinite and meerschaum; and amber.

Painted caves and engraved rocks

Rocks and cave walls on which stone age man painted (pictographs) or engraved (petroglyphs) by 'pecking' with a flint burin or other stone tool are artefacts only in a peripheral sense. Only in the case of a small rock or boulder transported from its original site could the question arise of petrology aiding provenance. Nevertheless, it is worth mentioning some of the rocks that have been used for this art form, especially since the texture and colour of the rock have on occasions been incorporated into the design.

The most famous of all stone age art occurs in the Franco-Cantabrian province, which includes the Lascaux caves of the Dordogne, of south-west Europe and North Africa, and might even extend into Palestine. Bandi, Breuil, Berger-Kerchner, Lhote, and Holm (1961) describe the paintings, which are deep in the caves on walls, with few exceptions of limestone, which as a surface lends itself to paint; thin films of travertine, or calcareous sinter, as well as small white beady efflorescences in the calcite, have 'fixed' the paintings firmly in many instances. Manganese dioxide (MnO_2) is perhaps the most common pigment, accompanied by the ochres (oxides and hydroxides of iron – hematite, limonite, and goethite), copper oxide, TiO_2, and red chalk (Newesely and Melaau 1978). The artists painted animals and humans, sometimes by the light of torches: flat, grooved slabs of schistose sandstone used to hold greasy, bituminous, or resinous material. The cave art of this region includes the painted pebbles of Mas-D'Azil, Ariège, with the famous spear thrower; similar examples are found at Birseck in Switzerland.

Franco-Cantabrian art includes some engravings; in the Spanish Levant, paintings again predominate but rare petroglyphs do occur. Both are executed on overhanging rock walls or on shallow rock shelters. In the Maghrab and Sahara regions the reverse is true: there are many engravings with some paintings. The petroglyphs are executed mainly on sandstone, a few occurring on quartz rock and granite or on any other suitable surface; the subjects are animals and humans. The paintings are in shallow 'caves' or beneath overhangs – there are no true caves in the Sahara – and they are also on sandstone (for example, Ordovician–Silurian sandstone in the Tassili-n-Ajjer), while the Hoggar granite is also used. They are accompanied by some small stone sculptures of animals and human heads.

Saudi Arabia has inscribed rocks – red sandstone and granite – which also bear drawings of elephants and of human hands and arms. In Nubia and upper Egypt rock peckings occur on sandstone and basalt: those on the latter retain their freshness longer. Western Sudan and the Sahara have Neolithic carved stones, up to 40 cm in size, of granite, gneiss, limestone, and sandstone (Milburn 1974). Engraved rocks are found in limestone and sandstone in the Welsh borderlands, Northumberland, and Scotland, usually of the cup and ring type. Also in northern Scotland are the unique Pictish painted pebbles dating from the first millenium AD (Ritchie 1971–2); Scandinavia, northern Russia, Sicily, and Turkey have engraved rocks, and for over 2000 years refugees have lived – and built their churches – in caves hollowed out of the soft, zeolite-rich volcanic tuff, from Mt Erciyes, at Cappadocia, Anatolia, Turkey. Similarly, some Dravidians were cave dwellers, and ornamented their walls with carvings. Zanskar (Ladakh) and Indonesia have rock paintings, and both art forms occur all over the American continent. At Writing-on-Stone, Alberta, Canada, sandstone is decorated, and in central Washington granite and basalt are used as painting surfaces whilst basalt is also engraved. Engravings are found in Georgia on granite and chlorite schist; in California on porous obsidian; at Black Canyon, in the Mojave Desert, on basalt boulders; and in Colombia. There are pecked quartzite cobbles in Virginia.

Attempts have been made at Grimes Point, Great Basin, Nevada, to date some of the petroglyphs by analysing their patination of 'desert varnish' (Bard, Asaro, and Heizer 1978). The varnish consists of oxides and hydroxides of Fe and Mn, as well as Si, Al, Ca, Mg, Na, and K; samples were removed from a test boulder by scraping from areas of fixed size and analysed by neutron activation. The oxide concentrations are proportional to thickness and thus to age; where petroglyphs are covered with appreciable coats of varnish, indicating repatination of the rock after pecking, they must be old; where they are clear, and penetrate to the fresh rock, they are young.

Australian aboriginal engravings occur all over that country under overhanging rocks, which include limestone, sandstone, diorite, and granite. They portray many types of animal, and include the Wondjina anthropomorphous figures. The paintings and engravings of Millstream station, Pilbara, Western Australia, include petroglyphs on fine-grained lithic sandstone at Gregory Gorge, Fortescue Valley. The stone is generally resistant to weathering but the artist made use of the soft clayey surface, highly suitable for pecking, resulting from the dissolution of dolomite and the alteration of feldspar to clay, these minerals being present in the rock (Clarke, Dix, Dortch, and Palmer 1978). The Melanesian–Micronesian people of Manus, in the Admiralty Islands between Papua New Guinea and Queensland, left petroglyphs carved on boulders, and pictographs in a cave site. After the Mediterranean rock art, however, it is in east, central, and southern Africa that one encounters the second most prolific region of rock painting and engraving.

The rock paintings of central Tanganyika were first described in detail in about 1930 (Culwick 1931) but a set of more recent papers (Fosbrooke 1950) reviews the subject in detail. Centred mainly around Kondoa but also at Singida and elsewhere, the paintings occur in 'boulder caves' in typical east

African bush country. In the Kondoa area the rocks are gneiss, whilst near Singida they are granite. Both pink and grey granite are used and sometimes the rock colour has been incorporated into the pictures. The paintings are accompanied by granite 'shapes': a primitive form of sculpture. Laterized amphibolite, effectively providing iron oxides such as hematite and limonite, seems to have been used successfully as a pigment; animals and human figures form the main, ubiquitous subjects of the artists, portrayed schematically rather than naturalistically.

Paintings and engravings are found on rocks in the ruined city of Engaruka, near Arusha, northern Tanganyika, where cup-mark engravings on rocks accompany stone walls and burial cairns; in the Serengeti Plain; and in central Africa, in Zambia, Zimbabwe, Swaziland (as at Sibebe), and Lesotho, where shelters, caves, and 'kopjes' of granite, basalt, and other rock types are used, accompanied by grooved rocks.

In the western Transvaal Bandi et al. (1961) describe three regions of rock engravings and peckings. To the north, granite caves predominate; dolerite occurs in the central region; and the southern part is circled by galleries of carved sandstone. Some of the most important engravings are carved on in situ rocks at the summits of exposed hills. However, fragments of, for example, dolerite are also used and in the mountain massifs there are rock 'galleries'. The subjects are animals, with fewer carvings of humans. In Botswana and Griqualand the best and most widely used surface is amygdaloidal dolerite, followed by other dolerites (and diabase), dolomite, sandstone and quartzite, and Dwyka conglomerate. At Vosburg, Cape Province, dolerite is commonly engraved with pictures of animals, human figures, and other subjects, whilst petroglyphs and pictographs occur on boulders both in open veldt and in kopjes, and in overhangs of gabbro and diorite.

Finally, a remarkable use to which rock has been put has been reported from west and east Africa. Rock 'gongs' – ringing or sounding rocks – are slabs or boulders, perhaps with cup-marks (cup-shaped depressions), of dolerite, granite, gneiss, or other suitable rock types. When struck with a fist-sized stone, they emit a clear metallic or ringing sound. Rock gongs occur near rock shelters, accompanied by artefacts. The stone chimes of ancient China served a similar purpose.

Megalithic stone circles, standing stones, and burial chambers

Megalithic and henge type arrangements of standing stones are found all over the world (Daniel 1980). There are well over 900 stone circles in the British Isles, of which perhaps 60 are important (cf. Burl 1976; Burl and Piper 1979; Wainwright 1969); others may remain to be discovered. The average recumbent stone weighs about 20 tonnes; however, at Old Keig, Aberdeen, there is one weighing 54 tonnes. Most of the monuments are built of local stone, commonly limestone, sandstone, granite, or gneiss. They incorporate both boulders and mason-dressed slabs and pillars. Little has been written concerning the petrology of the rocks employed, the principal exception being, of course, Stonehenge.

Stonehenge (Stone 1924) is built on the Chalk downs of Salisbury Plain in Wiltshire, southern England. It originally consisted of an outer circle of 60 sarsen stones ('greywethers'); a bluestone circle of 60 stones; a sarsen horseshoe of five trilithons; and an inner horseshoe of 19 bluestones. The sarsens (Whalley and Chartres 1976; Bowen and Smith 1977) are either concretionary slabs or boulders of siliceous sandstone, a silcrete or 'duricrust' formed of the sands of the Eocene Reading Beds, cemented together probably by interlocking secondary overgrowths of silica rather than by a normal siliceous matrix. The sarsens often contain pebbles, flints, and, rarely, shells, derived from the underlying and eroded Chalk, when they are known as 'puddingstones'. They occur sporadically on the nearby Marlborough Downs and can thus be regarded as of local origin; large tabular slabs of sarsen stone were also quarried locally. Some 45 sarsens remain at Stonehenge; some of them have incised petroglyphs.

The bluestones, however, are of a totally foreign nature unknown in the Cretaceous–Tertiary rocks of south-east England. Wales, Shropshire, the Mendip Hills, Devon, and Cornwall have all been suggested as possible sources. Stukeley (1740) first examined the rocks in thin section, whilst Story-Maskelyne (1878) described the rocks and published analyses of the dolerite (diabase) and rhyolite (Table 4.2), without resolving the problem of their source. It remained for Thomas (1923) to give the first full petrological account relating an artefact and its provenance. By comparing thin sections of the bluestones with rocks known to the Geological Survey of Great Britain from other parts of the country, he established that the bluestones almost certainly originated in the Preselau Hills of Pembrokeshire, a distance of some 280 km from Stonehenge. He further concluded that there was no evidence of glacial transportation, as opposed to fluvioglacial or ice-fed river transport, since the former did not extend this far south. However, Kellaway (1971) cited other occurrences, such as Heytesbury, Lake, and Stanton Drew, to support his contention that glacial transport, not human activity, could have been responsible for bringing the bluestones, and the sarsens, to Stonehenge.

Thus, Thomas contended that the raw material for the bluestones must have been transported by man, by land or land and sea, nearly 320 km.

The original horseshoe contained 59 bluestones; now only 32 remain. Of these 28 are of ophitic, chloritic, partly porphyritic 'diabase', later to be known as the spotted dolerite or 'preselite', whilst the other four are of locally spherulitic rhyolite. Fragments of rock found at Stonehenge also include basic ashes, tuffs and agglomerates, greywackes, argillaceous flag-

Table 4.2. Chemical analyses of the Stonehenge spotted ('diabase') dolerite and rhyolite, from the Preselau Hills, Pembrokeshire

	'diabase'	rhyolite
SiO_2	51.7	77.4
Al_2O_3	12.1	13.5
Fe_2O_3		
(total iron)	15.3	3.5
MgO	4.08	1.3
CaO	10.0	1.8
Na_2O	2.8	0.73
K_2O	1.02	0.6
H_2O	2.6	1.3
Total	99.6	100.13

From: Story-Maskelyne (1878); analyst: Dr Prevost.

stones, and slates: all were identified by Thomas as occurring in the Carn Meini–Cil-maenllwyd area of the Preselau Hills. In a later account of Stonehenge, Atkinson (1956) identified an unspotted variety of the dyke dolerite, not recognized by Thomas, which lacked the characteristic pea-sized pink or white feldspars. He identified the stumps of horseshoe rocks composed of volcanic ash and thus summarized the true bluestones as having consisted of four rock types:

> spotted dolerite
> unspotted dolerite
> rhyolite
> volcanic ash.

The Altar Stone, a partly calcareous and partly siliceous, pale green micaceous sandstone, is also foreign to the area. Thomas recognized it as a facies of the Old Red Sandstone which also occurs in Pembrokeshire; in view of the garnet grains found in it, North (1938) considered that it could well have derived from the Cosheston Beds, just north of Milford Haven. Jones (1956) noted 22 gateposts near Cardigan made of the Carn Meini spotted dolerite, accompanied by others of the local Cilgerran slate. Because of their foreign nature, Jones regards it as probable that the stones once formed part of a stone circle and were not imported for gate construction. Atkinson (1974) provided a footnote to the Stonehenge story by reporting a boulder of hornblende schist at Silbury Hill near Avebury, which is not the same as the spotted dolerite (preselite). But boulders of preselite do occur, with sarsens, at Boles Barrow, a Neolithic long barrow near Heytesbury, and at Lake, south of Amesbury.

The late Neolithic Avebury monuments, also in Wiltshire, consist of a ring of sarsen henges with two inner circles, the whole enclosed by a Chalk bank, linked to the West Kennet and the vestigial Beckhampton Stone Avenues, also of sarsens (Smith 1965; Burl 1979). Nearby Windmill Hill has yielded a wealth of Chalk carvings as well as flint implements, dolerite maceheads, axes, tools, and querns fashioned from a variety of English igneous, metamorphic, and sedimentary rocks well known to artefact petrologists, in addition to sarsens from the Marlborough Downs; the tool rocks, on the other hand, are mainly imported and are discussed elsewhere. Similarly, the dry stone walls are built of Great Oolite limestone or Forest Marble, which at their nearest point occur at Frome, some 40 km to the west. The 100 m Long Barrow is built of sarsens, topped with Chalk rubble, with the spaces infilled with flat limestone slabs – again Oolite from the Frome district and also Corallian, occurring at Calne at its nearest point, 11 km away. Also in Wessex are the Neolithic Durrington Walls, near Stonehenge, with its Chalk bank once the largest Stone Age henge construction in Britain; the nearby Woodhenge; the Kingston Russell stone circle, Abbotsbury, and the Nine Stones circle, Winterbourne Abbas, both near Dorchester; the Bronze Age Remstone stone circle, between Corfe Castle and Studland; and the Stanton Drew stone circles of Somerset. The latter have three circles of stones, avenues, and a cove, similar to that at Avebury; imported stone includes Old Red Sandstone, Inferior Oolite, and sarsens. The limestone Rollright Stones of Oxfordshire are almost the only example of standing stones in southern central England.

The standing stones and circles of south-west England are made of local granite; for example, in Devon, Scorhill and the Down Tor circle, and in Cornwall, the Boscawen-Un circle (which also has one quartz stone), the Merry Maidens, Trippet Stones, the Lanyon, Quoit tomb, and the Men-an-Tol megalith. A most unusual type of 'stone circle' is the White Ladder on the Moor, south-west Exmoor. This is a quarter mile long avenue of diminutive quartz stones, of which more than 70 have been found, terminating in a small burial cairn. Stone rows are common on Dartmoor.

Henge-type forts and burial chambers occur in northern Britain, especially in the Lake District (Cumbria), and in the Isle of Man. These include Long Meg (red sandstone), Swainside (porphyroblastic slate), Grey Croft (lava), Carles and the Castle Rigg stone circle (rhyolite and slate). Rudston, Yorkshire, has a well known menhir, and in Derbyshire there are the Arbor Low circle of limestone and the Barbrook stones (Millstone Grit sandstone). In north Wales, at Penmaenmawr, Gwynedd, there is a Druids' Circle, built of other than local rocks, probably glacial erratics such as dolerite and volcanic ash with some rhyolite, perhaps from the Snowdon area (Griffiths 1960). Tools from the local Graig Lwyd augite granophyre or felsite and other rock types are associated with the Penmaenmawr circles. Cromlechs also occur in Anglesey and Pembrokeshire.

Standing stone circles, built around stone cairns, cists, henge monuments, and burial chambers are especially common in Scotland. These are often of gneiss, granite, or sandstone, sometimes of greenschist, have cup-marks, and usually lack horizontal lintel or 'hanging' stones. They include the standing sandstone pillars at Machrie Moor, Arran; and in Lewis the Precambrian Lewisian gneiss was used at Callanish, Cnoc Fillibhir, and Garynahine. The north-east has Strichen, and the Clava Cairns of Inverness; Aberdeen has several circles of pink or red granite at Cullerlie, Loanhead of Daviot, and Sunhoney, but the monster at Old Keig, Aberdeen, weighing 54 tonnes is of sillimanite gneiss. In Fifeshire there are the sandstone Balbirnie and the granite Girdle Stones. The monuments of the Orkney and Shetland Islands are well known. Consisting of chambered cairns, Maeshowe and other tombs, circles, the Pictish Ring of Brodgar of flagstones, the Skara Brae village, Viking burial ships, dolmens, standing stones, and crosses, they are built of the main local rock, Old Red Sandstone, with lesser amounts of granite and basalt and occasional use of schist, gneiss, quartzite, limestone, gabbro, and serpentine. Collins (1976) ascribes the Stones of Stenness, Orkney, to the Middle Old Red Sandstone Stromness Flags, blue-grey calcareous flagstones perhaps from Arion and Vestra Fjold, where the ancient quarry still contains monolithic blocks. Ancient dry stone forts (duns) and defensible homesteads, circular dwellings some 17 m across, built of dry stone walls within outer walls also of stone and known as brochs, some of them vitrified (see Chapter 5), are a feature of early man in north and west Scotland, as at Glenelg and Dun Carloway, Lewis, and Burrian, Gurness, and Bu Broch, Stromness, in Orkney; some 500 are known. Rocks and stones with cup and ring engravings, Pictish symbols, and other incised engravings occur; red and other sandstones, granite, and limestone were used, with associated slate stone balls and tools of flint. Ireland has several stone ring forts and circles, including passage tombs, burial cists, as at New Grange, Co. Meath, near Dublin (greywacke); The Lios (limestone and agglomerate); Ballynoe, Co. Down (Ordovician grit); and Dromberg, Co. Cork. Stone possibly imported from Spain and Portugal was decorated with sculpted heads and abstract designs. Finally, throughout Britain generally, many of the defensive earthworks, barrows, and tumuli consist of mounds of earth only, but some had enclosing circles and walls of Chalk, flint, and other large standing stones or boulders.

The stone prehistoric monuments of Denmark have been described comprehensively by Glob (1971), though with no details of rock types employed. The first dolmens, which formed the earliest buildings in Europe, were large stones, sometimes weighing up to 40 tonnes, placed on burial mounds, often in rectangular or circular outline. They were followed by 'giant' tombs or passage tombs, the megalithic cists or large stone graves of the Battle-axe people, and the Bronze Age mounds of earth or stones, the late Bronze Age adopting an arrangement of single or concentric stone circles around the graves. Cup-marks, as in Scotland, were engraved on the stones of cists, passage graves, and dolmens, together with more elaborate petroglyphs. The graves of the Iron Age, though lacking the barrow form, are also marked by stone circles, including the famous 'stone ships', so called because the elongated arrangement of the circle, with curved sides and tall 'bow' and 'stern' stones, bore an overall resemblance to the plan view of a Viking ship. The monoliths which accompanied the circles were not inscribed by early Bronze Age people; by the late Iron Age, Viking inscribed memorial stones appeared, as at Jelling churchyard, and Uppsala, in Sweden, bearing runic engravings. Some are famous; for example the Troll stone has a 'watching' runic stone mask or face. The Iron Age people also built stone cellars. Similar stone ships and dolmens are found in Norway and elsewhere in Scandinavia. Standing stone alignments and circles are known from all over the world. Well known examples are found at Carnac and Locmariaquer, in southern Brittany, where the extensive alignments, menhirs, and dolmens are of local granite. Flagstone monuments also occur in several forms in the southern Sahara region (Milburn 1974). Sculpted menhirs occur in southern France, northern Italy, Spain, and the Channel Islands. Burial chambers are most common in France, as at Gavrinis, and Bagneux, Saumur, in the west; and also in Spain, Portugal, northern Germany, Scandinavia, and the British Isles. Megalithic temples, often with engraved stones, are found mainly in Malta and Gozo, and also in southern Italy.

Rock-cut tombs are common in the central Mediterranean countries, as at Sisante and the Ballearic Islands in Spain, together with other rock shelters and megalithic constructions (Kopper and Rossello-Bordoy 1974). These are usually of limestone, and this rock is also used for containers, funereal vessels, and querns. In Egypt stone circles of limestone and sandstone are found at Zi, and in Libya elongated double rows of stones were erected on a flat erosion surface of tufa. Basalt, granite, limestone, and sandstone monoliths are found in Ethiopia and columns of red sandstone, some of them phallic in design, are found in elliptical arrangements in Mali; north of the Gambia River are stone circles of shaped laterite blocks. Rock-cut tombs occur at Persepolis in Iran; megaliths and circles of granite, laterite, and other material are known from across the sub-continent of India and Pakistan from Kashmir to the south. In Indonesia megaliths, including stone circles, of basaltic and sedimentary rocks are found on many of the islands, amongst them Sumatra, Nias, Sulawesi – where there are also man-made cliff caves – and Sumba. Stone circles and dolmens have been described from Japan, Australia, and throughout America.

At Hopewell, Ohio, meteoritic nickel-iron has been found in burial mounds. At South Woodstock, Vermont, a system of underground stone platforms and chambers, upright stones, 'inscribed' rocks, and open 'cellar-holes' is ascribed to American Indians or even to early pre-Columbian Celtic or Iberian settlers. On a mesa overlooking the Animas River in Aztec, New Mexico, there are four parallel rows of cobblestone arcs, 250 metres long, known as the 'Old Indian Racetrack'. They may have been constructed by the Anasazi Indians but, despite the presence also of artefacts, their date or purpose is not known.

Early walls, crosses and grave slabs, and milestones

Most of the rocks used for constructing walls, crosses, grave slabs, and milestones are of local origin and little has been written concerning their petrology, except for Roman milestones and Highland grave slabs and crosses which have been the subjects of special study. Granite has been much used for drinking troughs and fountains.

Early walls

The early Greeks devised the technique of building walls known as Cyclopean, because of the great size of the blocks of stone used, weighing up to several tonnes each; the best example is at Tiryns, in the Argolid; that at Messene has large lintels only. The walls were only roughly trimmed, piled up, and the interstices filled with small pebbles, pieces of rock, and clay. The technique is similar, in fact, to that of 'flint knapping', used by the Romans and earlier: the flint nodules were roughly shaped, piled up, and held together with lime mortar. Ancient city walls, for example that surrounding the old city of Peshawar in north-west Pakistan, were often constructed of mud and brick. The old city of Jerusalem has a 2000 year old protective wall some 14 m thick – a 137 m section was discovered in 1977 – and this is more than three times as thick as the present wall, built 400 years ago by the Turks. The wall of Ka'aba, in the Grand Mosque at Mecca, has a 'celestial' Black Stone set in it: possibly it is a meteorite (Khan 1938). However, it is mainly the material used in dry stone walls that is considered here, in which suitably sized rounded or flat boulders are piled up to a height of four or five feet to form the wall, generally with no attempt at shaping and with no form of cement; the skill of the builder is sufficient to ensure a very considerable degree of permanency.

Dry stone walls occur in hill country all over Britain, and are best seen in Scotland, the Cheviot and Pennine Hills, the Lake District, north and south Wales, the Mendips, and in south-west England on Exmoor, Dartmoor, Bodmin Moor, and the Scilly Islands. Many types of rock are employed: granite in Scotland and Dartmoor; slates and volcanic rocks in Wales and the Lake District; Millstone Grit and other sandstones and limestones in the north; and so on, choice being largely governed by the local availability of durable stone. Similar constructions are found in Europe and many other countries; an interesting example is reported from the Transvaal, of Iron

Age date, and the Bantu of around AD 400 also built beautiful dry stone walls of granite around their circular fort, the Acropolis, of Zimbabwe. The Great Wall at Santa Valley, Peru, is 85 km long, incorporating 40 hilltop fortresses, and the Inca built colossal walls at Cuzco.

Two of the most interesting walls are those of China and northern England. The Great Wall of China extended for a total of some 6325 km, including branches and bends, or 3460 km along the main line (Needham 1971). It was constructed during the days of the first Han emperors (140–86 BC) in sections, with intermittent towers and fortresses, of round boulders, loess, and earth, and only locally, in valley bottoms and on passes, of masonry – either hewn stone or brick which formed foundations and facings, and sometimes even the entire wall. Iron and wood were used occasionally for reinforcement. The wall was rebuilt during the Ming Dynasty (1368–1644 AD) only in those parts necessary to keep out the Tartars, using a greater proportion of masonry; the present line dates from this period. The temples near to it are of granite and limestone, whilst sandstone and conglomerate also occur locally; it is therefore probable that all four rock types were employed in the wall.

Hadrian's wall, stretching for 118 km across northern Britain, from Solway Firth to the mouth of the River Tyne, was built to demarcate Roman territory and to protect it from the northern tribes. It extends across the country and in the east incorporates the great igneous intrusion of quartz dolerite known as the Whin sill. The wall is built on the sill where this aided construction, since the sill itself forms in part a natural rampart. To the west, the builders also used the local Carboniferous Limestone and some sandstone. The design was simple: double stone facings, filled with rounded boulders, rubble and mortar, with turf as a binding agent. The Roman walls in the southeast of England and East Anglia have been mentioned. In London, favourite stones were the Cretaceous Kentish Rag and ferruginous sandstone, and in East Anglia Chalk and flint.

Crosses and grave slabs

Crosses, dating from early Christian times or often earlier, and usually bearing engraved inscriptions, are best known from Scotland, Ireland, Wales, the Isle of Man, northern England, and Cornwall, but are known elsewhere in the south – for example at Thanet and Chichester – and from Europe. The use of local stones, such as granite, sandstone, and limestone predominated. For example, the early granite crosses, and medieval clapper bridges, of Cornwall are particularly notable. North (1938) noticed that an early cross from Cardiff did not resemble the local rocks but was made of an oolitic limestone similar to those of Bath and the Cotswolds. However, he concluded that it was not imported but derived from a very restricted local development of the Jurassic Lower Lias, of littoral type, occurring at St

Fagans, two miles north of Coed Riglan. Rutland (1976) discussed a carved stone forming the base of a modern cross in the graveyard at Aylestone, Leicester. The stone, thought to be a Christian triskele, probably predating the Roman conquest, is carved from a local sandstone unusually rich in white mica.

Phemister (1956) first identified the eighth or ninth century St John's Cross of Iona as being carved of calc-chlorite-albite schist, now thought to derive from the Loch Sween area, probably from Doide. In Dunbartonshire inscribed crosses of red and grey Carboniferous sandstone, and also of granite, and a sculpted slab of grey sandstone, are associated with a stone circle of greenschist, and in Renfrewshire sandstone has been used for Christian crosses.

Collins (1977), however, undertook the first petrological study of the late medieval monuments of the West Highlands of Scotland. More than 600 of these crosses, graveslabs, and effigies survive, dating probably from the fifteenth and sixteenth centuries, when the area was under the Lords of the Isles. The distribution map shows that the carvings stretch from the Outer Hebrides south to Arran, 90 per cent of them being south of Ardnamurchan Point and eighteen on the island of Iona. Collins described ten rock types, of which the most important is a calc-chlorite-albite schist, used for virtually all the carvings from the Kintyre, Oronsay, and Loch Sween workshops, and the majority of those from the Iona school, occurring from Lewis to Kintyre. Its origin is traced to the east shore of Loch Sween, where it forms part of the Dalradian sequence of the Caledonian metamorphic belt and was used in the construction of Castle Sween and Kilmory Chapel. The Loch Awe monuments and a few of those from Iona are of black pyritous slate from the Easdale and Ballachulish slate belts; this dark grey graphitic slate is notable for its pyrite cubes, reaching 0.5 cm across. Mainly the work of the Loch Awe school, they are found in their area of origin. Grave slabs of epidiorite (greenschist or 'greenstone') of Loch Awe type have been found in that district, together with an Iona school slab, at Clachan, Kintyre. This dark green rock appears igneous unless sheared, when it is schistose; crystals or 'knots' of hornblende and plagioclase are visible in both types. It may have been quarried from Kilmartin or from Eilean nan Leac, an island in Loch Sween. Slabs from the Loch Awe school composed of tremolite-chlorite schist occur at Kilchrenan; this is another dark green rock which may derive from Achnamady, west of Kilchrenan. Another Loch Awe type grave slab at Glendaruel (Cowal) is of schistose grit, a Dalradian rock common in the Cowal area. Black, coarse-grained plagioclase amphibolite, the hornblende crystals measuring up to 5 mm in length, was used between 1500 and 1600 by an independent workshop, probably situated in southern Harris, for carving effigies of men in armour, grave slabs, and a font in Skye and Harris. The rock probably comes from the Rodel area of southern Harris. Grave slabs of biotite-muscovite schist are found in northern and western Skye. This coarse-grained mottled grey rock, sometimes containing pink garnets, probably comes from the Lewisian rocks of the Outer Hebrides. Hornblende schist, a dark green schistose rock probably also of Lewisian age, was used for a sixteenth century effigy of a man in armour from Skeabost Island, Skye. Sandstone was rarely used for these monuments but was the material for the effigy of the Abbot Dominic in Iona Abbey church, and the carved voussoirs and panels on Alexander MacLeod's tomb at Rodel. The rock resembles the Carsaig sandstone used for the dressings of Iona Abbey and Nunnery. The final rock in Collins' account, chlorite-talc schist, is pale green and schistose, also containing calcite; it was used for an effigy of a man in armour in the graveyard at Kirkton, 7 km east of Kyle of Lochalsh. The work is a crude imitation of the effigy at Rodel, southern Harris, and must have been produced by a local carver. The rock probably derived from a quarry 3–4 km away, on the south side of Loch Alsh, in the Lewisian of the Glenelg district. Collins concludes with the opinion that the calc-chlorite-albite schist was a highly suitable material – not too difficult to carve, available in large flat slabs, yet not too fissile or easily weathered – and was thus prized by the sculptors of the Iona, Kintyre, and Oronsay schools; also it could be quarried from sites convenient for sea transport. In the case of the Loch Awe school, on the other hand, the carvers were probably itinerant, relying on local rocks for their work wherever they travelled.

Milestones

Milestones, generally constructed from local stones, have been the subject of two papers by Sedgley (1970; 1975), who has conducted an extensive petrographic study of Roman milestones in Britain. In the north of England the Romans used mainly Millstone Grit, sandstone from the Yoredale series, and Coal Measures sandstones, sometimes feldspathic, of Namurian and Westphalian ages. Other material used included Triassic Keuper Sandstone, Penrith Sandstone, St Bees Sandstone, and Carboniferous and other quartzites. In north Wales they again favoured Millstone Grit, using also the Cefn-y-Fedw Sandstone and igneous rocks such as dolerite, rhyolite and other lavas, and greenschist (metamorphosed dolerite). Two Caernarvon stones, dating from the times of Hadrian and of Severus and Caracalla, are of pebbly quartzite probably derived from the Millstone Grit of Llangollen, 64 km distant. Carboniferous rocks also predominate in south Wales: Millstone Grit – always a much favoured stone – and Upper Coal Measures sandstone. In the Cambridge area, the rocks employed include the Jurassic Barnack Freestone and Rag and Lincolnshire and other limestones; clunch, a locally named hard facies of the Lower Chalk; and Keuper Sandstone, transported from some distance away. In Berkshire two stones are of Great Oolite. Rock from the Lower Greensand was used for a stone near Worthing, whilst five milestones in the Hampshire and Dorset area are of Chilmark (Portland) stone or Bembridge Limestone, probably transported from the Isle of Wight. Finally, in south-west England, the Romans used granite for four of the known milestones from Cornwall, one from the Bodmin Moor granite and the others from local outcrops. The fifth known example is of a slaty silty sandstone from the metamorphosed Devonian sediments of the Tintagel area. Thus, whilst the Romans made obvious and sensible use of local material for their milestones, there is evidence of transport in some cases, including the use of stone ferried across the Solent. Many other examples occur throughout Europe. Later milestones were also fashioned from a variety of local rocks.

Classical marble statuary, sarcophagi, and inscriptions

Most of the petrological work applied to the provenance of artefacts has concerned the smaller items, such as flint and obsidian axes and tools, jade axes, and honestones. A considerable amount of work has been carried out, however, on chips and powder scrapings of marble from statues, sarcophagi, and inscribed slabs in order to establish their source. Like flint, obsidian, and jadeite, marbles are very hard to categorize individually. They can be divided into groups but within such groups require very sophisticated techniques to identify them positively. The following account traces the development of the petrological study of marbles from the early 'geological', stratigraphic, and simple petrographic approaches; through petrofabric study; trace element analysis; to isotopic studies, using first the stable isotopes of carbon and oxygen, to the most recent development using the radiogenic isotopes of strontium. The value of such studies in permitting the accurate 'fingerprinting' of marble artefacts and fragments is obvious, not only for establishing provenance but also for sorting and matching fragments for restoration, detecting forgeries, and for providing approximate dates. Previously the matching of fragments, for example, depended entirely on the expert eye of the archaeologist.

Pliny, Diocletian in his *Price Edict*, as well as Theophrastus, Strabo, and Pausanias frequently mentioned the classical marbles from Paros and elsewhere, although they never mentioned Naxos, an island which now exports marble; this stone in fact is thought to have been used for statuary purposes from the seventh to sixth centuries BC. Diocletian considered the subject from an economic viewpoint, giving contemporary values for the marbles having allowed for quarry location and accessibility to the sea. Among the early scientific accounts of marble, that of Lepsius (1890) stands out for the comprehensive way in which it handled its restricted topic – Greek marbles – and, in the present context, because it included a full discussion of the use of marbles in statuary. After describing stones from Thessalia, the Peloponnese,

Euboea, Attica, Paros, and Naxos (Fig. 4.1 and Table 4.1), Lepsius discusses the sculptures of Athens and elsewhere and the provenance of their stones. He included two partial analyses of the classical Pentelic (Attic) and Cycladic marbles, which are notable for the presence of 0.12 per cent Fe_2O_3 in the former, whilst no iron was detected in the island samples. Hull (1872 p. 130) quotes an analysis of Carrara marble from Italy, with 0.29 per cent Fe_2O_3. Thus a simple – and probably unreliable – chemical distinction between the iron-bearing and the iron-free marbles was attempted a hundred years ago.

Petrographic studies began with Washington (1898), distinguishing between Parian and Pentelic marbles mainly by texture. Parian marble, like Carrara, is coarse-grained, being formed of a mosaic of large ($c.$ 0.15–2.0 mm) interlocking crystals of calcite. This gives them their 'brilliant' lustrous surface, noted much later by Lawrence (1972) when reviewing the classical marbles from the point of view of their suitability as sculptural stone. Parian marble replaced Naxian as the leading sculptural material (sixth to fifth centuries BC) and was used for the Hermes of Olympia and the Venus de Milo. Pentelic marble, on the other hand, has large crystals in a fine-grained matrix, a porphyroblastic texture compared by Lepsius with the porphyritic texture of fine-grained igneous rocks. It can often be recognized by its grain size, streaks of mica, the colour of its patina, and its rusty weathering texture, caused by the relatively high iron content. It is worth noting that the remoter parts of Greece and the Greek colonies in southern Italy and Sicily had no marble of note; the sculptors therefore used limestone: in Selinus, a rich city, marble heads and arms were fixed to limestone metopes in its Doric temple E (Lawrence 1972). The similar acrolithic technique was also used throughout Greece, however, with clothed torsoes fashioned of wood or clay and projecting heads, hands, and feet alone made of marble or other stone, or even of ivory.

Martin (1965) and Papageorgakis (1967) gave good accounts of the geological features of the marbles, and other rocks, used in Greek architecture, and Monna and Pensabene (1977) detailed descriptions of the classical marbles from the Anatolian region of Turkey. The ancient Greek quarries were described by Dworakowska (1975). The late 1940s saw the first of a series of papers describing the structural and stratigraphic aspects of Greek marbles. Thus, Marinos (1948) outlined the geological history of the Aegean marbles, concluding that their texture, twinning, and resistance to weathering, amongst other properties, varied with their geological and structural position; the geologically 'deeper' the marble, the larger, more even, and clearer the calcite grains and therefore the more preferable for sculptural use. Ward-Perkins (1951) used a different method to trace the source of the archaeological marbles used in building in Tripolitania during the Severan period of the Roman empire, which derived from Carrara,

Greece, Phrygia, and north Africa. He relied on quarry marks on blocks and columns, a consignment 'note', and masons' marks; using quarry marks, for example, he identified six north African marbles: Africano; Synnadic; Portasanta; Numidian (giallo antico); Carystian (cipollino); and Tean. When describing Greek inscribed stones, it has been customary over the last hundred years to include a physical description of the material. The early epigraphers Pittakis and Rangabé attempted to distinguish between the island varieties and the Attic Pentelic and Hymettian marbles. They used colour and shade only, ignoring grain size, and could not agree on a classification. This was hardly surprising since the geological structure of Attica has still not been finally resolved. Lepsius gave an account of the stratigraphy in 1890, based on upper Hymettian and lower Pentelic marbles, and it was not until 1929 that Kober added a third formation. Much of the marble is allochthonous, or 'foreign', due to folding, faulting, and thrusting, and this, of course, compounds the problem; Kober even questioned the separate identity of the Hymettian and Pentelic stones.

Hertz and Pritchett (1953), both of the US Geological Survey, suggested a combination of colour, grain size, structural features, and accessory minerals in the marbles as a method of distinguishing between them. After describing their system, they tested it and found it generally satisfactory. Herz (1955a) summarized the Attic marbles from Mounts Pentelikon and Hymettus as including five general types: (i) marble breccias and mylonized marbles; (ii) schistose marbles; (iii) dolomitic marbles; (iv) white, medium- to coarse-grained marble, aesthetic 'Pentelic'; and (v) banded marbles, aesthetic 'Hymettian'. The type locality for Pentelic marble was the ancient quarry of the Spilia Daveli on the southern slope, and for Hymettian the Roman quarries along the west side of Kakorhevma; the latter is banded in white or light grey and bluish layers and is finer-grained than the Pentelic marble. By comparison, the Parian lychnite marble is pure crystalline coarse-grained rock, translucent through 35 mm as against 15 mm for the best Pentelic stone (Lepsius 1890).

Weiss (1954) took structural analysis a stage further, describing in detail the procedure for petrofabric analysis when applied to marbles. He warned that the apparent simplicity of the method was deceptive, adding that these principles and techniques cannot be applied except by an experienced worker with a knowledge of structural petrology. Further, they are highly time-consuming and should only be used when simpler methods have failed; they have now been replaced by the trace element and isotope determinations described below. Summarizing the contribution made by petrofabric analysis Weiss suggested that a knowledge of the orientation of each fragment alleged to belong to a single block of marble could go a long way towards confirming its authenticity, and also perhaps towards establishing the source of the whole block.

Using stereographic projection techniques, the orientation in space of any one piece of rock, and thus of its component fragments, provides a 'fabric picture'. The orientation of a specimen is generally fixed by three directions: (i) the 'compromise' β-axis deduced from the [0001]-axis orientation of the grains of calcite and the megascopic lineation, where present; (ii) and (iii) the statistical maxima of points of compression and tension deduced from twinning upon $\{01\bar{1}2\}$. Previous work shows that in a block of marble of considerable size, sufficient to contain most statuary, epigraphic, and building pieces, these three directions tend to have an approximately constant orientation. By selecting fragments of closely similar fabric picture, and arranging them in the correct relative orientation, it is possible to restore a flat slab such as an inscribed stele (Fig. 4.3); in the case of a statue the problem is possible but much more difficult, because of the third dimension of depth. Weiss pointed out that his account was a preliminary one describing a new and untried technique; applied to seven Greek marbles, he obtained strong and distinctive fabric pictures from each, and regarded the method as having considerable potential.

Fig. 4.3. Hypothetical reconstruction of a fragmental stele using petrofabric analysis. Symbols within strain ellipses indicate fabric planes and poles. Fragments 4, 7, and 10 clearly do not belong to the stele. (After Weiss 1954.)

At the same time as Weiss was conducting his study, Herz (1955b) was engaged in a similar investigation using orientated specimens from quarries in Naxos, Paros, and Delos in the Cyclades, and Mounts Pentelikon and Hymettus, and three epigraphic fragments. Herz prepared fabric diagrams in which the poles to $\{01\bar{1}2\}$ composition planes (cf. the work of Weiss) were plotted, using from 150 to 400 poles per diagram. Herz considered that his work, also preliminary, showed promising results: the three epigraphic fragments, two from one slab, one from another, gave similar diagrams, all resembling that of the Pentelic marble, which came from the ancient Spilia Daveli quarry. Thus Weiss and Herz, working simultaneously but unknown to each other, reached the same conclusion: that the technique of petrofabric analysis was preliminary but promising. However, as already mentioned, chemical methods have in fact replaced them, probably largely due to the time-consuming and specialized nature of petrofabric determinations.

Bautsch and Kelch (1960) described some layers of rock off the coast of Sicily; having decided that they might not be *in situ* but derive from a sunken ship carrying building stone, they sought to establish their provenance. Using conventional thin-section techniques such as grain size and, by staining, the calcite–dolomite ratio, they reached no conclusive results and largely brought to an end the era of petrographic methods in establishing marble provenance.

Renfrew and Peacey (1968) discussed the classical techniques of visual description and thin-section study – grain size, accessory minerals, colour, lustre, and texture, practised since the days of Lepsius – and concluded after studying 84 white – not coloured – marbles, from 30 sources (Fig. 4.1), that no definitive classification or division can be reached by these methods. Pointing out how recrystallization and shearing can totally alter the appearance of a marble, both in hand specimen and thin section, they urge that more scientific methods be used and the earlier categories abandoned. Among the methods they recommend are long wave ultraviolet study, at 366 μm. They found that all but their Rhodes marbles flouresced violet, unless weathered, whereas those samples from Rhodes fluoresced a salmon pink and could thus be easily distinguished. Using cathode luminescence, they found that their samples could be divided into five pattern groups. No data were presented, but petrofabric study and trace element determination, perhaps by neutron activation analysis, were also recommended as potentially successful methods. Ashmole (1970) similarly urged the application of science, tempered with common sense, to the establishment of the sources of the classical marbles of the Aegean.

Rybach and Nissen (1965) conducted the first important chemical study of the Mediterranean marbles. Some 230 fresh samples (c. 300 mg of each) of white or near white marbles from quarries in Attica, the Aegean, and

Anatolia were analysed for sodium and manganese by instrumental neutron activation analysis, using the heavy water reactor DIORIT. The results showed manganese contents of between 0.5 and 200 p.p.m., and sodium of between 2 and 300 p.p.m.; the values were similar in samples from the same quarries. The manganese concentrations, especially when combined with other data, enabled some marbles used by the Greeks to be distinguished. Other chemical techniques, attempted at the same time, were far less effective. Manganese concentrations (Fig. 4.4) are highest in Pentelic (30–700 p.p.m.) and Vresthena (180–600 p.p.m.) marbles, and lowest in marbles from Marmara (0.5–4 p.p.m.) and Paros (1–7 p.p.m.). Very generally, Attic marbles as a group seem to be highest in manganese. However, when using this element care must be taken that the sample is typical and not in any way enriched in manganese: for example, containing the mineral piemontite. Homogeneity was checked in samples from the same quarry and also from the same hand specimen, from Marmara, Işçihissar, and Pentelikon; homogeneity is greatest in the Marmara samples. Young and Ashmole (1968) carried out semi-quantitative analysis of the elements Fe, Si, Pb, Al, Mn, Mg, Ca, Sn, Cu, Ag, Zn, Na, Ni, Sr, Ti, K, Ba, and V, by optical emission spectroscopy, on the Boston Relief and the Ludovisi Throne, in the Boston Museum. They compared the results with measurements on marbles from Thasos, Siphnos, Naxos, Paros, and Pentelikon; a

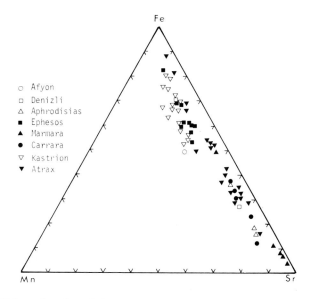

Fig. 4.4. Triangular plot of Fe, Mn, and Sr, used to distinguish between classical marbles. (See text; after Conforto *et al.* 1975, and Gast *et al.* 1979.)

match was clearly noted between the artefacts and the dolomitic Thasian marble, largely on the basis of their high magnesium contents. X-ray diffraction traces and thin-section study also indicated a dolomitic source. However, in the case of non-dolomitic marbles, a match would almost certainly not have been obtained on the strength of this type of comparison. Andreae, Oehelschlagel, and Weber (1972) measured Al, Si, Na, K, Mg, Fe, Mn, and Sr in fragments (left side, head, and right side) from a sarcophagus from the Acropolis, now in Frankfurt and Kassel Museums, and obtained results which supported the archaeological contention that, despite the lack of proportional relationship between the figures in the two fragments, they came from the same original. They supplemented their argument with a statistical analysis of the value of mineralogical and geochemical tests applied to this particular problem. In a recent personal communication (S. Walker 1979), however, it seems that the results of recent carbon and oxygen isotope analysis arranged by P. C. Bol suggest that the two fragments are incompatible, in agreement with the opinion of Drs Walker and Bol and other German scholars; Dr Walker is nevertheless of the opinion that the two fragments consist of the same type of marble but were not cut from the same block.

A recent chemical investigation is that of Conforto, Felici, Monna, Serva, and Taddeucci (1975), who investigated marbles from Carrara and also from the Aegean and Anatolia; these authors also determined the proportion (wt per cent) of insoluble residue in the samples. After measuring Fe, Mn, Al, Si, and Ba by optical emission spectroscopy, and K, Sr, and Ti by X-ray fluorescence, on 137 samples (Table 4.1), they concluded that most of these elements (K, Si, Al, Fe, Mn, Ti, Sr) can be used to discriminate between certain groups of marbles. Conforto *et al.* also group their samples into six colour classes, on the assumption that trace element contents correlate with colour. Only in one group, however, coloured white to light grey, do trace element abundances distinguish sampled areas: Fe, Mn, and Sr can be used to distinguish between Ephesos, Marmara, and Carrara marbles (Fig. 4.4).

Lazzarini, Moschini, and Stievano (1980*a*, *b*) conducted a study on the four groups of classical marble – Tuscany (Carrara), continental Greece, Greek islands, and Anatolia – in which combined petrographic, chemical (Ca/Sr ratio), and archaeological–historical data were used to provide criteria for distinguishing unambiguously between them. Specimens were collected from as many quarries as possible, especially those known or thought to have been used in Greco-Roman times, and their colour banding and veining, grain sizes, accessory minerals, and petrography studied. Thin-section examination of the texture included study of the crystal shapes and sizes, twinning, and metamorphic effects. The Ca/Sr ratio was determined by XRF (Table 4.1). Concluding, like Renfrew and Peacey (1968), that no single method can positively distinguish marbles, the authors claim that the combination of techniques can do so and support their contention by success-fully testing artefacts of known Naxian and Marmara stone.

To summarize, chemical characteristics seem to have only limited value in distinguishing between the classical marbles. Most notably, Marmara (Proconnesian) marble can probably be identified on the basis of very low manganese and iron and high strontium content, whilst the dolomitic Thasian rock is readily distinguishable by its high content of magnesium. Until more data are available, greater precision is unlikely to be achieved; further, the supersession of chemical techniques by stable and strontium isotope measurements may well have rendered chemical methods out of date.

Thermoluminescence – a method commonly used in determining the age and provenance of obsidian and pottery – has rarely been applied to marble, although some have claimed that the method could be equally effective in the case of marble, flint and chert, and basalt. Glow curves of samples from Greek quarries generally produced only a single peak so that no positive characterization of samples was possible; Afordakos, Alexopoulos, and Miliotis (1974) applied artificial thermoluminescence to artefact samples to increase the diagnostic value of the method. Since marble blocks from a single quarry vary considerably in their thermoluminescent characters, iso-lation of a source is not possible. In the case of fragments of an artefact, similar patterns do not prove that they originated in the same block since they could merely have come from the same quarry, Since differences within a single block are small, however, the technique can be used to confirm that fragments with major differences could not have come from a single block. The method was useful in restoring statues from fragments found in a shipwreck near the island of Antikythera.

Craig and Craig (1972) laid the framework for stable isotope determina-tions in marbles (Table 4.1). Making use of the fact that within rocks there are local variations in the isotopic ratios $^{13}C/^{12}C$ and $^{18}O/^{16}O$, they collected 170 quarry samples from Naxos, Paros, Pentelikon, and Hymettus. The specimens were taken from different parts of the quarries used by the ancient Greeks, from sites actually worked, and 35 per cent were analysed for C and O isotopes, as well as Sr and Mg concentrations. Ten archaeo-logical samples were also studied. The value of this work is clearly shown in Fig. 4.5; when $\delta^{13}C$ and $\delta^{18}O$ are plotted, the Parian, Pentelic, and Hymettian marbles form clusters, providing distinct isotopic fields for these rock types. As was hoped, isotopic equilibration seems to have occurred within the limited extent of quarries to give nearly homogeneous areas. The distinction between marbles from Mounts Pentelikon and Hymettus goes far towards confirming Lepsius' (1890) contention that the two marbles are different – the upper and lower – and not the same formation repeated by folding or faulting. Two types of marble occur on Naxos, both outcropping

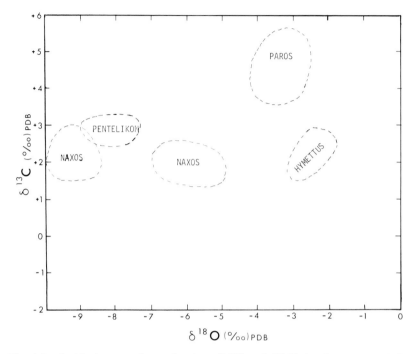

Fig. 4.5. Stable isotope determinations ($\delta^{13}C$ and $\delta^{18}O$) for four types of Greek classical marble. (After Craig and Craig 1972).

at each of the two quarry localities. The high $\delta^{13}C$ of the Parian marble suggests an origin as a chemical precipitate; its high purity supports this suggestion, whereas its trace element composition could provide no such indication. The ten archaeological samples had values showing two to have had a Naxian origin (high $\delta^{18}O$); two a Pentelic, including the 'Theseion' sample in the Athenian Agora (about 450 BC); and one a Parian – the Treasury of Siphnos at Delphi. The sources of five samples could not be established, including a specimen from Caesarea, Israel, suspected of being Hymettian marble imported by the Romans. Other source localities, therefore, remain to be 'fingerprinted' by isotope analysis. Manfra, Masi, and Turi (1975) applied the same techniques to the classical marbles from western Anatolia. Rocks from five localities – Marmara, Ephesos, Aphrodisias, Denizli, and Afyon – were measured; unfortunately, clustering was far less distinct than in the case of the Greek samples. However, if only white and slightly coloured marbles are included, reasonably clear fields are obtained for rocks from Marmara and Aphrodisias (Fig. 4.6). Those from Ephesos fall approximately into two groups and overlap the.

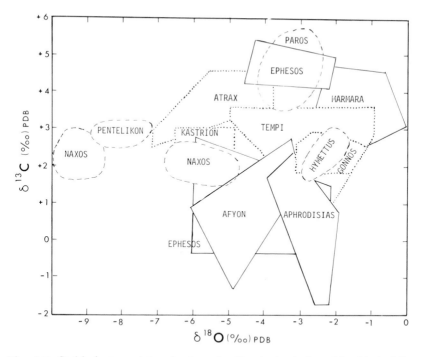

Fig. 4.6. Stable isotope determinations for Greek classical marbles (dashed lines; Craig and Craig 1972); Anatolian marbles (solid lines; Manfra *et al.* (1975); and Thessalian marbles (dotted lines; Germann *et al.* 1980); after Germann *et al.* (1980).

fields of Naxos and Paros. Manfra *et al.* suggest that some of the Ephesos and Marmara marbles, like those of Paros, might have a chemical origin.

Ideally, with the addition of isotope 'fields' for Carrara (for which two pairs of values were given by Baertschi (1957) (see Table 4.1)) and the other important Greek and Turkish marbles, a single diagram should go far towards identifying the origin of all the classical marble for which $\delta^{13}C$ and $\delta^{18}O$ had been measured. Unfortunately, this state of affairs has not been reached.

The method has been tested further, as described, in three papers by Herz and Wenner (1978), Coleman and Walker (1979), and Germann, Holzmann, and Winkler (1980). Herz and Wenner selected fragments from six classical stelae stored in the Epigraphical Museum and Agora Museum, Athens. The problem was to determine whether pairs of fragments, and in two cases three fragments, allegedly from a total of six stelae, were in fact derived from these artefacts; associations which had been debated by archaeologists for many years. The fragments were first subjected to hand lens examination for geological features such as foliation, lineation, grain size, accessory minerals, and colour. Isotopic ratios for carbon and oxygen were then determined. The first pair had similar structural features and isotopic ratios, compatible with a common origin. On the basis of isotope measurements, their source could not have been the classical quarries from Mounts Hymettus or Pentelikon, but could lie in unknown quarries in the upper part of Mount Pentelikon (H. Craig, personal communication to Herz and Wenner). The second case comprised three fragments: structural observations suggested that one piece came from a different stele than the second and third, but all three had similar isotopic ratios. The conclusion was that two stelae were made from marble from the same Hymettian quarry at about the same time; possibly a single slab was split to make the two artefacts. The third case again concerned three fragments, of which only two were analysed isotopically. Geological criteria were in agreement for all three, and isotopic ratios for the two analysed; the ratios were not suggestive of an origin in Pentelic or Hymettian quarries. In this case, it was notable that workings on the backs of the samples varied greatly, indicating the danger of using this feature as a diagnostic criterion. In the fourth case, the pair of fragments had similar geological features and isotopic ratios, suggestive of a common – Pentelic – origin. The fifth case showed structural features which allowed both fragments to have a common origin, but the isotopic ratios suggested that one derived from Mount Hymettus, the other from Mount Pentelikon. Finally, in the sixth case, a similar result obtained: agreement from geological but not from isotopic data. Thus, of the six cases examined, Herz and Wenner (1978) were able to conclude that a common origin applied in three. They noted:

> 'that the ancient quarrymen took advantage of the fact that marble tends to split most easily along its foliation planes as well as along its more prominent lineations. Thus any inscription with a foliation plane parallel to its face and a lineation perpendicular to the lettering direction, running from top to bottom, was orientated that way by the quarrymen for ease of cutting. Most of the stelae have the same orientation; all that can be said about two separate inscriptions with similar foliation and lineation features is that their geological structures permit an association' (p. 1072).

Only if other geological features agree, as well as isotopic ratios, can fragments be ascribed to an origin as part of the same original stele. Coleman and Walker (1979) compared the isotopic ratios of samples from two complete Attic sarcophagi from the same tomb at Ierapetra, Crete, which were believed to be Pentelic. A fragment of less certain identity was also measured. The isotope data suggested that whilst one is Pentelic, the other is probably made of a local stone with a strong superficial resemblance to Pentelic marble. The third, less certain, fragment is unlike the other two and appears to be made of Proconnesian (Marmara) marble. Fragments from two apparently Proconnesian, finely worked lions' heads were measured and both have isotopic ratios compatible with a Marmara origin. Determinations on a number of fragments from Sidamara sarcophagi raised technical problems and proved inconclusive. Their appearance is similar and had led to the suggestion that they derived from a single sarcophagus made of an unidentified Turkish marble, but detailed examination showed minor differences both of style and of finish which were supported by the inconclusive nature of the isotopic data. From this study, however, the authors were able to demonstrate several important points. The common art-historical assertion that all Attic sarcophagi are carved from Pentelic marble is clearly erroneous. Fragments of an object apparently carved from one block can probably be safely restored if they are isotopically and geologically compatible; the way the blocks were handled is also extremely important, similar techniques indicating a strong likelihood that they came from the same workshop or group of workshops.

Germann, Holzmann, and Winkler (1980) and Gast, Germann, and Eilert (1979) studied marbles from hellenistic funeral stelae from museums (mainly Larisa) in eastern Thessalia, and from quarries in the Larisa area (Papageorgakis 1963). The isotope ratios were determined and also the trace elements Fe, Mn, Mg, and Sr (by atomic absorption spectroscopy); in addition the marbles were studied petrographically in thin section (see also Germann 1978). Two main marble-producing areas can be distinguished on geological grounds: the western margin of the Larisa basin, near Atrax, and a group of localities on the eastern fringe: Kastrion, Tempi, and Gonnos. The Atragian marbles are coarse-grained, with more or less equant twinned crystals (Table 4.1); those from the eastern areas are highly cleaved, with the calcite crystals in a preferred orientation indicated by elongation, flattening, and bending. In each case the accessory mineral content is similarly low. The isotope data, on the other hand, separate the marbles into two groups: Atrax and Kastrion, and Tempi and Gonnos. The chemical results for Mg, Sr, and, partially, Mn, isolate marble from Gonnos from the other three; see also Fig. 4.4. Of the nine museum samples for which the isotopic ratios were determined only two could be assigned unequivocally to a source, Kastrion, with a possible third to Tempi, on the combined isotope, chemical, and petrographic evidence. Germann et al. (1980) therefore concluded that marbles even within small quarrying areas may be heterogeneous; that isotope data for marbles from widely separated areas (Gonnos, Hymettus, Marmara, Carrara) may be very similar and often in conflict with the geological evidence; and that trace element contents may be highly variable within marbles from a single area, whilst petrographic textures or fabrics are less liable to be so. Attempts to correlate marble artefact fragments with each other or with their sources should therefore be based on extensive field work to establish the range of, and variation within, possible source areas, followed by isotopic, chemical, and petrographic study, possibly aided by multivariate analysis.

The Thessalian isotope data have also been superimposed on the diagram of Craig and Craig (1972), in which sharply delineated fields are apparent for four of the classical marbles. It is clear (Fig. 4.6) that the considerable overlap which results in the isotopic fields for most of the marble groups greatly reduces the value of the method for the determination of marble provenance and fragment matching. However, as these last three papers show, isotopic analysis has profound implications for the study of artefacts, especially when attempting to match fragments; archaeological observations can in many cases be confirmed and in others contradicted. The greatest problems arise in attempting to establish sources; here only a probability can be asserted if the isotopic, chemical, and geological data for an artefact match those of a known source. The problem has been reviewed by Germann (1978), who includes a bibliography of German as well as other studies in the field, and by Herz and Wenner (1981).

The most recent archaeometric technique to be applied to archaeological raw material is that of strontium isotope analysis. Gale (1979) and his co-workers have applied the technique of $^{87}Sr/^{86}Sr$ determination to gypsum (alabaster), marble, and obsidian. No results on marble have yet been published but it seems clear that analysis of stable and Sr isotopes, taken together with geological and geochemical data, form the most promising techniques yet attempted for the determination of the provenance of marble used in classical archaeological artefacts.

Aspects of Indo-Pakistani sculpture

Gandhara sculpture, the Greco-Buddhist or Romano-Buddhist religious art form of the first to sixth centuries AD, is so called after the ancient name of the Peshawar Valley, Pakistan, where it was first recognized in the ruins of shrines and monasteries. It is found between the Afghan border with the Soviet Union and the Panjab in Pakistan. The largest quantities come from sites around Peshawar and the Swat Valley to the north; considerable but lesser amounts are from eastern Afghanistan and the Rawalpindi District of the Panjab. The sculpture consists mainly of cult images (Buddhas and Bodhisattvas or saviour deities) and architectural panels formerly covering the walls of the shrines, stupas, and monasteries, carved with Buddhist legends and decorative motifs (Fig. 4.7). Rock carving also occurs, such as the two giant heads of the Buddha carved in a cliff of augen gneiss on the south side of the road running east from Charbagh to Malam Jabba, Swat.

Though much work in stucco has survived, stone carvings predominate with examples of mica, talc, chlorite (as at Butkara), hornblende, and quartz

Fig. 4.7. A Gandharan frieze, of bluish grey schist, north-west Pakistan. The texture of the schist is clearly visible on fractured surface. (Reproduced by kind permission of W. Zwalf and the Trustees of the British Museum).

schists, as well as steatite, claystone, phyllite, slate, limestone, and sandstone (Marshall 1960). The majority, however, are of a bluish grey, or greenish grey, mica schist, homogeneous in texture, and hard enough to withstand wear and tear; at the same time the stone is soft enough to be capable of the delicate carving often achieved by the Gandhara sculptors.

Courtois (1962–3) examined ten specimens of schist (*phyllade*) and found them to fall into two groups. The first, variously bluish grey carbonate-chlorite-muscovite-sericite-quartz schists, with accessory rutile, apatite, garnet, epidote-zoisite, and magnetite, came from central Afghanistan, from the Kapisa Plain region, i.e. at the southern foot of the Hindu Kush. The chlorite is pale green; one example contained albite. The second group derived from the Peshawar region, as well as examples from Hadda, in eastern Afghanistan, and from Ranigat, east of Peshawar in Buner. This is the more common bluish grey chloritoid-muscovite-sericite-quartz schist, with accessory carbonaceous material, biotite, and rare hematite. The presence of blue needles of chloritoid distinguishes these rocks from the vast majority of low grade metamorphic schists.

Lahanier (1976) described the head of a barbaric king in the Gandhara style, from the Musée Guimet, as composed of chlorite-muscovite-quartz schist; semi-quantitative XRF analysis revealed trace amounts of strontium, manganese, and chromium. For comparison, he examined two more Gandhara schist objects, one of them from Hadda, the other without findspot, and found them to be carved of the same rock. Both contained strontium and manganese, as well as rubidium, arsenic (in one), and nickel (in one).

A fragment of the common bluish grey sculpted rock has been examined and analysed by the present writer, and confirmed as a chloritoid-paragonite-muscovite-quartz schist, with some plagioclase, biotite, and carbonaceous material. The chloritoid occurs as small laths or needles uniformly distributed throughout the rock. From the thin-section and chemical analysis (Table 4.3) it should be quite easy to confirm or reject the similarity between the sculptural rocks and samples from any suspected source area: chloritoid-bearing alumina-rich mica schists are not particularly common (Kempe 1982).

Nevertheless, so far as is known, the precise locality of the quarries from which this rock was obtained has never been established. In a letter to Sir Mortimer Wheeler, then Director General of Archaeology in India, dated 27 April 1948, Dr W. D. West, then Director of the Geological Survey of India, wrote that it was:

'a carbonaceous micaceous schist, a type that is rather common amongst the older rocks of the north-west Himalay, e.g. in the Salkhala Series that forms much of the country extending south-west of Nanga Parbat for 60 miles. As regards the Swat Valley, we know very little about its geology

Table 4.3. Chemical analyses of the Gandhara bluish grey mica schist, and the Asoka stone porphyritic microgranite, north-west Pakistan

	A			B	
%		p.p.m.		%	p.p.m.
SiO_2	56.9	Be	4	74.60	—
TiO_2	1.26	Cr	110	0.40	nil
Al_2O_3	25.0	Li	115	11.33	25
Fe_2O_3	2.73	Ni	30	2.33	15
FeO	3.28	Cu	70	1.00	43
MnO	0.13	Zn	95	0.16	200
MgO	0.86	V	190	0.47	nil
CaO	0.28	Sr	205	0.14	40
Na_2O	1.40	Ba	780	4.46	750
K_2O	2.58	Rb	110	4.40	19
H_2O^+	4.89	F	620	0.23	—
P_2O_5	0.06	Nb	—	0.03	250
CO_2	0.49	Zr	—	0.12	1250
C	0.33	Y	—	—	100
Others	0.25				
Total	100.44			99.67	

A. Gandhara bluish grey mica schist (Kempe 1982). Analyst: V. K. Din.
B. Asoka stone aegirine-riebeckite porphyritic microgranite, Shahbazgarhi (average of two analyses) (Kempe 1973). Analysts: C. J. Elliott, V. K. Din, and A. J. Easton.
Methods: XRF, AAS, and CHN analysis.

[and specimens collected by two geologists in 1914 and] a few years ago . . . are not of this type.'

Rather more is now known about the geology of Swat, although far from all; it seems most plausible that the schist should come from this area, and it has in fact been suggested that there may be quarries at Kafar Kot (Kafir Kot or Kote) in southern Swat, or at Ranigat, in Buner (Courtois 1962–3). A source near the Takht-i-Bahi monastery (Fig. 4.8), in Mardan District, has also been suggested but the monastery itself, however, seems to be constructed of rock from the local Lower Swat-Buner Schistose Group, a formation of siliceous schists and other related rocks, or from the Swabi-Chamla Sedimentary Group. Alternatively, the sculptural material may come from Afghanistan or the tribal areas between that country and Pakistan; there are widespread chlorite-mica-quartz schists in Afghanistan but none known to the writer to contain chloritoid. As Marshall (1960) observed: 'the quarries where the stones were hewn must also be located.'

One of the rocks on which King Asoka the Mauryan (*c.* 273–232 BC) proclaimed his royal edicts, engraved in a local form of Middle Indian, occurs south-west of Swat, at Shahbazgarhi, Mardan district; north of the Indus River, this area alone has such rocks, although others have been found

Fig. 4.8. Ruins of the Gandhara monastery at Takht-i-Bahi, north-west Pakistan. (Reproduced by kind permission of R. Knox.)

in the south. What makes it remarkable in the present context is that the rock is an alkaline porphyritic microgranite (Kempe 1973), a rare rock distinctive for its sodium-rich minerals (Fig. 4.9 and Table 4.3).

Turning to the eastern side of India, petrographic examination of a number of significant pieces of sculpture has provided some assistance in the consideration of provenance. No positive sources have been established but tests on the sculptures, stylistically eastern Indian and indeed apparently Bihari, have served to dispel the widespread belief that the sculptural stone is basalt, showing it in fact to be black-painted chlorite or mica schist, or sometimes sandstone or limestone, all rocks which outcrop in Bihar. Three examples – a quartz-sericite-biotite schist with small tourmalines; a chlorite-sericite-quartz schist containing tiny grains of an unidentified mineral of the zircon-thorite-xenotime series; and the (unusual) presence of gypsum in a sandstone – illustrate how rare accessory minerals can sometimes 'fingerprint' a schist or other common rock and, if a similar source rock can be located, establish provenance.

Objects in steatite and soapstone

Steatite and soapstone, both soft and aesthetically pleasing, have been in use since pre-Dynastic Egyptian times for carving seals, bowls, vases, lamps,

Fig. 4.9. The Asoka stone, Shahbazgarhi, north-west Pakistan. (From Kempe 1973.)

plaques, and figurines. Its ability to withstand high temperatures and thermal shock has also led to its extensive use for smoking pipes, cooking pots, and for crucibles and moulds for molten metallic copper (Dayton 1978). Dayton also claims that the first glazed objects, such as beads, scarabs, and stamp seals, were probably made of steatite. Crushed steatite was used also in faïence paste.

Steatite refers strictly to a rock composed mainly of talc ($Mg_3Si_4O_{10}(OH_2)$), whereas soapstone, a rock with a greasy or soapy feel, can contain the mineral assemblage talc plus any of the following: chlorite, amphibole, phlogopite, antigorite, magnetite, and carbonates. The two types occur together or separately, steatite, of course, usually containing small amounts of one or more of the other 'soapstone' minerals. For convenience, they are treated together and in fact the terms are often used synonymously. In origin, both rock types occur in small masses in many parts of the world, deriving from the hydrous metamorphism of ultrabasic igneous or impure, carbonate-rich sedimentary rocks; in the former case they are often associated with the harder related rock, serpentinite.

One of the most important collections of 'steatite' carvings, of the early third millenium BC, occurs at Tepe Yahya, south-east Iran, and includes the unique green soapstone figurine some 28 cm in height. Kohl (1976) and Kohl, Harbottle, and Sayre (1979) used neutron activation, X-ray fluorescence, and atomic absorption analysis, as well as thin-section microscopy,

X-ray diffraction, and emission and Mössbauer spectroscopy to identify, group, and establish the source of the Tepe Yahya carvings. This became important after 1971 when it appeared that many were rich in iron, talc being a magnesian mineral; it turned out that half the specimens were in fact chlorite. Other examples from Ur and Tarut were found to be, respectively, calcite, and phlogopite and serpentinite. The chlorites from the Arabian peninsula fall into two distinct groups, suggesting two separate sources in eastern Arabia. Precise identification of these chlorite artefacts and their sources is, however, proving very difficult.

The Pre-hispanic peoples (AD 650–1100) of the Mucuchíes area, Mérida State, in the Venezuelan Andes carved winged (batwing) pendants from serpentinite (antigorite, the principal constituent mineral, has the composition $Mg_6Si_4O_{10}(OH)_8$) and steatite (Wagner and Schubert 1972) in an area unlikely to contain these materials. Petrographic and X-ray diffraction examination show that the serpentinite consists of antigorite, with minor talc, magnetite, and carbonates, and the steatite of talc with lesser amounts of antigorite, chlorite, magnetite, and carbonate minerals. Other artefacts of the region were made from jadeite and nephrite, and chert and agate. The function of the pendants is highly conjectural: use as musical instruments, ornaments, totems, sacred symbols, and currency have all been suggested. Wagner and Schubert, speculating on their source region, consider the Guajira Peninsula of Colombia and the Western Caribbean Mountains of Venezuela as the most likely, as serpentinite and some steatite occur there, with the Sierra Nevada de Santa Marta, Colombia, and the Caribbean islands of Cuba, Hispaniola, and Puerto Rico as other possibilities. Soapstone was used by the Maya civilization in Mexico, Guatemala, and Honduras.

Perhaps the most important series of petrological investigations on steatite-soapstone artefacts so far conducted have been those of R. O. Allen and his co-workers. Allen, Luckenbach, and Holland (1975) and Luckenbach, Holland, and Allen (1975) (see also: Holland and Allen 1977; Allen and Pennell 1978) used instrumental neutron activation analysis in an attempt to establish the sources of aboriginal north American artefacts by relating them chemically to known quarry sources of the stone. Soapstone was used in the eastern United States during late Archaic and possibly early Woodland times for the manufacture of lugged bowls, and later for smoking pipes and decorative pieces. Known sources of this rock only occur in limited parts of the United States; in the east they are found as lenses in a narrow tectonic belt from Alabama to Newfoundland, just east of the Appalachian Mountains, in the Piedmont region. To help in the understanding of pre-historic trade patterns, Allen et al. (1975) chose specimens from the eastern Piedmont to see whether significant differences occur among them, and whether artefacts from sites across the mountains in the Shenandoah Valley,

Virginia, could be correlated with them. Owing to the variable mineralogy of the talcose rocks, resulting from the degree and style of their metamorphism, as well as variations in the mineralogy and chemical composition of the original material, their trace elements also show very considerable ranges; however, their rare earth element concentrations appear much more constant. Up to 22 trace elements were analysed in a total of 55 1 g samples from 29 different quarries in Virginia, Maryland, Pennsylvania, and North Carolina; a total of 53 different fragments from 28 sites in Virginia, Maryland, New York, and New Jersey were also analysed. The results were then presented graphically, normalized to chondritic values. It was found that the rare earth elements (REE), from lanthanum to lutecium, showed very similar patterns, but differing magnitudes, or absolute amounts of the elements, in samples taken both from one quarry and from different quarries in the same area. The patterns observed in specimens from eight different quarries are shown in Fig. 4.10, in the case of the Montgomery County quarry, the range is shown and can be taken as fairly typical of ranges in other such quarry groups. A similar pattern emerges when samples from artefacts are analysed and plotted. Two typical patterns, from bowls found at different sites in the Shenandoah Valley, Virginia, are also shown in Fig. 4.10 and it can be seen that there is a close match between one of them and the Madison County quarry specimen, some 45 miles away (M), and between the other and the Albemarle County quarry specimen (A). The match suggests transport of the material from quarry to site and in each case the gap through the Blue Ridge Mountains is the route suggested. Luckenbach *et al.* (1975) showed that artefactual material found in the Coastal Plain area of the eastern Piedmont did not match material from the Albemarle and Nelson Counties region but probably came from the Chula quarry in Amelia County (C in Fig. 4.10). Other Coastal Plain specimens do not match any quarry specimens so far tested. One interesting specimen from a site in Isle of Wight County has a similar rare earth pattern to specimens from quarries in south-eastern Pennsylvania. If the artefact did in fact derive from material from this quarry, it could have travelled more than 320 km by canoe down the coast of Chesapeake Bay.

Allen *et al.* (1975) also applied the technique to broken soapstone bowl sherds in an attempt to determine whether all originated in the same artefact. Five sherds from the same level of the Indian Head site in New Jersey gave similar patterns but differing absolute amounts of the elements (Fig. 4.11). This result suggests derivation at least from the same quarry, but the elemental differences between sherds from the same artefact have been found to be smaller than most of those shown here so that only the top two fragments probably originated from the same bowl. However, the technique can clearly be used in some instances to identify fragments from the same artefact. In the case of the other trace elements, Allen *et al.* (1975) use

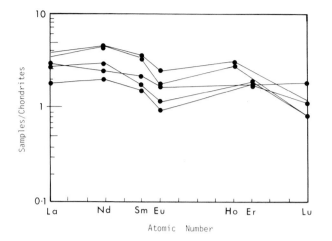

Fig. 4.11. Normalized REE concentrations for steatite bowl fragments from the Indian Head site, Salem County, New Jersey. While all the fragments probably originated from the same quarry, only the top two are thought to derive from the same bowl. (After Allen *et al.* 1975.)

Eskimo, and Norse in the Labrador–Newfoundland region for plummets, oil lamps, cooking pots, amulets, and spindle whorls. So far, over 50 soap-stone source regions of varying size have been differentiated on the basis of their REE patterns but artefact analysis suggests that others remain to be discovered. Over 60 Eskimo and Indian artefacts have been analysed and their rare earth patterns suggest that at least eight sources were used over the past 4000 years; only four of these have been located. Two quarry areas in Labrador have been sampled, at Freestone Harbour in the Davis Inlet area, south of Nain, and at Moores Island, near Okak, north of Nain. On Newfoundland, the large outcrops at Fleur-de-Lys were sampled, as well as an outcrop 1.6 km from the L'anse aux Meadows site. The REE patterns from the Okak and L'anse aux Meadows specimens are shown in Fig. 4.12, together with four artefacts. The patterns suggest that the Norse spindle whorl found at L'anse aux Meadows came from the L'anse quarry, as well as the 4000 year old Maritime Archaic Indian plummet from Rattlers Bight. Most of the plummets from this Indian region, however, have similar REE patterns but which differ from those of any of the quarry specimens analysed. Other Maritime Archaic plummets from Windy Tickle, Davis Inlet, have patterns matching the outcrop at Freestone Harbour. Of the two Eskimo cooking vessel samples, from a Dorset site in the Nain region, one matches each of the quarry samples plotted. The Dorset Eskimo used both the Labrador quarries in the Nain region extensively from 2700 to 1400 years ago; 10 per cent of the specimens analysed indicate that they also made use

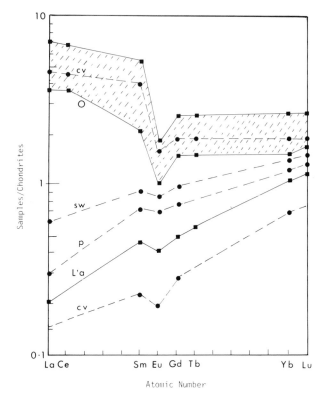

Fig. 4.12. Normalized REE concentrations for soapstone samples from northern Canadian quarries (solid lines and squares). The shaded area represents the range of values for outcrops in the Okak region of Nain, Labrador (O); and the lower quarry sample is from L'anse aux Meadows, Newfoundland (L'a). Artefacts are shown by broken lines and solid circles. The top artefact (cooking vessel, cv) matches the Okak quarry samples; and the lower three artefacts (spindle whorl, sw; plummet, p; and another cooking vessel, cv) the L'anse quarry sample. (After Allen *et al.* 1978.)

of the Newfoundland quarries worked earlier by the Maritime Archaic Indians. The problem remains, however, that nearly half of the 30 Dorset artefacts analysed do not match any from the four quarries.

Soapstone artefacts also occur at the Dorset sites at Arnapak and in Greenland, at Tyara; slate and nephrite were also used by the Dorset Eskimo. These examples perhaps link with the uses of steatite by the Vikings (Wainwright 1962) and the occurrence of steatite – and also clay – vessels in Bronze Age short cists in Orkney and, in lesser numbers, in Shetland.

Finally, talcose rock has also been used by early civilizations in Greece, for example at Akrotiri and Mycenae; at Lemba in Cyprus; at Tel Zerror, where a famous bowl, some 7 cm across, was found; in Sardinia; and throughout Egypt and northern Sudan. It was used by the Hittites; at the Fosse Temple in Palestine; for seals, including cylinder seals, in Mesopotamia; and in Aden, for lamps and bowls. It was in common use by the early peoples of the Indian sub-continent, for example at Harappa, for seals, and at Kish and Mohenjo-daro for dishes. Steatite was a commonly used material for sculpted figures, bowls, and other objects in West Africa, whilst the Zimbabwe settlement of southern Africa carved huge bird pillars and also vases from soapstone.

Colossal heads and smaller New World carvings

In addition to the small heads and other objects carved from basalt, andesite, and other rock types by the people of the pre-Columbian civilizations of central and south America, the Mesoamericans were notable for using stone for miniature 'thin stone heads' and also for 'colossal heads', associated with their cities, temples, and pyramids. Since the first colossal stone head was discovered at Hueyapa, in 1858, a total of eleven, attributed to the 1000 BC Olmec branch of the Mayan culture from south-eastern Mexico, has been described (Fig. 4.13; Heizer and Smith (1965)). It was at San Andrés Tuxtla, some 24 km from Hueyapa, that the famous Tuxtla Statuette was found at the turn of the century: the jadeite figurine of a bald Indian priest wearing a mask in the form of a duck's bill over the lower half of his face.

The petrography of the basalt used for the two heads from near Tres Zapotes, near Hueyapa (Fig. 4.13), has been reported in detail by Heizer, Smith, and Williams (1965). Their account refers to colossal head no. 2, which stands 1.5 m high and weighs 7.7 tonnes. Head no. 1 is larger, being 1.8 m high and weighing 10.2 tonnes. The heads (Fig. 4.14) were carved from huge spheroidally weathered boulders of a distinctive picritic basalt occurring on the slopes of Cerro El Vigía, formerly named Cerro Santiago, some 8 km from the Tres Zapotes locality. The rock is notable for its abundant olivine and augite (pyroxene) phenocrysts, though in highly variable proportions, and the corresponding paucity of large plagioclase feldspar crystals. In hand specimen the olivine crystals are pale green, the augites black; in thin section the augites exhibit oscillatory zoning, from colourless to green. The crystals range from 0.5 to 5.0 mm in length, some augites reaching 2.5 cm across, and together make up some 50 per cent of the rock by volume. Labradorite plagioclase constitutes some 40 per cent of the rock, the laths never exceeding 1.0 mm in size, and the remaining 10 per cent consists of minute granules and needles of augite, apatite, magnetite, and hematite. The rock has a specific gravity of 2.70. Four stelae, A, B, C, and D, have also been found at Tres Zapotes, of which A is 5.2 m long, together

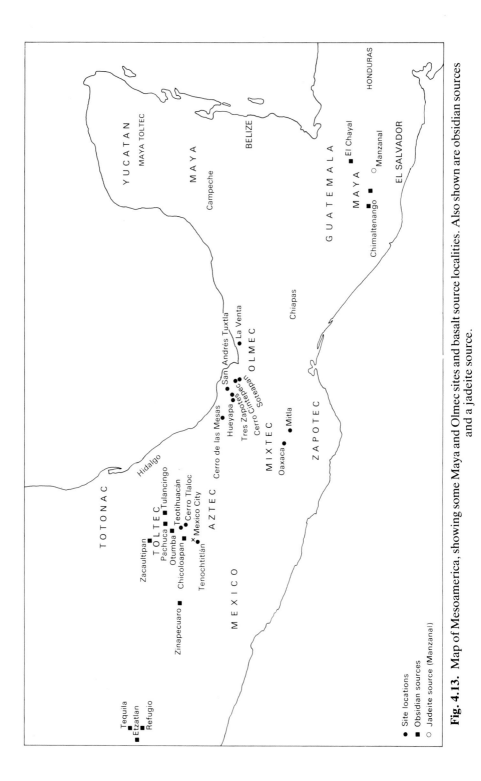

Fig. 4.13. Map of Mesoamerica, showing some Maya and Olmec sites and basalt source localities. Also shown are obsidian sources and a jadeite source.

Fig. 4.14. Olmec colossal head from Mexico; the heads stand 1.5 m or more high and were carved by Olmecs from picritic basalt. (Reproduced by kind permission of the Mexican National Tourist Council.)

with monument 9, monument F, the 'Frog Altar', and the 'Jaguar Throne'. Most of these are carved of the same basalt as head no. 2; stele (or monument) C, however, is made of the same rock as stele 3 of La Venta, whence came four colossal heads.

The La Venta basalt contains small phenocrysts of olivine, but none of augite or plagioclase, and probably derives from the northern end of the Tuxtla Mountains. It is one of many rocks from this area described by Williams and Heizer (1965a) and Curtis (1959); other La Venta basalts include a dense olivine-augite rock used for columns, a porphyritic olivine basalt for stele 2, and a dense olivine basalt, without plagioclase phenocrysts, used for monument 5. There are three monuments carved from a hornblende-augite andesite from La Unión volcano, and other andesites and basalts used for sculptures of an origin other than Olmec. Williams and

Heizer (1965a) quote Curtis' list of rock types from La Venta, which include pumpellyite, muscovite-actinolite, and actinolite schists; actinolite-epidote gneiss; quartzite; meta-andesites and metadiorites; serpentinite; jadeite rock; and limestone; together with basalt and andesite they were used for celts, cists, pavements, columns, and monuments. To this list Heizer *et al.* (1965) added chlorite-muscovite and chlorite-actinolite-epidote-albite-sphene schists, also from monuments; sandstone was also used.

From San Lorenzo Tenochtitlan come five colossal heads; the rock used for these is a porphyritic iddingsite-augite basalt from Cerro Cintepec and Soteapan, used also for colossal head no. 2 (previously monument 2), six altars, and three monuments from La Venta. The stelae and monuments from Cerro de las Mesas are of andesite and tuff; stele 3 of hornblende-augite tuff; stele 4 and monument 6 of a pilotaxitic, porphyritic 'oxyhornblende'-hypersthene andesite; stelae 8 and 9 of a tridymite-rich 'oxyhornblende' andesite; and stele 10 of a fine-grained hornblende andesite.

The colossal sculptures at or near Teotihuacán (Heizer and Williams 1965) are all carved in Cerro Tlaloc andesite, from some 25 km south of the site. This rock is pilotaxitic, porphyritic andesite, with resorbed hornblende crystals. Oscillatory-zoned labradorite-bytownite plagioclase feldspar constitutes 25–30 per cent of the rock, hypersthene 6 per cent, hornblende 3 per cent, augite 4 per cent, magnetite 2 per cent, and the groundmass, containing some cristobalite, 55–60 per cent. Amongst the sculptures is the unfinished figure, carved from a huge boulder, named the Idolo de Coatlichán (Heizer and Williams 1963); it is 7.1 m long, 3.8 m wide, 4 m thick and, assuming a specific gravity of 2.43, calculated as weighing 197 tonnes. There is also the 4 m high Diosa de Agua, or Water Goddess, carved from the same rock and weighing 24 tonnes, and the sculptured boulder or mutilated sculpture in the Avenue of the Dead at Teotihuacán, known as the prostrate monolith and weighing 6 tonnes.

Rhyolitic or rhyodacitic ignimbrite, previously referred to as trachyte, was used for the buildings at Mitla and other Oaxacan cities, whilst purplish, porphyritic, vesicular pyroxene andesite was employed for huge lintels and jambs (Williams and Heizer 1965b). Limestone, as well as sandstone and grey slate, were other building stones and the ignimbrite was used for hammerstones, picks, flakes, scrapers, and other tools. The Oaxacans used greenstone, alabaster, and onyx for stelae and slabs, and jadeite and serpentinite for figurines, masks, and bowls; they also painted murals on stone (Paddock 1966). In the Mayan lowlands, limestone is plentiful and was the principal building and monumental stone, and some of the quarries are known; sandstone, grey slate, and ignimbrite were also used. Two unusual stelae, however, occur at Ichpaatun and Calakmul. The first, stele 1, is of quartz-muscovite-chlorite-garnet-graphite schist or phyllonite; and the second, stele 9, of grey 'semischist' containing pyrite, muscovite, and graphite (Graham and Williams 1971).

In addition to the Olmec colossal heads of Mexico, together with stelae and monoliths, similar associations occur in Honduras and Guatemala, using porphyritic basalt, as well as granite and sandstone. The Maya–Toltec centre of Yucatan, Mexico, had pyramids and temples, with associated sculpture, whilst at Polol, near Tikal, and at Quiriguá, eastern Guatemala, monuments and stelae of schist, rhyolite, and sandstone occur, the preferred monumental stone for the Acropolis changing with time from rhyolite to sandstone. From Colombia, through Ecuador and Peru – where there are also Inca colossal walls at Cuzco – to the southern Andes, monoliths and stelae of basalt and sandstone are known, whilst the central Americans of 500 BC also carved monolithic statues and sarcophagi from basalt and andesite.

The Indians of north and south America produced little monumental sculpture on the scale of the Olmec colossal heads (Douglas and D'Harnoncourt 1941; Kubler 1962), but there are many examples of the sculptor's art from all over the continent. Early lamps from the Uyak site, Kodiak Island, Alaska (Heizer 1956), were of diorite and granite, with a fair number of sandstone examples and rare use of basalt, andesite, soapstone, and diabase. Tools of all kinds, as well as balls, beads, sharpening stones, and other objects were made of slate, limestone and marble, gypsum, jet, lignite, and cannel coal. Basalt was used on the Columbia River, Oregon, and limestone in the north-west, for example by the Haida, for heads and totem poles; the Haida also carved argillite.

The east coast people carved ornamental stone pipes, such as a duck sitting on a fish, from soapstone, chlorite schist, and serpentinite. In Illinois grey banded slate was used for carving birds, and the people of Ohio carved pipes decorated with otters, cats, dogs, bears, wolves, and elaborate figures from catlinite ('pipestone'). The Hopewell people carved ornaments such as flat hands, figures, and claws from sheets of mica, and figurines in iron-rich schist. The use of stone for smoking pipes by early American people is well covered by Moorehead (1900): as well as black, grey, yellow, and green steatite and soapstone, serpentinite, catlinite, shale, slate, chlorite schist, alabaster, limestone, sandstone, granite, tuff, pumice, and jasper were employed; a similarly varied list was used for tools. The Browne site from southern California has yielded the frog and tadpole effigies of diorite – (?)charmstones – accompanied by tools and also ornaments of serpentinite, chlorite schist, soapstone, and hematite (Greenwood 1969). Also from southern California come cogstones of igneous rocks – basalt and granite – and sedimentary rocks – mudstone, siltstone, limestone, and sandstone. Igneous rocks were preferred in the ratio two to one, and steatite was never used for this purpose although popular for ornamental carving. The use of the cogstones is not known; possibly they were ceremonial. From the Hollywood area are known handstones, millstones, and cobble hammers of sandstone and granite, as well as quartzite, mica schist, and siltstone. The Uto-Aztecan people carved fish, jars, and other objects from soapstone. Ornaments from the Ventana cave, Papaqueria, Arizona, were carved from basalt, rhyolite, argillite (claystone), schist, and steatite; steatite is widely recorded also from elsewhere in north America as artefact material. Cruciform objects of unknown use carved of serpentinite, limestone, mudstone, slate, tufa, quartzite, flint, chalcedony, obsidian, pitchstone, and basalt are known from southern Arizona, Texas, and Mexico, and from Sonora, Mexico, come smoking pipes of tubular sandstone. Also in the south, the people of Tennessee carved figures of sandstone, up to 46 cm high; those of Oklahoma used red bauxite for large pipes; bowls of limestone were carved in Alabama; and in Georgia axes and 60 cm tall images were made of stone.

The greatest use of stone was of course in Mesoamerica (Feldman 1973). The Olmecs of Mexico used basalt, green serpentinite for ceremonial axes, turquoise, onyx marble for the Teotihuacán jaguar, and jadeite; they fashioned tools from obsidian and vesicular lava. The later Aztecs and Toltecs used basalt, porphyry for the famous mask, serpentinite, onyx, turquoise, jadeite, obsidian, and quartzite; they also inscribed stone. Particularly famous are the Toltec stone macaws, while granite heads are known from the city of Tonalá. In Guatemala and Honduras, the Maya people carved limestone and sandstone in relief; for smaller objects they used jadeite, serpentinite, chlorite schist, amphibole rock, and steatite, and for tools flint (chert), obsidian (often imported), quartzite, limestone, and granite. Rock crystal (quartz) was used for the enigmatic 'Skull of Doom'. One major source of Mayan jade is thought to be San Agustin Acasaguastlan, south-east Guatemala. The Guatemalan Olmec head, 9.5 cm high, was of pale green micaceous schist (pseudojade) and jadeite was used by the Olmecs of Costa Rica. This latter material from Guápiles in north-east Costa Rica was first used for celts; when found to be a valuable stone it was fashioned by string sawing into carved animals, anthropomorphic human figures, and other ornaments, now classified into groups according to their relationship to other cultures. Some of the material was not true jade: it included saussurite, 'bowenite' (serpentine), and chalcedony. Stone was also used in Panama, Colombia, and Ecuador. Further south, early building was of adobe and stone; there are also the Tiahuanaco stone statues of Bolivia, whilst onyx and andesite were employed along the Amazon. In Peru – with the colossal walls at Cuzco – the Nazcas used marble and the Incas built of sandstone blocks, also using turquoise and obsidian, in their cities such as Machu Pichu. The Nazcas of Peru and Chile, as at Cerro Unitas, carved giant figures and animals into the natural rock surface of hillsides like the early British white horses carved from the Chalk downs.

Finally, stone was used in association with the ceremonial ballgames of central and south America. The Guatemalan highland cities – built of tufa, limestone, and schist – had ballgame courts, the hacha being made of granite. In Mexico, the horseshoe yokes were carved of grey-green andesite, and also of alabaster and 'greenstone'. And in southern south America, bolas – also used in east Africa, for hunting – and other discoidal objects were made of tuff, basalt, and argillite (claystone). As a footnote, an interesting account of the mines and mining techniques of the Chalchihuites culture, dating from about AD 100, of Zacatecas, Mexico, has been given by Weigand (1968). These people mined weathered chert/flint, associated with sandstone, and also rhyolite and hematite. Flint and rhyolite were used for tools, the weathered material for carving, and the hematite as a pigment. Although none has been found, it is possible that jadeite and turquoise were also mined.

Stone sculpture in Africa (Allison 1968) is nearly all confined to west Africa, the main exception being the animals and figures carved in steatite, with some serpentinite, granite, and sandstone, which accompany the 1.5 m long steatite pillars, surmounted with carved birds, heads, and the steatite and sandstone phallic pillars, of the southern city state of Zimbabwe. Two stone heads are known from Kimberley and others from elsewhere in South Africa. The best known stone sculpture in west Africa is found in Nigeria, carved from granite, gneiss, basalt, quartz, limestone, and sandstone, as well as steatite. The Yoruba monuments at Ife include granite standing stones, such as those at Opa Oranmiyan, and granite-gneiss figure carvings. The region is also known for the pedestal stools, shaped like cotton reels, with one single loop like a cup handle, standing some 33 to 51 cm high and carved from quartz, and also from granite and steatite. Other Yoruba carvings include the Images of Esiè, 20 to 122 cm tall (averaging 60 cm), while the eastern Nigerian Akwanshi decorated boulders of basalt, as well as limestone and sandstone, with carvings, and also fashioned phallic columns. The Nomoli of Sierra Leone and the Potman of Guinea carved heads, some of them large, as well as figures, from steatite, chlorite schist, and amphibolite, and also used granite, dolerite, and sandstone. Further south, the Mintadi of the Congo used granite of the Naqui massif, tuff, sedimentary rocks, and steatite for figures up to some 60 cm in height, whilst the people of Angola also sculpted in steatite. In east Africa, the Ethiopians used limestone for monoliths and altars, and the Zambians mica schist for bowls and other vessels. The Njoro River cave of Kenya has yielded bowls of lava and tuff, together with pestles and grindstones of a variety of rock types, mainly quartzite, schist, and igneous rocks.

The statues of Easter Island (Heyerdahl and Ferdon 1961), in the southern Pacific Ocean, are the most famous of a group of stone monuments –

temples and statues – from the Polynesian Islands, other examples of which include figure carvings from New Zealand, Hawaii, the Society Islands, including Tahiti and its pyramid, the Marquesas, Tuamotu, Austral, the Cook Islands, and Tonga, with its trilithon, the pillars of which weigh 30 to 40 tonnes. These monuments are nearly all carved of the prevailing basalt (some of it soft and vesicular), andesite, dolerite, and tuff, but the best documented from the petrological viewpoint are the Easter Island heads (Bandy 1937). Dating from AD 700, there are some 600 known statues carved from the Rano Roraka tuff (maea matariki), whilst a further 150 lie unfinished in the quarries. What is thought to be the largest statue is 11.4 m long, with the face 4.3 m long, and 2.5 m wide and 1.3 m thick at the chest. Allowing a specific gravity for the average rock of 2.1 (the pure tachylyte is 1.7), an average of three calculations gave a weight for the complete statue of some 65 tonnes. Estimates of up to 400 tonnes have been published for some statues but a maximum of 100 tonnes is probably realistic. Construction of the statues is thought to have ended with the civil war, which destroyed much of the island's culture, in about AD 1700. A few other types are known, and it is these which are mainly to be found in the museums of the west; the statues were carved of a coarse (doleritic), vesicular, glassy alkali basalt; three others are of the Puna Pau red scoria.

The Rano Roraka tachylyte andesitic tuff contains inclusions measuring up to 1 m across. It weathers to a rough surface, the hard bands standing out from the purer, and softer, tachylyte pumice. The tachylyte glass is greenish yellow, weathering greenish grey, with a specific gravity of 1.70 or less. It contains many phenocrsyts of augite, olivine, and plagioclase feldspar (An$_{70-53}$), with some iddingsite – from altered olivine – and magnetite. Zeolites fill many of the vesicles. The refractive index of the glass is 1.566 ± 0.002, equivalent to a SiO_2 content of 52 per cent; an analysis of the tuff is given in Table 4.4. The statues are accompanied by painted and carved rocks, mainly of tuff; the petroglyphs are of fish, turtles, flowers, and trees, with many bird men (the bird god) and other humans. There are also small statuettes and figurines carved of the Rano Roraka tuff, basalt, red scoria, and pumice. Many tools and implements have been found, some bearing petroglyphs, of obsidian, basalt, andesite, scoria, pumice, and coral; basalt was used as a sharpening and polishing stone, pumice for abrading. Foundation stones remain, bearing holes used for wooden upright supports.

Further west, the Melanesian group of islands off northern Queensland have carved stone figures from the Torres Strait and Banks Island, New Guinea, the New Hebrides, the coral and other figures from the Solomon Islands, and 'chalk' (limestone) carvings from New Ireland and New Britain. To the north-east, the Micronesian city site at Nan Madol, Temwen, Madolenihmw Harbour, Ponape Island, in the eastern Caroline group (8°N, 160°W), has a system of houses and tombs, tunnels, and chambers with

Table 4.4. Chemical analysis of the
Rano Roraka tachylyte tuff,
Easter Island

SiO_2	45.52	(51.81)
TiO_2	2.40	(2.73)
Al_2O_3	14.32	(16.30)
Fe_2O_3	6.92	(7.87)
FeO	5.14	(5.85)
MnO	0.20	(0.23)
MgO	2.98	(3.40)
CaO	5.88	(6.69)
Na_2O	2.89	(3.29)
K_2O	1.34	(1.52)
H_2O^+	4.81	
H_2O^-	7.22	
P_2O_5	0.27	(0.31)
CO_2	0.30	
Total	100.19	(100.00)

Figures in brackets indicate analysis recalculated on a
water-free basis. From Bandy (1937); analyst: [M.]
Raoult.

basalt column walls, filled with coral rubble, which lasted until the eighteenth century.

Apart from the obvious relationship with the megalithic heads and temples
of the other Polynesian Islands mentioned above, it is tempting to compare
the Easter Island colossal heads with those of meso- and south America.
Among others, Heyerdahl (1980) has speculated on such links extending
from Ur, the royal city of the Sumerians, built of sun-baked bricks in the
rockless Euphrates Valley, to the 5000 year old megalithic stone builders of
the Nimrud pyramid, near Nineveh, and the limestone city, Jidda, of the
Hittites; to the limestone buildings of Dilmun (Bahrain) and to Egypt, with
its pyramids, sphinxes, obelisks, and huge sandstone and granite heads.
Stretching to the Indus Valley civilization of Mohenjo-daro, and the stone
builders of pre- and Inca Peru and Bolivia, the list could be almost endless:
there are the carved heads and figures in west Africa and the Ethiopian
monoliths; huge monuments occur near Fort Victoria, in southern Africa, in
the Acropolis of the principal example of the 150 'Zimbabwe' city states
spread across Moçambique and Zimbabwe; and in Indonesia. The Buddh-
ists left the Asokan pillars in India; also monuments in Sri Lanka; Java; and
China, where 32 paired stone figures of turtles, griffins, elephants, camels,
and human figures, of Ming Dynasty age, line the road 65 km north of
Peking. In Siberia there are the babas or 'grannies' of the steppes, exhumed
from tumuli; in Turkey heads taller than the average man are found at
Adiyaman, south of Malatya; and finally, in north-western Europe, there

are the megalithic monuments of Great Britain, Denmark, France, and elsewhere.

Other Old World sculpture

A huge range of materials has been used by man, ever inventive, for carving life-size statues and an infinite variety of smaller objects. It is the purpose of this final section to list geographically some of these uses, excluding America, the Pacific Ocean, and Africa, which are covered in the previous section. The complete omission of Australia results from a lack of ornamental stone carvings, as distinct from the tools and other artefacts used by the Aboriginals and described elsewhere. It can be little more than a list because only minimal petrological information is available, the clearly defined fields in which detailed petrological work has been carried out being considered elsewhere in this book. The one exception is gypsum; strontium isotope determinations of this mineral and their implications are discussed below. Thus, what follows is a catalogue of rock types, with the whole subject of pebbles omitted, taken from the examples mentioned in the literature. Many will have been omitted, unintentionally, and many of the rock names given may be in error; this seems to the author to be unavoidable.

Very early British carvings include the Berkshire gravel pit flints 'carved' into birds and animals; the Wiltshire boulder of calcareous sandstone with three heads and the similar yellow sandstone boulder from Yorkshire. Incised Chalk plaques occur at Avebury, along with phalli, cups, dishes, and figurines; the latter have been compared with the Dolní Věstonice clay 'Venuses'. Similar carvings, as well as pendants and oil lamps (compared with those of Grimes' Graves) are found at Windmill Hill, whilst symbolic Chalk axes occur at Woodhenge, and incised plaques at Stonehenge Bottom (Vatcher 1969). The Romans also used Chalk for loam weights. Also, perhaps, the prehistoric white horse 'carved' into the Chalk at Uffington, near Lambourn, Berkshire, should be included and the Romano-British Cerne Abbas giant in Dorset. The five other British white horses (Westbury, Cherill, Alton Barnes, Marlborough, and Pewsey) are all modern, dating from the eighteenth century onwards, and leading to many other recent 'petroglyphs' including the Napoleonic army crests on Marlborough Downs and the United States presidents carved out of the Precambrian granite at Mount Rushmore, in the Black Hills of South Dakota. Other petroglyphs and similar carved rocks have been mentioned in association with stone circles and similar monuments, but the first British sculptures of note seem to be those of the Romans. Their use of Purbeck Marble as a building stone has already been chronicled (Beavis 1971), and they made good use of this material from perhaps the early part of the first century until about AD 150. From London to Chester, at a variety of sites in south-eastern England, there have been finds of mortaria; an occulist's stamp from Colchester; a candelabrum foot from Gloucester; basins from the Fishbourne palace and villa, Chichester; a dish from Rockbourne Down; pestles from Silchester; cists from Studland; a 'disc'; and quernstones. Better known are the tombstones, and other religious, military, and civil inscriptions from a variety of south-eastern sites. Other limestones, such as the oolites, were used by the Romans in Gloucester, as for the Romano-Celtic head at the Bon Marché site. The Romans also inscribed and sculpted sandstone, such as the Silchester ogham (Fulford and Sellwood 1980) and the limonitic rock of the Newcastle area (Robson 1969). Sandstone and granite were also used for early figure carving in Ireland and elsewhere; for example, Feehan (1979) described a beautiful 55 cm high figure of a kneeling woman, of unknown origin, carved from the local conglomeratic sandstone, from the Slieve Bloom Mountains, Co. Offaly. Smith (1967) identified the stone used for a mace-head from Dorchester, Oxfordshire, as a diopsidic epidote-hornblende schist from Cornwall. The Saxons in England followed the Romans in their use of Purbeck Marble, for example for sculpting their bishops in Wells Cathedral, and probably no other British rock has been used to such an extent for cathedral statuary and other sculpting, as noted by Gardner (1951), although Belgian marble and other stones were imported for medieval use. Portland Limestone has been used only occasionally for massive statues, such as C. H. Smith's copy of the Farnese Hercules in the Institute of Geological Sciences, Keyworth, Nottinghamshire, since it is much harder and lacks the delicacy of the Purbeck and other, genuine, marbles.

Amongst the unusual materials used for carving in Britain is the Jurassic Kimmeridge Shale. Calkin (1955, 1973) described Romano-British objects dating from the second to fourth centuries AD, including armlets and armlet cores (coal money), spindle whorls, dishes, trays (see also Baker 1971), bowls, pins, and table tops and legs, from Colliton Park, Dorchester, and other sites in Dorset. This shale has a high kerogen content and was used also as a fuel. The Caergwrle bowl, in Cardiff Museum, may also be of the same kerogen-rich clay material (bituminite?) (Green, Smith, Young, and Harrison 1980). Shale, as well as jet and lignite, have been used for beads. In rather more recent use, several clay-pipe kilns have been excavated in the London area, dating from the seventeenth and eighteenth centuries. The material used has been examined and reviewed by Young (1982), who concludes that the clays – mainly composed of kaolinite, illite, and quartz – probably originated in the Poole–Corfe–Wareham region of Dorset or in the western end of the Isle of Wight, all of Tertiary age.

All over the world, local stones have been used for carving; only where sculpture has become a serious art form has the importation of stone become a major factor. The Mediterranean peoples were lucky indeed in their marbles, porphyries, and alabasters, and the middle and southern Americans in their jadeite and steatite. So, in northern France, schist was engraved, and in Baltic Sea countries, and also in Sicily, amber was carved into beads and other small objects. This fossil resin – often enclosing small insects trapped on its once sticky surface – was used in Finland, together with slate and soapstone for cists and statuettes; in Poland for beads; and in northern Russia, together with flint, alabaster, and serpentinite, and also porphyry, rock crystal, and marble imported from the Urals and the Caucasus, for carving figurines (see Beck, Adams, Southard, and Fellows 1971; Rice 1980).

Spain and Portugal had to make do with limestones and sandstones for sculptural purposes, and even employed schist. From East Germany, Austria, and Czechoslovakia, as well as France, Italy, Siberia, and the Ukraine, come the Dolní Věstonice and other baked clay or soft stone 'Venuses': fertility symbol female figures and heads. One of the rarest sculptural rocks is massive kersantite lamprophyre, used at Plougastel-Daoulas in Brittany for the 1602–4 Calvary group statue of Christ before Pilate(Wimmenauer 1973), one of several on this theme. Of the more orthodox materials, Italy, Britain, Spain, France, Egypt, and north and south America have good sculptural alabaster, the French being the harder, 'plaster of Paris', variety; England has fluorite of the 'blue john' variety; Ireland rock crystal; whilst the people of Saxony used agalmatolite, the Norwegians steatite, and the Swedes employed a porphyry for carving vases.

In the Mediterranean, the Etruscans used tufa, sandstone, limestone, and 'neufro' (a porous lava), and the Greeks and Romans of course used marble on a grand scale for statues and building as well as porphyry, limestone, and sardonyx. At Saliagos, in the Cyclades, the 'Fat Lady' was carved in marble, and at Troy there are limestone stelae and objects carved of nephrite, rock crystal, and obsidian. At Akrotiri there are vessels and lamps of limestone, marble, gypsum, serpentinite, steatite, rock crystal, granodiorite, and micaceous sandstone; a large jar, 55 by 40 cm, of red impure marble is probably of the Laconian *rosso antico* from Crete, used by the Minoans. For their vases, the Minoans used blue-grey mottled serpentinite, (which accounted for nearly half the known total of objects), red and white marbles, banded tufa, dolomitic limestone, limestone, conglomerate, breccia, calcite, orange stalactite, Mediterranean and Egyptian alabaster, sandstone, basalt, gabbro, diorite, trachyte, dark green mottled lapis lacedaemonius porphyry from Sparta, obsidian, chlorite schist, rock crystal, and steatite (Warren 1969); and the Mycenaeans limestone, alabaster, serpentinite, 'pudding-stone', steatite, and lapis lacedaemonius porphyry. In Crete, as in Babylon, black porphyry, syenite, diorite, and mottled limestone were also used and in Cyprus the neo-Hittites employed sandstone; the chalcolithic figurines of Lemba in Cyprus are of limestone and green steatite.

The massive form of gypsum known as alabaster was used widely in the Middle Bronze Age in Minoan Crete for paving floors, benches, and dadoes. In was also employed in the Argolid citadels of Mycenae and Tiryns on the mainland of Greece. Controversy has existed for many years over the source of the gypsum used in Mycenae; it has been suggested that alabaster imported by boat from the abundant Cretan sources (Fig. 4.1) was used, but also that the source lay nearer to hand, in the less abundant deposits of the west coast of Greece, especially the Ionian island quarries of Kefallinia and Zakinthos. Gale (1979) and his co-workers have determined the strontium isotope ratios ($^{87}Sr/^{86}Sr$) for six specimens from the Minoan quarry at Gypsadhes, south of Knossos; four from the quarry near Ayia Triadha; and for specimens from Myrtos and Fournou Korifi, Crete. Nine specimens from the west coast of Greece, together with two from Kefallinia and one from Zakinthos were also determined. It is clear from Fig. 4.15 that the Cretan alabasters have strontium isotope ratios very close to those of artefact samples used both in Crete, at the Minoan Palaces of Knossos, Ayia Triadha, and also at Phaistos; and in the Megaron porch and vestibule, as well as the bull reliefs in the Treasury of Atreus, in Mycenae; the specimens from the quarries of western Greece, on the other hand, have very different values. Gale has concluded, therefore, that the Mycenaean material, like the Minoan, derived from Crete and was imported by boat.

Around Carthage, the Phoenicians used alabaster also, and the Predynastic Egyptians carved anthropomorphic figurines of alabaster, clay, breccia, limestone, marble, slate, serpentinite, soapstone, greenschist, basalt, rock crystal, onyx, mother of pearl from shells, and even lead. The Egyptians made wide use of basalt, granite, porphyry, obsidian, sandstone, quartzite,

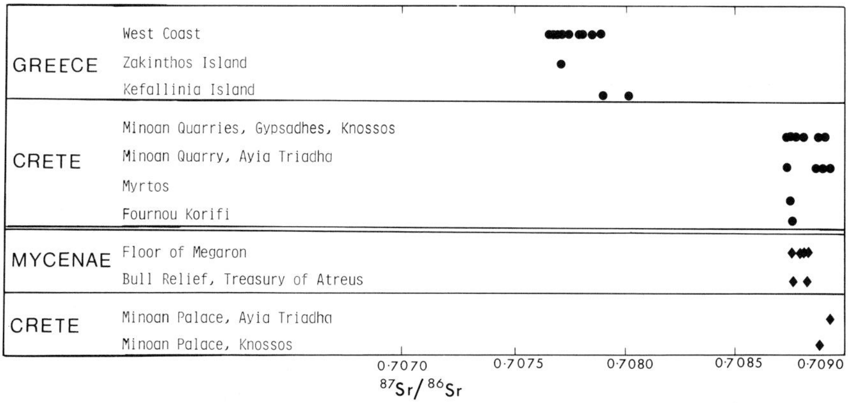

Fig. 4.15. Strontium isotope ratios for Greek and Cretan alabasters (solid circles), and Mycenaean and Minoan artefacts (solid diamonds). (After Gale 1979.)

breccia, schist, serpentinite, and steatite, with dolomite, limestone, diorite, and gypsum for vases in the northern Fayum desert. In the south and in northern Sudan steatite, sandstone, and granite were utilized for stelae, and the last two rock types for sculpture. The Nubians also employed serpentinite, and other rocks used in the Sudan included mudstone, chert, and chalcedony. The Fosse Temple of Palestine has pots of alabaster, calcite, steatite, and serpentinite; and the 24 cm long Hittite sphinx of Syria is of basalt. Dolerite was used in Sumeria, as in the case of the BC 2100 statues of Gudea. Seals in this region were made of steatite, basalt, greenschist, and jadeite, and bowls carved of alabaster, calcite, limestone, sandstone, marble, basalt, and andesite. The Babylonians, amongst others, employed clay tablets as a writing surface. In Aden, lamps and bowls were fashioned of soapstone and probably of basalt. A great variety of rocks were used in Arabia and other parts of western Asia: alabaster in the south; grey and green chlorite schist and limestone for bowls and statues in Iran, where the Parthians also used marble and alabaster; and dolerite and hornblende granite for statues in Iraq, as in the Parthian city of Hatra.

In the Indian sub-continent, schist, granite, quartz, and chert were employed, especially, as already described, the bluish grey schist, phyllite, limestone, and stucco of Gandhara. The Harappan culture used steatite for seals, lapis lazuli for beads, stone for vessels, and for sculpture, sandstone and ironstone. Wide use was made by the Mughals and others of alabaster, soapstone, serpentinite and rodingite (both often termed 'jade'), true jade, garnet, turquoise, rock crystal, onyx, agate and the other chalcedonies, as well as marble. The Biharis painted on mica. Schist, sandstone (including the spotted red Mathura sandstone from Uttar Pradesh), limestone, basalt, microdiorite, and many other rocks were used for statues, as well as granite and gneiss in the cave temples. Tombs in Sri Lanka were of charnockite (granulite) and on the island of Socotra, altar stones of limestone, whilst the Khmer sculptors of Angkor Wat and Bayon, Cambodia, employed 'polished' sandstone. The use of jade in China is also legendary, for amulets, vases, figurines, images, pagodas, and all forms of carving; agalmatolite, steatite, turquoise, and malachite were also used. Jade was also employed in Japan, as well as granite and other rock types, whilst andesite was used in Java and a few Tibetan sculptures are of schist.

Acknowledgements

The author is extremely grateful to R. K. Harrison, who read the manuscript and made many helpful criticisms and suggestions, and to G. F. Elliott, P. Hughes-Stanton, S. Walker, and W. Zwalf, all of whom criticized relevant sections, again most constructively.

References

Afordakos, G., Alexopoulos, K., and Miliotis, D. (1974). Using artificial thermo-luminescence to reassemble statues from fragments. *Nature* **250**, 47–8.

Allen, R. O. and Pennell, S. E. (1978). Rare earth element distribution patterns to characterize soapstone artifacts. *In* G. F. Carter (ed.) Archaeological chemistry – II. *Advances in Chemistry Series* **171**, 230–57.

—— Luckenbach, A. H., and Holland, C. G. (1975). The application of instrumental neutron activation analysis to a study of prehistoric steatite artifacts and source materials. *Archaeometry* **17**, 69–83.

—— Allen, K. K., Holland, C. G., and Fitzhugh, W. W. (1978). Utilisation of soapstone in Labrador by Indians, Eskimos and Norse. *Nature* **271**, 237–9.

Allison, P. (1968). *African stone sculpture*. Lund Humphries, London.

Andreae, B., Oehlschlegel, G., and Weber, K. (1972). Zusammenfügung der Fragmente eines Meleagersarkophags in Frankfurt und Kassel. *Jahrbuch Deutsches Archaeologische Instituts* **87**, 388–432.

Arkell, W. J. (1947). *Oxford stone*. Faber and Faber, London.

Ashmole, B. (1970). Aegean marble: science and common sense. *Annual of the British School at Athens* **65**, 1–2.

Atkinson, R. J. C. (1956). *Stonehenge*. Hamish Hamilton, London.

—— (1974). The Stonehenge bluestones. *Antiquity* **48**, 62–3.

Baertschi, P. (1957). Messung und Deutung relativer Häufigkeitsvariationen von ^{18}O and ^{13}C in Karbonatgesteinen und Mineralien. *Schweizerische Mineralogische und Petrographische Mitteilungen* **37**, 73–152.

Baker, R. S. (1971). A circular Kimmeridge Shale tray from Wareham. *Proceedings of the Dorset Natural History and Archaeological Society* **92**, 148–50.

Bandi, H.-G., Breuil, H., Berger-Kirchner, L., Lhote, H., and Holm, E. (1961). *The art of the stone age*. Methuen, London.

Bandy, M. C. (1937). Geology and petrology of Easter Island. *Bulletin of the Geological Society of America* **48**, 1589–1610.

Bard, J. C., Asaro, F., and Heizer, R. F. (1978). Perspectives on the dating of prehistoric Great Basin petroglyphs by neutron activation analysis. *Archaeometry* **20**, 85–8.

Bautsch, H.-J. and Kelch, H. (1960). Mineralogisch-petrographische Untersuchungen an einigen in der Antike als Baumaterial verwendeten Gesteinen. *Geologie* **9**, 691–700.

Beavis, J. (1971). Some aspects of the use of Purbeck Marble in Roman Britain. *Proceedings of the Dorset Natural History and Archaeological Society* **92**, 181–204.

Beck, C. W., Adams, A. B., Southard, G. C., and Fellows, C. (1971). Determination of the origin of Greek amber artifacts by computer-classification of infrared spectra. In: R. H. Brill (ed.): *Science and Archaeology*. MIT Press, Cambridge, Mass., 235–40.

Boëthius, A. and Ward-Perkins, J. B. (1970). *Etruscan and Roman architecture*. Penguin Books, Harmondsworth.

Bowen, H. C. and Smith, I. F. (1977). Sarsen stones in Wessex: the Society's first investigations in the Evolution of the Landscape project. *Antiquaries Journal* **57**, 185–96.

Burford, A. (1969). *The Greek temple builders at Epidauros*. Liverpool University Press.

Burl, A. (1976). *Stone circles of the British Isles*. Yale University Press, New Haven.

—— (1979). *Prehistoric Avebury*. Yale University Press, New Haven.

—— and Piper, E. (1979). *Rings of stone: the prehistoric stone circles of Britain and Ireland*. Frances Lincoln, Weidenfeld and Nicholson, London.

Burnham, S. M. (1883). *Limestones and marbles: their history and uses*. S. E. Cassino, Boston.

Calkin, J. B. (1955). Kimmeridge coal money. The Romano-British shale armlet industry. *Proceedings. Dorset Natural History and Archaeological Society* **75**, 45–71.

—— (1973). Kimmeridge Shale objects from Colliton Park. *Proceedings. Dorset Natural History and Archaeological Society* **94**, 44–8.

Clarke, J., Dix, W. C., Dortch, C. E., and Palmer, K. (1978). Aboriginal sites on Millstream station, Pilbara, Western Australia. *Records of the Western Australian Museum* **6**, 221–57.

Coleman, M. and Walker, S. (1979). Stable isotope identification of Greek and Turkish marbles. *Archaeometry* **21**, 107–12.

Collins, G. H. (1976). Appendix 5–Geology of the Stones of Stenness, Orkney. In: J. N. Graham Ritchie: The Stones of Stenness, Orkney. *Proceedings of the Society of Antiquaries of Scotland* **107**, 44–5.

—— (1977). Appendix 1. Petrology. In: K. A. Steer and J. W. M. Bannerman: *Late Medieval monumental sculpture in the West Highlands*. Royal Commission on the Ancient and Historical Monuments of Scotland, Edinburgh 44–5.

Conforto, L., Felici, M., Monna, D., Serva, L., and Taddeucci, A. (1975). A preliminary evaluation of chemical data (trace element) from classical marble quarries in the Mediterranean. *Archaeometry* **17**, 201–13.

Courtois, L. (1962–3). Examen minéralogique de quelques roches de monuments gréco-bouddhiques. *Arts Asiatiques* **9**, 107–13.

Craig, H. and Craig, V. (1972). Greek marbles: determination of provenance by isotopic analysis. *Science* **176**, 401–3.

Culwick, A. T. (1931). Some rock-paintings in central Tanganyika. *Journal of the Royal Anthropological Institute* **61**, 443–53.

Curtis, G. H. (1959). The petrology of artifacts and architectural stone at La Venta. *Bulletin of the Bureau of American Ethnology* **170** (Appendix 4), 284–9.

Daniel, G. (1980). Megalithic monuments. *Scientific American* **243** (1), 64–76.

Davey, N. (1961). *A history of building materials*. Phoenix House, London.

Dayton, J. (1978). *Minerals, metals, glazing and man*. Harrap, London.

Douglas, F. H. and D'Harnoncourt, R. (1941). *Indian art of the United States*. Museum of Modern Art, New York; Simon and Schuster, New York.

Dunning, G. C. (1949). The Purbeck Marble industry in the Roman period. *The Archaeological News Letter* **1** (11), 15.

Dworakowska, A. (1975). *Quarries in Ancient Greece*. Polish Academy of Sciences, Wroclaw.

Elsden, J. V. and Howe, J. A. (1923). *The stones of London*. Colliery Guardian Co., London.

Emery, K. O. (1960). Weathering of the Great Pyramid. *Journal of Sedimentary Petrology* **30**, 140–3.

Feehan, J. (1979). An early stone sculpture from Co. Offaly, Eire. *Antiquity* **53**, 146–8.

Feldman, L. H. (1973). Stones for the archaeologist. *Contributions, University of California Archaeological Research Facility* **18**, 87–104.

Fosbrooke, H. A. (ed.) (1950). Tanganyika rock paintings. *Tanganyika Notes and Records* **29**, 1–61.

Fulford, D. M. and Sellwood, B. (1980). The Silchester ogham stone: a reconsideration. *Antiquity* **54**, 95–9.

Gale, N. H. (1979). Gypsum, marble, obsidian; can their provenance be determined by strontium isotope determinations? *International Symposium on Archaeometry and Archaeological Prospection, London, Abstracts* **19**, 18.

Gardner, A.(1951). *English and Medieval sculpture*. Cambridge University Press.

Gast, R., Germann, K., and Eilert, E. (1979). Petrographische und Geochemische Untersuchungen zur Herkunftsbestimmung von Marmoren Hellenistischer Grabstelen Thessaliens. *'La Thessalie', Collection de la Maison de l'Orient Méditerranéen* **6**, série archéologique **5**, 51–62.

Gautschi, A. and Quervain, F. de (1978). Die Schweremineralmethode als Mittel zur Herkunftsbestimmung von Sandsteinen historischer Bild- und Bauwerke. *Schweizer Archäologie Kunstgeschichte* **35**, 190–3.

Germann, K. (1978). Probleme und Möglichkeiten, geowissenschaftlicher Herkunftsnachweise für Marmore. In: H. W. Hennicke (ed.): *Mineralische Rohstoffe als Kurlturhistorische Informationsquelle*. Verein Deutscher Emailfachleute, Hagen, 173–90.

—— Holzmann, G., and Winkler, F. J. (1980). Determination of marble provenance: limits of isotopic analysis. *Archaeometry* **22**, 99–106.

Glob, P. V. (1971). *Danish prehistoric monuments*. Faber and Faber, London. [Translated Bulman, J.]

Gnoli, R. (1971). *Marmora Romana*. Edizione dell'Elefante, Rome.

Graham, J. A. and Williams, H. (1971). Two unusual Maya stelae. *Contributions, University of California Archaeological Research Facility* **13**, 161–6.

Green, H. S., Smith, A. H. V., Young, B. R., and Harrison, R. K. (1980). The Caergwle Bowl: its composition, geological source and archaeological significance. *Reports of the Institute of Geological Sciences* **80/1**, 26–30.

Greenwood, R. S. (1969). The Browne site: early milling stone horizon in southern California. *Memoirs of the Society of American Archaeology* **23**, ix + 72.

Griffiths, W. E. (1960). The excavation of stone circles near Penmaenmawr, north Wales. *Proceedings of the Prehistoric Society* **26**, 303–39.

Heizer, R. F. (1956). Archaeology of the Uyak site, Kodiak Island, Alaska. *Anthropological Records of the University of California* **17**, 1–199.

—— Smith, T. (1965). Olmec sculpture and stone working: a bibliography. *Contributions, University of California Archaeological Research Facility* **1**, 71–87.

—— Williams, H. (1963). Geologic notes on the Idolo de Coatlichán. *American Antiquity* **29**, 95–8.

—— —— (1965). Stones used for colossal sculpture at or near Teotihuacán. *Contributions, University of California Archaeological Research Facility* **1**, 55–70.

—— Smith, T., and Williams, H. (1965). Notes on colossal head no. 2 from Tres Zapotes. *American Antiquity* **31**: 102–104.

—— Stross, F., Hester, T. R., Albee, A., Perlman, I., Asaro, F., and Bowman, H. (1973). The Colossi of Memnon revisited. *Science* **182**, 1219–25.

Herz, N. (1955a). Geology of the building stones of ancient Greece. *Transactions of the New York Academy of Science, Series II* **17**, 499–505.

—— (1955b). Petrofabrics and classical archaeology. *American Journal of Science* **253**, 299–305.

—— Pritchett, W. K. (1953). Marble in Attic epigraphy. *American Journal of Archaeology* **57**, 71–83.

—— Wenner, D. B. (1978). Assembly of Greek marble inscriptions by isotopic methods. *Science* **199**, 1070–2.

Herz, N. and Wenner D. B. (1981). How to pinpoint marble sources with the aid of isotopic signatures. *Archaeology* **34**, 14–21.

Heyerdahl, T. (1980). *The Tigris Expedition*. Allen and Unwin, London.

—— Ferdon, E. N. Jr. (ed.) (1961). Archaeology of Easter Island. *Monographs of the School of American Research and the Museum of New Mexico* **24** (1), xi + 559.

Holland, C. G. and Allen, R. O. (1977). Tracking soapstone artifacts with rare earth trace elements. *Rocks and Minerals* **52**, 67–9.

Howe, J. A. (1910). *The geology of building stones*. Arnold, London.

Hull, E. (1872). *A treatise on the building and ornamental stones of Great Britain and foreign countries*. Macmillan, London.

Jones, O. T. (1956). The blue-stones of the Cardigan district. *Antiquity* **30**, 34–6.

Jope, E. M. (1948–9). Abingdon Abbey craftsmen and building stone supplies. *Berkshire Archaeological Journal* **51**, 53–64.

—— (1953). History, archaeology and petrology. *Advancement of Science* **9**, 432–5.

—— (1964). The Saxon building-stone industry in southern and midland England. *Medieval Archaeology* **8**, 91–118.

—— Dunning, G. C. (1954). The use of blue slate for roofing in mediaeval England. *Antiquaries Journal* **34**, 209–17.

Kellaway, G. A. (1971). Glaciation and the stones of Stonehenge. *Nature* **233**, 30–5.

Kempe, D. R. C. (1973). The petrology of the Warsak alkaline granites, Pakistan, and their relationship to other alkaline rocks of the region. *Geological Magazine* **110**, 385–404.

—— (1982). Nature and source of the Gandhara sculptural schist. *Journal of Archaeological Science* **9**, 25–8.

Khan, M. A. R. (1938). On the meteoritic origin of the Black Stone of the Ka'bah. *Popular Astronomy* **47** (7), 1–5.

Kober, L. (1929). Beiträge zur Geologie von Attika. *Sitzungsberichte Akademie der Wissenschaften in Wien* 138 Abth 1: 299–327.

Kohl, P. L. (1976). 'Steatite' carvings of the early Third Millenium BC. *American Journal of Archaeology* **80**, 73–5.

—— Harbottle, G., and Sayre, E. V. (1979). Physical and chemical analyses of soft stone vessels from southwest Asia. *Archaeometry* **21**, 131–59.

Kopper, J. S. and Rossello-Bordoy, G. (1974). Megalithic quarrying techniques and limestone technology in eastern Spain. *Journal of Field Archaeology* **1**, 161–70.

Kubler, G. (1962). *The art and architecture of ancient America*. Penguin, Harmondsworth, Middlesex.

Lahanier, C. (1976). Laboratoire de Recherche des Musées de France examen au laboratoire d'une tête de roi barbare (Appendix). In: F. Tissot: Remarques iconographiques a propos d'une tête de roi barbare du Gandhara. *Arts Asiatiques* **32**, 80–1.

Lawrence, A. W. (1972). *Greek and Roman sculpture*. Jonathan Cape, London.

Lazzarini, L., Moschini, G., and Stievano, B. M. (1980*a*). A contribution to the identification of Italian, Greek and Anatolian marbles through a petrological study and the evaluation of Ca/Sr ratio. *Archaeometry* **22**, 173–82.

—— —— —— (1980*b*). A contribution to the identification of Italian, Greek and Anatolian marbles through a petrological study and the evaluation of Ca/Sr ratio. Some examples of identification of ancient marbles through a petrological study and the evaluation of Ca/Sr ratio. *Quaderni della Soprintendenza ai Beni Artistici e Storici di Venezia* **9**, 1–58.

Lepsius, G. R. (1890). Griechische Marmorstudien. *Abhandlungen der Preussischen Akademie der Wissenschaften zu Berlin. Philosophie-Historische Klasse*, 1–135.

Lucas, A. [Revised Harris, J. R.] (1962). *Ancient Egyptian materials and industries.* 4th edn. Edward Arnold, London.

Luckenbach, A. H., Holland, C. G., and Allen, R. O. (1975). Soapstone artifacts: tracing prehistoric trade patterns in Virginia. *Science* **187**, 57–8.

Manfra, L., Masi, U., and Turi, B. (1975). Carbon and oxygen isotope ratios of marbles from some ancient quarries of Western Anatolia and their archaeological significance. *Archaeometry* **17**, 215–21.

Marinos, G. P. (1948). Notes on the structure of Greek marbles. *American Journal of Science* **246**, 386–9.

Marshall, J. (1960). *The Buddhist art of Gandhara.* Cambridge University Press.

Martin, R. (1965). *Manuel d'Architecture Grecque. Volume 1: Matériaux et techniques.* A. and J. Picard, Paris.

Milburn, M. (1974). Some stone monuments of Spanish Sahara, Mauritania and the extreme south of Morocco. *Journal de la Société des Africanistes* **44**, 99–111.

Monna, D. and Pensabene, P. (1977). *Marmi dell'Asia Minore.* Consiglio Nazionale della Ricerche, Rome.

Moorehead, W. K. (1900). *Prehistoric implements.* Robert Clarke, Cincinnati, Ohio.

Murray, J. W. (1965). The origin of some medieval roofing slates from Sussex. *Sussex Archaeological Collections* **103**, 79–82.

Needham, J. (1971). *Science and civilisation in China. Volume 4, part III, Civil engineering and nautics.* Cambridge University Press.

Newesely, H. and Melaau, R. (1978). Manganknollen – Malstifte von Höhlenzeichnungen des Paläolithikums (Elektronenmikroskopischstrukturchemische Untersuchungen. In: H. W. Hennicke (ed.): *Mineralische Rohstoffe als Kulturhistorische Informationsquelle.* Verein Deutscher Emailfachleute, Hagen, 220–33.

Nisbet, H. C. (1974). A geological approach to vitrified forts. Part I. The archaeological and scientific background. *Science and Archaeology* **12**, 3–12.

North, F. J. (1938). Geology for archaeologists. *Archaeological Journal* **94**, 73–115.

Paddock, J. (ed.) (1966). *Ancient Oaxaca.* Stanford University Press.

Papageorgakis, J. E. (1963). [Ancient marble quarries of Thessalia.] *Praktika Akademias Athenon* **38**, 564–72 [In Greek].

—— (1967). Die in der Marmorindustrie nutzbaren Gesteine Griechenlands. *Annales Géologiques des Pays Hélleniques* **18**, 193–270.

Pellerin, F. M. (1980). La pétrophysique: une branche de la pétrographie directment applicable à l'altération des pierres en oeuvre. *GP News Letter [ICOMOS Stone Committee]* **1**, 3–9.

Phemister, J. (1956). In: R. B. K. Stevenson: The chronology and relationships of some Irish and Scottish crosses. *Journal of the Royal Society of Antiquaries of Ireland* **86**, 88.

Quervain, F. de (1979). *Steine schweizerischer Kunstdenkmäler.* Manesse, Zurich.

Rankine, W. F. (1949). Pebbles of non-local rocks from Mesolithic chipping floors. *Proceedings of the Prehistoric Society* **15**, 193–4.

Renfrew, C. and Peacey, J. S. (1968). Aegean marble; a petrological study. *Annual of the British School at Athens* **63**, 45–66.

Rice, P. C. (1980). *Amber: the golden gem of the ages.* Van Nostrand Reinhold, New York.

Ritchie, A. (1971–2). Painted pebbles in early Scotland. *Proceedings of the Society of Antiquaries of Scotland* **104**, 297–301.

Robinson, J. E. and Bishop, A. C. (1980). Geological walks around St Paul's. *Proceedings of the Geologists' Association* **91**, 241–60.

Robson, D. A. (1969). A note on the geology of the Roman inscribed and sculptured stones on exhibition in the Museum. *Archaeologia Aeliana* **47**, 167–8.

Rutland, R. A. (1976). A carved stone from Aylestone, Leicester. *Antiquity* **50**, 234–6.

Rybach, L. and Nissen, H.-U. (1965). Neutron activation of Mn and Na traces in marbles worked by the ancient Greeks. In: *Radiochemical Methods of Analysis: Volume I.* International Atomic Energy Commission, Vienna, 105–17.

Sedgley, J. P. (1970). Some problems connected with the petrographic examination of stone artefacts. *Science and Archaeology* **2/3**, 10–12.

—— (1975). The Roman milestones of Britain: their petrology and probable origin. *British Archaeological Report* **18**, 1–56.

Shackley, M. (1977). *Rocks and man.* Allen and Unwin, London.

Smith, I. F. (1965). *Windmill Hill and Avebury: excavations by Alexander Keiller 1925–1939.* Clarendon Press, Oxford.

Smith, W. Campbell. (1967). Source of the stone used in a mace-head from Dorchester, Oxfordshire. *Proceedings of the Prehistoric Society* **33**, 455–6.

Stone, E. H. (1924). *The stones of Stonehenge.* Scott, London.

Story-Maskelyne, N. (1878). Stonehenge: the petrology of its stones. *Wiltshire Archaeological and Natural History Magazine* **17**, 147–60.

Stukeley, W. (1740). *Stonehenge: a temple restored to the British Druids.* Innys and Manby, London.

Thomas, H. H. (1923). The source of the stones of Stonehenge. *Antiquaries Journal* **3**, 239–60.

Tucker, D. G. (1976). The slate quarries at Easdale, Argyllshire, Scotland. *Post-medieval Archaeology* **10**, 119–30.

Vatcher, F. de M. (1969). Two incised Chalk plaques near Stonehenge Bottom. *Antiquity* **43**, 310–11.

Wagner, E. and Schubert, C. (1972). Pre-hispanic workshop of serpentinite artifacts, Venezuelan Andes, and possible raw material source. *Science* **175**, 888–90.

Wainwright, F. T. (1962). *The Northern Isles.* Nelson, London.

Wainwright, G. J. (1969). A review of henge monuments in the light of recent research. *Proceedings of the Prehistoric Society* **35**, 112–33.

Walker, S. (1979*a*). A sanctuary of Isis on the south slope of the Athenian Acropolis. *Annual of the British School at Athens* **74**, 243–57.

—— (1979*b*). Corinthian capitals with ringed voids: the work of Athenian craftsmen in the second century AD. *Archäologischer Anzeiger (Deutsches Archäologisches Institut)*: 103–29.

Ward-Perkins, J. B. (1951). Tripolitania and the marble trade. *Journal of Roman Studies* **41**, 89–104.

Warren, P. (1969). *Minoan stone vases.* Cambridge University Press.

Washington, H. S. (1898). The identification of the marbles used in Greek sculpture. *American Journal of Archaeology* **2**, 1–18.

Waterman, D. M. (1970). Somersetshire and other foreign building stones in Medieval Ireland, c. 1175–1400. *Ulster Journal of Archaeology* **33**, 63–75.

Weigand, P. C. (1968). The mines and mining techniques of the Chalchihuites culture. *American Antiquity* **33**, 45–61.

Weiss, L. E. (1954). Fabric analysis of some Greek marbles and its applications to archaeology. *American Journal of Science* **252**, 641–62.

Whalley, W. B. and Chartres, C. J. (1976). Preliminary observations on the origin and sedimentological nature of sarsen stones. *Geologie en Mijnbouw* **55**, 68–72.

Williams, H. and Heizer, R. F. (1965*a*). Sources of rocks used in Olmec monuments. *Contributions, University of California Archaeological Research Facility* **1**, 1–39.

—— —— (1965*b*). Geological notes on the ruins of Mitla and other Oaxacan sites, Mexico. *Contributions, University of California Archaeological Research Facility* **1**, 41–54.

Williams, J. H. (1971). Roman building-materials in south-east England. *Britannia* **2**, 166–95.

Wimmenauer, W. (1973). Lamprophyre, Semilamprophyre und anchibasaltische Ganggesteine. *Fortschritte der Mineralogie* **51**, 3–67.

Wood, E. S. (1963). *Field guide to archaeology*. Collins, London.

Young, B. R. (1982). A note on the provenance of pipe-clays from three archaeological sites in London. *In* P. Davey (ed.), The archaeology of the clay tobacco pipe. vol 7. *British Archaeological Reports*, 307–10.

Young, W. J. and Ashmole, B. (1968). The Boston Relief and Ludovisi Throne. *Bulletin of the Boston Museum of Fine Arts* **66**, 124–66.

5. The Celtic vitrified forts

K. Fredriksson, E. Youngblood Anthony, and
B. J. Fredriksson

Introduction

Vitrified forts, the peculiar remnants of some Celtic fortifications, have intrigued archaeologists, geochemists, and historians, among others, since their discovery over 200 years ago (see Pennant 1769; West 1776 and Williams 1777 in Nisbet 1974; see also Mackie 1976). As early as the seventh century BC, the Celtic tribes which roamed throughout Europe built hillforts with timber-laced and stone-filled walls (e.g. Finavon; see Mackie 1969). Some of these were burned, perhaps partly causing vitrification of the building stones, and leading to the term vitrified forts. Remains of these forts have been found, for example, in Germany, France, possibly Sweden, and abundantly in Scotland where there are more than 60 (Mackie 1976, p. 444).

Nisbet (1975), listing the building stones used in the construction of the Scottish forts, stated that whilst 44 per cent of the rocks were sandstone and conglomerate, 56 per cent were pelitic and hornblende gneiss, granulite, mica and psammitic schist, and quartzite. Other materials used included hornfels, granite and granite gneiss, and the common basic igneous rocks basalt, dolerite and andesite.

Vitrification is indicated where cobbles and rock fragments have been welded and fused together by glassy material; also observed, at high magnification, is internal melting where individual mineral grains within the building stones are transformed into, or encased in, glass. The very large volume of vitrified masses which have sometimes been observed is surprising; they can reach several cubic metres. Excavations of fort walls have revealed that vitrification occurred within the core or interior portion of the walls (Fig. 5.1; see also Nisbet 1974 pp. 5–6). This finding is supported by the geochemical study discussed below, in which it is concluded that vitrification occurred under reducing conditions. Vitrified material which is found on the faces or sides of walls has presumably fallen from above and blanketed the original face (H. C. Nisbet, pers. comm. 1977).

Because of the sustained high temperatures, more than 900 °C, necessary to produce such vitrification, researchers have considered many possibilities

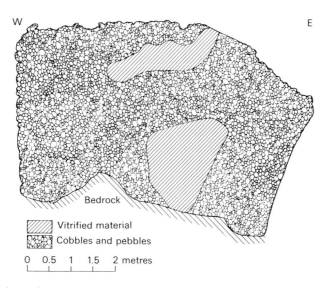

Fig. 5.1. Schematic cross-section of an excavated wall (the inner rampart) at Craig Phaidrig showing distribution of vitrification. Note that the vitrification is restricted to inner portions of the wall. Modified from Small and Cottam (1972).

regarding their origin. Early observers suggested that the vitrified material was volcanic or the result of lightning (see Nisbet 1974). However, it is now well established that the walls were originally part of forts, and that they were timber-laced. An analogy has been made with the *murus gallicus* reported by Caesar during his Gallic conquests. Nisbet (1974) argued that, because of the extreme age of some forts, such as Finavon, it is not valid to assume a similar age or style of construction for all vitrified forts. Some (e.g. Duff 1961) have been of the opinion that, although the walls were originally part of forts, the melting and vitrification was not *in situ*. This view is untenable in the light of the internal melting exhibited (see below), and it can reasonably be concluded that vitrification was the result of *in situ* melting of stones in timber-laced walls.

However, to accept this conclusion does not resolve one of the most fundamental and controversial questions of the vitrified forts: whether the firing was deliberately constructive, perhaps to strengthen the walls, or destructive, or even fortuitous, possibly associated with some form of smelting, ore extraction, or similar process. Nisbet (1974) states that most archaeologists currently prefer some variation of the hypothesis that the firing was caused by enemies, and therefore that the intent was destructive. A recent detailed study in support of the destructive hypothesis is that of Mackie (1976). On the other hand, Brothwell, Bishop, and Wooley (1974)

believed that the planning and care necessary to achieve vitrification imply
that the process was constructional, and they listed a number of basic facts
and questions regarding the vitrification.

Certainly, it seems that the Celts were capable of the necessary technology,
for associated artefacts recovered reveal that these nomads, often considered barbarians, were quite sophisticated technologically; they worked
metals, produced and used mercury, made glass, and were craftsmen in
wood, although variations among the tribes apparently existed (Herm
1977). (For a more complete summary of the history of the vitrified forts, see
Nisbet 1974; Cotton 1954; and Youngblood, Fredriksson, Kraut, and
Fredriksson 1978.)

In an attempt to elucidate the origin of the remnant vitrified fort walls,
Daubrée (1881a, b); Christison, Anderson, and Ross (1905); and Brothwell
et al. (1974) analysed glasses from the melted rock and reported that their
chemical compositions precluded the specific addition of fluxing agents.
Brothwell et al. (1974) also supported Childe and Thorneycroft's (1937a)
suggestion that the rocks melted in situ, and believed that temperatures near
1100 °C would have been necessary to produce the vitrification observed
(Fig. 5.2). In a more comprehensive petrological and geochemical study of
various vitrified fort glasses and parent rocks, Youngblood et al. (1978)
demonstrated that in situ partial melting could produce the glasses, and that
temperatures ranging from about 900 °C to 1100 °C must have been
achieved. Their results also reaffirmed the contention of previous re-

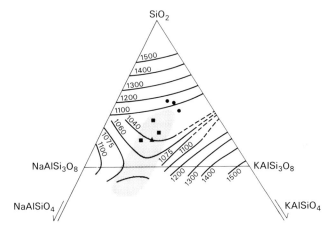

Fig. 5.2. Plot of glasses from vitrified forts in part of the anhydrous weight per cent
normative system SiO_2–$NaAlSiO_4$ (Schairer 1950). The positions of isotherms and
their temperatures are indicated; the shaded area constitutes the low temperature
trough. ● Arisaig; ■ Cullykhan (Castle Point); ▲Glen Nevis. (After Brothwell et al.
1974.)

searchers that no fluxing agents were selectively added. However, in contrast to the previous reports, they found a consistently higher FeO/Fe_2O_3 ratio in the glasses than in the parent rocks and concluded that firing occurred under confined and strongly reducing conditions.

In this chapter the analytical techniques employed by Youngblood *et al.* (1978) are expounded, particularly with regard to archaeological research, and some of their results summarized and discussed. Although the motive for firing the walls is still speculative, the use of geochemical data to establish constraints on the conditions necessary to produce such enigmatic monuments as the vitrified forts is discussed. Forts for which data are presented are: Braes (Stirlingshire, Scotland; National Grid Reference (NGR) NS809957); Chateauvieux (France, 46°5′ N, 2°4′ E); Donnersberg (Germany, 49°38′ N, 7°55′ E); and Finavon (Angus, Scotland; NGR N0507557).

Petrology and chemistry

The study of Youngblood *et al.* (1978) was designed to compare the degree of vitrification among forts built of different types of rock but, foremost, to determine the relations between the parent rock and the resulting glasses for each fort. Their intention was to deduce the conditions that could have produced the vitrification, e.g. temperatures, duration of firing, chemical reactions including oxygen fugacities, etc., which would allow them to identify possible construction aims and techniques.

Microscopy

Polished thin sections were prepared of a large number of samples to a thickness of 10 μm or less by using improved techniques which allow for higher resolution than in standard petrographic thin sections (Beauchamp and Williford 1973). The extent of vitrification, ranging from minor partial melting to complete fluidity, and the optical properties of the glasses produced, including their relationships with the remaining minerals, were determined microscopically. Specimens from two forts constructed of widely different rock types and with grossly varying degrees of vitrification are shown in Figs 5.3 and 5.4. In the Donnersberg fort, a salic or acid (rhyolitic) rock, rich in silica and alumina, with about 75 weight per cent silica (SiO_2), was used. Vitrification is restricted to thin surface glazing, which welded the rock fragments (Fig. 5.3a); minimal internal partial melting is also observed (Fig. 5.3b). At Finavon a femic or basic rock, rich in iron and magnesium oxides, with only about 47 wt per cent SiO_2, was used; here the vitrification is much more advanced (Fig. 5.4a) and includes flowing of glass with extensive melting even inside large individual blocks (Fig. 5.4b). However, caution must be exercised in attempting to estimate temperatures

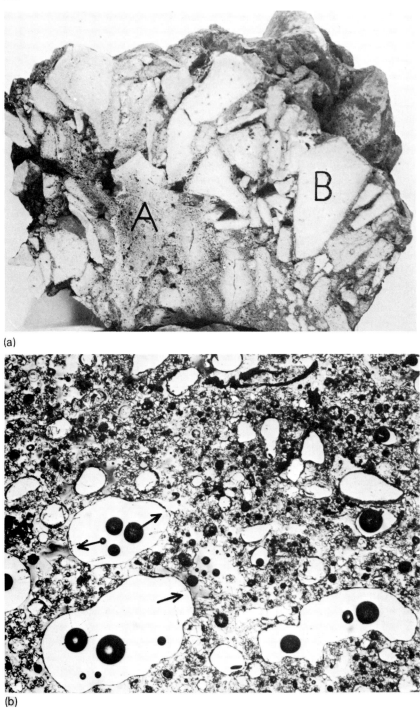

(a)

(b)

merely from the degree of melting observed. Rocks of different chemical compositions will begin to melt at different, so-called solidus temperatures, as is evident in Fig. 5.4, where extensively melted material is fused against distinctly less melted material. Although as a rule more acid or salic rocks have lower solidus temperatures than more basic or femic types, this difference is less than between the liquidus, i.e. total melting, temperatures for different rock types. Thus, unless the lithological or chemical composition of the original rock is known, it cannot be immediately concluded that samples showing a higher degree of vitrification were heated to higher temperatures.

Glass analysis

On the basis of these petrographic studies a wide range of representative samples of glasses and parent rocks were selected for chemical analysis by electron microprobe techniques. The glasses were analysed in ultrathin polished section by microprobe according to accepted mineralogical methods (Keil 1967). Analysed natural glasses and minerals were used for standards; special precautions were taken to avoid deterioration of the glasses (especially depletion or enrichment of alkalis) due to heating and electrostatic charging (Fredriksson 1967).

A few glass analyses, designated by a 'G' following the symbol for the fort, are given in Table 5.1. Clearly the glasses have a wide range in composition even within a single specimen (note the difference between dark, brown, and light glasses designated a, b, and c, respectively, in Table 5.1.). Yet these differences are much less than those between the country rocks used for the different forts.

Rock analysis

A novel technique originally developed for the analysis of very small (≤ 1 mg) samples of meteorites and minerals (De Gasparis, Fredriksson, and Brenner 1975) was employed by Youngblood *et al.* (1978) for determining the bulk chemical composition of the parent rocks, again using the

---

Fig. 5.3. (a) Donnersberg (DO14). Surface of a cut sample illustrating the textural variations among the rhyolite fragments from dense, barely glazed parts (B) to more melted, now frothy and vesicular portions (A). This gradation in textures is evidence for *in situ* local melting. Length of sample is about 20 cm.
(b) Photomicrograph of a thin (10 μm) section of Donnersberg sample DO14A (the area A in Fig. 5.3.(a)) which demonstrates the slight degree of melting and the minimal amount of interstitial glass (indicated by arrows) even in the more melted portions. The large ovoids are vesicles. Note the segregation of clear and dark coloured glasses with different compositions and formed from varying proportions of alkali and iron-magnesium minerals, e.g. feldspars and biotite, respectively. (See Table 5.1. for comparison of chemical compositions of clear and dark glasses.) Lack of mixing implies small scale disequilibrium, and that temperatures barely exceeded the solidus. Length of section is 3.65 mm.

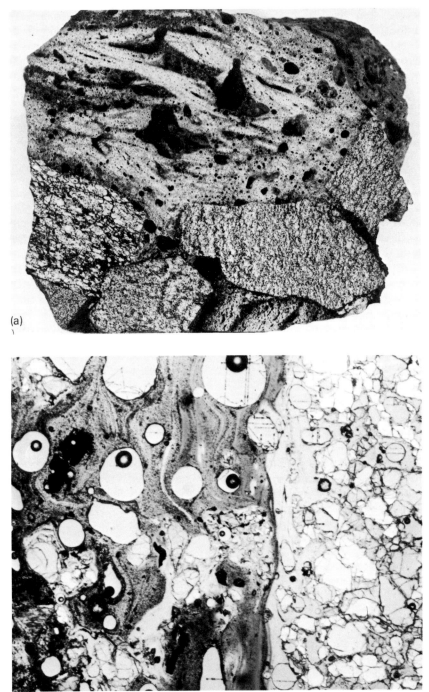

(a)

(b)

electron microprobe. Although in the case of the vitrified forts ample material was available, this method was selected because of speed and economy. The desirability and applicability of this technique to archaeological samples, which are often scarce, has prompted the following brief description.

The sample was crushed and ground to pass through a 200 mesh sieve. A representative aliquot of some 100 mg was carefully split and ground in a boron carbide micro-mortar to less than 5 μm. Several samples of a few milligrams were pressed into 2 to 3 mm diameter, less than 0.1 mm thick pellets between tungsten anvils at 20 to 30 kilobars pressure. The pellets were mounted on conductive discs with silver paint and coated with a carbon film according to normal procedures (Keil 1967) for electron probe analysis of non-conductors. In order to compensate for inhomogeneities and grain size variations, a beam spot size of about 50 μm was used and the sample moved at about 10 μm/s for 3 to 5 counting periods of 20 seconds each. The standards were pressed pellets of well analysed rocks; accuracy of the analyses, as deduced from analyses of different standards, was within the normal range for electron probe analysis, i.e. 2 to 5 per cent of reported values. A few of the 'bulk rock' analyses, designated by a 'P' (for pellet or parent) reported by Youngblood et al. (1978) are given in Table 5.1. It should be noted that the analysed 'parent rocks' in most cases were samples from the vitrified walls and thus slightly melted. However, the bulk composition of large blocks appears to be unchanged.

Perhaps one of the most informative aspects of the petrographic work was the discovery of 'wood casts' (Fig. 5.5a), containing small spherules of pure iron (as ascertained by electron probe analysis), near the previous boundary with wood (Fig. 5.5b). These spherules were apparently produced by reduction, similar to that which occurs in volcanic lavas in contact with trees (Kanehira and Shimazaki 1971). Because electron probe analysis is not suitable for distinguishing between ferrous and ferric iron, Youngblood et al. (1978) resorted to wet chemical analysis to determine the FeO/Fe_2O_3 ratios in glasses and parent rocks. For fresh, unweathered samples (rare

---

Fig. 5.4.(a) Finavon (F10). Cut surface showing distinct textural differences between the upper, highly vesicular portion and the lower portion consisting of angular gneissic fragments. Both parts exhibit partial melting, although to different degrees. Apparently the source materials differed. The vesiculation may be the result of burning and melting of substances used as fill in between the rocks in the walls. Length of sample is about 8 cm.
(b) Photomicrograph of a thin (10 μm) section of a Finavon sample (F2). The right-hand third of the section consists predominantly of quartz and feldspars with small amounts of interstitial glass. The left two-thirds, corresponding to the upper part of Fig. 5.4(a), consists of flow banded vesicular glass with only a few mineral grains. Length of section is 3.65 mm.

Table 5.1. Chemical compositions in weight percent oxides of vitrified fort samples

	SiO$_2$	Al$_2$O$_3$	FeO	MgO	CaO	Na$_2$O	K$_2$O	TiO$_2$	P$_2$O$_5$	"	Total
B1P	84.2	2.30	1.05	0.05	0.13	0.02	0.30	0.08	—		88.1
B3P	46.6	12.3	11.5	5.42	4.02	3.84	0.88	2.16	0.50		87.4
B4P	80.4	3.92	4.74	0.35	0.24	0.07	0.11	0.13	<0.1		89.9
B2G[b]	54.4	15.8	15.0	5.11	1.29	1.76	0.97	2.88	—		98.0
B2G[a]	56.6	16.2	13.6	2.70	1.31	2.10	0.64	5.37	0.6–1.0		99.2
B2G[c]	64.7	18.7	5.95	2.20	0.94	3.41	0.73	0.12	0.8		97.6
B2G[c]	70.4	19.5	1.47	0.65	0.74	7.44	0.94	0.01	0.06		101.2
B2G[a]	47.9	11.1	20.0	13.5	0.66	1.54	0.25	1.57	0.47		97.1
CH1P	66.2	14.9	3.58	1.79	2.08	3.08	4.11	0.59	—		96.3
CH1Ga[a]	56.9	23.1	5.79	2.84	2.95	3.85	5.26	1.00	0.4		102.1
CH1Gb[c]	62.7	21.6	3.48	1.47	1.43	3.32	7.60	0.42	—		102.0
DO10P	72.3	15.2	0.78	0.18	0.35	3.30	5.60	—	<0.01		98.1
DO14AP	72.3	15.2	0.78	0.18	0.35	3.30	5.60	<0.01	<0.01		97.7
DO14BP	71.8	15.0	1.13	0.36	0.15	2.80	5.95	<0.01	<0.01		97.1
DO14AG[b]	60.0	14.3	2.29	4.14	9.19	2.20	3.93	0.45	2.94		99.4
DO14BG[c]	62.8	19.0	1.97	0.32	0.47	4.41	7.08	0.01	0.01		96.1
DO12G[c]	74.3	12.7	1.09	0.69	2.82	3.35	5.59	0.07	0.15		100.7
DO12G[b]	64.1	17.9	5.02	2.49	0.38	4.07	4.98	1.89	0.10		100.9
F7P	48.5	15.9	13.3	8.43	5.14	2.59	1.36	1.03	0.1		96.3
F8P	45.8	14.2	15.4	8.57	6.83	1.74	0.25	1.27	0.1		94.2
F2G[b]	65.4	20.3	2.41	1.81	0.84	4.03	5.36	0.58	0.5		101.3
F2G[c]	69.3	19.4	1.09	0.79	0.55	5.49	5.43	0.08	0.04		102.1

Symbols are as follows: CH, Chateauvieux; DO, Donnersberg; B, Braes; F, Finnavon. The letter P signifies a pellet (parent rock) analysis; G, glass analysis in thin section. The letter a denotes dark glass; b, brownish glass; c, light glass. This table illustrates the type of data used to calculate the normative minerals for Fig. 5.6. For a complete tabulation of data, see Youngblood et al. (1978).

these 2000 year old structures), the glasses showed a consistently higher FeO/Fe_2O_3 ratio than the parent rocks, clearly indicating reducing conditions during vitrification.

Interpretation

Youngblood *et al.* (1978) presented extensive chemical data for a total of eleven forts. Included here are selected data for four of the forts which are representative of the trends found in this study. The electron probe analyses of glasses and parent rocks given in Table 5.1 were used to calculate the normative mineral compositions for the ternary diagrams shown in Fig. 5.6.

Before the interpretation of specific data is discussed, several points should be emphasized regarding the use of ternary diagrams to depict chemical data. Firstly, the apices represent combinations of normative minerals, i.e. not actual phases present, but rather calculated 'potential' phases which might crystallize from a melt of the determined composition under certain conditions. These norm calculations are described by Cross, Iddings, Pirsson, and Washington (1903) and Barth (1952). Secondly, ternary diagrams are only two-dimensional. Major components are combined and normalized to 100 per cent and minor components are usually disregarded. Clearly, such diagrams are only significant if the components selected represent a major fraction of those in the system. Thus it is advantageous to use the complex normative minerals rather than oxides, for they also reflect interaction between the elements; for example, calcium may be partitioned between salic and femic minerals. Thirdly, these diagrams should not be confused with *equilibrium* diagrams frequently used by petrologists to illustrate phase relations in different chemical systems at various temperatures and pressures, and also melting and crystallization sequences. In vitrified forts, the parent rocks and glasses are not in equilibrium.

Figure 5.6(a) illustrates the difference between parent rocks and early glasses formed by chemical reaction and partial *in situ* melting of minor incompatible phases. These glasses are in gross *disequilibrium* with the bulk rock and with each other even in the same thin section. This is also indicated by the segregations of dark and light glasses (Fig. 5.3(b)). However, each individual glass may be considered in *local equilibrium*, and thus the conditions necessary for melting, e.g. temperature, pressure, and redox potential, may be evaluated by comparison with known systems of similar chemistry. Thus, limiting conditions of the physical processes necessary to obtain vitrification, as well as devitrification and crystallization, may be deduced.

Figure 5.6(a) shows the trends in normative mineral composition between glasses and parent rocks for two forts (Chateauvieux and Donnersberg) built with salic (silica-rich) rocks. For both there is a consistent decrease in normative quartz and increase in normative feldspars from parent rocks to

(a)

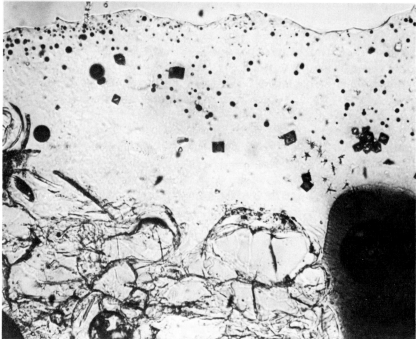

(b)

glasses. Some of the glasses also show an increase of the normative femic (iron-magnesium) minerals. Figure 5.6(b) depicts the rock-to-glass relations for the Finavon fort in which a more femic (silica-poor) rock was used. There is a decrease in the glasses of normative femic minerals and an increase in the salic minerals quartz and feldspars. Also included in Fig. 5.6(b) are data for a fourth fort, Braes, which was constructed of rocks of widely differing composition. The normative compositions of the glasses are intermediate between those of the rocks, but this is not due to mixing of the glasses formed from these rocks. Rather, the scatter represents chemical reactions and *in situ* partial melting of various proportions of minerals or chemically different rock fragments which were incompatible at elevated temperatures. Thus, in salic rocks, the first glasses formed are more femic, while femic rocks first produce small amounts of salic glasses. As larger amounts of glass are formed, the glass composition approaches that of the bulk rock. A corollary is that, initially, partial melting may produce small amounts of relatively similar glasses in very different rocks and at similar temperatures; thus almost any rocks could yield vitrified walls if fired at adequate temperatures, i.e. in the 900 °–1100 °C range or lower if the conditions discussed below, which would result from higher water vapour pressures, were applicable. Still, for vitrification to occur, the temperatures must be high, and the fires kept burning for a long time, certainly longer than would be possible given a reasonable estimate of wood to stone ratio in a timber-laced wall (Childe and Thorneycroft 1937*a*). Childe and Thorneycroft (1937*b*) calculated the amount of timber required to vitrify the Rahoy fort as over 66 tonnes; experiments conducted in Scotland in 1980 by Dr Ian Ralston demonstrated that large quantities – lorry loads – were required to produce only very small amounts of vitrification.

The possible explanation lies in the reducing conditions demonstrated during the vitrification which imply a confined, slow, and oxygen-starved fire. Combustion under reducing conditions would resemble that in a wood gas generator or charcoal kiln. The wood could produce gases, such as methanol (CH_3OH), by direct distillation, and perhaps also by the reaction $H_2O + C = H_2 + CO$, etc. These gases would in turn burn at even higher temperatures and produce localized vitrification and welding with more modest energy requirements than would be required for total melting.

Fig. 5.5.(a) Glassy wood cast of oak in a sample from Chateauvieux (CH1) is evidence for a timber-laced construction. Length of section is 7 cm.
(b) Photomicrograph of a thin (10 μm) section of the wood cast in (a). Clear glass (top), once in contact with the wood, contains black spherules of pure metallic iron, suggesting that vitrification occurred in a reducing environment. The square grains are spinels segregated from the glass. Fracturing of quartz grains, lower centre and left, is another indication of the high temperatures reached ($\sim$ 1000 °C). Length of section is 0.6 mm.

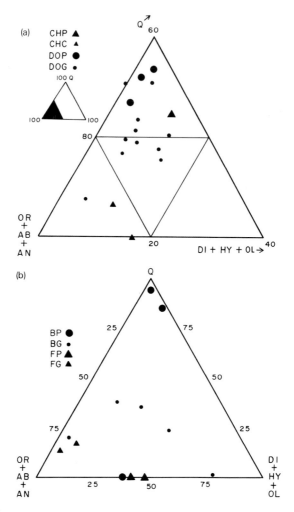

Fig. 5.6.(a) Portion of a ternary diagram for glasses and their salic (silica- and alumina-rich) parent rocks from Chateauvieux (CH) and Donnersberg (DO). The apices are the salic normative minerals: quartz ($Q = SiO_2$), and feldspars (orthoclase $= OR = KAlSi_3O_8$; albite $= AB = NaAlSi_3O_8$; and anorthite $= AN = CaAl_2Si_2O_8$), and the femic (for iron-magnesium) minerals: hypersthene $= HY = FeSiO_3$; diopside $= DI = (Ca,Mg)SiO_3$; and olivine $= OL = (Mg, Fe)_2SiO_4$. Sample designations are as in Table 5.1. Note the trend of the glasses, CHG and DOG, away from their parent rock compositions, CHP and DOP, and towards the feldspar and femic apices. Points displaced toward the femic apex represent darker glasses. (See Table 5.1.)

(b) Ternary diagram for glasses and parent rocks from Braes (B) and Finavon (F). Sample designations are as in Table 5.1; apices labelled as in (a). Note the trend for Finavon glasses (FG) away from the parent, femic, composition (FP) and towards feldspar and quartz. For Braes where parent rocks (BP) vary grossly, the glasses (BG) are intermediate because different rocks tend to produce similar glasses as a result of initial 'low' temperature partial melting, *not* because of mixing.

Evidence supporting this hypothetical process is found in the wood casts, which required slow combustion for their preservation, and in the iron spherules, which were formed by various reactions between iron components, carbon, and carbon monoxide, e.g. $Fe_2O_3 + C = 2FeO + CO = Fe + FeO + CO_2$, etc. An interesting analogy in primitive technology has recently been demonstrated for iron smelters in Tanzania (Schmidt and Avery 1978). The smelting process included preheating and roasting of the ore in a confined pit containing wet wood. The combustion allows for formation of iron according to the reactions given above. The cross-section drawn by Schmidt and Avery (1978) might well serve as a crude model of what is envisaged here as having been the construction of the now vitrified fort walls with the burning timbers acting as draft channels (corresponding to the 'tuyéres'). Finally, in these smelters temperatures up to 1600 °C are achieved, supporting the contention that the temperatures necessary for confined local vitrification (smelting) are feasible given the proper conditions.

This discussion implies that there was no addition of fluxing agents which would change the major element chemical compositions of the glasses. However, some of the glasses do show anomalous enrichment of phosphorus (Table 5.1). These increases cannot be adequately explained by the melting of phosphate minerals such as apatite which were available in the parent rocks. Thus, the anomalously high phosphorus content of some glasses does suggest that organic materials, perhaps bones and refuse, were added to the walls, rendering the structures much more densely packed than a simple rock-filled timber frame. This observation, combined with the reducing conditions, which suggest that the walls were covered by sod or debris, has led to the hypothesis that the construction of the walls was much more elaborate than was previously believed.

Minor and trace elements

Except for some titanium and phosphorus analyses reported by Youngblood *et al.* (1978), no attempts seem to have been made to compare the distribution of minor elements among glasses, parent rocks, and organic remnants in the vitrified forts. It is well known in geochemical prospecting for ores (e.g. Goldschmidt 1937; Fredriksson and Lindgren 1967) that minor and trace elements are grossly differentiated by different rocks and minerals, and also among different plant specimens. Thus it is suggested that in future work on vitrified forts the distribution and relative concentration of elements such as B, F, Cl, Ti, Cr, Mn, Ni, Cu, As, Ba, Pb, and others should be determined. Such analyses might well reveal the characters and proportions of soil, plants, and other organic components incorporated in the glasses from vitrified forts as compared with the rocks used in their building.

168

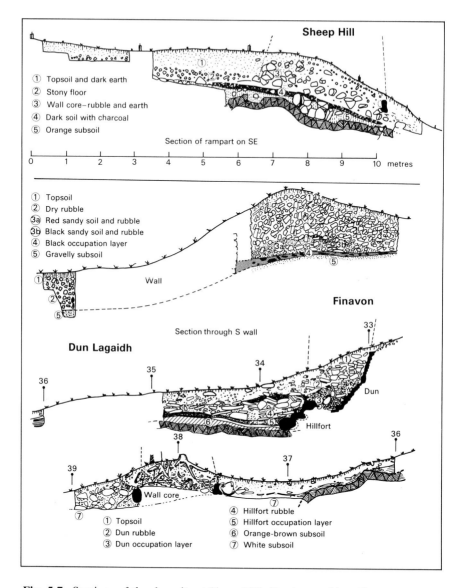

Sheep Hill

① Topsoil and dark earth
② Stony floor
③ Wall core—rubble and earth
④ Dark soil with charcoal
⑤ Orange subsoil

Section of rampart on SE

0 1 2 3 4 5 6 7 8 9 10 metres

① Topsoil
② Dry rubble
③a Red sandy soil and rubble
③b Black sandy soil and rubble
④ Black occupation layer
⑤ Gravelly subsoil

Wall

Finavon

Section through S wall

Dun Lagaidh

Dun

Hillfort

Wall core

① Topsoil
② Dun rubble
③ Dun occupation layer
④ Hillfort rubble
⑤ Hillfort occupation layer
⑥ Orange-brown subsoil
⑦ White subsoil

Fig. 5.7. Sections of the deposits at Sheep Hill, Dunbartonshire; Finavon, Angus; and Dun Lagaidh, Ross and Cromarty. The black areas indicate the vitrified material. (After Mackie 1976.)

Conclusions

Interpretation of the chemical data obtained for parent rocks and glasses from vitrified forts establishes several facts concerning the origin of these forts. First, melting and vitrification definitely occurred *in situ*. There is no evidence that fluxing agents had a significant role in the melting process. Thus, the temperatures achieved during vitrification must have been in the range of those for natural basaltic and granitic systems, i.e. 900–1100 °C, or lower if substantial water pressures were sustained. Second, the anomalous enrichments of phosphorus suggest that, in addition to stones, the walls contained organic, more combustible materials. The presence of metallic iron spherules, which imply reducing conditions during vitrification, suggest that the walls were densely packed and probably covered by rather impervious materials, such as sod. Thus the Celts may have employed sophisticated techniques in the construction of their hillfort walls. Whether or not vitrification was intentional cannot be determined definitely at this time; however, it does appear that the Celts anticipated or planned for the fires. In order better to understand the vitrification process, it would be desirable to know what type of woods or brush and other combustible materials were incorporated into the walls, and trace element analyses might answer this question. It would also be helpful to have more precise excavational data on wall construction (Fig. 5.7). Thus, although geochemical studies alone may not ultimately resolve the questions concerning the origin of the vitrified forts, they can provide useful constraints on the conditions involved in the vitrification process.

Acknowledgement

We wish to thank F. Hueber for identifying the charred oak cast in Fig. 5a and extend our appreciation to V. Krantz for the photographs in Figs 3a, 4a, and 5a. The Smithsonian Research Foundation provided partial financial support.

References

Barth, T. F. W. (1952). *Theoretical petrology*. Wiley, New York.
Beauchamp, R. H. and Williford, J. F. (1973). Metallographic methods applied to ultrathinning lunar rocks, meteorites, fossils, and other brittle materials for optical microscopy. In: J. L. McCall and W. M. Mueller (ed.): *Metallographic specimen preparation*. Plenum, New York, 233–49.
Brothwell, D. R., Bishop, A. C. and Woolley, A. R. (1974). Vitrified forts in Scotland: a problem in interpretation and primitive technology. *Journal of Archaeological Science* **1**, 101–7.

Childe, V. G. and Thorneycroft, W. (1937a). The experimental production of phenomena distinctive of vitrified forts. *Proceedings of the Society of Antiquaries of Scotland* **12**, 44–55.

—— —— (1937b). The vitrified fort at Rahoy, Morvern, Argyll. *Proceedings of the Society of Antiquaries of Scotland* **12**, 23–43.

Christison, D., Anderson, J. and Ross, T. (1905). Report on the Society's excavations of forts on the Poltalloch Estate, Argyll, in 1904–1905. *Proceedings of the Society of Antiquaries of Scotland* **39**, 270–85.

Cotton, M. A. (1954). British camps with timber-laced ramparts. *Archaeological Journal* **111**, 26–105.

Cross, W., Iddings, J. P., Pirsson, L. V. and Washington, H. S. (1903). *Quantitative classification of igneous rocks.* University of Chicago Press.

Daubrée, R. A. (1881a). Examen mineralogique et chimique de materiaux provenant de quelques forts vitrifies de la France. *Revue Archaeologique* **41**, 18–28.

—— (1881b). Examen des materiaux des forts vitrifies de Chateau-Meignan (Mayenne) et du Puy-de-Gaudy (Creuse). *Revue Archaeologique* **42**, 275–8.

De Gasparis, A. A., Fredriksson, K. and Brenner, P. (1975). Composition of individual chondrules in ordinary chondrites. *Meteoritics* **10**, 390–2.

Duff, D. G. (1961). Vitrified forts – how were they built? *Scots Magazine* 1961, 254–7.

Fredriksson, K. (1967). Standards and correction procedures for microprobe analysis of minerals. *Proceedings International Conference on X-Ray Optics and Microanalysis.* **4th**: 305–9.

—— Lindgren, I. (1967). Anomalous copper content in glacial drift and plants in a copper mineralized area of the Caledonides. In: A. Kvalheim (ed.) *Geochemical prospecting in Fennoscandia.* Interscience, New York, 193–202.

Goldschmidt, V. M. (1937). The principles of distribution of chemical elements in minerals and rocks. *Journal of the Chemical Society* **1937**, 655.

Herm, G. (1977). *The Celts.* Weidenfeld and Nicolson, London.

Kanehira, K. and Shimazaki, Y. (1971). Native iron in basalt surrounding tree-molds at Mt. Fuji, Japan. *Neues Jahrbuch für Mineralogie. Monatshefte* **1971** (3), 124–30.

Keil, K. (1967). The electron microprobe X-ray analyzer and its application in mineralogy. *Fortschritte der Mineralogie* **44**, 4–66.

Mackie, E. W. (1969). Radiocarbon dates and the Scottish Iron Age. *Antiquity* **43**, 15–26.

—— (1976). The vitrified forts of Scotland. In: D. W. Harding (ed.): *Hillforts: later prehistoric earthworks in Britain and Ireland.* Academic Press, London, 205–35.

Nisbet, H. C. (1974). A geological approach to vitrified forts. Part I. The archaeological and scientific background. *Science and Archaeology* **12**, 3–12.

—— (1975). A geological approach to vitrified forts. Part II. Bed rock and building stone. *Science and Archaeology* **15**, 3–16.

Schairer, J. F. (1950). The alkali–feldspar join in the system $NaAlSiO_4$–SiO_2– $KAlSiO_4$. *Journal of Geology* **58**, 512–17.

Schmidt, P. and Avery, D. H. (1978). Complex iron smelting and prehistoric culture in Tanzania. *Science* **201**, 1085–9.

Small, A. and Cottam, M. B. (1972). Craig Phaidrig. *Occasional Papers. University of Dundee, Department of Geography* **1**, 1–57.

Youngblood, E., Fredriksson, B. J., Kraut, F. and Fredriksson, K. (1978). Celtic vitrified forts; implications of a chemical–petrological study of glasses and source rocks. *Journal of Archaeological Science* **5**, 99–121.

6. Petrology of stone axes and tools

W. A. Cummins

History of implement petrology

Introduction

Research into the petrology of stone implements may be divided into several stages. The initial motivation for such work comes from the realization that tools are often made of stone which is foreign to the area in which they are found. Over three hundred years ago, Sir William Dugdale (1656), writing about a flint axe from Oldbury, in Warwickshire, commented on the fact that flint does not occur within forty miles of the location of the find spot. Similar observations have been repeated many times, and suggest the possibility of prehistoric trade. This possibility receives further support from the discovery of mines and quarries, and factories for the production of stone tools, on a scale far beyond the needs of the local population. For any further study of prehistoric trade, the products of different factories must be identifiable among the artefacts found in the surrounding areas. This is essentially a petrological problem.

Petrological examination of stone tools has two basic aims, and these have often been pursued simultaneously. The first is to identify the products of known factories, and the second to acquire petrological data leading to the discovery of previously unknown sources of raw material. With some rock types, notably certain flints and cherts, excellent results have been obtained by macroscopic examination of the artefacts. At the other extreme, the macroscopic identification of different types of greenstone presents almost insuperable problems. Greenstone suffers from weathering, and the surface characteristics of a greenstone artefact will depend on the chemical nature of the soil or other environment in which it has been buried. Implements made from an individual greenstone source may show a great range of surface features, due to weathering; whereas implements from different greenstone sources, but from the same archaeological environment, may look almost identical. Microscopic examination of thin sections is the obvious method to apply to such implements. But, since this involves cutting slices from the implements, there is liable to be a conflict between petrologists and museum curators, concerned with the conservation of their collections. The resolution of this conflict is part of the history of implement petrology (Grimes 1979).

Microscopic petrology has proved to be a very effective tool for distinguishing the products of different centres of production among collections of stone tools. Its application is not universal, however, and it is least effective when dealing with very fine-grained homogeneous rocks, such as flint and chert, or with volcanic glasses, like obsidian. For such rocks, which were used for fine blades, points, microliths, etc., all over the world, chemical analysis is now widely used (Shotton and Hendry 1979). In special circumstances other methods, such as oxygen isotope analysis, have also been used (Stiles, Hay, and O'Neil 1974).

The development of methods for the petrological identification of stone tools is, of course, only part of the story. During the past sixty years, petrological studies of stone tools have been carried out in many parts of the world, on all scales, ranging from the identification of single artefacts to regional research projects. Petrological reports on stone tools are often published as appendices to archaeological excavation reports, and may throw light on the cultural contacts of the tool users at the site in question. Regional projects on implement petrology are undertaken with broad aims, such as the determination of 'early trade routes and other factors of economic and social importance' (Keiller, Piggott, and Wallis 1941), or 'in the hope of supplementing the ethno-historical literature' and gaining 'new information on the economic life of the prehistoric inhabitants and their trade, barter or exchange, at least in so far as this is reflected in the distribution of durable raw materials' (Binns and McBryde 1972).

A regional implement petrology survey should yield three basic kinds of information, essential for the study of prehistoric trade: the recognition of a number of petrological groups among the artefacts of the area; the geological source and, ideally, the actual quarries or production centres for each of the groups; and the distribution of tools emanating from each centre of production. Even when all this information is assembled, the interpretation of the data may still present considerable problems. In geology, there is the principle of uniformitarianism, commonly expressed in the simple statement that *the present is the key to the past*. This principle can be applied to the physical aspects of archaeology, such as the wearing down of mounds and banks, the silting up of ditches, and the formation of lynchets. But, if it were to be applied to the behavioural aspects of archaeology, such as trade and communications, one would have to ask the question – 'which present?'

In the western desert of Australia, 'a man visiting a geographical site associated with his ancestral mythical species – the rabbit-eared bandicoot, for example – would collect stones from the site that could later be made into various stone tools. He would pass them on to other members of his patrilineage as a token of their mutual affiliation and as sacred 'relics' of the mythical event that occurred at that sacred site, somewhat like a pilgrim sharing a piece of the True Cross. A form of intralineage exchange thus exists where pieces of chert, quartzite, and other stones are exchanged and eventually come to rest as discards in camp-sites hundreds of miles from their source.' (Gould 1979).

Further east, in Victoria, the greenstone of Mount William was extensively quarried for making axeheads. '-The outcrops were owned by a group of the Wurndjeri tribe, and only members of a certain family were permitted to work them. The last man responsible for working the quarry, Billi-billeri, died in 1846' (McBryde 1979, p. 117). 'Barak, a nephew of Billi-billeri, told Howitt that members of tribes neighbouring the Wurndjeri sent messengers to Billi-billeri if they required stone. A price was discussed and Billi-billeri worked the stone for them. Rugs, weapons, and ornaments were exchanged for it, three pieces of stone for one possum skin rug. This evidence suggests that Mount William stone was acquired at the initiative of those requiring it. . . . The outcrops were not worked as a commercial enterprise for which a network of supply was created, but in response to demand'. (McBryde 1978, p. 364).

These and other ethno-historical examples make one aware of the range of models which should be considered, when attempting to interpret prehistoric distribution patterns. Binns and McBryde (1972, p. 2) strike a suitable note of caution when they remark that, while implement petrology surveys will yield 'objective and precise information on source areas and distribution . . ., they cannot, of course, answer the questions raised by the anthropological literature on the nature of the exchange involved.'

Mines, quarries, and factories

From about 1860 onwards, flint mines were being discovered in several European countries, particularly England, Belgium, and France. Nearly all were sited on the Upper Cretaceous Chalk. Their presence was indicated by surface features related to the shafts and spoil heaps. Archaeological excavations, such as those carried out by Canon Greenwell at Grimes Graves, in Norfolk, revealed the true nature of such sites. Clark and Piggott (1933) published a map showing the distribution of these mines, and also a list of references to papers on their discovery and investigation.

Stone axe factories, based on a variety of fine-grained rocks which can be flaked like flint, have been revealed by their abundant and characteristic debris of rough-outs and waste flakes. The first to be reported was near Cushendall, in Northern Ireland (Knowles 1903). A similar factory was later discovered on Rathlin Island, off the Antrim coast, some 25 km north of Cushendall (Jope 1952). Then Hazzledine Warren found the important axe factory near Penmaenmawr, in North Wales (Warren 1919; Houlder 1956). Information on the Great Langdale axe factories, in the English Lake

District, was not published until 1949, though they had been known for some years before then (Bunch and Fell 1949; Houlder 1979). In Scotland, an axe factory has been found near Killin, north of Loch Tay (Ritchie 1968), but little detailed information has yet been published. On a much smaller scale than these axe factories are the quarries at Mynydd Rhiw, in North Wales (Houlder 1961), and on the Beorgs of Uyea, Shetland (Scott and Calder 1954).

In some parts of the world, the 'Stone Age' ended so recently that the working of quarries for stone tools is still remembered. In New Guinea, for example, stone for making axes was being quarried as late as the 1940s and 1950s (Chappel 1966). Chappell examined ten such quarries during 1963–4, of which three had been visited before, two were reported to him by an anthropologist, and five had been found by himself, by following up local information gathered during the course of his fieldwork. In Australia, the 'Stone Age' ended over a hundred years earlier, and only the great Mount William quarry, in Victoria, is recorded in the ethno-historical literature (McBryde 1979). Other stone axe quarries in the greenstone belt of Victoria (McBryde 1979), and also in New South Wales (Binns and McBryde 1972), were discovered by their archaeological traces, in the same way as the British stone axe factories. Stone age axe and tool factories are known, too, from the Indus River Region of Pakistan.

Macroscopic implement petrology surveys

In Poland flint from several different geological formations was exploited for the manufacture of stone axes and other tools. About 1920, S. Krukowski began to distinguish the different types of flint among assemblages of implements from central Poland, and to plot their distribution. From 1922 onwards he had the collaboration of a geologist, J. Samsonowicz. Between them, they traced the several flint types to their geological sources, and located the prehistoric mines from which they were extracted. A recent general account of this Polish work, with references to the earlier work, is given by Sulimirski (1960).

The *Chocolate Flint*, distinguished by its characteristic colour, is one of the best Polish materials. This is an Upper Jurassic flint, and has been traced to limestones of Late Oxfordian (possibly lowest Kimmeridgian) age, formerly referred to as Upper Astartian, along the north-eastern flanks of the Holy Cross Mountains, in central Poland. Neither the limestones themselves, nor the residual clays derived from them, are anywhere exposed at the surface. The Quaternary cover is of variable thickness, but is seldom more than about four metres deep in areas where prehistoric mines were sunk. A recent account of work on the chocolate flint is given by Schild (1976).

The *Banded Flint* is another Upper Jurassic flint, distinguished by 'thin parallel bands of various shades of grey, yellowish, brownish and some other colours' (Sulimirski 1960). Like the chocolate flint, it too has its source along the north-eastern flanks of the Holy Cross Mountains, but at a slighly lower horizon in the Oxfordian (Lower Astartian). The best quality material was mined at various places in the district of Opatow. The mines at Krzemionki, discovered by J. Samsonowicz, are among the most extensive in Europe, with well over 700 pits.

The *Świeciechów Flint* is of Upper Cretaceous age, and is distinguished by its abundant white spots – and sometimes darker stains – in a generally grey matrix. The source of this flint is in Lower Turonian strata, separated from the Upper Jurassic flint mining area to the west by the River Vistula (Balcer 1976, Fig. 1). Recent petrographic work has shown that the white spots and dark stains are due to calcite and opal, respectively, in the mainly chalcedonic flint (Balcer, 1976, p. 180).

Other varieties of Polish flint, which can be distinguished and traced to their sources, include the *Milky Flint* of the north-west, and the *Black* or *Black and Grey Flint* of the south-east (Sulimirski 1960). In France, the honey-coloured flint from Grand Pressigny is another important and widely recognized type (Sherratt 1976).

In England, the best flints were obtained from the Upper Cretaceous Chalk. The black flints of East Anglia and southern England are easily distinguished from the white flints of Yorkshire and Lincolnshire (Shotton and Hendry 1979, p. 77), though it is not possible to make a macroscopic distinction between, for example, the products of the Grimes Graves flint mines, in Norfolk, and those at Cissbury, in Sussex. The Upper Jurassic Portland chert was used, mainly in Mesolithic times, in southern England and, 'once this blue-grey, lead-coloured chert has been seen, it is readily recognised' (Rankine 1951). Black chert, from the Carboniferous Limestone, has also been distinguished on Mesolithic sites (Radley and Mellars 1964).

In Norrland, in northern Sweden, where there is no local supply of flint, quartz was used extensively. The great amount of quartz recovered from archaeological excavations in the Vasterbotten area suggested quarrying in the vicinity. Consultation, first with a mining geologist, and later with a blaster who had worked in an abandoned feldspar quarry and also conducted some independent prospecting, revealed several quartz veins in the area, which showed evidence of prehistoric quarrying with the aid of fire setting (Broadbent 1973).

Macroscopic identifications have met with considerable success when applied to flint, chert, and quartz, as indicated above, and microscopic examination has added little or nothing to these results (e.g. Schild 1976). When applied to other rocks, of more complex composition, however, macroscopic examination provides very little information and is quite inadequate for provenance studies (Grimes 1979).

Microscopic implement petrology surveys

From about 1920 onwards, archaeologists in various parts of Europe were consulting their geological colleagues about the petrological identification and possible geological provenance of stone implements. The results of such a collaboration have already been considered in the study of Polish flint implements by Krukowski, the archaeologist, and Samsonowicz, the geologist. During this same period, a number of fruitful and quite independent petrological investigations, involving the microscopic examination of thin sections, were carried out on stone implements other than flint. Štelcl and Malina (1975, pp. 105–7), in their book on 'Petro-archaeology', give a useful bibliography of this work. Two examples will be considered here as representative of this period.

In Finland the petrological study of stone implements was begun by Professor P. Eskola. In 1919, at the suggestion of the archaeologist A. Europaeus, he undertook a petrological examination of the shaft-hole axes of Finland. During his absence abroad in 1922–3, he handed the project over to his colleague, A. Laitakari, who later published the results of their work (Laitakari 1928). Thin sections were taken, when permitted, from broken specimens, but most of the identifications were made macroscopically, with the aid of a hand lens. The most striking results of their work related to the typologically distinctive boat-axes, 80 per cent of which were made of dolerite. Among these dolerite boat-axes, olivine dolerite formed a particularly abundant and distinctive petrological group, whose geological provenance is located in the area south of Pori, in south-western Finland. This olivine dolerite of Satakunta (Satakunta-diabas) accounts for nearly 60 per cent of all the boat-axes and almost 90 per cent of certain types (Laitakari 1928, p. 17).

In Norway, the first petrological study of stone implements followed immediately on the discovery of a stone axe factory on the island of Bømlo, about 90 km south of Bergen. Professor H. Shetelig, who had been studying a Neolithic site near the southern tip of the island, was impressed by the great quantity of waste flakes and rough-outs he found. This was in complete contrast to other Neolithic dwelling sites in western Norway, where finished tools were the norm and such waste material very rarely occurred. Shetelig then enlisted the help of N. H. Kolderup in Bergen, to try to locate the source of the raw material used in this stone industry. Macroscopic inspection showed that the material was 'greenstone', for which it would be difficult to find a source without more detailed analysis. Fortunately, there was no lack of material from which thin sections could be taken, and these formed the basis of Kolderup's investigation (Kolderup 1925).

Microscopic examination showed the rock to be a spilite, in which the original igneous texture and mineralogy were very little altered. This eliminated the possibility of a source on the island of Bømlo itself, where all the volcanic rocks are metamorphosed, so that the greenstones and greenschists show very little trace of their igneous textures. West of the southern point of Bømlo is a group of small islands called Espevaer, on which greenschist is the dominant rock type. In these islands there is abundant evidence of Neolithic activity, but the greenschist is still too highly metamorphosed to be matched with the spilite of the axe factory. A little to the north lies another group of islands, Nordoerne, in which the grade of metamorphism is so low that it is difficult to believe that they form any part of the Caledonian fold belt of Norway (Kolderup 1925, p. 166). Three of these islets, Joöen, Sölö, and Hespliholmen, were geologically promising as sources of spilite. On Joöen, the spilite is much darker than that used in the axe factory. On Sölö, the outcrops of spilite are all at a low level, and were probably below sea-level during the Neolithic period. Finally, on Hespliholmen, a suitable source was found *and also the quarry from which the stone had been extracted.* The flat quarry floor was about 5 m above sea-level, and Kolderup (1925, p. 170) estimated that about 70 m^3 of stone had been removed. The quarry was probably close to sea-level when it was in operation, and has since been raised to its present level by the isostatic uplift of this part of Norway, following the melting of the Scandinavian ice cap.

The implement petrology survey in Britain had its effective origin about ten years later than these early investigations in Finland and Norway, and the history of its development has recently been recorded by Grimes (1979). It differs from earlier work in several respects. From regional beginnings in the south-west, it developed into a national survey, involving a considerable team of archaeologists and geologists; it is a long-term project, with comprehensive aims; and microscopic examination of thin sections has been, from the very outset, regarded as the standard basis for petrological identifications. In 1936, the South Western Group of Museums and Art Galleries appointed a sub-committee to consider the petrological identification of stone implements and, after the examination of over two hundred axes, they produced their first report (Keiller *et al.* 1941). In this report, nine petrological groups, were established, of which three could be identified with the products of known axe factories. Group VI (Fig. 6.1), a fine-grained epidotized tuff, was identified with D.M.S. Watson's axe factory at Stake Pass, north of Great Langdale, in the Lake District. Group VII, a fine-grained augite granophyre, was derived from Hazzledine Warren's axe factory near Penmaenmawr, in North Wales. Group IX, a porcellanite resulting from the thermal metamorphism of an inter-basaltic soil horizon or bole, had come all the way from W.J. Knowles' axe factory near Cushendall, in Northern Ireland. Of the other groups, by far the most

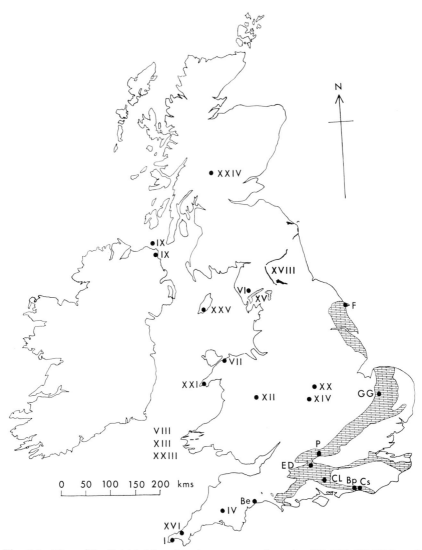

Fig. 6.1. Map of the British Isles, showing stone axe factories (VI, VII, IX, XXI, and XXIV), geological sources of stone axes and shaft-hole implements (I, IV, VIII, XII, XIII, XIV, XV, XVI, XVIII, XX, XXIII, and XXV), flint mines (Bp, Cs, ED, GG, and P), and flint implement factories (Be, Cl, and F). The outcrops of the more extensive source rocks – the Whin Sill (XVIII), the Upper Silurian Coniston Grit (XV), and the Ordovician igneous rocks of Pembrokeshire (VIII, XIII, and XXIII) – are shown on the map, and also the Upper Cretaceous Chalk, on which the flint industry is based. The petrological groups for stone implements (Roman numerals) are listed on page 180. Groups which are neither widespread, nor even locally abundant, have been omitted. The flint mines are Blackpatch (Bp), Cissbury (Cs), Easton Down (ED), Grimes Graves (GG), and Peppard (P). Beer (Be) and Clanfield (Cl) are surface working sites (Sieveking *et al*. 1972, p. 153). In Yorkshire, where the Chalk is rather hard, flint implement factories around Flamborough Head (F) made use of blocks and nodules of flint, derived from the boulder clay cliffs along the coast (Sheppard 1920; Moore 1964; Manby 1979).

important was Group I, a greenstone, whose source in Cornwall was not precisely located (Table 6.1).

It is only since this first report that the grand scale of the axe factories in the Langdale and Scafell Pike area of the Lake District has been appreciated (Houlder 1979). Similarly, the dominance of Group VI axes over almost the whole of England has only recently become well known (Cummins 1979). In the light of these observations, it is interesting to look back at the comments made on Group VI axes almost forty years ago. 'Perhaps the most interesting discovery made is the recognition of over a dozen exports from a very small and hitherto almost unknown axe factory in the Lake District. . . . It is noteworthy that, apart from a Dorset specimen, all come from the upper Thames and north Wiltshire region. The connection between this area and Cumberland comes as an archaeological surprise, and now the axes have pointed the way we may discover further evidence of trade contacts between the two regions' (Keiller *et al*. 1941, p. 68).

The South Western team continued to make progress during the next decade, and produced two further reports (Stone and Wallis 1947; 1951). As time went on, and their work became more widely known and valued, they responded to an increasing number of requests for petrological identifications from other parts of the country. Many of these were incorporated in their fourth report (Evens, Grinsell, Piggott, and Wallis 1962). Meanwhile, the Council for British Archaeology had set up an Implement Petrology Committee, under the chairmanship of Professor W. F. Grimes, to organize similar work over the whole country.

The next important results came from the west Midlands, with the recognition of four new petrological groups. The first of these, Group XII, is a picrite, whose source was traced to a very limited outcrop near the village of Hyssington, about 15 km west of Church Stretton, on the Welsh Border (Shotton, Chitty, and Seaby 1951). Unlike the earlier groups recognized in the south-west, the products of Group XII were entirely shafthole implements – axe hammers and battle axes. Among the other new groups, Group XV, a sub-greywacke probably from the Upper Silurian Coniston Grits in the southern Lake District (Shotton 1959), was an important raw material for axe hammers in north-western England (Roe 1979, p. 29).

Following the fourth South Western report, a series of other regional reports appeared; Yorkshire (Keen and Radley 1971); East Anglia (Clough and Green 1972); Lincolnshire, Nottinghamshire, and Rutland (Cummins and Moore 1973); Derbyshire and Leicestershire (Moore and Cummins 1974); London and Middlesex (Celoria 1974; Stanley 1976); and a fifth report on the South Western counties (Evens, Smith, and Wallis 1972).

A complete annotated list of British petrological groups is given by Clough and Cummins (1979, p. 127), with general accounts of the distribution of the more important groups of stone axes by Cummins (1979) and of

Table 6.1. British implement petrology groups

Group I Uralitized gabbro, epidiorite, or greenstone. Source in Mount's Bay area, near Penzance, Cornwall. Widely distributed and abundant.

Group Ia Close to Group I.

Group II Epidiorite or greenstone. Source near St Ives, Cornwall. Rare.

Group IIa Close to Group II.

Group III Epidiorite or greenstone. Source near Marazion, Cornwall. Rare.

Group IIIa Close to Group III.

Group IV Altered picrite. Source near Callington, Cornwall. Locally abundant in the south-west.

Group IVa Sheared greenstone, close to Group IV.

Group V Calc-silicate hornfels. Source said to be probably near St Ives, Cornwall. Very rare.

Group VI Epidotized intermediate tuff. Factories in Great Langdale and Scafell Pike area of the Lake District. Widely distributed and very abundant.

Group VII Augite granophyre. Factories in the Penmaenmawr area, Caernarvonshire, e.g. Graig Lwyd. Widespread and abundant in some areas.

Group VIIa Later given full group status as Group X (*qv*).

Group VIII Silicified tuff. Source in south-west Wales. Widely distributed and locally abundant.

Group VIIIa Close to Group VIII.

Group IX Porcellanite. Factories at Tievebulliagh and Rathlin Island, County Antrim, Ireland. Widespread but relatively uncommon outside Ireland.

Group X Fine dolerite. Factories near Sélédin, Brittany. Rare in Britain. Equivalent to Dolerite Type A. An earlier Group X and Group Xa have been superseded.

Group XI Fine silicified tuff. Source in Great Langdale area of the Lake District. Rare.

Group XII Picrite. Source near Hyssington, on the Shropshire-Montgomeryshire (Powys) border. Axe hammers and battle axes only. Abundant in the west Midlands.

Group XIII Spotted dolerite or preselite. Source in the Preselau Hills, Pembrokeshire (Dyfed). Rare, but important as 'Bluestones' of Stonehenge.

Group XIV Camptonite. Source near Nuneaton, Warwickshire. Rare.

Group XV Micaceous sub-greywacke. Source in southern Lake District. Widespread and locally abundant (particularly as axe hammers).

Group XVI Epidiorite or greenstone. Source near Camborne, Cornwall. Locally abundant in the south-west.

Group XVII Epidiorite or greenstone. Source near St Austell, Cornwall. Rare.

Group XVIII Quartz dolerite. Source in the Whin Sill, northern England. Widespread and locally abundant (particularly as axe hammers).

Group XIX Greywacke. Source probably in Cornwall. Rare.

Group XX Epidotized ashy grit. Source in Charnwood Forest, Leicestershire. Widespread and locally abundant.

Group XXI Baked shale. Factory at Mynydd Rhiw, Caernarvonshire. Rare.

Group XXII Riebeckite felsite. Factory in Shetland. Unknown outside Shetland, though possible examples from mainland Scotland await thin-sectioning.

Group XXIII Ranges from graphic pyroxene granodiorite (Group XXIIIa) to quartz dolerite (Group XXIIIb). Source area between Preselau Hills and St David's Head, Pembrokeshire (Dyfed). Group XIII is an individual rock type which falls within the petrological and geographical range of Group XXIII. It might have been classed as a sub-group of XXIII but for its prior publication as a group in its own right. Rare.

Group XXIV Calc-silicate hornfels. Factory near Killin, Perthshire.

Group XXV Altered quartz diorite. Source south-west of Douglas, Isle of Man. Locally important but as yet unknown outside Isle of Man.

Group XXVI Carbonate mudstone. Source Lower Jurassic of North Yorkshire. Locally important, but not widespread.

the various types of shafthole implements by Roe (1979). One slightly disappointing and perhaps surprising feature of all this work is that, although five of the petrological groups have been identified with the products of *known axe factories*, none has actually led to the discovery of a *new factory*, even where, as with Group XII, the source has been very precisely located. This may, in part, be due to production by methods other than flaking, which would leave less recognizable waste (Coope 1979).

In France, petrological work on stone axes began in Brittany, an area which has close cultural and geological links with the south-western peninsula of England. Professor P.-R. Giot, of the Institut d'Anthropologie Generale at Rennes, who initiated the programme, joined the Prehistoric Society (in whose *Proceedings* most of the British results were being published) in 1950. During the all important early years of his work he had the enthusiastic collaboration of a geological colleague, Professor J. Cogné. A preliminary macroscopic examination of over 3000 stone axes from Brittany showed that over two thirds of them were made of 'greenstone', strongly suggesting a centre of production somewhere in central Brittany (Giot 1951).

This preliminary work was quickly followed by a programme of thin-sectioning and microscopic identification, the results of which were published almost annually in the *Bulletin de la Société Préhistorique Française* (Cogné and Giot 1952, 1953, 1954, 1955, 1957; Giot 1959). It soon became apparent that there was one distinctive and dominant petrological group among the Breton greenstone axes. Dolerite Type A is a fine-grained, strongly epidotized dolerite, much finer than most of the Armorican greenstones. The search for the source of dolerite Type A was greatly facilitated by the publication of a paper on the greenstone of the Laniscat–Merleac anticline (Nicolas and Sagon 1963), in which a few fine-grained dolerite outcrops were described and considered to be the chilled upper margins of thick spilitic lava flows. A match for dolerite Type A was soon established and 'the neighbouring fields, immediately prospected, produced an impressive mass of flakes of all sizes and a fair series of rough-outs closely comparable with those of the well-known British and Irish stone-axe factories (Le Roux 1971). Here, as at Penmaenmawr, the fine-grained chilled margin of an igneous body was selected, so that the rock could be 'roughed out' by the very rapid flaking technique.

Hornblendite Type C is another important Breton group. Like its British ultrabasic equivalent, the Group XII picrite, it was employed almost exclusively for the manufacture of shaft-hole implements, chiefly battle axes. It is derived from a restricted outcrop in southern Finistere but, since the outcrop has been extensively quarried and, more recently, built over, there seems little hope of locating the actual prehistoric quarry or factory. Finds of broken or complete rough-outs are common, however, in the vicinity of the modern quarry (Le Roux 1979).

The Breton studies are gradually being extended radially outwards into neighbouring areas of France. Minor local petrological groups are recognized, but Breton axes, in particular those of dolerite Type A, continue to be important. In Touraine, for example, sixteen new groups were defined, mostly various kinds of dolerite and amphibolite (Le Roux and Cordier 1974). The axes which could not be referred to definite petrological groups were also mainly dolerite and amphibolite. A full bibliography of the French literature on the subject is given by Le Roux (1979).

In Australia, the study of stone axe petrology began in the New England area of northern New South Wales, resulting in two most valuable reports by Binns and McBryde (1969, 1972). As a result of the examination of over 500 stone axes, mostly in thin section, ten petrological groups were established, of which six were divided into three or more sub-groups.

Group 2B, a meta-greywacke of volcaniclastic origin, with very little quartz, is by far the most abundant group. It is clearly identified with material from the largest known axe quarry in the area, on Mount Daruka, north of Tamworth. The rock being exploited belongs to the Devonian Baldwin Formation. Group 2B axes were widely distributed, and are found over 500 km from the quarry.

Two other groups, both small, were identified with the products of known quarry sites. Group 3D, a thermally metamorphosed vitric tuff, represents the products of a quarry near Uralla, about 20 km SSW of Armidale. Group 8C, a distinctive fine laminated amphibolite, is derived from a quarry near Tia, about 55 km SSE of Armidale. This last quarry was not discovered till 1970, when the land was cleared for grazing. Both these small groups have a very localized distribution around their respective quarry sites.

Group 6, described as a pyrometamorphosed bole, is a highly distinctive rock in thin section, very similar to the British Group IX. As in Ireland, the source for such axes had to be located where a Tertiary basaltic soil had been metamorphosed by a later igneous intrusion. This, and the concentrated distribution of Group 6 axes, limited the area to be searched. The axe factory was found, as a direct result of the implement petrology survey, on Gragin Peak near Warialda, about 150 km NW of Armidale. Though most of the Group 6 axes are concentrated fairly close to the source, a few have been carried distances of well over 100 km.

Following the completion of the New South Wales survey, Mcbryde turned her attention southwards to the stone axes of Victoria. Here, the centre of interest was the great Mount William axe quarry, about 35 km north of Melbourne, well known from the ethno-historical literature. The project was complicated at an early stage by the discovery of several other quarries in the greenstone belt of Victoria. The petrological task of distinguishing between the products of these quarries was taken on by Alan Watchman.

Axe stone, quarried at eight different localities in the area, included andesite, diabase, porphyry, hornfels, volcaniclastic rocks, altered pyroclastics, and metagabbro. Products of most of the quarries can be readily distinguished in thin section, on the basis of their mineralogy and texture (Watchman 1979). At Mount William, however, an actinolite-cummingtonite hornfels was worked, almost identical with the rock quarried at Mount Camel, some 50 km further north. For many axes, a clear distinction between these two sources could not be made by microscopic petrology, and geochemical methods had to be employed. On the distribution maps (McBryde 1978, 1979) different symbols are used to indicate whether the identification was made by macroscopic examination, microscopic examination, or trace element analysis.

In south-western Australia, J. E. Glover has made a petrological study of flaked stone tools; of particular interest in this work is the distinction between different chert types in thin section. The most interesting of these is a fossiliferous chert, used extensively in the Perth Basin. This chert is a silicified limestone, in which bryozoa are the most abundant fossils. Fourteen different bryozoa have been identified, nine of them at specific level, and this fauna clearly indicates an Eocene age for the rock. The Eocene age is confirmed by the presence of the Middle to Late Eocene foraminifer, *Maslinella chapmani*, in two of the flakes (Glover and Cockbain 1971). Photographs of this chert, showing microfossils in thin section, have been published by Glover (1974). The nearest outcrops likely to yield such cherts are in the Plantagenet Group, over 500 km away along the south coast; further away, near Eucla, Eocene chert is known to have been quarried in pre-historic times.

Since 1971, chert artefacts have been examined from a number of sites along the south coast. Though superficially similar to the fossiliferous chert flakes from the Perth Basin, these are quite distinct under the microscope and much less fossiliferous. The south coast chert artefacts are clearly derived from the local Plantagenet Group (Glover 1975a, b), so it becomes necessary to look elsewhere for the source of the fossiliferous chert. In the Perth Basin, the relative abundance of the fossiliferous chert in assemblages of stone tools increases westwards, towards the open sea, thus suggesting the existence of a submerged source in that direction (Glover 1975a, b). Such dating evidence as is available suggests that the fossiliferous chert source, wherever it was, was in use during the period 19 000 to 12 000 BP, that is before the post-glacial eustatic rise in sea-level. During this period, the sea-level was probably about 90 metres lower than now, and the coast line would have been about 40 km west of Perth. In the now submerged coastal belt of that period, there may well have been a source of fossiliferous Eocene chert. Current knowledge of the submarine geology of this area is insufficient either to confirm or refute this suggestion (Glover 1975a, b).

Microfossils in chert, such as those from Western Australia, are generally impossible to extract, hence the necessity for studying them in thin section. Occasionally, however, the chert (or flint) may be so decayed that it can be crushed, and the microfossils extracted (Curry 1963). Decayed flints from a Middle Pleistocene deposit near Westbury-sub-Mendip, in Somerset, which contained Acheulian flint artefacts, have yielded Coniacian (Upper Chalk) foraminifera (Bishop 1974, p. 307; 1975).

In New Guinea, J. Chappell carried out an independent and highly individual study of the stone axe factories of the eastern Highlands. He began, late in 1963, by journeying through the Highlands with the object of locating all the quarries, and other sites, where stone axes had been made in the recent past. He then made a detailed study of the petrology of these sources, the aim being to distinguish between their products. Finally, he applied this petrological knowledge to the analysis of six assemblages of stone tools collected by anthropologists. All the main quarries, and several of the minor sources, are sited in the thermal aureoles of granodiorite intrusions, where fine-grained Mesozoic greywackes and interbedded argillites have been altered to tough hornfelses. A few minor sources occur in hard bands away from the aureoles. Representative thin sections were taken from all the sources. The lithological similarity between the various sources was so great, however, that special methods had to be devised to enable a distinction between their products to be made.

Chappell listed a number of lithological characters, some macroscopic and others microscopic, and tabulated their occurrence in rocks from the various sources (Chappell 1966, Table 1). These characters, with their possible variations, were: rock type; regional metasediment or hornfels; colour; hardness on Mohs' scale; toughness, on a scale from 1 to 5; cleavage: none, weak, or good parallel; fracture: conchoidal or hackly; bedding: none, fine irregular, fine laminar, turbidite, indistinct, or clear; veins: characteristic, rare, or very uncommon; texture: metasedimentary, relict sedimentary, fine granular, interlocking laths, etc.; dominant minerals: epidote, albite, actinolite, etc.; other minerals; and grain size: mud, silt, fine sand, or sand.

With the aid of this table, Chappell was able to assign 90 per cent of the axes he examined to one or other of the known sources by means of macroscopic examination. Thin sections were taken from those which gave ambiguous results on macroscopic examination. Thin sections were also taken from some which gave clear identifications, in order to give some control to the method. As with many prehistoric examples, it was found that a small number of the known sources was responsible for the production of a very large proportion of the total output.

Chemical analysis in implement petrology

The potential of chemical analysis as an aid to implement petrology was realized long ago by Laitakari (1928), in his study of the shaft-hole axes of Finland. He made chemical analyses of two dolerite axes and two naturally occurring dolerites, with which he compared them. These analyses (Laitakari 1928, p. 30) showed good correlation between each axe and the dolerite with which it was being compared, and also a very clear distinction between the two types of dolerite. There was, however, no hope of more general application of chemical analysis to stone axe studies until more rapid methods became available.

More recently optical emission spectroscopy and atomic absorption spectroscopy have been used for the chemical analysis of flint (Sieveking, Craddock, Hughes, Bush, and Ferguson 1970; Sieveking, Bush, Ferguson, Craddock, Hughes, and Cowell 1972) and jasper (Blackman 1974). X-ray fluorescence has been applied to volcanic rocks (Higashimura and Warashina 1975; Warashina, Kamaki, and Higashimura 1978) and thermally altered basic igneous rocks (Watchman 1979). Neutron activation analysis has been used on flints and cherts from many areas (Aspinall and Feather 1972; de Bruin, Korthoven, Bakels, and Groen 1972; Ives 1974; Luedtke 1974; 1979; Arps 1978). Also, oxygen isotope analysis has been applied to chert artefacts from Olduvai Gorge (Stiles *et al.* 1974).

In England, G. de G. Sieveking initiated the analytical study of flint axes, an important group of artefacts which had been deliberately avoided in the petrological survey organized by the Implement Petrology Committee of the Council for British Archaeology (Grimes 1979). Sieveking enlisted the help of a team of scientific colleagues, P. T. Craddock, M. J. Hughes, P. Bush, and J. Ferguson. They commenced their study by analysing material from seven flint mines and axe factories (twenty samples from each), all situated on the Chalk outcrops of south-eastern England and western Europe (Sieveking *et al.* 1970, Fig. 1), to which four more were added at a later date (Sieveking *et al.* 1972, Fig. 1). Analysis by optical emission spectroscopy yielded quantitative data on five elements, but the sensitivity of the method was low, and the reproducibility of the results poor. They eventually analysed for eight elements, using atomic absorption spectroscopy for calcium, magnesium, aluminium, and iron; flame photometry for sodium and lithium; and solution spectrophometry for phosphorus. Flint is almost pure silica so, in this context, these are all trace elements and their abundances are given as parts per million (p.p.m.).

Of the seven sites studied in the first report, two could be distinguished from all the others by the abundance of single elements. Spiennes, in Belgium, at the north-eastern end of the Paris Basin, was characterized by high phosphorus values, while Grand Pressigny, in France, at the south-western end of the Paris Basin, was rich in iron. The phosphorus and iron values at these two sites, respectively, showed negligible overlap with other sites (Sieveking *et al.* 1970). The addition of extra sources in the second report reduced the significance of these single element distinctions. Beer, in Devon, the most westerly of the British flint axe factories, showed a considerable overlap in phosphorus values with Spiennes, and in iron values with Grand Pressigny (Sieveking *et al.* 1972, Appendix A). Flints from Beer, however, can be distinguished from Spiennes and Grand Pressigny flints, and indeed from all the other sites, by their very high aluminium values. In general, it was found necessary to consider all eight elements and, for this purpose, multivariate statistical analysis was employed, which showed that 'all the sites so far investigated . . . can now be sufficiently differentiated' (Sieveking *et al.* 1972, p. 153). Closely adjacent sites, such as Cissbury and Blackpatch, only five miles apart on the South Downs in Sussex, tend to have greater chemical similarities than more distant sources.

'The main archaeological results of this programme will be available only when a high proportion of all provenanced flint axes found in Britain, at sites which are not flint mines or sources of raw material, have also been analysed' (Sieveking *et al.* 1972, p. 154). With a total of between 7000 and 8000 flint axes of known provenance in British museums (Sieveking *et al.* 1972 p. 165), this target seems a very distant prospect. Results so far seem to indicate that axes found in the vicinity of flint mines, such as Grimes Graves in Norfolk, were derived from those mines; and that flint axes from well dated archaeological contexts were in use during the period of operation of the flint mines to which they have been attributed (Bush and Sieveking 1979). No details have been published.

The chemical characterization of flint mine products from England and western Europe has also been studied by Aspinall and Feather (1972), using neutron activation analysis. They analysed material from eight of the flint sources studied by Sieveking *et al.* (1972). Their analyses yielded quantitative data on fifteen elements: Na, Cs, Sc, Ta, Cr, Fe, Co, La, Ce, Sm, Eu, Tb, Yb, Th, and U, and qualitative data on nine others. Apart from sodium and iron, which also appeared in the analyses of Sieveking *et al.*, these elements are only present in minute quantities, seldom exceeding one part per million. The precision and reproducibility of the analyses were good, but significant variations in trace element concentrations were found, not only between different flints from the same source, but also between different samples taken from the same specimen of flint. When subjected to this sort of analysis, flint is seen to be no longer as homogeneous as it appears.

The results for six elements and five ratios were presented graphically for each site, relative to the values for Cissbury, which was chosen arbitrarily as a standard (Aspinall and Feather 1972, Fig. 1). Differences between flint sources showed up as visual patterns on these diagrams. Thus, 'in a some-what subjective sense, all available data have been used. . . . The wide scatter of data for a particular element is well shown in Figure 1, where, for every site, very few 'mean concentration' points are situated further than two standard deviations from the value "unity" appropriate to the Cissbury standard' (Aspinall and Feather 1972 p. 48). Like Sieveking *et al.* (1970, 1972), they found clear distinctions between Grand Pressigny and Spiennes and the British sites. Distinctions between the various British sites proved more difficult, particularly between Cissbury and Blackpatch, the two adjacent sites in Sussex.

In Holland, neutron activation analysis was used to characterize the products of three European flint sources (de Bruin *et al.* 1972): Grand Pressigny, in France, and Rijckholt, in Holland, both of which were also included in the British studies (Sieveking *et al.* 1972; Aspinal and Feather 1972), and Hov, in Denmark. The analyses yielded quantitative data on fourteen elements which, after statistical analysis, resulted in good distinctions between the three sources. In Holland, as in England, distinction between closely adjacent flint sources is difficult. At the Linear Pottery sites at Elsloo, Stein, and Sittard, most of the chert (flint) artefacts can be recognized macroscopically as coming from the Gulpen Formation, a division of the Maastrichtian Chalk (Arps 1978, p. 100). There were, however, several possible sources of this raw material, including the flint mine at Rijckholt, where the flint was extracted from the solid Chalk; the quarries at Banholt, Mheer, and Rullen, where the flint was taken from residual deposits (eluvia) overlying the Chalk; and the gravel deposits of the River Maas. Neutron activation analyses were carried out on between 40 and 50 samples from each flint source. The analyses showed that only the flint from Rijckholt had well defined chemical characteristics. Flint from the other quarries, in residual deposits, and from the river gravels had a more varied composition. As a result, the analyses failed to distinguish between the different sources of flint in the Gulpen Formation (Arps 1978, p. 102).

In North America, cherts and jaspers from a wide range of geological formations were exploited in prehistoric times. 'Cherts from different sources are often visually distinctive, and archaeologists working in a particular geographic region quickly become familiar with the most common local chert types. Thus site reports frequently mention that the lithic assemblage is made of chert from a particular source or sources, and it might seem that visual inspection alone is an adequate identification technique' (Luedtke 1979, p. 745). With the current interest in chemical methods of identification, there is a tendency to reject macroscopic identifications as 'subjective, non-quantifiable, and liable to observer perceptual and judgmental errors' (Ives 1974).

Luedtke (1979) has given a lucid account of chert source identification.

The samples which formed the basis for this discussion consisted of 88 chert artefacts from Late Woodland sites in Michigan, and 155 chert samples from the five most important sources for this period and area. The sources considered in this study, which were all well separated from one another, either geographically or stratigraphically, were: the Norwood Chert, from the Middle Devonian of Michigan; the Bayport Chert, from the Upper Mississippian of Michigan; the Upper Mercer Chert, from the Lower Pennsylvanian of Ohio; the Indiana Hornstone, from the Upper Mississippian of Indiana; and the Kettle Point Chert, from the Middle Devonian of Ontario. Quantitative data on 22 trace elements from these samples were obtained by neutron activation analysis.

Luedtke (1979, p. 750) distinguished three types of error, which may in source identification studies. In any such study, there may be a number of known sources to be considered, and also a number of unknown sources, or sources which for some reason are excluded from the study. Type 1 error is the identification of an artefact as coming from one known source, whereas it actually came from another known source. This type of error is particularly liable to occur when two or more sources are geographically and stratigraphically close to one another and, consequently, produce very similar cherts. Such sources are the Cissbury and Blackpatch flint mines, in Sussex (Sieveking *et al.* 1970; 1972; Aspinall and Feather 1972), and the several sources of the Gulpen Flint, in Holland (Arps 1978). Type 2 error is the identification of an artefact as coming from an unknown source, when it actually came from one of the known sources. This type of error may result from inadequate characterization of the source material. Chemical changes in the artefacts, due to weathering, may also result in type 2 errors. Type 3 error is the opposite of type 2, namely the identification of an artefact as coming from one of the known sources, when it actually came from an unknown source. Type 3 error is very liable to occur, so long as any important sources remain undiscovered, especially if such unknown sources are similar to any of those known.

Luedtke found that the best results were obtained by discriminant analysis of log-transformed data for all the trace elements studied (Luedtke 1979, Table 4); the quality of the results was significantly reduced if the number of elements analysed was reduced (Luedtke 1979, Table 6). Visual (macroscopic) identifications were also made of the 88 chert artefacts analysed. These macroscopic identifications were of three kinds: definite attribution to one of the five sources; probable attribution to one of the known sources; and definite exclusion from any of the known sources, i.e. identification as unknown. The basis for comparison of the different techniques of identification was the 'consensus identification', resulting from the use of a variety of techniques (Luedtke 1979, p. 752). If the definite macroscopic identifica- are taken by themselves, it appears that visual inspection is not as efficient as the best chemical analysis. If, however, 'all the "probable" assignments are treated as definite ones, the percentage of correct assignments for visual identifications jumps to 88.6 per cent, a value equal to discriminant analysis [of log-transformed trace element data]. Therefore it can be concluded that for these sources and this identifier, visual inspection was a relatively effective means of identifying sources of chert artefacts' (Luedtke 1979, p. 753).

An entirely different method of chert source characterization, which has been used in East Africa, employs the determination of oxygen isotope ratios (Stiles *et al.* 1974). In this area, the chert nodules are of Pleistocene age, formed by the silicification of layers of magadiite, a hydrous sodium silicate mineral, in saline lake deposits. The oxygen isotope ratios in the chert nodules vary with the salinity of the lake water in which they were formed, higher $^{18}O/^{16}O$ ratios indicating higher salinity (O'Neil and Hay 1973). This method was used to compare material from a chert implement factory with naturally occurring chert nodules in a nearby exposure. The factory chert was found to have generally lower $^{18}O/^{16}O$ ratios than the nodules in the chert bed, thus confirming the differences noted by macroscopic examination, and suggesting that it was formed in waters of lower salinity. 'Most likely this means that the source lay to the south, farther from the centre of the lake, in an area not now exposed by erosion. Palaeogeographic considerations suggest that the source(s) were located no more than 1 km from the factory site, and the distance was probably much less than this' (Stiles *et al.* 1974, p. 291).

In western Japan, the most important raw material for making stone implements was sanukite, a type of hypersthene andesite which 'generally occurs as boulders (a few tens of cm in diameter) in soil' (Higashimura and Warashina 1975, p. 170). When fresh, sanukite is black and glassy, with a good conchoidal fracture. It weathers rather rapidly to a grey colour. Samples were collected from eight sources of natural sanukite, and powdered samples analysed by X-ray fluorescence. The data obtained for seven elements, potassium, calcium, titanium, rubidium, strontium, yttrium, and zirconium, were expressed as ratios: K/Ca, Ti/Ca, Rb/Sr, Y/Sr, and Zr/Sr. Samples of sanukite artefacts from a prehistoric site at Ikegami were analysed in the same way, and successfully correlated with the nearest source, some 20 km away at Nijosan (Higashimura and Warashina 1975, p. 174).

Higashimura and Warashina then experimented with non-destructive analysis. A sanukite block from the Nijosan source was broken, to obtain small pieces of different shape. 'Five samples were taken, each being 5–10 cm^2 in surface area and 0.3–1 cm in thickness. Every sample was measured twice, first on one surface and then turned over' (Higashimura and Warashina 1975, p. 174). The results compared very well with the powdered sample analyses. They then applied this non-destructive method of analysis to sanukite flakes from a number of excavated archaeological sites, all in the vicinity of the Nijosan source (Higashimura and Warashina 1975, Fig. 1). All but one of these flakes was correlated with the Nijosan source, though the quality of the correlation was adversely affected by surface weathering on some samples (Higashimura and Warashina 1975, pp. 176–7).

This Japanese work was extended considerably by Warashina *et al.* (1978), who analysed more than 100 artefacts from 36 archaeological sites. They used the non-destructive method, but 'when flakes of sanukite implements were studied, the surface layer was chipped off to obtain fresh surfaces in order to avoid the effect of weathering suffered after being buried' (Warashina *et al.* 1978, p. 284). Most of the archaeological sites investigated belonged to two important areas of ancient local civilizations, Yamato in the east, and Kibi in the west (Warashina *et al.* 1978, Fig. 1). The Nijosan source is situated in the middle of the Yamato area, and is the most important source of sanukite for that area. Artefacts from the Kibi area do not come from any of the sources studied; they show strong group characteristics and must come from an individual source which has yet to be located (Warashina *et al.* 1978, Fig. 3). Over 90 per cent of the artefacts analysed were traced to definite sources, including the unknown Kibi source.

In Australia, the great Mount William axe quarry, north of Melbourne, is situated in the lower part of the Cambrian Heathcote Greenstone, a formation which was also exploited in two smaller quarries near Mount Camel, some 50 km further north (McBryde 1979, Fig. 3). Both these sources produced axes of actinolite-cummingtonite hornfels, some of which could not be distinguished either in hand specimen or under the microscope (Watchman 1979). Trace element analysis was therefore employed as a supplementary method, to determine the source of those axes which had defied petrological identification. 21 source rocks and 69 axe samples were analysed by X-ray fluorescence for eight elements: rubidium, strontium, yttrium, zirconium, lead, nickel, copper, and zinc. Unfortunately, even in terms of trace element geochemistry, the 'hornfelses from the two quarries are not sufficiently distinct to allow classification of all the axes' (Watchman 1979, p. 125). However, using statistical methods which take all eight elements into consideration, it was possible to attribute most of the 69 axes analysed to the appropriate source.

Interpretation

This history of the development of implement petrology would be incomplete without some reference to the interpretation of the results. To what extent have these results matched up to the aims and aspirations expressed in the early stages of the work? What has been learned, as a result of implement petrology, about exchange mechanisms, early trade routes, or about other factors of economic or social importance?

The most fundamental and important result of implement petrology surveys in several parts of the world is that a large proportion of the stone tools used in an area are the products of a small number of factories (mines, quarries, etc.). Some of these factories are small and serve the area immediately surrounding them. Others are much larger, and their products are still abundant hundreds of kilometres away. Good examples of such large factories include the Langdale (Group VI) axe factory in England (Houlder 1979; Cummins 1979), the Plussulien (Type A) axe factory in Brittany (Le Roux 1979), the Mount William axe quarry in Victoria (McBryde 1979), and the Mount Daruka (Group 2B) axe quarry in New South Wales (Binns and McBryde 1972).

Trade routes may be revealed by relative concentrations of stone implements along natural waterways or ridgeways. The abundance of stone axes in the Thames Valley of England is a good example. One problem of interpretation is to distinguish between the several possible causes of such a concentration. It may be related to a concentration of the Neolithic population and, therefore, of stone axes *in use*; or to prehistoric trade and, therefore, to a high proportion of stone axes *in transit*. It may also result from an accidental bias in the stone axe collections, resulting from a concentration of gravel working, dredging, road making, building, etc., in the valley, in which case it has no prehistoric significance whatever.

The proportion of near perfect and complete axes in the Thames collections is in marked contrast to the fragmentary material usually recovered during excavations of Neolithic habitation sites. Here too, however, there may be an element of bias in the collections. A collector of stone axes might have been unwilling to accept broken specimens when complete ones could be obtained. Adkins and Jackson (1978), in an excellent discussion of the Thames material, concluded that most of the axes were accidentally lost in the river, 'whether as part of the possessions of an immigrant group, part of the stock of a trader, or, perhaps more frequently, as part of the equipment of a villager embarked on a local expedition' (p. 10). Perhaps the clearest example of a stone axe lost in a river during transit is the rough-out from the River Trent, near Nottingham (Cummins 1978). This axe is of Group VII rock, from Penmaenmawr in North Wales: it had never been used. One surface had been worn smooth by the passage over it of abrasive sand as it lay on the river bed. The other side was as fresh and sharp as the day it was flaked (Cummins 1978, Plates 1 and 2).

For further interpretation of distribution patterns, it is clearly necessary to consider the nature of the samples on which they are based. The samples are generally small, both in relation to the size of the area studied, and in terms of the time span during which the tools were in use. They are also generally far from random, having been influenced by a great range of factors, including the distribution of museums, collectors, excavated archaeological sites, and modern centres of population, and variations in the intensity and character of road making, gravel digging, agriculture, and many other activities. The non-random nature of the sample is compounded by the fact that collectors tend to flock to areas where available information suggests that there is a good chance of making finds.

Cummins (1974; 1979), in an attempt to overcome the effect of non-random sampling, prepared contoured *relative* frequency distribution maps for the major stone axe groups of England and Wales. These maps, while lacking the detail of the original distribution patterns, brought out 'significant features of the distributions which have hardly, if at all, appeared on previously published maps' (Cummins 1974, p. 201). Most of the groups have distributions centred around their respective sources, as would be expected from a simple model for primitive trade (Fig. 6.2). Two groups, however, were found to have distributions centred several hundred kilometres from their source areas (Fig. 6.3). Both these groups are numerically important and, between them, account for more than a third of the stone axes in England and Wales (Cummins 1974, Figs 2, 3; 1979, Figs 7, 8). It appears that, for these two groups, trade took place in two stages: bulk carriage from the source to a secondary centre of distribution; and local distribution from the secondary centre. In both cases, the sources are in western, hard rock areas, and the secondary centres in eastern, soft rock areas.

The distribution patterns, by themselves, do not establish whether the motivation for this bulk trade came from the producers or from the consumers. The producers were working in areas of abundant raw materials, where the local demand may have been very limited, and 'successful trade, therefore, depended on finding and exploiting distant markets' (Cummins 1974, p. 204). The consumers, on the other hand, were living in areas of relatively high population density, but without a good supply of stone for axes. They might, therefore, have 'sent prospecting expeditions into the highland zone to try and remedy this deficiency. Location of a suitable rock source might have been followed directly by exploitation, without any need for trade. Indeed, there may have been no native population to trade with. Such exploitation would probably have been accompanied early by the establishment of a permanent colony in the source area' (Cummins 1979, p. 10). The reality of such bulk trade in Neolithic Europe is well attested by the great hoards of Danish flint axes found in northern Sweden, over a thousand kilometres from their source (Becker 1952). These were presumably lost at sea, and are now found some twenty to thirty kilometres inland, because of the post-glacial isostatic uplift of Scandinavia. The largest of these hoards contained 175 axes.

Petrological examination of the stone implements from individual archaeological sites might be expected to demonstrate the use of relatively poor quality local stone, alongside better quality imported material. The ratio

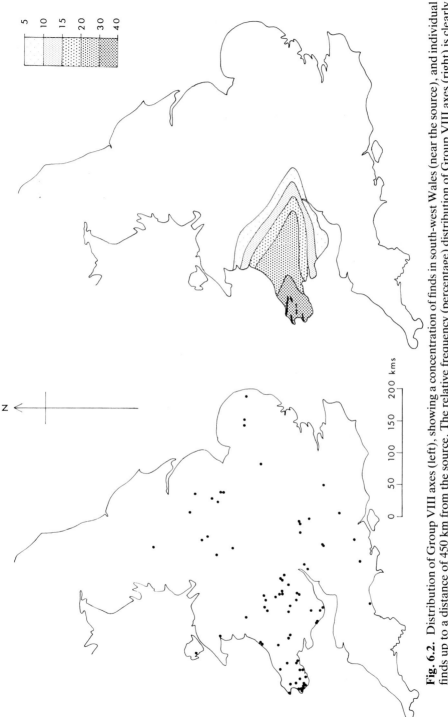

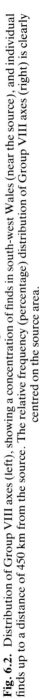

Fig. 6.2. Distribution of Group VIII axes (left), showing a concentration of finds in south-west Wales (near the source), and individual finds up to a distance of 450 km from the source. The relative frequency (percentage) distribution of Group VIII axes (right) is clearly centred on the source area.

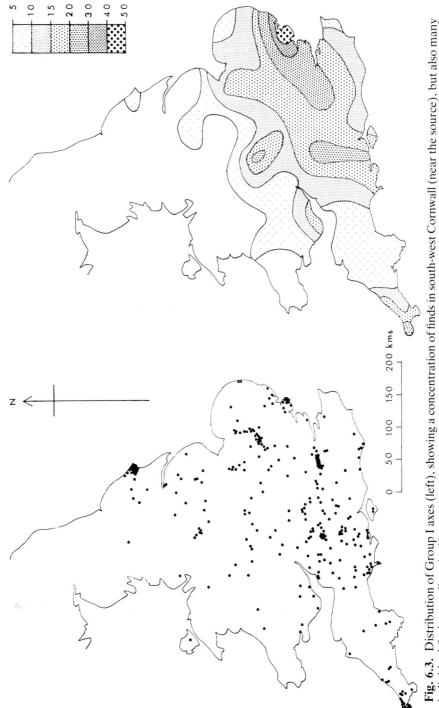

Fig. 6.3. Distribution of Group I axes (left), showing a concentration of finds in south-west Cornwall (near the source), but also many individual finds as well as significant concentrations up to 550 km from the source. The relative frequency (percentage) distribution of Group I axes (right) is complex, but mainly centred several hundred kilometres to the east of the source area.

between the two would depend on the wealth of the inhabitants and the extent of their communications with the outside world. The reverse situation, where poor quality imported stone is used in significant proportions, alongside excellent local stone, would seem unlikely. And yet, this is just what has been found at Puntutjarpa, a site in Western Australia, dating from about 10 000 years BP (Gould 1979, p. 35). The most important tools at this site were the adzes and micro-adzes. Most of these were made of a local white chert, shown in laboratory experiments to hold a better edge than any other chert used on the site. But, in spite of the local availability of this excellent chert, a quarter of the adzes and micro-adzes on the site were made of imported chert of inferior quality, some of it brought from as far as 320 km away. Even if they were unaware of the superiority of the local chert, the inhabitants of this site can hardly have thought that the imported material was actually better, in any functional sense. Ethnographic evidence, however, suggests that these imported cherts may have had a religious or spiritual value, which might well have outweighed their relative inferiority in the material sense. They may have been collected at a sacred site, perhaps associated with an ancestral mythical species (Gould 1979).

In Brittany, Le Roux (1979) has used the stone axe industry as a basis for studying the demography and economy of the Neolithic population. This was possible for two reasons: some 5000 axes have been studied in an extensive implement petrology survey of Brittany and adjacent parts of western France, an area of about 60 000 km²; and the source of the Type A dolerite axes, which account for about 40 per cent of these, has been excavated. The Type A dolerite quarry and axe factory at Plussulien was in operation over a period of 1500 years, from about 5200 BP. An estimate of the volume of quarry and factory waste produced during this period, combined with some experimental work on axe manufacture, suggests an annual output of some 5000 axes. This in turn, taking all the other groups of axes into account, implies an annual consumption of between 12 000 and 13 000 axes in the area studied. Making some reasonable guesses about axe use, Le Roux estimates the population density in this area to be of the order of 1 per km². He goes on to consider the work force required at the quarry, and the size of the population which might have supported it, and concludes that the Plussulien axe factory may have been at the centre of a tribal territory of about 1500 km².

These figures of Le Roux are, of course, only estimates, liable to revision. There are several variables involved in them, about which there is too little information. The importance of this work in the history of implement petrology is that it shows how a comprehensive survey, combined with information from excavations, dating, and experimental archaeology, can yield quantitative data for a study of a prehistoric society.

Stone implement petrology

Introduction

The choice of rock type for the manufacture of stone tools is dependent on three main factors: its suitability for the purpose in mind; the ease with which it can be worked to the required shape; and its availability.

The physical properties of a rock determine, for example, how well a sharp cutting edge will stand up to prolonged use, or how long a heavy hammer stone can be used before it breaks up under repeated impacts. The physical properties also determine how easily the rock can be shaped, whether by flaking (knapping), sawing, pounding, or grinding. The final choice is likely to be a compromise, as the most suitable rock may also be the hardest to work. Such quality decisions can seldom have been made in isolation, and a choice must often have had to be made between utilizing a relatively poor quality local stone and acquiring good tools by trade from a more distant source.

More than forty years of petrological work on stone tools in Britain has shown that a very wide range of rock types – igneous, sedimentary, and metamorphic – was employed. Within this range, however, a few rock types were much more commonly used than all the others. The makers of stone tools were well aware of the physical properties of the rock types, with respect to the tools they were producing. The rock types selected varied from area to area (Fig. 6.4) according to availability. The selection also depended on the type of artefact (Fig. 6.5), either because of different functional requirements, or because of constraints imposed by different methods of manufacture.

In view of the range of tool types to be considered in this chapter, the petrological data are assembled under several broad typological headings.

Pebbles and pebble-derived tools

Unmodified pebbles are among the most basic of tools, and are found on many archaeological sites. Signs of wear may indicate the use to which they were put; for example, abraded edges on hammer-stones, and smoothed surfaces on pebbles used for grinding or polishing. Pebbles used as hammers were often modified to make them more effective. They might be pitted, to provide better hand grip (Miles 1963, p. 74); grooved and pitted, so that a handle could be fixed (Miles 1963, p. 76); or perforated for hafting (Roe 1979). Pitted pebbles might also find a use as drill caps for bow drills (Miles 1963, p. 89).

Many of the earliest artefacts – tools that were made, rather than stones that were used – show evidence of manufacture by striking flakes off pebbles or cobbles (e.g. Leakey 1971*a*). For this reason, it is convenient to consider

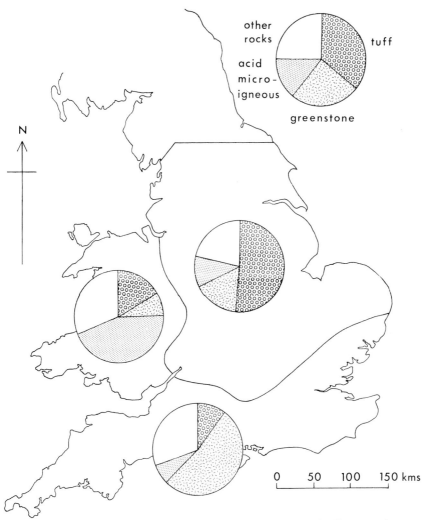

Fig. 6.4. Map of England and Wales, showing the proportion of different rock types used for stone axes in three major provinces. The provinces (Cummins 1980, Fig. 8) are 'Six Land', covering most of northern and central England, in which Group VI axes are dominant; 'West Land', consisting of Wales with Herefordshire and part of Shropshire, in which Group VII axes are more abundant than Group VI axes; and 'South Land', in which Group I axes are more abundant than Group VI axes. The rock types are divided as follows: Tuff, including Groups VI and XX, covers all types except for fine-grained acid varieties; Greenstone, including Groups I, II, III, IV, XVI, and XVII, covers a wide range of altered basic igneous rocks; acid micro-igneous rock, including Groups VII and VIII, covers a variety of fine-grained siliceous rocks such as rhyolite, acid tuff, and felsite. The map illustrates the regional (souce rock availability) control on stone implement petrology. The main sources for 'Six Land' were in Northern England; for 'West Land' in Wales; and for 'South Land' in Cornwall. The proportions for these three provinces combined are shown in the key to the ornament. *Note*: Flint and chert are not included in the data for this map, which is based on 'stone' axes which have been petrologically examined (Cummins 1979).

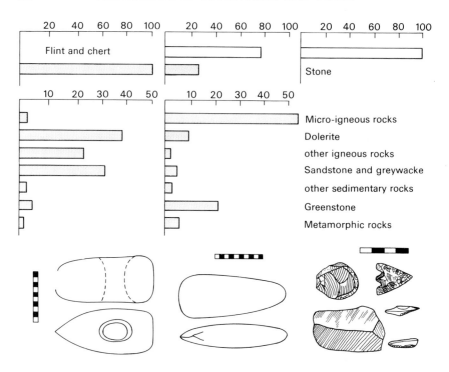

Fig. 6.5. Raw materials used for stone implements in England and Wales. The implement types considered are: (i) blades and points (top); (ii) axes (middle); and (iii) axe hammers (bottom). The scales of the drawings are in centimetres. The rock types used for these implements are classified in two stages. First (left), they are divided into flint and chert (blank), and 'stone' (stippled). Then (middle), the rock types used for the 'stone' implements are further sub-divided. These bar diagrams have percentage scales. Micro-igneous rocks include tuffs (e.g. Group VI) and lavas and rapidly chilled intrusive rocks (e.g. Group VII), all of which can be shaped by flaking (flint technology). This diagram shows the control exerted by implement type on the choice of raw materials.

much of the early Palaeolithic material under this general heading.

Flint is the classic rock type for Palaeolithic tools, and northern France is the classic area for their study. It is no accident that such widely used terms as Chellian, Abbevillian, and Acheulean are based on sites in the river valleys of northern France. The Seine and the Somme have their catchment areas in the Cretaceous and Tertiary strata of the Paris Basin, and the pebbles in their gravels are largely of flint, derived from the Cretaceous Chalk. South-eastern England has a broadly similar geology, and a similar wealth of Palaeolithic sites. There is a close correlation between the distribution of early Palaeolithic sites in Britain and the occurrence of flint-bearing gravel deposits. Less than one per cent of all the early Palaeolithic tools found in Britain were found north-west of a line from the Wash to the Bristol Channel (D.A. Roe 1968). Shotton (1968, p. 478), however, has pointed out out that this distribution may be controlled as much by climatic factors as by the availability of flint.

The almost complete dominance of flint in the Palaeolithic industries of England and France has two possible explanations: the settlement patterns may have been largely controlled by the distribution of this vital raw material for tool making; and flint tools may have found their way into museum collections, in greater numbers than other kinds, because of their superior quality. The great collections of early Palaeolithic tools in the museums of England and France are not the result of careful archaeological excavations, but were made during the course of gravel quarrying, in the days before this was mechanized. The collections are thus biased in favour of the best tools. The flaking quality of flint is so vastly superior to that of the available alternatives that it was flint tools which caught the eye of the gravel digger and collector. Furthermore, the lack of such good tools from other areas will not have encouraged anyone to search there for such tools as might have been found.

In summary then, flint (a variety of chert) was an extremely important raw material in early Palaeolithic times, and was used wherever available. Its distribution may have exerted some control over settlement patterns, though this would be difficult to prove. Its importance has certainly been exaggerated by the non-random manner in which the great national collections were accumulated.

Quartzite, like flint, is a very stable rock type, both chemically and physically. Quartzite pebbles are thus a common component of gravel deposits in many sedimentary and metamorphic areas, and may have passed through several cycles of erosion and sedimentation. The flaking quality of quartzite, however, is very poor by comparison with flint.

Quartzite was used in the early Palaeolithic of Czechoslovakia, and the poor quality and indeterminate typology of the tools was a direct result of this (Neustupny and Neustupny 1961). It was also used for about half the tools at the stratified site at Vertesszollos, in Hungary (Kretzoi and Vertes 1965). The quality of the artefacts at Vertesszollos has 'emphasised the potential problem of recognition of such early industries in gravels or similar deposits where such material is most likely to be represented' (Coles and Higgs 1969, p. 325). In the English Midlands, quartzite is the main rock type to be used as an alternative to flint for Palaeolithic tools, as the latter becomes scarcer towards the west (Posnansky 1963). Similarly in Brittany, west of the Paris Basin, quartzite was used for early Palaeolithic tools (Giot, L'Helgonach, and Mounier 1979). In southern Russia, too, in the area around the Black Sea and the Caspian, quartzite was used (Sulimirski 1960).

On a world map, quartzite would probably be the most widespread raw material used for early Palaeolithic artefacts. It was used in many parts of Africa, including such well known sites for early hominid remains as Olduvai Gorge in Tanzania (Leakey 1971a), and Sterkfontein (Robinson and Mason 1957) and Swartkrans (Brain 1970; Leakey 1970) in South Africa. Quartzite tools have also been found at the Kalambo Falls (Howell and Clark 1964), and in the Sangoan industries of the Limpopo and Zambesi basins (Coles and Higgs 1969), all in the eastern half of southern Africa; and, in smaller proportion, at Baia Farta (Clark 1966), further west. In India, quartzite tools are dominant in a number of areas: the Narmada Valley, north of Bombay (Wainwright and Malik 1967), and Pushkar (Allchin and Goudie 1974), in the west; Madras (Allchin 1963), in the east; and the Soan Valley, in the Punjab (Movius 1948), in the north. Elsewhere in Asia, early Palaeolithic tools of quartzite have been recorded from Malaya (Walker and Sieveking 1962), Cambodia (Saurin 1966), and the Shansi Province of China (Cheng 1966), and later Palaeolithic examples from Thailand (Heekeren and Knuth 1967). Palaeolithic artefacts of quartzite are also known from Peru (Lanning 1970).

Pebble hammers with shaft-holes are widespread in Britain, and the majority of them are made of quartzite (Roe 1979). Many of these quartzite pebbles have a long history. From their Palaeozoic source rocks, they accumulated as pebbles in the Triassic Bunter Pebble Beds, whence they were eroded and redistributed by ice, during the Pleistocene Period; they are now being redistributed again by modern rivers. There are good Mesolithic associations for such tools (Rankine 1949), but they also occur on Neolithic, Bronze Age, Iron Age, and Roman sites (Roe 1979). Since quartzite pebble hammers, like quartzite pebbles, are almost indestructible, it is difficult to be sure whether these later associations are primary or secondary.

Quartz pebbles are common, for similar reasons to quartzite, and were fairly widely used for early Palaeolithic tools. In the Olduvai Gorge (Leakey 1971a), and at Baia Farta (Clark 1966), quartz tools are more abundant than quartzite; and at the Nakapapula rock shelter site, in Zambia (Phillipson 1969), they are completely dominant. They also occur in association with early hominid remains at Choukoutien (Movius 1948). Elsewhere, quartz tools have been recorded from Cambodia (Saurin 1966), Ceylon (Coles and Higgs 1969), and Brittany (Giot, l'Helgouach, and Monnier 1979).

Chert and *jasper* pebbles are stable, like other forms of silica, and both have better flaking qualities than quartz and quartzite. Chert was used at many of the Palaeolithic sites mentioned above, in connection with quartzite and quartz. In Africa, chert tools have been recorded from the Olduvai Gorge (Leakey 1971a), the Kalambo Falls (Howell and Clark 1964), Baia Farta (Clark 1966), and the Nakapapula rock shelter (Phillipson 1969).

Chert was very important in the lower part of Bed II in the Olduvai Gorge succession, but is almost totally absent at other levels (Leakey 1971a, pp. 263–4). This is because the chert was obtained from contemporary lake deposits, which were only accessible during a short period of lowered water level (Hay 1971). Chert tools were associated with the early hominid remains at Choukoutien (Movius 1948). They have been found together with jasper tools in Ceylon (Coles and Higgs 1969), and in Ecuador and Chile (Lanning 1970).

Silicified wood, found in Tertiary deposits in parts of south-east Asia, provided raw material for Palaeolithic tools in Cambodia (Saurin 1966), Burma and Java (Movius 1948).

Sandstone is less well cemented than quartzite. As a result, sandstone pebbles are less stable than quartzite pebbles and wear away more rapidly. Also, the flaking qualities of sandstone, except for the most indurated types, are much inferior to those of quartzite, and any edge produced would tend to be unstable. Not surprisingly, in view of this, early Palaeolithic artefacts of sandstone are rarely reported. Sandstone tools were found associated with the early hominid remains at Choukoutien (Movius 1948), and later Palaeolithic artefacts made from sandstone pebbles are found in Sumatra (Coles and Higgs 1969).

Pebble hammers with shaft-holes were often made from the tougher varieties of sandstone, such as *greywacke* and *sub-greywacke*. In England, a number of these belong to a petrological group (Group XV), whose source is in the Silurian Coniston Grits of the Lake District (Shotton 1959). A factory (or factories), presumed to be in the source area, was responsible for a considerable output of axe hammers and other artefacts. The suggestion that this petrological grouping indicates contemporaneity with the axe hammers (Roe 1979, p. 36) is, unfortunately, not valid. The pebble hammers are made from pebbles, whose derivation from the source area is second or third hand. The distribution of Group XV pebble hammers (Roe 1979, Fig. 15) is related to that of glacial erratics from the southern Lake District (Harmer 1928, Plate 5), and they were presumably made from river pebbles derived from glacial deposits.

Limestone is soluble in acidic water and is much softer than quartz. Limestone pebbles, therefore, tend to be rather shortlived, and are not usually found far from their source outcrops. Limestone does not, at first sight, seem to be a particularly suitable raw material for the manufacture of tools. It flakes fairly well, however, and as far as hardness is concerned, its value would depend on its use: it is harder than meat, for example! Limestone tools were associated with the early hominid remains at Choukoutien (Movius 1948). In South America, Palaeolithic tools were made of silicified limestone in Chile (Lanning 1970), but this, of course, is harder than ordinary limestone and might be termed chert. In north

Karnataka, in India (Paddaya 1977), over 90 per cent of the Acheulean artefacts at one site were of limestone, and here it was a matter of definite selection from the available material. The bed-rock at this site was granite, overlain by 'gravel and rubble', of which limestone formed 41 per cent, granite 33 per cent, and other rocks, including chert, shale, quartzite, quartz, schist, dolerite, and sandstone, made up the remaining 26 per cent.

Dolomite artefacts were associated with early hominid remains at Makapansgat, in South Africa (Brain, Lowe, and Dart 1955).

Volcanic rocks tend to be fine-grained and have good flaking qualities. As pebbles, they are much less durable than quartzite or flint, and rarely occur at any distance from their source. Where available, volcanic rocks were commonly used for making early Palaeolithic tools. Such volcanic artefacts are best known in East Africa, where there has been much recent volcanic activity, abundant early hominid occupation, and a wealth of modern research, initiated over fifty years ago by L. S. B. Leakey.

Basalt, andesite, trachyte, trachyandesite, phonolite, and *nephelinite* were used in the Olduvai Gorge, and at other sites in Tanzania and Kenya (Hay 1971; Leakey 1966; 1971*a, b*; Leakey, Hay, Thurber, Protsch, and Berger 1972). *Basalt* and *ignimbrite* were used in Ethiopia for Oldowan and Acheulian tools, and at least some of the ignimbrite seems to have been quarried from the outcrop (Clark and Kurashina 1979). *Basalt* was also used for making hand axes in the Jordan Valley (Bar-Yosef 1975) and in Israel and the Middle East it was widely used alongside flint (Gilead 1970).

In South America, *basalt, felsite,* and *welded tuff* were used in Chile (Lanning 1971). In south-east Asia, *basalt* was employed in North Vietnam (Borisovski 1967), *rhyolite* in Cambodia (Saurin 1966), and *silicified tuff* in Burma and Java (Movius 1948). *Trachyte* palaeoliths have been recorded from Greece (Dakaris, Higgs, and Hay 1964), and in England, one of *basalt* from Gloucestershire (Evens *et al.* 1972) and one of *andesite* from Derbyshire (Posnansky 1963).

Metamorphic rocks hardly appear in the records of early Palaeolithic industry. *Hornfels* was used in the Shansi Province (Coles and Higgs 1969) and *slate* was among the rock types used at the early hominid sites at Choukoutien, in China (Movius 1948). *Granite gneiss* was occasionally used in the Olduvai Gorge (Hay 1971).

Summary. The range of rock types used in the manufacture of early Palaeolithic tools is very limited. There are two reasons for this. Firstly, siliceous rocks and minerals, such as flint, chert, quartz, and quartzite, are much more stable than all other rock types. Pebbles of these materials are more durable, and therefore more abundant, than pebbles of other rocks. Secondly, fine-grained rocks are more easily worked by flaking than coarse-grained rocks. Thus, volcanic rocks and hornfels would have been easier to work than the coarser-grained intrusive igneous and regional metamorphic rocks.

If we consider pebbles used, more or less unmodified, as hammers, polishers, etc., then the second factor no longer applies. Little systematic petrological work seems to have been done on such objects. Detailed research would almost certainly be unrewarding, though hand specimen identification would be useful. In England, Evens, Grinsell, Piggott, and Wallis (1962) listed petrological identifications for 1200 objects, mainly from the south-western counties. Of these, 26 are listed as pebbles, cupped pebbles, and pebble rubbers. The rock types include the following, in order of abundance: greenstone, sandstone, dolerite, granite, quartzite, slate, greywacke, microgranite, schorl rock (tourmalized granite), and schist. Other implements listed, which may have been largely pebbles, include a burnisher, hammers, a maul, mullers, polishers, pounders, and rubbers. The addition of these would increase the number of pebbles identified to 68. The general pattern remains essentially unaltered, but with the addition of four extra rock types: conglomerate, hornfels, limestone, and rhyolite.

Blades and points

This section covers a wide range of tools, including knives, sickles, saws, arrow and spear points, microliths, awls, burins, and scrapers. The main common factors linking all these tools are sharpness and precision of manufacture – factors which place severe constraints on the rock types that can be used. The ancestors of such precision tools were in use early in Palaeolithic times, and it was quite clear to the early inhabitants of Olduvai Gorge that quartz, quartzite, and chert were vastly superior to volcanic rocks for such tools (Leakey 1971a, p. 264). Recent experimental work at Olduvai Gorge (Jones 1979) has shown that quartzite tools, when used for skinning and cutting meat, remain sharp for longer than similar tools made of the local volcanic rocks. Furthermore, when blunted, such quartzite tools can easily be sharpened by secondary flaking. Basalt cannot be resharpened by secondary flaking and phonolite, though it produces very sharp edges and can be resharpened, is brittle and much more quickly blunted than basalt or trachyandesite.

It should not be forgotten that a variety of raw materials, other than stone, may have been used for blades and points. In Brazil, for example, knives were made of split toucan beaks, split peccary teeth, and ground bamboo, and even the lower jaws of piranha fish were used for cutting tools (Lathrop 1970, p. 62). In North America, arrow and spear points were made of elk-horn, bone, ivory, and wood, as well as of stone (Miles 1963, p. 29).

Glass has excellent flaking properties and, after the arrival of the European settlers, bottles and other sources of manufactured glass were widely exploited both in North America and Australia. A beautiful yellow bottle glass spearhead from northern Australia is illustrated by G. Clark (1967, Fig. 50), and Miles (1963, p. 29) has figured some North American examples. *Obsidian* (Chapter 7) is the most important natural glass and was widely used by prehistoric man, in spite of the fact that obsidian edges are more rapidly blunted than chert edges (Greiser and Sheets 1979). *Tektites* were utilized in the areas where they occur. Thus on the island of Luzon, in the Philippines, two per cent of the blades and flakes are of tektite, in an assemblage dominated by obsidian (Bellwood 1978, p. 73). Flaked tektites are also found on some central European sites (Williams and Nandris 1977). Libyan *desert glass* was also used by prehistoric man (Oakley 1952; Olsen and Underwood 1979). In Western Australia, pieces of *lechatelierite*, a silica glass formed by the action of lightning on sand, are found on some prehistoric sites, but there is no clear evidence that they were ever utilized by man (Glover 1975b).

Flint, chert, and jasper are fine-grained siliceous rocks, composed largely of chalcedony and cryptocrystalline quartz. They are considered together here, for two reasons: they have broadly similar properties; and there are problems of nomenclature, both in the archaeological and in the geological literature.

There is no lack of literature on late Palaeolithic, Mesolithic, and Neolithic blades and points, but most of it is concerned with typological matters. Petrology generally receives no more than a passing mention, under such headings as 'flint industry' and 'chipped stone industry'. The two may well be synonymous: there is no means of telling, because flint, after all, is a stone. Furthermore, 'flint' is not necessarily any more informative than 'chipped stone', if it is used 'in an archaeological rather than a mineralogical sense, to include various kinds of stone that can be flaked easily' (Bandi 1969, p. 107). The implication of Bandi's disarmingly candid statement about his own usage is that flint has a clearly defined petrological meaning. Unfortunately, this is not so; flint is a variety of chert. In Britain, use of the term 'flint' is restricted to the chert nodules in the Upper Cretaceous Chalk. Similar nodules in the Upper Jurassic Portland Beds are always called chert. Tarr's (1938) suggestion that the term flint should be discarded, or reserved for prehistoric flint implements, has had considerable influence (Pettijohn 1957; Gary, McAfee, and Wolf 1972). Thus, many 'flint' artefacts may have their geological provenance in chert formations.

More durable than obsidian, and flaking better than quartz or quartzite, flint and the other varieties of chert were the most valuable raw materials for the manufacture of blades and points. They were quarried; they were mined; they were transported for hundreds of miles. A vast amount of time and energy was expended in making them available as widely as possible. Among prehistoric blade and point assemblages, they are the dominant raw materials over most of Europe, North Africa, the Middle East, North

America, and parts of Australia. To such an extent are they dominant, that it is simpler to list the areas where they are *not* dominant, under various other petrological headings.

Chalcedony, agate, bloodstone, carnelian, and *opal* are fine-grained siliceous minerals, all of which may be semi-precious stones. For prehistoric technology, they had similar properties to chert. Agate, carnelian, and chalcedony artefacts have been reported from various parts of India (Coles and Higgs 1969; Allchin, Goudie, and Hedge 1978; Khatri 1962). Arrowheads of agate are known from Oregon and Washington, in the USA, where they are referred to as 'Oregon gem points' (Miles 1963, p. 29). Chalcedony was used in various parts of southern Africa (Clark 1970), eastern Australia (McBryde 1979, p. 115), western Australia (Clarke, Dix, Dortsch, and Palmer 1978) and in the East Indies (Coles and Higgs 1969; Bellwood 1978). In South America, chalcedony and opal were used in Ecuador (Meggers 1966, p. 35). Bloodstone, from the island of Rhum, was used along the west coast of northern Scotland (Ritchie 1968).

Silcrete and *polymorphic sandstone* are siliceous rocks composed largely of quartz grains, cemented together by chalcedonic silica. Silcrete is widespread in the duricrust of Australia, and is also found in southern Africa. Watts (1978) has provided a recent petrographic study of Australian silcretes. The term 'polymorphic sandstone', first used by Cornet (1894) for a Tertiary formation in the Belgian Congo, was later used for similar rocks in Angola. The most distinctive rock type in these formations is a chalcedonic quartz sandstone (Furon 1963, pp. 288, 298). Because of their chalcedonic cement, these rocks flake like cherts. Silcretes were widely used in Australia (Dickson 1973; Dortch 1977; Dortch and Gardner 1976; Hughes, Sullivan, and Lampert 1973; Sullivan and Simmons 1979). In Western Australia, silcrete was less important than chert and quartzite (Glover 1974). In southeastern Australia, it was more popular than quartz, which was used in areas where silcrete was unobtainable (Sullivan and Simmons 1979, p. 52). Silcrete quarries are known in Victoria (Sullivan and Simmons 1979, Fig. 1) and Western Australia (Clarke *et al.* 1978). Silcrete is a fairly new term in Australia, and there has been some confusion with quartzite, among the coarser varieties, and with chert at the finer end of the range (Sullivan and Simmons 1979). Silcrete was also used in southern Africa (Clark 1970, p. 136, 163), and polymorphic sandstones in the Congo and Angola regions of Africa (Clark 1970, p. 136, 163, 176; Cahen 1978).

In *silicified wood* the original organic structure is replaced by opal or chalcedony. This material was used in the Sudan, in north Africa (Clark 1970, p. 190); in eastern Australia (Dickson 1973); and in the western USA (Miles 1963, p. 29).

Quartz, apart from the best quality rock crystal, does not flake as well as chert. But 'despite its rather unattractive properties quartz will of necessity be used in areas where more desirable stones cannot be found locally or acquired by trade' (Dickson 1977). In Africa, quartz artefacts are mainly found south of the Sahara. Clark (1970) illustrates examples from Ghana (p. 201), Rhodesia (p. 131, 179), Zambia (p. 177), Nigeria (p. 174), East Africa (p. 173), and South Africa (p. 163), as well as from one locality in the north (p. 190) and van Noten (1977) has recently described a quartz microlith assemblage from Matupi Cave, in Zaire. In Australia, quartz was used in the east (Moore 1970), south-east (Sullivan and Simmons 1979), south (Pretty 1977), and west (Glover 1974). It was also used in China (Coles and Higgs 1969, p. 407), and in India and Ceylon (Coles and Higgs 1969, p. 380–1; Misra 1974). In northern Europe, quartz tools are found in Finland (Kivikoski 1967), northern Norway (Indrelid 1975, 1978), northern Sweden (Broadbent 1973), northern Scotland (Knox 1954), and Shetland (Ritchie 1968,p. 136).

Quartzite is less widely used than quartz for blades and points, because its flaking is poorer and less predictable. Quartzite tools, in this category, have been recorded from southern Africa (Clark 1970, pp. 131, 136), from various parts of Australia (Glover 1976; McBryde 1973; O'Connell 1977), from New Mexico (Bryan and Butler 1940), from Norway and Sweden (Indrelid 1978), and from Lepenski Vir, on the Danube (Srejovic 1972).

A variety of other fine-grained rock types have been employed for the manufacture of blades and points by fine flaking. These include *pitchstone* in Scotland (Ritchie 1968); fine *porphyry* in Sweden (Broadbent 1978), glassy *andesite* and *basalt* in New Mexico (Bryan and Butler 1940), *rhyolite* in eastern Australia (Dickson 1973), *basalt* in Norway and Sweden (Fitzhugh 1974), Ecuador (Meggers 1966, p. 31), and in New Zealand (Moore 1976), flinty *mylonite* in Western Australia (Glover 1976), indurated shale in southern Africa (Clark 1970), and sub-greywacke in Western Australia (Clarke *et al.* 1978). Such unlikely rocks as *dolerite, granite,* and *schist* were also occasionally used (Glover 1974).

Chert (including flint and jasper), obsidian, and quartz, are undoubtedly the most important raw materials for prehistoric 'chipped stone industries'. Of these, experimental work suggests that chert is more durable than obsidian (Greiser and Sheets 1979), and easier to work than quartz (Dickson 1977). One might expect, therefore, that chert would be the most favoured raw material, and that obsidian and quartz would be used only in areas where chert was unobtainable. The three are in fact found in different, though not mutually exclusive, geological environments. Obsidian is restricted to geologically recent volcanic areas; quartz is found mainly in older igneous and metamorphic terrains; and chert is most commonly found in sedimentary rock sequences.

The broad distribution of chert, quartz, and obsidian 'chipped stone industries' is clearly related to the geological occurrence of the raw materials. Quartz artefacts are mainly found in the Precambrian shield areas of southern Africa, India, Australia, and Scandinavia. In North America, flint and chert arrowheads are generally dominant; but in the west, where there was much Cainozoic volcanic activity, obsidian takes over (Miles 1963, p. 29).

In areas where two or more of the main raw materials were available, it may be possible to assess their relative value to the prehistoric tool-maker. A Mesolithic site at Bagor, in north-western India (Misra 1974), yielded several hundred thousand microliths, mainly of chert and quartz. Quartz, for which there was a local source, was dominant in the waste material, indicating that it was worked on the site. Chert, which was not available locally, was none-the-less dominant among the finished tools, and was evidently imported as ready-made artefacts. Similar indications of pre-historic preference for chert over quartz come from Australia (Dickson 1977, p. 97). In Central America, the Maya used obsidian and chert (Greiser and Sheets 1979) or flint (Whitlock 1976). In the volcanic highlands, a site at Chalchuapa yielded 37 189 chipped stone artefacts, of which all but fifteen were of obsidian. At Barton Ramie, in the lowlands, 60 per cent of the artefacts were of chert. Selection of stone here was determined partly on the basis of flaking quality (obsidian flakes better than the local chert), and partly by function. Of the 31 scrapers at this site, not one was made of obsidian (Greiser and Sheets 1979, pp. 295–6). Similarly, at many sites in the Near and Middle East (Mellaart 1975), where both obsidian and chert/flint were available, sickle blades were very rarely made of obsidian.

Slate is much softer than the rocks discussed above, but was used to make a wide variety of knives and spearheads in Scandinavia, north-eastern North America, Greenland, Alaska, the north-west Pacific, and interior eastern Asia (Fitzhugh 1974). Slate artefacts are considered separately, under the general heading of blades and points, because they are the products of a different technology. They are made by cutting and grinding, rather than by flaking. The resultant edges are smooth, and not serrated as on flaked tools; they can easily be sharpened, like metal blades, by grinding. Such features are functionally advantageous to communities dependent on fish and marine mammals for their livelihood (Fitzhugh 1974, pp. 52–4). These circum-polar slate industries probably developed independently of the 'chipped stone industries' discussed above, and may be more closely related to bone and antler proto-types (Fitzhugh 1974, p. 52).

Axes and adzes

Axes and adzes are among the most familiar of prehistoric tools. Though it is natural to think of them in terms of tree felling and woodworking, similar tools may have been used as hoes, for tilling the ground, and the prehistoric butchers of Iraq seem to have used them for jointing meat (Kirkbride 1974,

p. 91). The artefacts considered under this heading are simple axes, adzes, celts, chisels, hoes, etc., without shaft-holes.

Such tools were not always made of stone. Bone chisels are recorded from Denmark (Becker 1962) and Spain (Phillips 1975). Becker experimented with modern reproductions of the Danish prehistoric bone chisels, and found them to be effective tools. On many of the Pacific islands, adzes were made from the shells of the giant bivalves *Tridacna* and *Hippopus*, and the gasteropod *Terebra* (Bellwood 1978). These shells were a readily available raw material and, though softer than stone, had the advantage of being easy to work, presumably by cutting and grinding, and easy to sharpen. Shells of the gasteropod *Strombus gigas* were similarly used in Colombia, in South America (Reichel-Dolmatoff 1965).

In some areas, such as West Africa, petrological examination of polished stone tools is inhibited because such objects, referred to as 'God's thunderbolts', have a ritual importance at the present time (Posnansky 1974).

Flint and chert were used to make axes, both of the flaked and the polished variety. Axe manufacture necessitated the use of large pieces of high quality flint, and was therefore restricted to outcrops of the Upper Cretaceous Chalk and other suitable source rocks, from which the flint was mined or quarried. Flint axes are abundant in south-eastern England. In the Thames Valley, they make up 67 per cent of a total of 369 axes described recently (Adkins and Jackson 1978). Further north, in Lincolnshire, Nottingham-shire, and Yorkshire, flint axes represent only about 25 per cent of the total (Moore 1979, p. 83; Manby 1979, p. 71), and they decrease rapidly west-wards, away from the Chalk outcrop. In France, flint axes are dominant in the Paris Basin, but become much less abundant westwards, towards the Palaeozoic areas of Brittany (Le Roux 1979, p. 50).

Greywacke is the only sedimentary rock, other than flint, which has any importance for the manufacture of stone axes. In Australia, greywacke axes are abundant in New South Wales (Binns and McBryde 1969; 1972: Groups 1 and 2) and they are also found in the North Island of New Zealand (Moore 1976, Fig. 5). Greywackes, more or less metamorphosed, were also important in New Guinea (Chappell 1966). In England and Wales, grey-wacke (including the small Cornish Group XIX) and sub-greywacke (includ-ing Group XV from the Lake District, mainly used for axe hammers), together account for no more than about two per cent of all the axes so far examined.

Micaceous sandstone, probably of Carboniferous age, was used for making 'shoe-last adzes' in Belgium. A factory where these tools were made has been excavated near Horion-Hozement, about 12 km west of Liege. Mate-rial recovered from several hut floors illustrated the stages of manufacture, including sawing (Dradon 1967).

Other sedimentary rocks used for axes include a variety of *sandstones,
sedimentary quartzites, siltstones, shales, mudstones,* and *limestones,* but
these are nowhere numerically important.

Basalt seems to be the most widely used volcanic rock. It was important or
dominant at several sites in the Lower Rhine and Meuse, in Holland and
West Germany (Bakels and Arps 1979, p. 59). Basalt axes were abundant in
the Barcelona area of Spain (Phillips 1975, pp. 112, 115). There were great
basalt axe quarries on Hawaii and neighbouring islands (McCoy and Gould
1977). In Australia, basalt was used in New South Wales (Binns and
McBryde 1972, Group 7) and also in the North Island of New Zealand
(Moore 1976). In the Near and Middle East, basalt axes were important at a
number of localities (Kirkbride 1972, p. 8; 1974, p. 91; Mellaart 1975,
pp. 135, 138, 203, 230). In England and Wales, basalt axes are uncommon,
forming under one per cent of the total.

Andesite was probably important as a raw material for axes in South
America. An andesite axe-head from the Caimito complex, in the Upper
Amazon, is illustrated by Lathrop (1970, Fig. 37); such axes are known as
Inca axes and are generally made of andesite. Monolithic axes, in which the
blade and handle are formed together from a single piece of stone, are found
in Colombia, and Reichel-Dolmatoff illustrates one of andesite (Reichel-
Dolmatoff 1965, Plate 50 and p. 152). Extensive use of andesite as a raw
material for making axes in South America is implied by these few examples.
In Central America, andesite and meta-andesite axes have been reported
from La Venta (Curtis 1959). In Australia an altered andesite was exploited
at Berrambool, in Victoria (McBryde 1979; Watchman 1979) and andesite
was the main rock used for adzes and chisels on Mindanao, in the Philippines
(Lynch and Ewing 1968). An axe of andesite has also been recorded from
East Africa (Brown 1969).

Tuffs were the dominant raw materials for stone axes (excluding flint) in
England and Wales. The largest group of axe factories in England is based
on a band of andesitic tuffs in the Borrowdale Volcanic Series of the Lake
District (Bunch and Fell 1949; Houlder 1979). The products of these
factories – Group VI axes – are dominant over a large part of England
(Cummins 1979). Rhyolitic tuffs – Group VIII – have a local importance in
South Wales (Cummins 1979, Fig. 4a). Elsewhere in the world, tuffs do not
seem to have been important in axe manufacture.

Dolerite, particularly fine-grained dolerite which, like basalt, can be
flaked, was popular for making axes in some areas. In Brittany, dolerite axes
are more abundant than any other kind, and most of these are of the
distinctive Type A, produced in the great axe factory at Plussulien (Le Roux
1979). In England and Wales about seven per cent of the stone axes (excluding flint) are of dolerite. About a third of these are of a fine-grained quartz
dolerite, probably derived from the Whin Sill of northern England (Group

XVIII), which was more important as a raw material for axe hammers. Coarser-grained dolerites and related rocks, ranging in composition from quartz dolerite to granodiorite (Groups XIII and XXIII) and derived from sills in South Wales, were locally important (Shotton 1972). Dolerite (diabase) was important in Finland (Kivikoski 1967, p. 40).

Augite granophyre was the raw material for an important group of axe factories in the Penmaenmawr area of North Wales (Houlder 1956). The chilled margin of these intrusions produced a fine-grained rock, which could be worked by flaking, followed by grinding. Products of these axe factories (Group VII axes) are abundant, not only in Wales, but also across large areas of England (Cummins 1979).

Other intrusive igneous rocks do not seem to have been widely used. In England and Wales, axes of the following rocks have been recorded, in decreasing order of abundance: gabbro, diorite, felsitic rocks (microgranite, microgranodiorite, microdiorite, felsite), granodiorite, granophyre, pyroxenite, syenite, porphyry, and granite. Of some three thousand stone axes (excluding flint) so far examined in England and Wales, gabbro reaches about 0.5 per cent, and granite less than 0.1 per cent. There is no indication, in the available literature, that such rocks were any more important for making stone axes in other parts of the world. A granite axe was, however, found at the Olmec site at Tres Zapotes, Mexico.

Greenstones – basic igneous rocks which have been more or less metamorphosed – were highly favoured for making stone axes in many parts of the world. They have undergone various degrees of metamorphism and are listed under a variety of names such as uralitized gabbro, greenschist, amphibolite, actinolitic amphibole schist, epidiorite, and hornblende schist. Owing to the fact that the word for schist in Russian and other languages may be translated into the more common English word 'slate', we also have hornblende slate and green slate. In France, the term *roche verte* is broad enough to cover dolerite as well (Le Roux and Cordier 1974, p. 347).

Amphibolite axes are important or dominant in the Linear Pottery sites of the Lower Rhine and Meuse, in Holland and West Germany (Bakels and Arps 1979, p. 59). At Hienheim, in Bavaria, all the axes were of amphibolite (Bakels and Arps 1979, p. 58), and in Czechoslovakia greenschist, amphibolite, actinolitic amphibole schist, etc., account for nearly all the axes at several sites (Štelcl, Kalousek, and Malina 1970; Štelcl and Malina 1975, pp. 180–5). In Brittany, epidiorites (Type B) made a significant contribution to stone axe production, particularly in the south (Le Roux 1979). In England, greenstone axe production was important in Cornwall, and greenstone axes – particularly Group I – are widespread and abundant all over southern England (Cummins 1979).

There are prehistoric greenstone quarries on the tiny island of Hespriholmen, off the west coast of Norway, south of Bergen (Clark 1952,

Plate XVa). These quarries supplied the raw materials for axe factories on the larger island of Bømlo (Clark 1952, pp. 244–5). The products of these factories are currently being studied, under the direction of Egil Bakka. Greenstone axes from Norway have been reported by Indrelid (1978, pp. 162–3). 'Green slate' axes are abundant in Finland and adjacent parts of Russia (Kivikoski 1967; Clark 1952, pp. 245–6). These implements, described petrologically as fine-grained greenschists (Laitakari 1928, p. 25), are the products of factories north of Petrosavodsk, on the shore of Lake Onega.

Greenstone, greenschist, and amphibolite axes have been recorded along the Mediterranean coast of France (Phillips 1975, pp. 54, 127) and northern Italy (Phillips 1975, p. 80; Bagolini and Biagi 1976a), where several have been discovered during recent excavations of Neolithic sites (Bagolini and Biagi 1976b, p. 52; 1977, p. 50; Bagolini, Balista, and Biagi 1977, p. 83). Greenstone axes seem to be dominant in Provence, southern France, but have not yet been subjected to petrological examination (Courtin 1974, pp. 25, 65, 158, 197, 268). Mme Ricq has recently started work on the stone axes of south-eastern France. Further east in the Mediterranean and in the Middle East, greenstone axes have been recorded from Yugoslavia, Greece, Turkey, Lebanon, the Levant, Iraq, and Syria (Kirkbride 1972, p. 8; Mellaart 1975, pp. 65, 95, 103, 135, 237, 251, 258).

In Australia, there were axe quarries at a number of places in the Cambrian greenstone belt of Victoria (McBryde 1979). The rocks have' suffered thermal metamorphism, and the dominant rock type extracted from the important Mount Wilson and Mount Camel quarries was an actinolite-cummingtonite hornfels (Watchman 1979). Greenstone axes were also made in New South Wales (Binns and McBryde 1972, Group 8).

Elsewhere in the world, greenstone or amphibolite axes have been recorded from central America (Sheels 1978; Curtis 1959), and from Ghana (Clark 1970, p. 201) and Burundi (Van Noten 1969).

Hornfels is the only type of metamorphic rock, other than greenstone, which was important in the manufacture of stone axes. In Northern Ireland, a metamorphosed inter-basaltic soil produced a tough *porcellanite*, which was exploited for axe production at Tievebulliagh, in County Antrim, and on Rathlin Island. The products of these axe factories (Group IX axes) were dominant in Northern Ireland, and are widespread in England, Wales, and Scotland (Jope 1952). A very similar rock was used in New South Wales, Australia (Binns and McBryde 1972, Group 6). *Cordierite hornfels*, with or without biotite, chiastolite, or garnet, was important in New South Wales (Binns and McBryde 1972, Group 5). Similar rocks were used in Britain, but have not been grouped or traced to any one source area. In Scotland, a *calc-silicate hornfels* was the basis for axe production near Killin, in Perthshire (Ritchie 1968). Products of this axe factory (Group XXIV axes) were important in Scotland, and spread into England, but details have not yet been published. Hornfels, and a range of metamorphosed clastic rocks, formed the basis of much of New Guinea's axe production (Chappell 1966). *Metasomatized argillite* was important in adze manufacture in New Zealand (Moore, Keyes, and Orchiston 1979).

Summary. Two facts emerge from this review of stone axe petrology; the range of rock types commonly used for making stone axes was very limited; and similar rock types were selected by different communities, even though they may have been separated by thousands of years and as many kilometres.

Many of the rocks used for making axes – flint, chert, tuffs, the chilled margins of igneous intrusions, hornfels – are fine-grained. Such rocks can be quickly roughed out by flaking, prior to the much slower process of grinding to the required shape. Grinding of the edges probably prevented damage to the blade by accidental flaking during use (Harding and Young 1979). Many flint axes in Britain were edge-ground only, or not ground at all (Manby 1979; Moore 1979). In the Thames Valley, about thirty per cent of the flint axes are described as flaked, or edge-ground only (Adkins and Jackson 1978). Flint was extremely difficult to grind because its hardness is so close to that of quartz, the only abrasive generally available to the prehistoric axe maker (Coope 1979).

The dominance of basic rocks among the igneous and meta-igneous rocks used is another striking fact. Many of these basic rocks – the basalts of Hawaii (McCoy and Gould 1977), the greenstones of Hespriholmen (Clark 1952), the Type A dolerite of Brittany (Le Roux 1979), and the green slate of Lake Onega (Clark 1952) – were fine enough to be roughed out by flaking, as shown by the great accumulation of waste at the factory sites. Others were too coarse to flake effectively. But, fine or coarse, basic rocks are dominant. The Neolithic inhabitants of Cornwall did not make axes of granite, in spite of the fact that granite is far more widespread in that area than greenstone. The reason is simple: the axes were ground, and the edges in particular beautifully polished; the abrasive used was quartz. In basic rocks, all the main mineral constituents are softer than quartz, and therefore relatively easy to grind (Coope 1979).

Shaft-hole implements

The axe hammers, battle axes, mace heads, and shaft-hole adzes of Britain and related areas (Roe 1979), the boat axes of Scandinavia (Kivikoski 1967, Fig. 20), and the banner stones of North America (Miles 1963, pp. 177–9), are included in this section. Some of them, notably the axe hammers, were obviously functional. Many of these show signs of wear at the hammer end and on the blade, and successful tree-felling experiments have been carried out with tools of this kind (Štelcl and Malina 1975, pp. 204–9). Others were prestige objects, of ceremonial rather than functional use (cf. jade axes Chapter 8).

Implements intended for ceremonial use only may be made from a wider range of materials than those of a purely functional nature. At the lower end of the scale, they only have to *look* good. This must be the explanation of the fired clay and pottery battle axes and mace heads that are occasionally found (Evens *et al.* 1962, no. 932; Milisauskas and Kruk 1978, p. 47; F. E. S. Roe 1968, p. 163). At the other end of the scale, the factory product – just the same as hundreds of others – might not be good enough for a powerful chieftain. Such a man would be in a position to have a battle axe or mace head made specially from a rock of his own choice. The remarkable Scottish battle axe with two intersecting quartz veins, showing up white against a dark background, and symmetrically arranged like a St Andrew's cross (Roe 1966, no. 461, Fig. 6b), is unlikely to be the product of an axe factory. There may be many other less obvious examples of 'specially commissioned work' among artefacts of this type. Banded rocks 'and others that were visually attractive' were popular for mace heads in Britain (Roe 1979, p. 30), and Miles (1963, p. 179) refers to the 'artistic choice of materials' for making banner stones in North America.

Greywacke was the dominant rock type used for axe hammers in southern Scotland, particularly in the south-west in the area of their maximum concentration (Roe 1979, p. 28). Work on the petrology of these axe hammers is in progress, but no petrological data have yet been published. *Micaceous subgreywacke*, derived from the Upper Silurian Coniston Grits of the Lake District (Shotton 1959, Group XV), is dominant among the axe hammers of north-western England, and was also used for battle axes and shaft-hole adzes in the same area (Roe 1979). In the axe hammers of this rock, the stratification is sometimes seen to be normal to the shaft-hole. It has been suggested (Coope 1979, p. 100) that beds of the right thickness were quarried and broken up, thus minimizing the amount of pecking and grinding required.

Dolerite was important in several areas. In northern England, the *quartz dolerite* of the Whin Sill (Evens *et al.* 1962, Group XVIII) was used. Group XVIII axe hammers and battle axes are dominant in eastern England, and this rock was also used for shaft-hole adzes and mace heads (Roe 1979). *Olvine dolerite* (diabase) from the Satakunta area, in south-western Finland, was the rock used for a vast output of boat axes (Laitakari 1928; Kivikoski 1967). Other *dolerites* (diabase) of less certain provenance were also used for boat axes in Finland (Laitakari 1928).

Picrite, from a limited source area in west Shropshire (Shotton *et al.* 1951, Group XII) was the main rock used for axe hammers and battle axes over much of central England and Wales (Roe 1979). In France, another ultrabasic rock – *hornblendite* – from Brittany was widely used for making battle axes (Le Roux 1979, Type C).

Greenstone was much less commonly used, in England, for axe hammers than for axes. The reason seems to be that axe hammers have a mainly northern distribution, whereas the greenstone source area is in the south-west. A limited number of battle axes and mace heads of Cornish green-stones are known (Roe 1979). In Czechoslovakia, *amphibolite* and *actinolitic amphibole schist* seem to have been just as popular for making axe hammers as axes (Štelcl and Malina 1975, pp. 184–5). These amphibolite axe hammers, possibly from Zobten (Sobotka) in Poland, are found as far to the west as Belgium and Holland (Van de Waals 1972). In Finland, a variety of metabasic rocks – *amphibolite, greenschist, uralite*, etc. – were used, though none of them came near to the dolerites in numerical importance (Laitakari 1928).

Other rocks used to make shaft-hole implements include *camptonite*, in central England (Shotton 1959, Group XIV; Roe 1979), *spessartite* and *porphyrite* in Czechoslovakia (Štelcl and Malina 1975, p. 185), and a variety of metamorphic rocks in Finland (Laitakari 1928). In North America, the banner stones were made of various intrusive igneous rocks in some areas, and of *slates* in others (Miles 1963, pp. 177–9). The banding in the slates as often symmetrically arranged, for the best visual effect.

In Britain, mace heads were sometimes made from rocks which were important in axe production, such as *flint*, Group I *greenstone*, Group VI *tuff*, Group VII *granophyre*, Group XVIII *quartz dolerite*, Group XX *ashy grit*, and Groups XIII and XXIII *quartz dolerite* to *granodiorite* (Roe 1979). The period of use of these mace heads seems to have overlapped with the last few hundred years of stone axe production (Smith 1979), and they were sometimes produced from the same rock sources. Battle axes, on the other hand, are petrologically much more closely linked with axe hammers (Roe 1979), with which they were probably contemporary (Smith 1979).

Summary. As far as the functional axe hammers are concerned, there is a very clear preference for a limited range of raw materials. The most popular rocks for these tools are basic and ultrabasic igneous and meta-igneous rocks. Next to these come the greywackes and sub-greywackes. The various fine-grained rocks used for axes are notable by their absence. Such fine-grained rocks, which can quickly be roughed out by flaking, would never stand up to heavy use as axe hammers. The hammer end would soon be destroyed by accidental flaking during use. The preference is clearly for heavy massive rocks, generally coarse-grained, and with a texture that makes them resistant to splitting or flaking.

Miscellanea

There are a great many stone tools which lie outside the scope of the preceding sections: arrow shaft smoothers, archers' wrist guards, pestles, mortars, bowls, moulds for bronze axes, etc. Some of these, such as the Californian pestles and mauls (Miles 1963, pp. 47, 75), have distinctive typology, suggesting the possibility of centralized production. Petrological examination of such tools may well prove rewarding. Three types of artefact have been selected for further discussion in this section, all of which are connected with the important business of producing material for clothing.

Spindle whorls and flywheels

Spindle whorls are the most familiar form of flywheel in archaeological collections. Their purpose was simply to give additional angular momentum to the spindle, so that the spin imparted to it by the fingers could be maintained. The flywheels used on pump drills are similar in form and function. Larger flywheels have also been described, and may have belonged to potter's wheels or lathes (Brailsford 1962). Such artefacts do not suffer damage from abrasion or impact during their use, so there is very little restriction on the materials to be used in their manufacture.

Apart from stone, spindle whorls are most commonly made of clay, baked clay, and pottery, including re-used potsherds. Bone spindle whorls are less common. The heads of the humerus and femur (the balls of ball and socket joints) were used in southern England during the Iron Age (e.g. Bulleid and Grey 1917, 1948; Brailsford 1962), and the patella of a whale was used for the flywheel of an Eskimo pump drill (Miles 1963). Wooden spindle whorls are probably under-represented in archaeological collections. One was recovered from a Roman well in Somerset (Rahtz and Greenfield 1977), and wooden flywheels were used on pump drills by the Pueblo Indians (Miles 1963).

It seems likely that adequate raw materials for making spindle whorls were available locally in most areas. While no detailed petrological study of the spindle whorls of any area has yet been undertaken, such information as is available is consistent with the use of local materials. Results from a selection of Iron Age sites in southern England will serve to illustrate this point. At Maiden Castle, in Dorset (Wheeler 1943), nearly all the spindle whorls were made of chalk, which was available on the site. At St Mawgans, in Cornwall (Threipland 1957), most were of slate (reported as 'schist'), of a type available within a few kilometres of the site. The Glastonbury and Meare Lake Villages, in Somerset (Bulleid and Gray 1917, 1948), produced a total of almost 450 spindle whorls, of which nearly three-quarters were of stone. About half of these were identified as Liassic limestone, which is the local bedrock and could have been obtained wherever it rose above the general level of the Lake, as on Meare Hill. The remainder were of sand-stone, which occurs in gravel deposits within a few kilometres of the sites.

Fossils have occasionally been utilized as spindle whorls, and may be added to the petrological data. Ammonites and a plesiosaur vertebra from the local Lias, with central perforations, were found in the Glastonbury and Meare Lake Villages (Bulleid and Gray 1917, 1948). At Bredon Hill, in Gloucestershire (Hencken 1938), a number of stone spindle whorls were described, without petrological data, but one fossil echinoid, with central perforation, was identified as a species occurring in the local Inferior Oolite limestone.

Weights

Weights and plummets have a variety of uses, such as holding down the rooves of houses and the tops of hay ricks, and include the net sinkers used in fishing, and the bolas weights, which have the same function in catching birds (Miles 1963, pp. 12, 38). The purpose, and even the identification, of weights may be far from certain on archaeological sites. Probably the most widely recognized are loom weights. Function seems to place little con-straint on the rock types from which stone weights should be made, and loom weights, which were used indoors, were commonly made of baked clay.

In the absence of any general study of stone weights, the results from a selection of sites in southern England may be reported. Loom weights were abundant in the Somerset lake villages, where they were all of baked clay (Bulleid and Gray 1917, 1953), and at Maiden Castle, in Dorset, where 90 per cent were of chalk and 10 per cent of clay (Wheeler 1943). In north Cornwall, a Bronze Age site at Trevisker (ApSimon and Greenfield 1972) and an Iron Age site at St Mawgans (Threipland 1956) produced crude perforated stones, which were interpreted as rick or thatch weights. These were of locally available shale (given its local name of 'shillet') and slate (recorded as 'schist' at St Mawgans). Rather more specialiazed than these, though for what purpose is not known, are two stone weights, each with the remains of an iron hook in the top, which were recovered from an Iron Age hillfort at Winklebury, in Hampshire (Smith 1977). These are of a white sandstone, which is traced to an outcrop of the Cretaceous Lower Greensand some 68 km to the west.

Bark cloth beaters

Bark cloth beaters were used in south-east Asia, the Pacific Islands, central and south America, and parts of Africa, mainly in areas where the art of weaving was not known. Many were made entirely of wood; others had stone beater-heads, attached to a wooden handle by means of springy rattan strips; and others again were monolithic stone tools, with the handle and head in one piece (Ling 1962). There are little published petrological data on bark cloth beaters, and their inclusion here is more on account of their potential for studies of prehistoric communications. Such highly evolved artefacts are likely to have been traded widely from a limited number of specialist factories.

Serpentine for bark cloth beaters is quarried in the highlands of Sulawesi. An account of their manufacture is given by Ling (1962, p. 208). The quarrying is done with axes, and the final shaping – cutting of grooves – with knives. The finished beater-head is then 'cooked' in water containing leaves of a particular kind, in order to strengthen its 'soul-stuff'. Then, while still warm, it is rubbed with wax to make it smooth and bright. These serpentine beater-heads were traded with the lowland people for other goods.

Other rock types used for bark cloth beaters include *sandstone* and *limestone* in Taiwan, *silicified limestone* in South China, and *andesite* in South China and on Mindanao, in the Philippines (Ling 1966, pp. 199, 200, 207; Lynch and Ewing 1968, p. 12). Bark cloth beaters of *andesite* and *felsite* have been recorded from Chalchuapa, El Salvador, in central America (Sheels 1978).

Acknowledgement

I am very much indebted to Mrs Fiona Roe, who has searched through a great deal of archaeological literature and abstracted petrological data for me. Without her unstinting help, much of the material on which this chapter is based would not have been seen.

References

Adkins, R. and Jackson, R. (1978). Neolithic stone and flint axes from the River Thames. *British Museum Occasional Paper* **1**, 1–72.

Allchin, B. (1963). The Indian stone age sequence. *Journal of the Royal Anthropological Institute* **93**, 210–34.

—— Goudie, A. (1974). Pushkar: prehistory and climatic change in western India. *World Archaeology* **5**, 358–68.

—— —— Hedge, K. (1978). *The prehistory and palaeogeography of the Great Indian Desert*. Academic Press, London.

ApSimon, A. M. and Greenfield, E. (1972). The excavation of Bronze Age and Iron Age settlements at Trevisker, St Eval, Cornwall. *Proceedings of the Prehistoric Society* **38**, 302–81.

Arps, C. E. S. (1978). Petrography and possible origin of adzes and other artefacts from prehistoric sites near Hienheim (Bavaria, Western Germany), Elsloo and Stein (Southern Limburg, The Netherlands). In C. C. Bakels: Four Linearband-keramik settlements and their environment: a palaeoecological study of Sittard, Stein, Elsloo and Heinheim. *Analecta Praehistorica Leidensia* **11**, 202–28.

Aspinall, A. and Feather, S. W. (1972). Neutron activation analysis of prehistoric flint mine products. *Archaeometry* **14**, 41–53.

Bagolini, B. and Biagi, P. (1976a). The origins of the Neolithic in northern Italy. In: G. Baillard (ed.): UISPP IX Congres, Colloque XXI La Neolithisation de l'Europe Occidentale, 58–73.

—— —— (1976b). Vlio, Campo Ceresole; Scavi 1976. *Preistoria Alpina* **12**, 33–60.

—— —— (1977). Ogetti "d'arte neolitica" nel Grippo del vlio di Paderna (Cremona). *Preistoria Alpina* **13**, 47–66.

—— Balista, C., and Biagi, P. (1977). Vlio, Campo Ceresole: Scavi 1977. *Preistoria Alpina* **13**, 67–98.

Bakels, C. C. and Arps, C. E. S. (1979). Adzes from Linear Pottery sites: their raw material and their provenance. In: T. H. McK. Clough and W. A. Cummins (ed.): Stone axe studies. *Research Report Council for British Archaeology* **23**, 57–64.

Balcer, B. (1976). Position and stratigraphy of flint deposits, development of exploitation and importance of the Świeciechów flint in prehistory. *Acta Archaeologica Carpathica* **16**, 179–99.

Bandi, H. G. (1969). *Eskimo prehistory.* Methuen, London.

Bar-Yosef, O. (1975). Early man in the Jordan Valley. *Archaeology* **28**, 30–7.

Becker, C. J. (1952). Die nordschwedischen flintdepots. Ein beitrag zur geschichte des neolithischen fernhandels in Skandinavien. *Acta Archaeologica* **23**, 31–79.

—— (1962). A Danish hoard containing Neolithic chisels. *Acta Archaeologica* **33**, 79–92.

Bellwood, P. (1978). *Man's conquest of the Pacific.* Collins, London.

Binns, R. A. and McBryde, I. (1969). Preliminary report on a petrological study of ground-edge artefacts from northern New South Wales, Australia. *Proceedings of the Prehistoric Society* **35**, 229–35.

—— —— (1972). A petrological analysis of ground-edge artefacts from northern New South Wales. Australian Institute of Aboriginal Studies Canberra. (*Publication no. 47.*)

Bishop, M. J. (1974). A preliminary report on the Middle Pleistocene mammal bearing deposits of Westbury-sub-Mendip, Somerset. *Proceedings of the University of Bristol Spelaeological Society* **13**, 301–18.

Bishop, M. J. (1975). Earliest record of man's presence in Britain. *Nature* **253**, 95–7.

Blackman, M. J. (1974). An analysis of jasper artefacts and source materials by atomic absorption and flame photometry. *Newsletter of Lithic Technology* **3**, 40 (abstract).

Borisovski, P. I. (1967). Problems of the Palaeolithic and of the Mesolithic of South East Asia. *Asian and Pacific Archaeology Series* **1**, 41–6.

Brailsford, J. W. (1962). *Hod Hill Vol. 1 Antiquities from Hod Hill in the Durden Collection.* British Museum, London.

Brain, C. K. (1970). New finds at Swartkrans australopithecine site. *Nature* **225**, 1112–19.

—— Lowe, C.van R., and Dart, R. A. (1955). Kafuan stone artefacts in the post-Australopithecine breccia at Makapansgat. *Nature* **175**, 16–18.

Broadbent, N. D. (1973). Prehistoric quartz quarrying in Norrland. *Fornvännen* **68**, 129–37.

—— (1978). Prehistoric settlement in northern Sweden: a brief survey and a case study. In: P. Mellars (ed.): *The early Post-Glacial settlement of Northern Europe.* Duckworth, London, 177–204.

Brown, J. (1969). Some polished stone axes from East Africa. *Azania* **4**, 160–66.

Bryan, K. and Butler, A. P. (1940). Artifacts made of the glassy andesite of San Antonio Mountain, Rio Arriba County, New Mexico. *Bulletin of the University of New Mexico* **349**, 27–31. (Anthropology series, v. 3, no. 4.)

Bulleid, A. and Gray, H.St.G. (1917). *The Glastonbury Lake Village.* Vol. 2. Taunton, 353–724.

—— —— (1948–1953). *The Meare Lake Village.* Taunton, (2 vols).

Bunch, B. and Fell, C. I. (1949). A stone axe factory at Pike of Stickle, Great Langdale, Westmorland. *Proceedings of the Prehistoric Society* 15, 1–20.

Bush, P. R. and Sieveking, G.de G. (1979). Geochemistry and the provenance of flint axes (synopsis). In: T. H. McK. Clough and W. A. Cummins (ed.): Stone axe studies. *Research Reports Council for British Archaeology* 23, 97.

Cahen, D. (1978). New excavations at Gombe (ex-Kalina) Point, Kinshasa, Zaire. *Antiquity* 51, 35–40.

Celoria, F. (1974). Preliminary list of Neolithic axes from the London region with petrographic data. *London studies* 1, 87–92.

Chappell, J. (1966). Stone axe factories in the Highlands of East New Guinea. *Proceedings of the Prehistoric Society* 32, 96–121.

Cheng, T. K. (1966). *New light on prehistoric China.* Heffer, Cambridge.

Clark, G. (1976). *The Stone Age hunters.* Thames and Hudson, London.

Clark, J. D. (1966). *The distribution of prehistoric culture in Angola.* Subsidios para a História Arquelogia e Etrografia dos Poros da Lunda Musev do Dundo, Lisbon.

—— (1970). *The prehistory of Africa.* Thames and Hudson, London.

—— Kurashina, H. (1979). Hominid occupation of the East-Central Highlands of Ethiopia in the Pleistocene. *Nature* 282, 33–9.

Clark, J. G. D. (1952). *Prehistoric Europe. The economic basis.* Methuen, London.

—— Piggott, S. (1933). The age of the British flint mines. *Antiquity* 7, 166–83.

Clarke, J., Dix, W. C., Dortch, C. E. and Palmer, K. (1978). Aboriginal sites on Millstream Station, Pilbara, Western Australia. *Record of the Western Australian Museum* 6, 221–57.

Clough, T. H. McK. and Cummins, W. A. (ed.) (1979). Stone axe studies. *Research Reports Council for British Archaeology* 23, viii + 137.

—— Green, B. (1972). The petrological identification of stone implements from East Anglia. *Proceedings of the Prehistoric Society* 38, 108–55.

Cogné, J. and Giot, P. R. (1952). Etude pétrographique des haches polies de Bretagne, I. *Bulletin de la Société Préhistorique Française* 49, 388–95.

—— —— (1953). Etude pétrographique des haches polies de Bretagne, II. *Bulletin de la Société Préhistorique Française* 50, 37–9.

—— —— (1954). Etude pétrographique des haches polies de Bretagne, III. *Bulletin de la Société Préhistorique Française* 51, 28.

—— —— (1955). Etude pétrographique des haches polies de Bretagne, IV. *Bulletin de la Société Préhistorique Française* 52, 401–9.

—— —— (1957). Etude pétrographique des haches polies de Bretagne V. *Bulletin de la Société Préhistorique Française* 54, 240–41.

Coles, J. M. and Higgs, E. S. (1969). *The archaeology of early man.* Faber and Faber, London.

Coope, G. R. (1979). The influence of geology on the manufacture of Neolithic and Bronze Age stone implements in the British Isles. In: T. H. McK. Clough and W. A. Cummins (ed.): Stone axe studies. *Research Reports Council for British Archaeology* 23, 98–101.

Cornet, J. (1894). Les formations post-primaires du basin du Congo. *Annales de la Société Géologique de Belgique* 21, 193–279.

Courtin, J. (1974). Le Neolithique de la Provence. *Mémoires de la Société Préhistorique Française* 11.

Cummins, W. A. (1974). The Neolithic stone axe trade in Britain. *Antiquity* 48, 201–5.

—— (1978). A Graig Lwyd stone axe rough-out from Holme Pierrepont, Nottinghamshire. *Transactions of the Thoroton Society* **82**, 66–8.

—— (1979). Neolithic stone axes: distribution and trade in England and Wales. In: T. H. McK. Clough and W. A. Cummins (ed.): Stone axe studies. *Research Reports Council for British Archaeology* **23**, 5–12.

—— (1980). Stone axes as a guide to Neolithic communications and boundaries in England and Wales. *Proceedings of the Prehistoric Society* **46**, 45–60.

—— Moore, C. N. (1973). Petrological identification of stone implements from Lincolnshire, Nottinghamshire, and Rutland. *Proceedings of the Prehistoric Society* **39**, 219–55.

Curry, D. (1963). On rotten flint pebbles in the Palaeogene of Southern England. *Proceedings of the Geologists' Association* **74**, 457–60.

Curtis, G. H. (1959). The petrology of artifacts and architectural stone at La Venta. *Bulletin of the Bureau of American Ethnology* **170** (Appendix 4), 284–9.

Dakaris, S. I., Higgs, E. S. and Hay, R. W. (1964). The climate, environment and industries of Stone Age Greece. *Proceedings of the Prehistoric Society* **30**, 199–244.

De Bruin, M., Korthoven, P. J. M., Bakels, C. C., and Groen, F. C. A. (1972). The use of non-destructive activation analysis and pattern recognition in the study of flint artefacts. *Archaeometry* **14**, 55–63.

Dickson, F. P. (1973). Backed blades and points. *Mankind* **9**, 7–14.

—— (1977). Quartz flaking. In: R. V. S. Wright (ed.): Stone tools as cultural markers. *Prehistory and material culture series Australian Institute of Aboriginal Studies* **12**, 97–103.

Dortch, C. E. (1977). Early and Late stone industrial phases in Western Australia. In: R. V. S. Wright (ed.): Stone tools as cultural markers. *Prehistory and material culture series Australian Institute for Aboriginal Studies* **12**, 104–32.

—— Gardner, G. (1976). Archaeological investigations in the Northcliffe District, Western Australia. *Records of the Western Australian Museum* **4**, 257–93.

Dradon, M. G. (1967). Decouverte d'ateliers de taille et de finition d'herminettes Omaliennes. *Helinium* **7**, 253–9.

Dugdale, W. (1956). *The Antiquities of Warwickshire*. London.

Evens, E. D., Grinsell, L. V., Piggott, S., and Wallis, F. S. (1962). Fourth report of the sub-committee of the South-western Group of Museums and Art Galleries on the petrological identification of stone axes. *Proceedings of the Prehistoric Society* **28**, 209–66.

—— Smith, I. F., and Wallis, F. S. (1972). The petrological identification of stone implements from south-western England. *Proceedings of the Prehistoric Society* **38**, 235–75.

Fitzhugh, W. (1974). Ground slates in the Scandinavian younger Stone Age, with reference to circumpolar maritime adaptations. *Proceedings of the Prehistoric Society* **40**, 45–58.

Furon, R. (1963). *Geology of Africa*. Oliver and Boyd, Edinburgh.

Gary, M., McAfee, R. and Wolf, C. L. (ed.) (1972). *Glossary of geology*. American Geological Institute, Washington DC.

Gilead, D. (1970). Handaxe industries in Israel and the Near East. *World Archaeology* **2**, 1–11.

Giot, P. R. (1951). A petrological investigation of Breton stone axes. *Proceedings of the Prehistoric Society* **17**, 228.

—— (1959). Étude petrographique des haches polies de Bretagne VI. *Bulletin de la Société Préhistorique Française* **56**, 43–5.

—— l'Helgouach, J. and Monnier, J. L. (1979). *Préhistoire de la Bretagne*. Ouest, Rennes, France.

Glover, J. E. (1974). Petrology of chert artefacts from Devil's Lair, Western Australia. *Journal of the Royal Society of Western Australia* **57**, 51–3.

—— (1975a). Aboriginal chert artefacts, probably from quarries on the continental shelf, Western Australia. *Search* **6**, 392–4.

—— (1975b). The petrology and probable stratigraphic significance of aboriginal artefacts from part of south-western Australia. *Journal of the Royal Society of Western Australia* **58**, 75–85.

—— (1976). The petrology and archaeological significance of mylonitic rocks in the Precambrian shield near Perth, Western Australia. *Journal of the Royal Society of Western Australia* **59**, 33–8.

—— (1979). The mineral properties and probable provenance of a 33,000 year old opaline artefact from Devil's Lair, South-western Australia. *Records of the Western Australian Museum* **7**, 369–74.

—— Cockbain, A. E. (1971). Transported aboriginal artefact material, Perth Basin, Western Australia. *Nature* **234**, 545–6.

Gould, R. A. (1979). Exotic stones and battered bones. *Archaeology* **32**, 29–37.

Greiser, S. T. and Sheets, P. D. (1979). Raw materials as a functional variable in use-wear studies. In: B. Hayden (ed.): *Lithic use-wear analysis*. Academic Press, London, 289–99.

Grimes, W. F. (1979). The history of implement petrology in Britain. In: T. H. McK. Clough and W. A. Cummins (ed.): Stone axe studies. *Research Reports Council for British Archaeology* **23**, 1–4.

Harding, A. and Young, R. (1979). Reconstruction of the hafting methods and function of stone implements. In: T. H. McK. Clough and W. A. Cummins (ed.): Stone axe studies. *Research Reports Council for British Archaeology* **23**, 102–5.

Harmer, F. W. (1928). The distribution of erratics and drift. *Proceedings of the Yorkshire Geological Society* **21**, 79–150.

Hay, R. L. (1971). Geologic background of Beds I and II: stratigraphic summary. In: M. D. Leakey (ed.): *Olduvai Gorge*, vol. 3. Cambridge University Press, 9–18.

Heekeren, H. R.van and Knuth, E. (1967). *Archaeological excavations in Thailand. Vol. 1: Sai Yok*. Munksgaard, Copenhagen.

Hencken, T. C. (1938). The excavation of an Iron Age Camp on Bredon Hill, Gloucestershire 1935–1937. *Archaeological Journal* **95**, 1–111.

Higashimura, T. and Warashina, T. (1975). Sourcing of sanukite stone implements by X-ray fluorescence analysis. *Journal of Archaeological Science* **2**, 169–78.

Houlder, C. H. (1956). The Graig Lwyd group of axe factories. In: *Caernarvonshire. Vol. I*. Royal Commission on Ancient and Historic Monuments, Wales and Monmouthshire, p. xli–lvii.

Houlder, C. H. (1961). The excavation of a Neolithic stone implement factory on Mynydd Rhiw in Caernarvonshire. *Proceedings of the Prehistoric Society* **27**, 108–43.

—— (1979). The Langdale and Scafell Pike axe factory sites: a field survey. In: T. H. McK. Clough and W. A. Cummins (ed.): Stone axe studies. *Research Reports Council for British Archaeology* **23**, 87–9.

Howell, F. C. and Clark, J. D. (1964). Acheulian hunter gatherers of sub-Saharan Africa. In: F. Bourlière and F. C. Howell (ed.): *African ecology and human evolution*. Methuen, London, 458–533.

Hughes, P. J., Sullivan, M. E. and Lampert, R. (1973). The use of silcrete by Aborigines in southern coastal New South Wales. *Archaeology and physical anthropology in Oceania* **8**, 220–25.

Indrelid, S. (1975). Problems relating to the Early Mesolithic settlement of southern Norway. *Norwegian Archaeological Review* **8**, 1–18.

—— (1978). Mesolithic economy and settlement patterns in Norway. In: P. Mellars (ed.): *The early post-glacial settlement of Northern Europe*. Duckworth, London, 147–76.

Ives, D. J. (1974). Activation analysis at the UMC Laboratory for Nuclear Archaeology: II Lithics. *Newsletter of Lithic Technology* **3**, 42 (abstract).

Jones, P. R. (1979). Effects of raw materials on biface manufacture. *Science* **204**, 835–6.

Jope, E. M. (1952). Porcellanite axes from factories in north-east Ireland. *Ulster Journal of Archaeology* **15**, 31–55.

Keen, L. and Radley, J. (1971). Report on the petrological identification of stone axes from Yorkshire. *Proceedings of the Prehistoric Society* **37**, 16–37.

Keiller, A., Piggott, S., and Wallis, F. S. (1941). First report of the sub-committee of the South-western Group of Museums and Art Galleries on the petrological identification of stone axes. *Proceedings of the Prehistoric Society* **7**, 50–72.

Khatri, A. P. (1962). Origin and development of Series II Culture of India. *Proceedings of the Prehistoric Society* **28**, 191–208.

Kirkbridge, D. (1972). Umm Dabaghiyah 1971: a preliminary report. *Irak* **34**, 3–15.

—— (1974). Umm Dabaghiyah: a trading outpost? *Irak* **36**, 85–92.

Kivikoski, E. (1967). *Finland*. Thames and Hudson, London.

Knowles, W. J. (1903). Stone axe factories near Cushendall, County Antrim. *Journal of the Royal Anthropological Institute* **33**, 360–6.

Knox, E. M. (1954). Pollen analysis of a peat at Kingsteps Quarry, Nairn. *Transactions and Proceedings of the Botanical Society of Edinburgh* **36**, 224–9.

Kolderup, N. H. (1925). Petrologische untersuchungen über das material für wekzeuge im westlichen Norwegen. *Tschermaks Mineralogische und Petrogaphische Mitteilungen* **38**, 165–74.

Kretzoi, M. and Vertes, L. (1965). Upper Biharian (intermindel) pebble industry occupation site in western Hungary. *Current Anthropology* **6**, 74–87.

Laitakari, A. von (1928). Die schaftlochaxte der Steinzeit, von geologische-petrographischem standpunkt. *Suomen Muinaismuistoyhdistyksen Aikakauskirja Finska Fornminnesföreningens Tidskrift* **38**, 1–38.

Lanning, E. (1970). Pleistocene man in South America. *World Archaeology* **2**, 90–111.

Lathrop, D. W. (1970). *The Upper Amazon*. Thames and Hudson, London.

Leakey, M. D. (1966). Primitive artefacts from Kanapoi Valley (Kenya). *Nature* **212**, 579–81.

—— (1970). Stone artefacts from Swartkrans. *Nature* **225**, 1222–5.

—— (1971a). *Olduvai Gorge Volume 3. Excavations in Beds I and II, 1960–1963*. Cambridge University Press.

—— (1971b). Discovery of post-cranial remains of *Homo erectus* and associated artefacts in Bed IV at Olduvai Gorge, Tanzania. *Nature* **232**, 380–3.

—— Hay, R. L., Thurber, D. L., Protsch, R. and Berger, R. (1972). Stratigraphy, archaeology, and age of the Ndutu and Naisiusu Beds, Olduvai Gorge, Tanzania. *World Archaeology* **3**, 328–41.

Le Roux, C. T. (1971). A stone-axe factory in Brittany. *Antiquity* **45**, 283–8.

—— (1979). Stone axes of Brittany and the Marches. In: T. H. McK. Clough, and W. A. Cummins (ed.): Stone axe studies. *Research Reports Council for British Archaeology* **23**, 49–56.

—— Cordier, G. (1974). Étude petrographique des Haches Polies de Touraine. *Bulletin de la Société Préhistorique Française* **71**, 335–54.

Ling, S. S. (1966). Stone bark cloth beaters of South China, South-east Asia and Central America. *Bulletin of the Institute of Ethnology Sinica* **13**, 195–212.

Luedtke, B. (1974). Characterisation of chert sources by neutron activation analysis. *Newsletter of Lithic Technology* **3**, 41, (abstract).

—— (1979). The identification of sources of chert artefact. *American Antiquity* **44**, 744–57.

Lynch, F. X. and Ewing, J. F. (1968). Twelve ground-stone implements from Mindanao, Philippine Islands. *Asian and Pacific Archaeology Series* **2**, 7–20.

Manby, T. G. (1979). Typology, materials, and distribution of flint and stone axes in Yorkshire. In: T. H. McK. Clough and W. A. Cummins (ed.): Stone axe studies. *Research Reports Council for British Archaeology* **23**, 65–81.

McBryde, I. (1973). Stone arrangements and a quartzite quarry site at Brewarrina. *Mankind* **9**, 118–21.

—— (1978). *Wil-im-ee-Moor-ring*: or, Where do axes come from? *Mankind* **11**, 354–82.

—— (1979). Petrology and prehistory: lithic evidence for exploitation of stone resources and exchange systems in Australia. In: T. H. McK. Clough and W. A. Cummins (ed.): Stone axe studies. *Research Reports Council for British Archaeology* **23**, 113–26.

McCoy, P. and Gould, R. A. (1977). Alpine archaeology in Hawaii. *Archaeology* **30**, 234–43.

Meggers, B. J. (1966). *Ecuador*. Thames and Hudson, London.

Mellaart, J. (1975). *The Neolithic of the Near East*. Thames and Hudson, London.

Miles, C. (1963). *Indian and Eskimo artefacts of North America*. Bonanza, New York.

Milisauskas, S. and Kruk, J. (1978). A Neolithic settlement in south-eastern Poland. *Archaeology* **31**, 44–52.

Misra, V. N. (1974). Bagor – a Late Mesolithic settlement in northwest India. *World Archaeology* **5**, 92–110.

Moore, C. N. (1979). Stone axes from the East Midlands. In: T. H. McK. Clough and W. A. Cummins (ed.): Stone axe studies. *Research Reports Council for British Archaeology* **23**, 82–6.

—— Cummins, W. A. (1974). Petrological identification of stone implements from Derbyshire and Leicestershire. *Proceedings of the Prehistoric Society* **40**, 59–78.

Moore, D. R. (1970). Results of an archaeological survey of the Hunter River Valley. *Records of the Australian Museum* **28**(2), 25–64.

Moore, P. R. (1976). The Tahanga Basalt: an important stone resource in North Island prehistory. *Records Auckland Institute and Museum* **13**, 77–93.

—— Keyes, I. W. and Orchiston, D. W. (1979). New records and an analysis of the side-hafted adze from New Zealand. *New Zealand Journal of Archaeology* **1**, 53–84.

Movius, H. L. (1948). The Lower Palaeolithic cultures of southern and eastern Asia. *Transactions of the American Philosophical Society* N.S. **38**, 329–420.

Neustupny, E. and Neustupny, J. (1961). *Czechoslovakia*. Thames and Hudson, London.

Nicolas, J. and Sagon, J. P. (1963). Nouvelles observations sur les roches vertes de l'anticlinal de Laniscat Merleac (C-de-N). *Bulletin de la Société Géologique de France* **7**, 844–51.

Oakley, K. P. (1952). Dating the Libyan Desert silica glass. *Nature* **170**, 447–9.

O'Connell, J. F. (1977). Aspects of variation in Central Australian lithic assemblages. In: R. V. S. Wright (ed.): *Stone tools as cultural markers*. Australian Institute of Aboriginal Studies, Canberra, 269–81.

Olsen, J. W. and Underwood, J. R. (1979). Desert glass: an enigma. *Aramco World Magazine* **30**(5), 2–5.

O'Neil, J. R. and Hay, R. L. (1973). O^{18}/O^{16} ratios in cherts associated with the saline lake deposits of East Africa. *Earth and Planetary Science Letters* **19**, 257–66.

Paddaya, K. (1977). An Acheulian occupation site at Hunsgi, Peninsular India: a summary of the results of two seasons of excavation (1975–6). *World Archaeology* **8**, 344–55.

Pettijohn, F. J. (1957). *Sedimentary rocks.* Harper, New York.

Phillips, P. (1975). *Early farmers of West Mediterranean Europe.* Hutchinson, London.

Phillipson, D. W. (1969). The prehistoric sequence at Nakapapula Rockshelter, Zambia. *Proceedings of the Prehistoric Society* **35**, 172–202.

Posnansky, M. (1963). The Lower and Middle Palaeolithic industries of the English East Midlands. *Proceedings of the Prehistoric Society* **29**, 357–94.

—— (1974). Aspects of early West African trade. *World Archaeology* **5**, 149–62.

Pretty, G. L. (1977). The cultural chronology of the Roonka Flat. In: R. V. S. Wright (ed.): *Stone tools as cultural markers.* Australian Institute of Aboriginal Studies, Canberra, 288–331.

Radley, J. and Mellars, P. (1964). A Mesolithic structure at Deepcar, Yorkshire, England, and the affinities of its associated flint industries. *Proceedings of the Prehistoric Society* **30**, 1–24.

Rahtz, P. A. and Greenfield, E. (1977). Excavations at Chew Valley Lake, Somerset. *Archaeological Reports Department of the Environment* **8**.

Rankine, W. F. (1949). Stone 'maceheads' with Mesolithic associations from south-eastern England. *Proceedings of the Prehistoric Society* **15**, 70–76.

—— (1951). Artefacts of Portland Chert in southern England. *Proceedings of the Prehistoric Society* **17**, 93–4.

Reichel-Dolmatoff, G. (1965). *Colombia.* Thames and Hudson, London.

Ritchie, P. R. (1968). The stone implement trade in third millennium Scotland. In: J. M. Coles and D. D. A. Simpson (ed.): *Studies in Ancient Europe.* Leicester University Press, 117–36.

Robinson, J. T. and Mason, R. J. (1957). Occurrence of stone artefacts with *Australopithecus* at Sterkfontein. *Nature* **180**, 521–4.

Roe, D. A. (1968). A gazetteer of British Lower and Middle Palaeolithic sites. *Research Reports Council for British Archaeology* **8**.

Roe, F. E. S. (1966). The battle axe series in Britain. *Proceedings of the Prehistoric Society* **32**, 199–245.

—— (1968). Stone mace heads and the latest Neolithic cultures in the British Isles. In: J. M. Coles and D. D. A. Simpson (ed.): *Studies in Ancient Europe.* Leicester University Press, 145–72.

—— (1979). Typology of stone implements with shaftholes. In: T. H. McK. Clough and W. A. Cummins (ed.): Stone axe studies. *Research Reports Council for British Archaeology* **23**, 23–48.

Saurin, E. (1966). Le Palaeolithique du Cambodge oriental. *Asian perspectives* **9**, 96–110.

Schild, R. (1976). Flint mining and trade in Polish prehistory as seen from the perspective of the Chocolate Flint of Central Poland. A second approach. *Acta Archaeologica Carpathica* **16**, 147–76.

Scott, L. G. and Calder, C. S. T. (1954). Notes on a chambered cairn and a working gallery, on the Beorgs of Uyea, Northmaven, Shetland. *Proceedings of the Society of Antiquities of Scotland* **86**, 171–7.

Sheels, P. D. (1978) Artifacts. In: R. J. Sharer (ed.): *The prehistory of Chalchuapa, El Salvador.* University of Pennsylvania.

Sheppard, T. (1920). The origins of the material used in the manufacture of prehistoric stone weapons in east Yorkshire. *Transactions East Riding Antiquarian Society* **23**, 34–54.

Sherratt, A. (1976). Resources, technology and trade: an essay in early European metallurgy. In: G. de G. Sieveking, I. H. Longworth and K. E. Wilson (ed.): *Problems in economic and social archaeology.* Duckworth, London, 557–81.

Shotton, F. W. (1959). New petrological groups based on axes from the West Midlands. *Proceedings of the Prehistoric Society* **25**, 135–43.

—— (1968). Prehistoric man's use of stone in Britain. *Proceedings of the Geologists' Association* **79**, 477–92.

—— (1972). The large stone axes ascribed to north-west Pembrokeshire. In: F. Lynch and C. Burgess (ed.): *Prehistoric man in Wales and the West.* Adams and Dart, Bath, 85–91.

—— and Hendry, G. L. (1979). The developing field of petrology in archaeology. *Journal of Archaeological Science* **6**, 75–84.

—— Chitty, L. F., and Seaby, W. A. (1951). A new centre for stone axe dispersal on the Welsh Border. *Proceedings of the Prehistoric Society* **17**, 159–67.

Sieveking, G. de G., Craddock, P. T., Hughes, M. J., Bush, P., and Ferguson, J. (1970). Characterization of prehistoric flint mine products. *Nature* **228**, 251–4.

—— Bush, P., Ferguson, J., Craddock, P. T., Hughes, M. J., and Cowell, M. R. (1972). Prehistoric flint mines and their identification as sources of raw material. *Archaeometry* **14**, 151–176.

Smith, I. (1979). The chronology of British stone implements. In: T. H. McK. Clough and W. A. Cummins (ed.): Stone axe studies. *Research Reports Council for British Archaeology* **23**, 13–22.

Smith, K. (1977). The excavation of Winklebury Camp, Basingstoke, Hampshire. *Proceedings of the Prehistoric Society* **43**, 31–129.

Srejovic, D. (1972). *Lepenski Vir.* Thames and Hudson, London.

Stanley, J. W. (1976). A preliminary description of thin sections of some Neolithic stone axes from the London region. *Science and Archaeology* **18**, 3–11.

Štelcl, J. and Malina, J. (1975). *Základy petroarcheologie.* Universita J.E. Purkine v Brne.

—— Kalousek, F. and Malina, J. (1970). A petro-archaeological study of a deposit of Neolithic stone tools at Stará Břecalv, Czechoslovakia. *Proceedings of the Prehistoric Society* **36**, 233–40.

Stiles, D. N., Hay, R. L., and O'Neil, J. R. (1974). The MNK chert factory site, Olduvai Gorge, Tanzania. *World Archaeology* **5**, 285–308.

Stone, J. F. S. and Wallis, F. S. (1947). Second report of the sub-committee of the South-western Group of Museums and Art Galleries on the petrological identification of stone axes. *Proceedings of the Prehistoric Society* **13**, 47–55.

—— —— (1951). Third report of the sub-committee of the South-western Group of Museums and Art Galleries on the petrological identification of stone axes. *Proceedings of the Prehistoric Society* **17**, 99–158.

Sulimirski, T. (1960). Remarks concerning the distribution of some varieties of flint in Poland. *Swiatowit Rocznik Katedri Arch. Pierwotnej i wczesnosredniowiecznej uniwersytetu Warszawskiego* **22**, 281–307.

Sullivan, M. E. and Simmons, S. (1979). Silcrete: a classification for flaked stone artefact assemblages. *The Artefact* **4**, 51–9.

Tarr, W. A. (1938). Terminology of the chemical siliceous sediments. *National Research Council Division of Geology and Geography Annual Report* **1937–1938**, (Appendix A exhibit A), 8–27.

Threipland, L. M. (1956). An excavation at St. Mawgen-in-Pyder, North Cornwall. *Archaeological Journal* **113**, 33–81.

Van der Waals, J. D. (1972). Die durchlochten Rössener Keile und das frühe Neolithikum in Belgien und in den Niederlanden. *Fundamenta* A3, Va., 153–184.

Van Noten, F. (1969). A ground axe from Burundi. *Azania* **4**, 166.

—— (1977). Excavations of Matupi Cave. *Antiquity* **51**, 35–40.

Wainwright, G. J. and Malik, S. C. (1967). Recent research on problems of archaeology and Pleistocene chronology in Peninsular India. *Proceedings of the Prehistoric Society* **33**, 132–46.

Walker, D. and Sieveking, G. de G. (1962). The Palaeolithic industry of Kota Tampan, Perak, Malaya. *Proceedings of the Prehistoric Society* **28**, 103–39.

Warashina, T., Kamaki, Y., and Higashimura, T. (1978). Sourcing of sanukite implements by X-ray fluorescence analysis II. *Journal of Archaeological Science* **5**, 283–91.

Warren, S. H. (1919). A stone axe factory at Graig Lwyd, Penmaenmawr. *Journal of the Royal Anthropological Institute* **49**, 342–65.

Watchman, A. (1979). Petrology of the greenstone quarries and their products. Appendix to McBryde, I. Petrology and prehistory: lithic evidence for exploitation of stone resources and exchange systems in Australia. In: T. H. McK. Clough and W. A. Cummins (ed.): Stone axe studies. *Research Reports Council for British Archaeology* **23**, 122–6.

Watts, S. H. (1978). A petrological study of silcrete from inland Australia. *Journal of Sedimentary Petrology* **48**, 987–94.

Wheeler, R. E. M. (1943). Maiden Castle, Dorset. *Report of the Research Committee of the Society of Antiquities* **12**.

Whitlock, R. (1976). *Everyday life of the Maya.* Batsford, London.

Williams, O. and Nandris, J. (1977). The Hungarian and Slovak sources of archaeological obsidian: an interim report on further fieldwork, with a note on tektites. *Journal of Archaeological Science* **4**, 207–19.

7. Petrology of obsidian artefacts

J. R. Cann

Introduction

Obsidian is a volcanic glass which fractures readily and predictably to give a sharp cutting edge. It was extensively used in the ancient world, principally to provide sharp blades for different kinds of cutting, but also for mirrors and as an ornamental material. Because of its superiority in use to most other natural competitors, and no doubt because of its splendid appearance, it was traded widely from its rather few sources and may, if it can be successfully characterized, give valuable information on patterns of cultural contact through time. In addition, when it is exposed to the weather, it hydrates slowly and predictably, forming a thin distinct surface layer. As this layer thickens with time, it can be used as a tool for dating as well as for the determination of provenance. Thus, obsidian can be a very informative material for archaeologists, and this chapter discusses it as a material, and describes how it can best be utilized in archaeological investigations.

Obsidian as a rock

Obsidian is a glass, a super-cooled liquid, which is liquid in all its properties except in its ability to flow easily. Its atomic structure is entirely disordered, and because of this it has no preferred directional properties and is physically quite isotropic; this is one of the reasons why it makes such effective tools, since flakes can be struck from a core in any direction.

Two factors control whether a volcanic rock forms as a glass or not: its chemical composition and its rate of cooling. To form glass effectively, crystallization must be prevented, and in obsidian this is very strongly helped by its high content of silicon and aluminium relative to other atoms. Silicon and aluminium, combined with oxygen, form long, branching, and tangled chains of silicate and aluminate tetrahedra, joined together, which do not break easily, and only become organized into a regular crystalline array very slowly. The liquid is also very viscous. Liquids less rich in silicon and aluminium (the *glass formers*) and richer in magnesium, sodium, and calcium (the *network modifiers*), such as basalt lavas, which are less viscous, form glasses much less readily.

Almost all liquids will form glasses if cooled rapidly enough, but for many liquids the cooling rates necessary are much faster than are commonly found in nature. The more fluid silicate liquids, such as basalt lavas, only form glass (sideromelane) in exceptional circumstances, such as during eruption underwater or when small drops of fountaining lava are blown away from the vent by the wind. Because of the high cooling rates required, basalt glass never forms very large lumps, and so was only of limited use in tool making.

Easier to make into glass are the silicate liquids rich in glass formers, in which the viscosity is high. These form glass under a wide range of the cooling rates at or near the Earth's surface. Even these liquids, however, will crystallize if they are intruded at any depth within the Earth because of the slower rate of cooling there.

Most natural liquids rich in glass formers are also rich in water and other volatiles. Usually, when such lava is erupted, it froths up to form pumice, or explodes to form small glassy fragments, to make tuff. Such lava, with abundant gas bubbles (vesicles), does not make good tools. It is, however, much commoner than vesicle-free volcanic glass. In order to produce this, the liquid must either have been formed with a very low water content, or it must have been degassed in some way before being erupted.

Glass is not a very stable material. At low temperatures a mixture of crystals is always more stable than a glass, and glasses will crystallize spontaneously if the atoms within them have the opportunity of diffusing through the glass and becoming ordered. Such an opportunity can be provided by the glass being reheated, or by hot water percolating through the glassy rock, dissolving and reprecipitating atoms. Since volcanoes generally have an abundance of heat and often produce plentiful hot water, the lifetime of volcanic glass is relatively short by geological standards, especially if it is buried by later lavas. Obsidian is thus almost entirely restricted to young volcanic areas, except where it has exceptionally escaped the later stage of crystallization. Very few obsidians are older than 10 million years, and many are less than 100 000 years old.

Lavas rich enough in silicon and aluminium to form glasses readily are erupted in many parts of the world. However, because of their normally high water content, obsidian is only rarely formed from them; when it does it may not necessarily either be called by that name or be suitable for tool-making. Lavas that form obsidian are usually members of the granite clan, though some are members of the syenite clan, producing less quartz and more feldspar than granites on crystallization. The commonest lavas of these two clans, when crystalline, are called respectively rhyolites and trachytes. The various names given to these lavas and their glassy equivalents, based on minor differences and geographic origin, that may be encountered in the

Table 7.1. Names of
volcanic rocks synonymous
with, or associated with,
obsidians in the field

Glassy rocks

* obsidian	marekanite
* pitchstone	vitrophyre
* perlite	hyalopsite
* pumice	hraftinna
lassenite	

Non-glassy rocks (often originally
glassy but now microcrystalline)

* rhyolite	* pantellerite
* rhyodacite	* comendite
* dacite	ponzite
liparite	* trachyte
domite	* ignimbrite
felsite	nevadite
dellenite	toscanite
tordrillite	sanukite
hornstone	gibelite
drakonite	macedonite
kaiwekite	shastalite
selagite	

* Names in common use today.

geological literature, are listed in Table 7.1. One distinction which is particularly relevant to archaeological characterization studies is that between peralkaline and peraluminous rhyolites and trachytes. *Peralkaline* lavas are those in which there are more sodium and potassium atoms than aluminium atoms, and *peraluminous* lavas are those in which the reverse is true.

In general, only genuine obsidian is suitable for tool-making, but since geologists have not been concerned with the same distinctions as those using the rock for artefacts, some obsidian has not been used for tools. Most commonly this has been because a particular rock was not totally glassy. Though many obsidians contain 95–100 per cent of glass, some contain 5–15 per cent of crystals formed in the melt before it was erupted at the Earth's surface. Not only do these act as centres around which clusters of small crystals can form in the glass, but they also disturb the even and predictable fracturing of the obsidian. Thus, the obsidian from Giali in the eastern Aegean, which contains about 5 per cent of feldspar crystals, was apparently not used for chipped stone tools although it was used for the manufacture of stone vessels in Bronze Age Crete (Renfrew, Cann, and Dixon 1965). Sometimes, the fragments of obsidian are too small to be able to be used effectively, since they occur as glassy lumps in tuff, but are still recorded by geologists. This is true of the obsidian of Antiparos, also in the Aegean, which was apparently used for beads, but occurred in pieces too small for the manufacture of blades (Renfrew *et al.* 1965).

Recognition of obsidian

Identification of obsidian sources is an important part of any study of the material. In a given area, local geological survey information will identify recently active volcanoes that have erupted lavas of the appropriate type (Table 7.1). Only a small proportion of these will have obsidian exposed on their flanks. The next task is to identify these.

One way of narrowing the search is to investigate the distribution of obsidian use near the volcanoes. In the immediate neighbourhood of sources, obsidian characteristically makes up more than 95 per cent of the chipped stone tools of Neolithic cultures (Renfrew, Dixon, and Cann 1966). This argument is somewhat circular, however, and in the end there will be no substitute for field surveying. Obsidian is formed as lava flows, though these can be broken up in explosive eruptions to give blocks of obsidian in tuff; however, obsidian flows do not have the same appearance as basaltic lava flows. Because the magma is very viscous, obsidian flows are more in the nature of domes, sometimes roughly hemispherical in shape, and usually about 50–200 m high, a hundred to a few hundred metres wide, and up to a kilometre or so long. The obsidian forms a coating on the outside of these flows, often interbanded with lava that has crystallized and looks stony rather than glassy (Friedman, Long, and Smith 1963). Domes and thick flows of acid lava can often be identified on aerial photographs, especially if vegetation is not too lush and, with practice, can be recognized readily on the ground.

There are, however, complicating problems. As a volcano erupts, its lavas continuously cover the older lavas and an obsidian source available a few thousand years ago may no longer be visible. Equally, obsidian sources visible now may not have been present then, as Bigazzi and Bonadonna (1973) have shown for two flows on Lipari. This is not a major problem, however, since the rate of production and burying of obsidian flows is slow compared with the time scale of a few thousand years, with which most archaeology is concerned.

Furthermore, obsidian may be eroded from the outcrop and transported by rivers for several kilometres. Man saw no particular virtue in quarrying from an outcrop, and very often used boulders from river beds. However, geologists tend to concentrate on outcrops, and may not examine material only present as transported boulders unless they are specifically looking for it.

There are several kinds of material that resemble obsidian more or less closely, particularly flint and chert, which are also extensively used for stone tools. Black varieties of chert have a strong superficial resemblance to obsidian, but their surface lustre is dull compared with the true glassy lustre of obsidian. Chert, too, though it is often translucent on thin edges, is never truly transparent as are many obsidians. Obsidian often shows a banding related to the presence of more or less abundant minute crystals, which may have been bent or swirled by the flow of the viscous liquid, and usually contains a few visible crystals of feldspar and some gas bubbles. Chert, as a sedimentary rock, lacks these features, but may contain fossils.

More difficult to distinguish from obsidian are other natural glasses. Sideromelane, the basalt glass (see above), only forms as small pieces, and can be distinguished from obsidian by its higher refractive index and the different crystals found in it. Tektites are small glassy meteorites, found in limited strewn fields, and are very rare even in these. Tektites occur as a variety of teardrop, button, and dumb-bell shapes, no more than a few centimetres across. These characteristic shapes, and a distinctive chemical composition, distinguish them readily from obsidian. More rare still are the silica-rich natural glasses such as the Darwin glass of Australia and the glass of the Libyan desert. These kinds of glass can occur in lumps of up to several kilograms, but they are nearly colourless and very different in composition from obsidian.

Man-made glasses may sometimes closely resemble obsidian. This is particularly true of the glassy slags resulting from some kinds of early metal-working. They contain crystalline inclusions very different from those found in obsidian, which can be identified in thin section. For all of these potentially confusing materials, a trace element analysis, of the kind used for characterization, is particularly effective in identifying whether a material is obsidian or not, because of the very characteristic range of trace element composition of true obsidian.

Sources of obsidian

The sources of obsidian (see Cann, Dixon, and Renfrew 1969, Fig. 105; also Figs 4.1 and 4.13) are always volcanoes that are still active or only recently extinct, which erupt acid lavas sufficiently rich in silicon and aluminium. Even in the best geologically surveyed areas, it is not clear that all sources have been identified, while in less well surveyed areas major obsidian flows may remain undetected. Some volcanic areas, such as Hawaii, erupt no silicic lavas, and thus are not capable of containing obsidian, but most do produce such lavas, either during the evolution of basaltic magma, or by melting the crust through which the lavas pass. Bearing in mind, then, that most volcanic environments are capable of bearing obsidian, there are certain broad rules concerning its occurrence.

The most characteristic environment of obsidian formation is that of the volcanic arcs or chains. Some of these chains lie 100–200 km inland, parallel to the margin of the continent, while others form chains of offshore islands, usually arc-like in plan, sometimes stretching far into the Pacific and other oceans. Consistently associated with these chains of volcanoes are offshore deep-sea trenches. The trenches mark the sites where slabs of ocean crust are slowly plunging back into the Earth, while the volcanoes, lying above these descending slabs, seem to be related to frictional heating of the slabs leading to melting as they plunge downwards.

Such volcanic arcs extend over much of Central America, down the west coast of South America, through the island chains of south-east Asia and Australasia, and up around Japan, Kamchatka, the Aleutians, and Alaska to reach western Canada, Washington, and Oregon, where the circle about the Pacific is almost complete. Arcs outside the Pacific include the Antilles chain in the Caribbean, and the Aegean.

Very similar volcanoes are found in chains across areas where oceans have been closed within the last 10 million years by the drift of the continents. These chains are not now at continental margins, nor do they have deep-sea trenches associated with them, but the volcanoes are of exactly the same type as in present day arcs. Areas that appear anomalous in this way include parts of the Alpine–Himalaya mountain belt, such as the Carpathian area of eastern Europe, central and eastern Turkey and adjacent areas, and points further east along this belt.

Within volcanic arcs, the most characteristic form of obsidian is peraluminous, defined above, which has a distinctive chemistry called *calc-alkaline*, marked as the name suggests by simultaneously high levels of calcium and alkalis. In terms of trace elements this is shown particularly by high levels of strontium and especially barium in some of the obsidians. Most obsidians formed in volcanic arcs belong to this class. Also occurring in volcanic arcs are some *alkaline* obsidians in which, either as a result of prolonged evolution, or because of a different mode of origin, the level of alkalis is high, but that of calcium is very low. These obsidians are also peraluminous. Some few volcanoes within volcanic arcs erupt mildly *peralkaline* lavas (defined above). These have been as yet little studied: the best known examples are Nemrut Dag, near Lake Van in eastern Turkey; Mayor Island in New Zealand; and Pachuca, Hidalgo, in Mexico. However, there are clearly several others, including some volcanoes in California (Christiansen and Noble 1965; Noble, Sargent, Ekren, Menhert, and Byers 1968) (Table 7.2).

The other important kind of plate boundary, the spreading plate boundary where the plates are moving apart and new crust is being generated, is also associated with obsidian, though it is quantitatively less important than the arcs. Much of this type of plate boundary is below sea-level, forming

Table 7.2. Major and trace element analyses of different types of obsidian

	(a)	(b)	(c)	(d)	(e)	(f)	(g)
SiO_2	75.33	73.15	76.38	72.22	74.7	69.56	62.61
TiO_2	0.27	0.28	0.07	0.23	0.22	0.49	0.81
Al_2O_3	12.58	13.68	12.65	14.41	10.1	9.62	11.01
Fe_2O_3	1.58	0.88	0.39	0.50	1.93	2.16	} 11.06
FeO	0.88	1.22	0.68	1.62	2.45	5.45	{
MnO	0.07	0.03	0.05	0.06	0.10	0.17	0.44
MgO	0.24	0.34	0.01	0.18	nil	0.02	0.15
CaO	1.25	1.26	0.56	0.84	0.20	0.47	0.90
Na_2O	4.02	3.96	4.06	5.28	5.60	6.66	7.84
K_2O	3.82	4.21	4.67	4.01	4.25	4.39	4.11
H_2O^+	0.31	} 0.45 {	0.23	0.12	0.29	0.13	—
H_2O^-	0.09		0.03	0.01	—	0.08	—
P_2O_5	0.02	0.02	0.01	0.03	0.01	—	0.05
F	—	—	0.08	—	—	—	—
Cl	—	—	0.07	—	—	0.21	—
Total	100.46	99.48	99.90	99.51	99.93	99.72	99.01
			p.p.m.				
Rb	55	168	192	150	134	120	218
Sr	200	121	5	64	0.3	12	13
Y	20	—	34	70	145	130	218
Zr	150	232	120	390	1100	1050	1380
Nb	<5	—	22	—	69	155	359
Ba	645	916	30	870	9	700	126
La	20	—	—	—	95	120	205
Ce	50	—	52	—	150	270	355

Missing elements not quoted in original sources.

(a) Calc-alkaline obsidian from Talasea volcano, New Britain (343 of Lowder and Carmichael 1970).
(b) Calc-alkaline obsidian from Medicine Lake volcano, California (Mertzman 1977).
(c) Alkaline obsidian from Glass Mountain, Mono County, California (MO3B of Noble *et al.*, 1972).
(d) Obsidian with peralkaline tendencies, Newberry Volcano, Oregon (54 of Higgins 1973).
(e) Peralkaline rhyolite obsidian, Mayor Island, New Zealand (5 of Ewart, *et al.*, 1968).
(f) Peralkaline obsidian, Fantale volcano, Ethiopia (Y346 of Gibson 1972).
(g) Peralkaline trachyte obsidian, Emuruangogolok volcano, Kenya (S63 of Weaver 1977).

mid-ocean ridges, and thus not of interest to archaeologists. However, spreading boundaries are found locally above sea-level, as in Iceland and East Africa, and there obsidian is found. The obsidian of Iceland is probably not archaeologically significant, but that of East Africa is very important. Here, splitting of the African continent has been going on very slowly for 25 million years, so slowly that only in Ethiopia has any separation, as opposed to stretching, occurred. Associated with this are many volcanoes, some of which erupt peralkaline obsidian (Bailey and Macdonald 1970, 1975; Gibson 1972; Macdonald, Bailey, and Sutherland 1970; Macdonald and Gibson 1969). Peralkaline obsidian is also characteristic of some oceanic islands occurring very near to the crest of the submarine mid-ocean ridges, such as Ascension Island and Bouvet in the Atlantic, and Easter Island and the Revillagigedos in the Pacific (Table 7.2).

Volcanoes also occur without any clear relation to plate boundaries; these are the intra-plate volcanoes, scattered apparently at random across the surface of the Earth. Many of these, such as Hawaii, do not produce obsidian, but important examples that do are Pantelleria in the Mediterranean (Carmichael 1962), Tibesti in Libya, the Canary Islands, and possibly some of the volcanoes in the western USA. Obsidian from these sources is usually more or less peralkaline. Related to the peralkaline chemistry of lavas is a higher content of iron, which gives the glass a green or brown colour in transmitted light, and high contents of zirconium, niobium, and other trace elements that behave similarly (Butler and Smith 1962; Macdonald and Bailey 1972) (Table 7.2).

Hydration of obsidian

As was first noted by Bonney (1877), obsidian absorbs water readily during exposure to weathering or, more rapidly, as volcanically heated waters pass through obsidian flows (Ross and Smith 1955; Friedman and Smith 1958; Chenebaux, Bordet, and Sabatier 1960; Nasedkin 1963). The result is first the formation of a hydrated glass called perlite, and eventually the crystallization of the glass to a microcrystalline rock. Both processes degrade both the physical properties and the appearance of the material. Hydration is the main reason why high quality obsidian is only found in geologically young rocks.

However, the earlier stages of hydration are the basis of the obsidian dating method (Evans and Meggers 1960; Friedman and Smith 1960; Friedman and Trembour 1978), and this has wide archaeological applications wherever obsidian forms a substantial part of the lithic debris. The initial stages of obsidian hydration occur as a distinct step. The obsidian, which usually contains 1 per cent or less of water, is converted to perlite, with 3–5 per cent of water, which forms a thin rind on the outside of the obsidian fragments and on the edges of cracks, separated from the anhydrous obsidian by a sharp boundary. As hydration progresses, the boundary migrates into the obsidian and the layer of perlite thickens. The gradual growth of the hydrated layer is the basis of the technique of obsidian dating. Under the right conditions, measurement of the thickness of the layer will enable a direct measure of age.

The layer is measured using a thin section of the fragment on a petrological microscope. The thin section must be prepared so that the fragile surface layer is not damaged, especially if the layer is at all thick, since hydration induces a volume change, and thus stresses, in the hydrated layer, which readily spalls off when thicker than a few micrometres. Encasing the specimen in epoxy resin may be necessary to reduce cutting stresses. The hydration layer can be recognized under high magnification (c. 400×) by the difference in its refractive index from that of the unhydrated glass, and also by the strain birefringence induced in it by the stresses produced during hydration. Measurement may be made using a micrometer eyepiece, photographically (Findlow and De Atley 1976), or using nuclear means (Lee, Leich, Tombrello, Ericson, and Friedman 1974). Several different measurements must be made on each sample, examining different parts of the specimen for evidence of spalling or retouching. Eventually, some estimate must be made of the realistic mean for the sample concerned.

Calibration of the thickness measured in terms of age is not easy. A universal calibration curve is not possible, because the rate of hydration varies considerably with environmental conditions, and even local calibration curves are not easy to make or to use. If the rate of reaction is controlled by diffusion of water through the hydrated glass, then the relationship between layer thickness (x) and time (t) should have the form:

$$x = kt^{1/2} \tag{7.1}$$

where k is the diffusion constant, which is related to temperature by the Arrhenius equation:

$$k = Ae^{-(E/RT)} \tag{7.2}$$

in which A is a constant, E the activation energy of the hydration reaction, R the gas constant, and T the temperature in Kelvin (Friedman, Smith, and Long 1966). A is related to the nature of the particular obsidian concerned, and E would be expected to vary somewhat, but much less, if the nature of the obsidian changed greatly. In any case, determination of k at three or four values of T for a particular type of obsidian would yield values of A and E, which would in turn allow k to be calculated for any T, and hence for hydration of this obsidian in an environment where T is known (Friedman 1976). Determination of k is possible by several methods by which the rate of uptake of water at different temperatures can be determined. Recently, Laursen and Lanford (1978) used the ^{15}N resonance nuclear reaction method to study hydration profiles in obsidian hydrated at 90 °C. Determination of T, the mean, long-term temperature of a piece of obsidian recovered from an archaeological site is not easy (Friedman 1976; Ambrose 1976; Friedman and Long 1976) and is discussed further below.

The alternative approach is to calibrate the hydration layer with carefully selected dates obtained by ^{14}C or some other independent means. In this way, empirical dates which are independent of theory can be obtained, though they are only valid in a restricted area and age range. Calibration curves obtained in this way may not show the theoretical square root behaviour (Findlow, Bennett, Ericson, and De Atley 1975; Meighan 1970;

Meighan, Foote, and Aiello 1968; Ericson, MacKenzie, and Berger 1976; Kimberlin 1976), and a number of different local hydration laws have been proposed on this basis, with the power of t in eqn (7.1) ranging between 0.3 and 1.

Friedman and Smith's (1960) original work used a hybrid method, which assumed square root dependence, but relied also on some radiocarbon dates for calibration, particularly to determine the elusive quantity T, the *in situ* temperature. This is certainly not an easy quantity to grasp. Friedman (1976) showed how strongly the temperature varies with depth and how, in the sun, surface temperatures may considerably exceed air temperatures. The integrated temperature history of a flake of obsidian would thus depend strongly on the rate of its burial below the top 10 cm or so of soil, and the presence of local shade during that particular period. Under the worst conditions, this might lead to a variation in apparent age by as much as 1000 years in 3000, and the variability often observed in rind thickness at a given horizon might be caused by such variation in mean temperature rather than by mixing from other horizons. Ambrose (1976) has suggested an ingenious method for measuring the rate of hydration at a particular site with a particular obsidian, but this itself shows the importance of environmental factors and the difficulty of obtaining an unequivocal estimate of the factors involved.

Another factor that influences hydration rate is the nature of the obsidian being hydrated. One fundamental factor appears to be primary water content of the obsidian. Friedman and Smith (1960) and Friedman *et al.* (1966) point out that the small glassy meterorites called tektites (see above) show no sign of hydration, despite having been exposed to water for several million years. On the other hand, obsidian hydrates even in environments of low relative humidity. This difference they attribute to the difference between the very low water content of the tektites (Friedman 1958; O'Keefe 1964) and the much higher primary water content of the obsidians. However, there is every reason to suppose that the water content of obsidian will be rather variable even within a single flow. Production of obsidian is, in geological terms, rather difficult to explain, and the role of water is one of its more enigmatic aspects. It seems likely that dehydration of the magma may be necessary to allow it to be extruded at the surface without frothing up, and in such viscous magma it seems entirely likely that water will be distributed inhomogeneously within it. The effect of such variation on hydra-rates could be important, but remains inadequately investigated.

Variation of hydration rates between sources has been well documented (Katsui and Kondo 1976; Kimberlin 1976; Friedman, Smith, and Clark 1969; Ericson and Berger 1976; Minor 1977; Mendoza 1981). The reason for this sort of variation is not clearly understood. An important factor might simply be variation in the content of primary water from source to source.

Other possible controls could be whether the obsidian is peralkaline or peraluminous, and the level of its silicon content. Whatever the cause, it is clear that the greatest care must be taken to distinguish obsidian from different sources if they are represented in a collection from one site. Provided the distinction can be made visually, there is little difficulty, but often the differences can only be detected by chemical means, which are expensive to apply, and can only be used on a limited number of samples.

The problems that have arisen with obsidian dating mean that its use must be carefully controlled. Its advantage is its speed and cheapness compared with radiocarbon dating, and this means that a much more dense coverage both vertically and laterally can be achieved within one site. However, a framework of radiocarbon dates is usually necessary to confirm that hydration is proceeding in a controlled and regular way. In addition the variation in hydration layer thickness caused by environmental and other factors limits the precision of the method and the accuracy of correlation between different parts of the same site. As with many technical innovations in archaeology and, for that matter, geology, obsidian dating is not the universal panacea that the optimists originally supposed, nor is it as poorly based as pessimists have occasionally suggested. Used responsibly by archaeologists properly informed of its strengths and weaknesses it can be one very valuable tool among many in unravelling problems of dating and of stratigraphy, as well as volcanology and geology (Michels 1969; Friedman and Peterson 1971; Friedman, Pierce, Obradovich, and Long 1973; Ericson 1975; Bell 1977; Leach 1977; Tebiwa, Aikens, and Minor 1978). Recent advances in the field have been reviewed extensively in Taylor (1976).

Characterization of obsidian

The term characterization applied to the assignment of archaeologically discovered obsidian to its source was only recently introduced (Cann and Renfrew 1964), but characterization had been attempted on obsidian for many years (cf. Ordoñez 1892). Appearance was the most immediately used characteristic, but it led to a fundamental error when Evans (1921, p. 87, 412) ascribed the white-spotted obsidian found archaeologically in Crete to a source far to the west in Lipari on the basis of its appearance. Trace element analyses have since demonstrated its source to be the island of Giali, lying north of Rhodes and north-east of Crete (Renfrew et al. 1965). Refractive index and density studies were used by Wainwright (1927) for Egyptian obsidian, but these too must be carefully controlled to be useful. Trace element studies show that all these techniques can be used to distinguish peralkaline obsidian from other obsidians. Peralkaline obsidian is characteristically green or brown when viewed in transmitted light, while alkaline and calc-alkaline obsidian is usually translucent in shades of grey (or rarely red). Peralkaline obsidian has in addition typically rather higher refractive indices than other obsidian ($c.$ 1.50 as opposed to $c.$ 1.49), and also a rather higher density ($c.$ 2.40 as opposed to $c.$ 2.35 g/cm³). In practice, the appearance is usually sufficiently decisive so that the other techniques do not need to be deployed.

The ready distinction of peralkaline obsidian from other types is particularly valuable where a site is supplied from two sources, one of them peralkaline, such as is the case in Malta (Cann and Renfrew 1964), where the sources are the islands of Pantelleria and Lipari, or some sites in Iraq where obsidian comes from the sources near Lake Van and from Cappodocia (Dixon 1976). In such cases, counts of the proportion of obsidian from the different sources can be made for all obsidian recovered, and can be charted level by level through the site, enabling quantitative estimates to be made of the variation in sources of supply, and thus perhaps contact, through time. Otherwise discrimination must be by trace elements, and must necessarily be incomplete.

Characterization by trace elements has been remarkably successful and has also been useful archaeologically in giving information about patterns of prehistoric contact and trade (Cann *et al.* 1969). Generalization about the method is difficult, since the particular approach used will depend on such factors as the analytical tools available and the particular range of sources required to be discriminated.

Trace element studies form a very substantial part of geochemical investigations today, and a complete review would be beyond the scope of this chapter, but some background needs filling in to allow useful patterns to be seen. Obsidian lava is formed at depth inside the earth during high-temperature ($c.$ 1000 °C) melting and crystallization reactions. The melts thus form in equilibrium with solid material, and the trace elements present are distributed between the melt and the solid phases depending on their chemical nature and the nature of the solid materials present. During this process, some elements (such as chromium, cobalt, and nickel) are strongly absorbed into the solids. These are called compatible elements, because they are essentially compatible with the crystallizing solids. Others, such as gallium and germanium, are approximately equally divided between the solid and the liquid. Yet others are termed *incompatible elements* because they are incompatible with the solid phases and are concentrated in the liquid. This incompatibility may take the form of the ions being too large for the available ionic sites in the solids, as in the case of rubidium, caesium, strontium, and barium. Alternatively, it may result from the ions possessing too high an ionic charge to fit into the crystal structure of the solid phase, such as the triply charged rare earth elements (e.g. lanthanum, cerium, and yttrium), the quadruply charged ions of titanium and zirconium, or the quintuply charged ions of phosphorus, tantalum, and niobium. Some ions are too small (beryllium and boron) or carry too low an ionic charge (lithium) to fit, but these are in the minority.

As a magma evolves within the earth, melting still further or crystallizing different solids, the nature of the solids changes, and crystals may form which accept the incompatible elements because of some particular features of their crystal structure. Thus, feldspar of a particular composition is a good host for the otherwise incompatible element strontium, as is mica for rubidium. After evolving for some while in equilibrium with such a solid, the content of the characteristically absorbed trace element is reduced in the liquid, and also relative to the other incompatible elements. Changes of this kind give a particular character to given obsidians and occur, too, in a regular way as liquids evolve by crystallization.

A good example is found in calc-alkaline magma series characteristic of volcanic arcs. The least evolved obsidians from such series are characteristically enriched in barium and strontium because of events further back in their history which are not well known, and anyway are not important here. Barium contents of 2000 p.p.m. and strontium contents of 200 p.p.m. are possible in such rocks. As the evolution of the liquids proceeds, they begin to precipitate feldspars which will first reduce strontium contents and later barium contents down to levels of only a few parts per million. Meanwhile, rubidium contents continue to increase, and so to begin with do zirconium contents. However, zirconium becomes saturated in peraluminous (calc-alkaline or alkaline) melts when it reaches levels of only 200 p.p.m. Small amounts of zircon begin to precipitate. The result of these effects is a characteristic evolutionary path from calc-alkaline obsidians to alkaline obsidians, in which barium, strontium, and zirconium are all low (Table 7.2).

Peralkaline rock series are quite different. Zirconium is much more soluble in peralkaline liquids, and often reaches levels of over 1000 p.p.m. before precipitation of zirconium-bearing solids begins. The series often starts with obsidians high in barium and strontium, and moderately enriched in zirconium. Barium and strontium are particularly rapidly depleted by crystallization of feldspars, while zirconium and niobium continue to increase to high levels.

The result of the operation of these processes is that the incompatible elements are particularly sensitive indicators of the provenance of obsidian, and can vary in characteristic ways depending on the history of the obsidian. This is illustrated by Fig. 7.1, which is exactly equivalent to the rubidium–strontium–zirconium triangle of Jack (1976), transformed to be more convenient for further plotting, in which the calc-alkaline series, the alkali rhyolites, and the peralkaline obsidians are all well distinguished. The separation is closely equivalent to that on the barium–zirconium graph, used originally by Cann and Renfrew (1964) and still a very effective way of

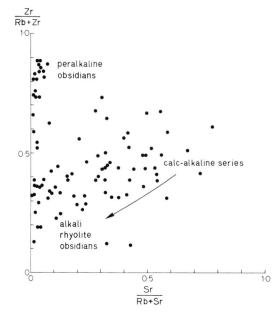

Fig. 7.1. Rb–Zr–Sr relations in obsidians. This diagram is topologically equivalent to the Rb–Zr–Sr triangle of Jack (1976), but is designed to be more easy for plotting. The obsidian analyses come from a large number of papers quoted elsewhere in this chapter.

separating obsidians (Fig. 7.2). Rb–Ba–Sr relations are shown on Fig. 7.3.

Application of trace element analysis to characterization depends to a large extent on the method of analysis available. These vary according to the range of elements covered, their speed and accuracy, and whether they are destructive or non-destructive. The original technique used was that of optical emission spectrography (Cann and Renfrew 1964). This covers a wide range of elements, though with variable precision and limit of detection. Precision may be as low as ± 30 per cent, which is on the margin for much successful characterization, and is particularly poor for elements such as rubidium, for which the lines lie in the infrared part of the spectrum. The method is destructive, but requires only 0.05 g of material, a quantity that can usually be spared in return for an analysis. Speed of analysis is comparable with other good methods. The second analytical method popular for obsidian is instrumental neutron activation analysis. It covers a wide range of elements, with very variable detection limits, but covering rather fewer than the preceding method, without rather complex procedures. It is particularly suitable for rare earth elements, manganese, scandium, tantalum, and thorium, and also provides rapid and precise analyses of the major elements sodium and iron. Precision is good, though it depends on the

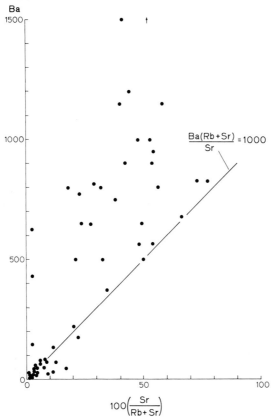

Fig. 7.2. Ba–Zr plot for obsidians. Analyses high in Ba are of calc-alkaline samples, those with more than 200 p.p.m. Zr are more or less peralkaline, and those low in Ba and Zr are alkaline obsidians. Very many fewer obsidians have been analysed for Ba and Zr than for Rb, Zr, and Sr because of the analytical techniques involved. The analyses come from several sources quoted elsewhere in this chapter.

sample geometry and the amount of time and trouble spent in counting. The method can be non-destructive of small samples, but it performs better if the samples are powdered and given a constant geometry. About 0.1 g is very adequate for an analysis, but 0.01 g will often suffice. Speed of analysis depends on the precision required, but it can be comparable with other techniques. The third important method is that of X-ray fluorescence. This can analyse for all elements of atomic number greater than 8, but is better for some elements than others, being particularly suited to elements with atomic numbers between those of nickel (28) and molybdenum (42), a span that includes the important group of elements rubidium, strontium, yttrium, zirconium, and niobium. Again, it can be used non-destructively for specimens up to 5 cm across, but performs much better on powdered specimens,

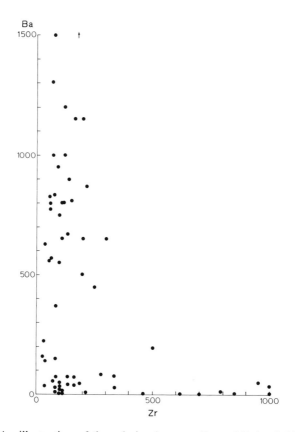

Fig. 7.3. An illustration of the relation between Ba and Sr in obsidians. To some extent Ba and (Sr/Rb + Sr) are interchangeable in plotting obsidian analyses. The analyses come from several sources quoted elsewhere in this chapter.

requiring a minimum of 0.4 to 1.0 g of powder. It seems best to use powdered specimens to analyse source material, but usually individual small flakes are better analysed whole as site material, because of the risk of mixing sources if several flakes are combined and powdered. Finally, atomic absorption spectroscopy has been widely used. This analyses solutions prepared by dissolving 0.2 g or more of powdered obsidian in hydrofluoric acid under controlled conditions. Sensitivity is excellent for some elements, but less good for others, including the potentially important element zirconium. Precision is good, at about ± 5 per cent, when well above the detection limit.

Also applied to obsidian analysis, though not yet extensively, have been the methods of proton inelastic scattering (Coote, Whitehead, and Mac-Callum 1972), proton induced X-ray emission (PIXE) (Nielson, Hill, Mangelson, and Nelson 1976), and Mössbauer spectroscopy (Longworth and Warren 1979).

Each method, then, has its advantages and disadvantages. In terms of the useful range of elements, optical emission spectroscopy and X-ray fluorescence have the advantage; for precision, neutron activation, atomic absorption spectroscopy, and X-ray fluorescence lead; and optical emission spectroscopy and neutron activation require the least powdered sample, if the analysis needs to be conducted in this way.

Once the analyses have been obtained, the question arises of their interpretation. Usually this involves two difficult and important questions, those of the indistinguishable sources and of the unknown sources. With many pairs of sources, discrimination can be achieved simply and visually by experimenting with bivariate scatter diagrams, and there is no doubt that this is the most powerful method, since the human eye is a far more able statistical tool than the computer. However, once bivariate diagrams are unable to separate sources (the case of indistinguishable sources), then discriminant analysis must be used to give a multivariate separation.

There is not space here to give a full consideration of the philosophy of discriminant analysis, but it should certainly be used with care. Remember that it can only assign unknowns to recognized sources, raising the important problem of the missing sources (see below). In addition it only searches linear combinations of the variables. In many rock series the most profound discriminators are ratios between variables. In order to include this as a possibility, the logarithms of the abundances must be used instead of raw abundance numbers. A logarithm transformation has the additional advantage that it changes the usual log-normal frequency distribution of geochemical data to a more or less normal distribution. Since traditional discriminant analysis assigns unknowns on the basis of multivariate normal distribution statistics, such assignments are likely to be more in accordance with actuality after transformation to a normal distribution. In cases where distinction is vital, making analyses on further elements is often a help, and such additional techniques as fission track dating have proved useful (see below). In addition, it sometimes pays to seek more precise methods of analysis, since homogeneity of obsidian sources is usually as great as the accuracy of the most precise techniques available, and thus subtle distinctions can be made which cannot be approached by the less precise techniques (Gale 1981).

The unknown source problem is more difficult to grasp. It usually appears as a group of analyses of archaeological material that do not fit into any group of analyses from known sources. A very good example is the obsidian consigned to Group 3 by Cann and Renfrew (1964), and reconsidered in some detail by Dixon (1976). So far, no clear sources are known for this obsidian, though it was widely traded in later Neolithic times in the

Mesopotamian region. The pattern of its distribution in the region shows that the source or sources must lie close to, but somewhat east of Nemrut Dag, from which a very characteristic peralkaline obsidian was obtained. Dixon (1976) concluded that there may be several different sources represented within Group 3, on the basis of the variation in composition of the artefacts, and attempted to associate them with particular volcanoes. However, even after more than ten years' work, and a very clear-cut problem, the situation is still unsatisfactory. At least in this case the existence of an unknown source was clear from a visual examination of the trace element analyses.

More severe problems are likely to arise when an unknown source is very close in composition to one already recognized. The degree to which discriminant analysis will show up the existence of material from an unrecognized source under these conditions will depend on a number of factors, such as the closeness of the sources in multivariate space, the closeness of other sources, and the dispersion of sources. Even when a slight systematic difference is noticed between a group of artefacts and the nearest source, this may mean no more than that the obsidian was collected from another part of the same flow, or from a nearby related flow (Bowman, Asaro, and Perlman 1973a, b). On the other hand, it may conceal an archaeologically very significant link.

The answer must be to maintain a constantly open mind on the question, and to remember that discriminant analysis is very vulnerable to the missing source problem, trying, as part of its nature, to conceal or minimize the extent of the problem. Very useful can be the consideration of information that has not been used in the discriminant procedure, such as distribution among sites and semi-quantitative data, including appearance. Additional analyses can be important, just as when two known sources are close, though they are usually expensive to acquire.

One other major method has been used to supplement trace element analyses in obsidian characterization studies: fission track dating. Most dating methods are too expensive and time consuming for routine work, though K/Ar dating was applied to Italian obsidian by Belluomini, Discendenti, Malpieri, and Nicoletti (1970). However, fission track methods are particularly suited to obsidian, because of the latter's homogeneous and isotropic nature, and because they are cheap enough to apply more or less routinely. The first applications were in the Mediterranean area (Bigazzi, Bonadonna, and Belloumini 1971; Bigazzi and Bonadonna 1973; Durrani, Khan, Taj, and Renfrew 1971), but other places where it has proved successful are Slovakia (Repčok 1977) and New Zealand (Rutherford 1978). Measurements have also been made in Japan (Watanabe and Suzuki 1969), although not directly applied to characterization. The philosophy behind the application of dating methods has been that sources indistinguishable by trace elements may have been erupted at times different enough to be distinguishable by fission track measurements, and the applications referred to above show that this aim can be successfully achieved. A similar approach involves precise measurement of the ratio of $^{87}Sr/^{86}Sr$ (Gale 1981) which, though relatively time consuming, can provide discrimination not possible by other methods.

Finally, there is the promise of thermoluminescence for achieving the same ends. Though so far not extensively applied to obsidian, it has been shown by Leach and Fankhauser (1978) to have a potential in separating sources in New Zealand, and by Huntley and Bailey (1978) for samples from sources in the north-west coastal region of Canada and the USA. Excellent summaries of obsidian characterization studies in both eastern and western hemispheres are given in Taylor (1976) and, additionally, of Mesoamerican material in Hester (1978).

Regional applications of obsidian characterization

Circum-Mediterranean region

Sources that might have supplied the general Mediterranean region range widely through Europe, Asia, and Africa (see Chapter 4, Fig. 4.1). One group lies in the area of southern Italy in the west Mediterranean, and one in Hungary and Slovakia. Three sources form a group in the Aegean, and another important source region is in central Anatolia. Further east, the sources in the area of Lake Van supplied a wide area, perhaps supplemented by sources lying further north in the fringes of the Caucasus. The Ethiopian sources appear to have supplied at least some of the needs of Egypt, and some obsidian occurs in the remote desert volcanoes of Tibesti, in north Africa. The general Mediterranean problem has been tackled by Cann and Renfrew (1964), and recently reviewed by Dixon (1976). Within the western Mediterranean, a complex and overlapping effort by a number of authors (Belluomini and Taddeuci 1971; Belluomini et al. 1970; Bigazzi et al. 1971; Bigazzi and Bonadonna 1973; Hallam, Warren, and Renfrew 1976; Longworth and Warren 1979; Gale 1981) has led to a clarification of sources used at different times and in different places. However, there are still unresolved problems about which sources in Sardinia were used, and how these fit into the overall scheme.

The region of Slovakia, northern Hungary, and the very western part of the USSR has the disadvantage of crossing three national boundaries. Nandris (1975) and Williams and Nandris (1977) reviewed the problem, in the light of their initial work, and Repčok (1977) contributed fission track dates for sources. Gale (1981) has provided Sr isotope measurements, as well as contents of Rb, Sr, and U. However, the extent to which different sources were used and traded has yet to be clearly established.

Within the Aegean, Renfrew *et al.* (1965) established a broad framework which has been little changed by later work by Aspinall, Feather, and Renfrew (1972), Aspinall and Feather (1978), Gale (1981), and Dixon (1976). Calc-alkaline Melian obsidian, with its characteristic pearly grey lustre, dominated the dispersion zone, and was widely traded, competing effectively with obsidian from Lipari, Turkey, and other parts of the Mediterranean well beyond the limits of the Aegean Sea. The white-spotted large-blocked obsidian from Giali was only used for specialist purposes, such as for stone vases in Minoan Crete, while the alkaline obsidian of Antiparos was a very minor source. (See also Cosgrove, Hodson, Renfrew, Warren, and Shelford 1982; Filippakis, Grimanis, and Perdikatsis 1981).

Within the region of Anatolia, Cappadocia, and Armenia, including parts of Turkey, Iraq, Iran, and the USSR, there seem to be two main groups of sources, one in central Turkey, and the other broadly in Armenia. Here identification of sources has been a major problem, but the work of Westerveld (1957), Renfrew *et al.* (1966, 1968), Wright (1969), Wright and Gordus (1969*a*, *b*), Innocenti, Mazzuoli, Pasquare, Radicat, and Brozolo (1975), Renfrew and Dixon (1976) has clarified the position greatly. However, there are still problems about the extent of sources in Iran (the enigmatic Group 3 source) and in the Armenian SSR, though these last may not have been widely traded to the south.

East Africa

Work here has been limited in extent, though it is clear that many sources exist within a broad region stretching from Afar, at the southern end of the Red Sea, to Kenya. Though Cann and Renfrew (1964) and Muir and Hivernel (1976) provided some analyses from this region, most work so far has been for purely petrological ends, though still useful for characterization (Bailey and Macdonald 1975; Dickinson and Gibson 1972; Gibson 1972; Macdonald and Gibson 1969; Weaver 1977; Weaver, Sceal, and Gibson 1972).

North America

Within the American continent, three areas have been investigated for obsidian characterization: the Pacific north-west, the western USA, and Central America. Though other areas, notably extensive tracts of the Andes, contain sources, no evaluation of these appears yet to have taken place. In the Pacific north-west, work is only just beginning but patterns are already emerging (Patton and Miller 1970; Laidley and McKay 1971; Nelson, D'Auria, and Bennett 1975; Wheeler and Clark 1977). California and the western parts of the USA have, on the other hand, been the subject of intensive study, both petrological and archaeogeochemical, for many years. Geological studies include the work of Noble and his co-workers, interested principally in the problem of the nature and genesis of peralkaline obsidians (Christiansen and Noble 1965; Noble *et al.* 1968; Noble, Korringa, Hedge, and Riddle 1972), as well as many other reports such as those of Gilbert, Christensen, Al-Rawi, and Lajoie (1968); Zielinski, Lipman, and Millard (1977); Mertzman (1977); Higgins (1973); and Creasey and Krieger (1978). Sometimes geological work spills over into an archaeological context, as in that of Bowman *et al.* (1973*a*, *b*) in the Borax Lake area, and Lipman, Rowley, Menhert, Evans, Nash, and Brown (1978) on the Mineral Mountains rhyolite of Utah. Earlier archaeological studies in the area include that of Parks and Tieh (1966); Gordus, Fink, Hill, Purdy, and Wilcox (1967); Gordus, Wright, and Griffin (1968); Griffin, Gordus, and Wright (1969); Stevenson, Stross, and Heizer (1971); Schrieber and Breed (1971); and Jack (1971). So far as California is concerned, two fine summaries have been produced in Taylor (1976) by Jack (1976), concentrating on geochemical aspects, and Ericson *et al.* (1976), dealing with descriptions of sources and the traditions of use from Indian accounts.

Mesoamerica

Within the broad area of Mesoamerica, two distinct regions have so far been identified as containing sources of obsidian (see Chapter 4, Fig. 4.13). One is in central Mexico, in the part of the central Mexican volcanic belt which reaches towards the Gulf of Mexico, and the other is in the volcanic belt running through Guatemala and El Salvador, about 800 km to the south-east. It is possible that other groups of sources exist in the difficult terrain of the southern part of this large area, but it has already been shown that obsidian from the known sources was traded widely as an economically important commodity in prehistoric cultures (Heizer, Williams, and Graham 1965), both in the northern part of the area (Spence 1967; Cobean, Coe, Perr, Turkian, and Kharkar 1971) and in the south (Hammond 1972; Sidrys 1976). The obsidian mines from the western region, centred on Hidalgo, have been discussed by Spence and Parsons (1967) and Charlton (1969), and from El Chayal, Guatemala, by Coe and Flannery (1964). Much of the work of characterization of source materials so far has been of an exploratory nature (Weaver and Stross 1965; Stross, Weaver, Wyld, Heizer, and Graham 1968; Stevenson *et al.* 1971; Wagner 1978). Studies of particular areas include reports from Nielson *et al.* (1976) and Nelson, Nielson, Mangelson, Hill, and Mathehy (1977) on trace elements in obsidians from the Campeche region of north-east Mexico; work on the Chiapas littoral zone by Nelson and Voorhies (1980); reports on obsidian in Guatemala by Stross, Asaro, Michel, and Gruhn (1977), Asaro, Michel, Sydris, and Stross (1978), and Mendoza and Jester (1978); and a paper by Stross, Bowman, Michel, Asaro, and Hammond (1978) on Belize. However the systematization of Mesoamerican obsidians has now advanced considerably and the general features of their characterization have been well developed (Stross, Hester, Heizer, and Jack 1976; Ericson and Kimberlin 1977). Hester (1978) published a compilation of archaeological studies on Mesoamerican obsidian containing a number of papers not mentioned above, and dealing with mines and quarries, early technology, and trace element characterization; hydration is not included but important references to this aspect are included in the eleven page bibliography.

New Zealand

Attempts to characterize the obsidians of New Zealand were among the earliest made. First efforts, using refractive indices, were unsuccessful, as in other parts of the world. However, Green, Brooks, and Reeves (1967) made a successful start using optical emission spectroscopy, and this was followed by a number of varied applications (Armitage, Reeves, and Bellwood 1972; Reeves and Armitage 1973; Ward 1974*a, b, c*; Leach and Anderson 1978). Again, a good summary is available in a paper by Reeves and Ward (1976), in Taylor (1976). Since then thermoluminescence has been applied by Leach and Fankhauser (1978) and fission track dating by Rutherford (1978).

In New Zealand, many sources have been identified, concentrated in the central and northern parts of North Island. Some are more or less peralkaline, especially the famous source on Mayor Island, while most are alkaline or calc-alkaline.

Oceania

Obsidian sources are widespread in the volcanic arcs of the western Pacific, but characterization studies are only just beginning (Key 1968; Ambrose and Green 1972; Osawa, Kiyota, Furuya, Fujikura, Sakakibara, and Kasuya 1974). An initial synthesis has been made by Smith, Ward, and Ambrose (1977).

Acknowledgements

I would like to thank C. Renfrew and J. E. Dixon for all their enthusiasm and inspiration for our work in the Mediterranean, and D. R. C. Kempe for his not inconsiderable contribution to this chapter.

References

Aikens, C. N. and Minor, R. (1978). Obsidian hydration dates for Klamath prehistory. *Tebiwa* **11**, 1–17.
Ambrose, W. (1976). Intrinsic hydration rate dating of obsidian. In: R. E. Taylor, (ed.): *Advances in obsidian glass studies.* Noyes, Park Ridge, N.J., 81–105.
—— Green, R. C. (1972). First millenium B.C. transport of obsidian from New Britain to the Solomon Islands. *Nature* **237**, 31.

Armitage, G. C., Reeves, R. D., and Bellwood, P. (1972). Source identification of archaeological obsidian in New Zealand. *New Zealand Journal of Science* 15, 408–20.

Asaro, F., Michel, H. V., Sidrys, R., and Stross, F. (1978). High-precision chemical characterization of major obsidian sources in Guatemala. *American Antiquity* 43, 436–43.

Aspinall, A. and Feather, S. W. (1978). Neutron activation analysis of Aegean obsidians. In: *Thera and the Aegean World* I. Thera and the Aegean World, London, 517–21.

—— —— Renfrew, C. (1972). Neutron activation analysis of Aegean obsidians. *Nature* 237, 333–4.

Bailey, D. K. and Macdonald, R. (1970). Petrochemical variations among mildly peralkaline (comendite) obsidians from the oceans and continents. *Contributions to Mineralogy and Petrology* 23, 340–51.

—— —— (1975). Fluorine and chlorine in peralkaline liquids and the need for magma generation in an open system. *Mineralogical Magazine* 40, 405–14.

Bell, R. E. (1977). Obsidian hydration studies in highland Ecuador. *American Antiquity* 42, 68–78.

Belluomini, G. and Taddeuci, A. (1971). Studi sulle ossidiane italiane III. Elementi minori. *Periodico di Mineralogia* 40, 11–40.

—— Discendenti, A., Malpieri, L. and Nicoletti, M. (1970). Studi sulle ossideiane italiane. II. Contenuto in ^{40}Ar radiogenico e possibilità di datazione. *Periodico di Mineralogi* 39, 469–79.

Bigazzi, G. and Bonadonna, F. (1973). Fission track dating of the obsidian of Lipari Island (Italy). *Nature* 242, 322–3.

—— —— Belluomini, G., and Malpieri, L. (1971) Studi sulle ossidiane Italiane IV. Datazione con il metodo delle tracce di fissione. *Bolletino della Società Geologica Italiana* 90, 469–80.

Bonney, T. G. (1877). On certain rock-structure, as illustrated by pitchstones and felsites in Arran. *Geological Magazine* (II) 4, 499–511.

Bowman, H. R., Asaro, F., and Perlman, I. (1973c). On the uniformity of composition in obsidians and evidence for magmatic mixing. *Journal of Geology* 81, 312–27.

—— —— —— (1973b). Composition variations in obsidian sources and the archaeological implications. *Archaeometry* 15, 123–7.

Butler, J. R. and Smith, A. Z. (1962). Zirconium, niobium, and certain other trace elements in some alkali igneous rocks. *Geochimica et Cosmochimica Acta* 26, 945–53.

Cann, J. R., Dixon, J. E., and Renfrew, C. (1969). Obsidian analysis and the obsidian trade. In: D. Brothwell and E. Higgs (ed.): *Science in Archaeology*. Thames and Hudson, London, 578–91.

—— Renfrew, C. (1964). The characterization of obsidian and its application to the Mediterranean region. *Proceedings of the Prehistoric Society* 30, 111–33.

Carmichael, I. S. E. (1962). Pantelleritic liquids and their phenocrysts. *Mineralogical Magazine* 33, 86–113.

Charlton, T. H. (1969). On the identification of pre-Hispanic obsidian mines in southern Hidalgo. *American Antiquity* 34, 176–7.

Chenebaux, J., Bordet, P., and Sabatier, G. (1960). Sur les conditions de formation des obsidiennes et des rétinites. *Compete Rendu Hebdomadaire des Seances de l'Académie des Science, Paris* 250, 1679–80.

Christiansen, R. L. and Noble, D. C. (1965). Black Mountain volcanism of southern Nevada. *Special Paper. Geological Society of America* 82, 246 (abstract).

Cobean, R. H., Coe, M. D., Perry, E. A., Turekian, K. K., and Kharkar, D. P. (1971). Obsidian trade at San Lorenzo, Tenochtitlan, Mexico. *Science* **174**, 666–71.

Coe, M. D. and Flannery, K. V. (1964). The pre-Columbian obsidian industry of El Chayal, Guatemala. *American Antiquity* **30**, 43–9.

Coote, G. E., Whitehead, N. E. and McCallum, G. J. (1972). A rapid method of obsidian characterization by inelastic scattering of protons. *Journal of Radioanalytical Chemistry* **12**, 491–6.

Cosgrove, M. E., Hodson, F., Renfrew, [A.] C., Warren, S., and Shelford, P. H. (1982). Characterization of Melian obsidian. In: [A.] C. Renfrew and J. M. Wagstaff (ed.): *An island policy: the archaeology of exploitation in Melos.* Cambridge University Press.

Creasey, S. C. and Krieger, M. H. (1978). Galliuro volcanics, Pinal, Graham, and Cochise counties, Arizona. *Journal of Research United States Geological Survey* **6**, 115–31.

Dickinson, D. R. and Gibson, I. L. (1972). Feldspar fractionation and anomalous $^{87}Sr/^{86}Sr$ ratios in a suite of peralkaline silicic rocks. *Bulletin of the Geological Society of America* **83**, 231–40.

Dixon, J. E. (1976). Obsidian characterization studies in the Mediterranean and Near East. In: R. E. Taylor (ed.): *Advances in obsidian glass studies.* Noyes, Park Ridge, N.J., 288–333.

Durrani, S. A., Khan, H. A., Taj, M., and Renfrew, C. (1971). Obsidian source identification by fission track analysis. *Nature* **233**, 242–5.

Ericson, J. E. (1975). New results in obsidian hydration dating. *World Archaeology* **7**, 151–9.

—— Berger, R. (1976). Physics and chemistry of the hydration process in obsidians. In: R. E. Taylor (ed.): *Advances in obsidian glass studies.* Noyes, Park Ridge, N.J., 46–62.

—— Kimberlin, J. (1977). Obsidian sources, chemical characterization and hydration rates in west Mexico. *Archaeometry* **19**, 157–66.

—— Hagan, T. A., and Chesterman, C. W. (1976). Prehistoric obsidian in California. II. Geologic and geographic aspects. In: R. E. Taylor (ed.): *Advances in obsidian glass studies.* Noyes, Park Ridge, N.J., 218–39.

—— Mackenzie, J.D., and Berger, R. (1976). Physics and chemistry of the hydration process in obsidians. I. Theoretical implications. In: R. E. Taylor (ed.): *Advances in obsidian glass studies.* Noyes, Park Ridge, N.J., 25–45.

Evans, A. (1921). *The Palace of Minos. Vol. 1. Macmillan, London.*

Evans, C. and Meggers, B. J. (1960). A new dating method using obsidian. Part II. An archaeological evaluation of the method. *American antiquity* **25**, 523–37.

Ewart, A., Taylor, S. R. and Capp, A. C. (1968). Geochemistry of the pantellerites of Mayor Island, New Zealand. *Contributions to Mineralogy and Petrology* **17**, 116–40.

Filippakis, S. E., Grimanis, A. P., and Perdikatsis B. (1981). X-ray and neutron activation analysis of obsidians from Kitsos Cave. *Science and Archaeology* **23**, 21–6.

Findlow, F. J. and De Atley, S. P. (1976). Photographic measurement in obsidian hydration dating. In R. E. Taylor (ed.): *Advances in obsidian glass studies.* Noyes, Park Ridge, N.J., 165–72.

—— Bennett, V. C., Ericson, J. E., and De Atley, S. P. (1975). A new obsidian hydration rate for certain obsidians in the American southwest. *American Antiquity* **40**, 344–8.

Friedman, I. (1958). The water, deuterium, gas and uranium content of tektites. *Geochimica et Cosmochimica Acta* **14**, 316–22.

—— (1976). Calculations of obsidian hydration rates from temperature measurements. In: R. E. Taylor (ed.): *Advances in obsidian glass studies.* Noyes, Park Ridge, N.J., 173–82.

—— Long, W. (1976). Hydration rate of obsidian. *Science* **191**, 347–52.

—— and Peterson, H. V. (1971). Obsidian hydration dating applied to dating of basaltic activity. *Science* **172**, 1028.

—— Smith, R. L. (1953). The deuterium content of water in some volcanic glasses. *Geochimica et Cosmochimica Acta* **15**, 218–28.

—— —— (1960). A new dating method using obsidian. Part 1. The method of obsidian dating. *American Antiquity* **25**, 476–93.

—— Trembour, F. W. (1978). Obsidian: the dating stone. *American Scientist* **66**, 44–51.

—— Long, W., and Smith, R. L. (1963). Viscosity and water content of rhyolite. *Journal of Geophysical Research* **68**, 6523–35.

—— Pierce, K. L., Obradovich, J. D., and Long, W. D. (1973). Obsidian hydration dates glacial loading? *Science* **180**, 733–4.

—— Smith, R. L., and Long, W. D. (1966). Hydration of natural glass and formation of perlite. *Bulletin of the Geological Society of America* **77**, 323–7.

—— —— Clark, D. L. (1969). Obsidian dating. In: D. Brothwell and E. Higgs (ed.): *Science in archaeology.* Thames and Hudson, London, 62–65.

Gale, N. H. (1981). Mediterranean obsidian source characterization by strontium isotope analysis. *Archaeometry* **23**, 41–51.

Gibson, I. L. (1972). The chemistry and petrogenesis of a suite of pantellerites from the Ethiopian rift. *Journal of Petrology* **13**, 31–44.

Gilbert, C. M., Christensen, M. N., Al-Rawi, Y., and Lajoie, K. R. (1963). Structural and volcanic history of Mono Basin, California–Nevada. *Memoir. Geological Society of America* **116**, 275–329.

Gordus, A. A., Wright, G. A., and Griffin, J. B. (1968). Obsidian sources characterized by neutron-activation analysis. *Science* **161**, 382.

—— Fink, W. C., Hill, M. E., Purdy, J. C. and Wilcox, T. R. (1967). Identification of the geologic origins of archaeological artifacts: an automated method of Na and Mn neutron activation analysis. *Archaeometry* **10**, 87–96.

Green, R. C., Brooks, R. R. and Reeves, R. D. (1967). Characterization of New Zealand obsidians by emission spectroscopy. *New Zealand Journal of Science* **10**, 675–82.

Griffin, J. B., Gordus, A. A., and Wright, G. A. (1969). Identification of the sources of Hopewellian obsidian in the middle west. *American Antiquity* **34**, 1–14.

Hallam, B. R., Warren, S. E., and Renfrew, C. (1976). Obsidian in the western Mediterranean: characterization by neutron activation analysis and optical emission spectroscopy. *Proceedings of the Prehistoric Society* **42**, 85–110.

Hammond, N. (1972). Obsidian trade routes in the Mayan area. *Science* **178**, 1092–3.

Heizer, R. E., Williams, H., and Graham, I. A. (1965). Notes on Meso-American obsidians and their significance in archaeological studies. *Contributions. University of California Archaeological Research Facilty* **1**, 94–103.

Hester, J. R. (ed.) (1978) Archaeological studies of Mesoamerican obsidian. Ballena Press, Socorro, N. M. *Ballena Press Studies in Mesoamerican Art, Archaeology and Ethnohistory* no. 3.

Higgins, M. W. (1973). Petrology of Newberry volcano central Oregon. *Bulletin of the Geological Society of America* **84**, 455–8.

Huntley, D. J. and Bailey D. C. (1973). Obsidian source identification by thermoluminescence. *Archaeometry* **20**, 159–70.

Innocenti, F., Mazzuoli, R., Pasquare, G., Radicat, D. L., and Brozolo, F. (1975). The Neogene calc-alkaline volcanism of central Anatolia: geochronological dates on Kayseri–Nigde area. *Geological Magazine* **112**, 349–60.

Jack, R. N. (1971). The source of obsidian artefacts in northern Arizona. *Plateau* **43**, 103–14.

—— (1976). Prehistoric obsidian in California. I. Geochemical aspects. In: R. E. Taylor (ed.): *Advances in obsidian glass studies*. Noyes, Park Ridge, N.J., 183–217.

Katsui, Y. and Kondo, Y. (1976). Variation in obsidian hydration rates for Hokkaido, northern Japan. In: R. E. Taylor (ed.): *Advances in obsidian glass studies*. Noyes, Park Ridge, N.J., 120–40.

Key, C. A. (1968). Trace element identification of the source of obsidian in an archaeological site in New Guinea. *Nature* **219**, 360.

Kimberlin, J. (1976). Obsidian hydration rate determinations on chemically characterized samples. In: R. E. Taylor (ed.): *Advances in obsidian glass studies*. Noyes, Park Ridge, N.J., 63–80.

Laidley, R. A. and McKay, D. S. (1971). Geochemical examination of obsidians from Newberry Caldera, Oregon. *Contributions to Mineralogy and Petrology* **30**, 336–42.

Laursen, T. and Lanford, W. A. (1973). Hydration of obsidians. *Nature* **276**, 153–6.

Leach, B. F. (1977). New perspectives on dating obsidian artefacts in New Zealand. *New Zealand Journal of Science* **20**, 123–38.

—— Anderson, A. J. (1978). The prehistoric sources of Palliser Bay obsidian. *Journal of Archaeological Science* **5**, 301–7.

—— Fankhauser, B. (1978). The characterization of New Zealand obsidian sources by use of thermoluminescence. *Journal of the Royal Society of New Zealand* **8**, 331–42.

Lee, R. R., Leich, D. A., Tombrello, T. A., Ericson, J. E., and Friedman, I. (1974). Obsidian hydration profile measurements using a nuclear reaction technique. *Nature* **250**, 44–7.

Lipman, P. W., Rowley, P. D., Mehnert, H. H., Evans, S. H., Nash, W. P., and Brown, F. H. (1978). Pleistocene rhyolite of the Mineral Mountains, Utah–geothermal and archaeological significance. *Journal of Research United States Geological Survey* **6**, 133–47.

Longworth, G. and Warren, S. E. (1979). The application of Mössbauer spectroscopy to the characterization of western Mediterranean obsidian. *Journal of Archaeological Science* **6**, 1–15.

Lowder, G. G. and Carmichael, I. S. E. (1970). The volcanoes and caldera of Talasea, New Britain: geology and petrology. *Bulletin of the Geological Society of America* **81**, 17–38.

MacDonald, R. and Bailey, D. K. (1972). The chemistry of the peralkaline over-saturated obsidians. *Professional Paper United States Geological survey* **440N**, 1–37.

—— Gibson, I. L. (1969). Pantelleritic obsidians from the volcano Chabbi (Ethiopia). *Contributions to Mineralogy and Petrology* **24**, 239–44.

—— Bailey, D. K., and Sutherland, D. S. (1970). Oversaturated peralkaline glassy trachytes from Kenya. *Journal of Petrology* **11**, 507–17.

Meighan, C. W. (1970). Obsidian hydration rates. *Science* **170**, 99–100.

—— Foote, L. J. and Aiello, P. V. (1968). Obsidian dating in west Mexico. *Science* **160**, 1069–75.

Mendoza, L. H. de (1981). Estimating a hydration rate for Chimatenango obsidian. *American Antiquity* **46**, 159–62.

—— and Jester, W. A. (1978). Obsidian sources in Guatemala: a regional approach. *American Antiquity* **43**, 424–35.

Mertzman, S. A. (1977). The petrology and geochemistry of the Medicine Lake volcano, California. *Contributions to Mineralogy and Petrology* **62**, 221–47.

Michels, J. W. (1969). Testing stratigraphy and artifact reuse through obsidian hydration dating. *American Antiquity* **34**, 15–22.

Minor, R. (1977). An obsidian hydration rate for the lower Columbia River valley. *American Antiquity* **42**, 616–19.

Muir, I. D. and Hivernel, F. (1976). Obsidians from the Melka-Kinture prehistoric site, Ethiopia. *Journal of Archaeological Science* **3**, 211–17.

Nasedkin, V. V. (1963). Volatile components of volcanic glasses. *Geochemistry International* 1964, 317–30. [Translated from the Russian.]

Nandris, J. (1975). A reconsideration of the south-east European sources of archaeological obsidian. *Bulletin of the Institute of Archaeology, University of London* **12**, 71–94.

Nelson, D. E., D'Auria, J. M., and Bennett, R. B. (1975). Characterization of Pacific northwest coast obsidian by X-ray fluorescence analysis. *Archaeometry* **17**, 85–7.

Nelson, F. W., Nielson, K. K., Mangelson, N. F., Hill, M. W., and Matheny, R. T. (1977). Preliminary studies of the trace element composition of obsidian artefacts for northern Campeche, Mexico. *American Antiquity* **42**, 209–25.

—— Voorhies, B. (1980). Trace element analysis of obsidian artifacts from three shell midden sites in the littoral zone, Chiapas, Mexico. *American Antiquity* **45**, 540–50.

Nielson, K. K., Hill, N. W., Mangelson, N. F., and Nelson, F. W. (1976). Elemental analysis of obsidian artefacts by proton particle-induced X-ray emission. *Analytical Chemistry* **48**, 1947–53.

Noble, D. C., Korringa, M. L., Hedge, C. E., and Riddle, G. O. (1972). Highly differentiated subalkaline rhyolite from the Glass Mountain, Mono County, California. *Bulletin of the Geological Society of America* **83**, 1179–84

—— Sargent, K. A., Ekren, E. B., Mehhert, H. H., and Byers, F. M. (1968). Silent Canyon volcanic center, Nye County. *Memoir. Geological Society of America* **110**, 65–75.

O'Keefe, J. A. (1964). Water in tektite glass. *Journal of Geophysical Research* **69**, 3701–7.

Ordonez, E. (1892). Algunas obsidianas de Mexico. *Memorias de la Sociedad Cientifica 'Antonio Alzato'* **6**, 33–45.

Osawa, M., Kiyota, S., Furuya, K., Fujikura, M., Sakakibara, Y. and Kasuya, H. (1974). Trace element abundances in obsidians and jadeites – a preliminary report on archaeological province studies. *Bulletin Tokyo Gakugei University* (IV) **26**, 188–208. [Japanese; English summary.]

Parks, G. A. and Tieh, T. T. (1966). Identifying the geographical source of artefact obsidian. *Nature* **211**, 289–90.

Patton, W. W. and Miller, T. P. (1970). A possible bedrock source for obsidian found in archaeological sites in northwestern Alaska. *Science* **169**, 760–1

Reeves, R. D. and Armitage, G. C. (1973). Source identification of archaeological obsidians in New Zealand. *New Zealand Journal of Science* **16**, 561–72.

—— Ward, G.K. (1976). Characterization studies of New Zealand obsidians: towards a regional prehistory. In: R. E. Taylor (ed.): *Advances in obsidian glass studies*. Noyes, Park Ridge, N.J., 259–87.

Renfrew, C., Cann, J. R., and Dixon, J. E. (1965). Obsidian in the Aegean. *Annual of the British School at Athens* 60, 225–47.

—— Dixon, J. E. (1976). Obsidian in western Asia; a review. In: G. de G. Sieveking, I. H. Longworth, and K. E. Wilson (ed.): *Problems in economic and social archaeology*. Duckworth, London, 137–50.

—— Dixon, F. E., and Cann, J. R. (1966). Obsidian and early cultural contact in the Near East. *Proceedings of the Prehistoric Society* 32, 30–72.

—— —— —— (1968). Further analysis of Near Eastern obsidians. *Proceedings of the Prehistoric Society* 34, 319–31.

Repčok, I. (1977). Fission tracks of uranium and possibility of its applications for dating examples of volcanic glasses. *Zap. Karpaty Ser. Min. Petrogr. Geochem. Loz.* 3, 175–96. [Slovak; English summary.]

Ross, C. S. and Smith, R. L. (1955). Water and other volatiles in volcanic glasses. *American Mineralogist* 40, 1071–89.

Rutherford, N. F. (1978). Fission track age and trace element geochemistry of some Minden rhyolite obsidians. *New Zealand Journal of Geology and Geophysics* 21, 443–8.

Schreiber, J. P. and Breed, W. J. (1971). Obsidian localities in the San Francisco volcanic field, Arizona. *Plateau* 43, 115–19.

Sidrys, R. V. (1976). Classic Maya obsidian trade. *American Antiquity* 41, 449–64.

Smith, I. E. M., Ward, G. K. and Ambrose, W. R. (1977). Geographic distribution and the characterization of volcanic glasses in Oceania. *Archaeology and Physical Anthropology in Oceania* 12, 173–201.

Spence, M. W. (1967). The obsidian industry of Teotihuacán. *American Antiquity* 32, 507–14.

—— Parsons, J. (1967). Prehistoric obsidian mines in southern Hidalgo. *American Antiquity* 32, 542–3.

Stevenson, D. P., Stross, F. H., and Heizer, R. F. (1971). An evaluation of X-ray fluorescence analysis as a method for correlating obsidian artifacts with source location. *Archaeometry* 13, 17–25.

Stross, F. H., Asaro, F., Michel, H. V., and Gruhn, R. (1977). Sources of some obsidian flakes from a paleoindian site in Guatemala. *American Antiquity* 42, 114–18.

—— Hester, T. R., Heizer, R. F., and Jack, R. N. (1976). Chemical and archaeological studies in Mesoamerican obsidians. In: R. E. Taylor (ed.): *Advances in obsidian glass studies*. Noyes, Park Ridge, N.J., 240–58.

—— Bowman, H. R., Michel, H. V., Asaro, F., and Hammond, N. (1978). Mayan obsidian: source correlation for southern Belize artifacts. *Archaeometry* 20, 89–93.

—— Weaver, J. R., Wyld, G., Heizer, R. H., and Graham, J. (1968). Analysis of American obsidians by X-ray fluorescence and neutron activation analysis. *Contributions. University of California Archaeological Research Facility* 5, 59–79.

Taylor, R. E. (ed.) (1976). *Advances in obsidian glass studies. Archaeological and geochemical perspectives*. Noyes, Park Ridge, N.J.

Wagner, G. A. (1978). Alters-und Herkunftsbestimmung Südamerikanischer Obsidianantefakte mittels Spaltspurenanalyse. In: H. W. Hennicke (ed.): *Mineralogische Rohstoffe also Kultur-historische Informationsquelle*. Vereins Deutscher Emailfachleute, Hagen, 200–205.

Wainwright, G. A. (1927). Obsidian. In: *Ancient Egypt*. British School of Archaeology in Egypt, London, 77–93.

Ward, G. K. (1974a). A paradigm for sourcing New Zealand archaeological obsidians. *Journal of the Royal Society of New Zealand* 4, 47–62.

—— (1974b). A systematic approach to the definition of sources of raw material. *Archaeometry* **16**, 41–53.

—— (1974c). Comparison of source and artifact characterization data using a generalised distance measure. *American Antiquity* **39**, 473–77.

Watanabe, N. and Suzuki, M. (1969). Fission track dating of archaeological glass materials from Japan. *Nature* **222**, 1057–8.

Weaver, J. R. and Stross, F. H. (1965). Analysis by XRF of some American obsidians. *Contributions. University of California Archaeology Research Facility* **1**, 89–93.

Weaver, S. D. (1977). The Quaternary caldera volcano Emuruangogolok, Kenya Rift, and the petrology of a bimodal ferrobasalt–pantelleritic trachyte association. *Bullétin Volcanologique* **40**, 209–30.

—— Sceal, J. S. C., and Gibson, I. L. (1972). Trace element data relevant to the origin of trachytic and pantelleritic lavas in the East African Rift System. *Contributions to Mineralogy and Petrology* **36**, 181–94.

Westerveld, J. (1957). Phases of Neogene and Quaternary volcanism in Asia Minor. *Report International Geological Congress* 20th (Seccion 1, Primer Tomo): 103–19.

Wheeler, M. E. and Clark, D. W. (1977). Elemental characterization of obsidian from the Koyukule River, Alaska, by atomic absorption spectrophotometry. *Archaeometry* **19**, 15–31.

Williams, O. and Nandris, J. (1977). The Hungarian and Slovak sources of archaeological obsidian: an interim report on further fieldwork, with a note on tektites. *Journal of Archaeological Science* **4**, 207–19.

Wright, G. A. (1969). Obsidian analysis and prehistoric Near Eastern trade 7500-3500 B.C. *University of Michigan Museum of Anthropology, Anthropological Papers* **37**, 1–97.

—— Gordus A. A. (1969a). Source areas for obsidian recovered at Munhata, Beisamoun, Hazorea and El-Khiam. *Israel Exploration Journal* **19**, 79–88.

—— —— (1969b). Distribution and utilization of obsidian from Lake Van sources between 7500 and 3500 B.C. *American Journal of Archaeology* **73**, 75–7.

Zielinski, R. A., Lipman, P. W. and Millard, H. T. (1977). Minor-element abundances in obsidian, perlite and felsite of calc-alkalic rhyolites. *American Mineralogist* **62**, 426–37.

References added in proof

Hughes, R. E. (1982). Age and exploitation of obsidian from the Medicine Lake Highland, California. *Journal of Archaeological Science* **9**, 173–85.

Michels, J. W. (1982). Bulk element composition versus trace element composition in the reconstruction of an obsidian source system. *Journal of Archaeological Science* **9**, 113–23.

8. Jade axes and other artefacts

A. R. Woolley

Since Neolithic times jade, when available, seems to have played a rather special role as a material for ceremonial axes, utilitarian bowls, small carvings, and a host of other objects and yet, of all the naturally occurring materials worked by man jade is probably the toughest. Chapman (1892) reported that a man might not live long enough to complete one of the nephrite axes fashioned by the inhabitants of New Caledonia. The German mineral dealer Krantz in 1860 also learned to his cost the intractable nature of jade. Having unsuccessfully tried to break a block of nephrite with sledge hammers he sent it to the Krupp Armaments Works at Essen to be broken under a huge steam hammer. The nephrite remained unbroken but the anvil on which the block was placed was ruined. The block was later fragmented by heating it to redness and immersing it in water. For such extraordinarily tough material to have been worked by early man indicates that it must have been held in very high regard indeed. The techniques used by modern Chinese jade carvers, essentially grinding using an abrasive, are outlined in Bishop (1906) and Webster (1975).

The word 'jade' refers to two distinct minerals, nephrite and jadeite, which are members of two large mineral families, the amphiboles and the pyroxenes. Nephrite and jadeite differ considerably in their chemical composition, physical properties, and in the geological processes by which they are formed although, as will be outlined later, they may occur in a closely related geological context. However, the mineralogical distinction between the two forms of jade necessitates separate treatment, which is followed in the rest of this chapter.

Nephrite

Chemical and physical properties

Nephrite is the name given to the fine-grained, tough, dense masses of the amphibole minerals tremolite and actinolite. The definition is thus essentially textural and nephrite is not a mineral species *sensu stricto*. Pure tremolite has the chemical composition $Ca_2Mg_5Si_8O_{22}(OH)_2$ and pure actinolite (strictly ferroactinolite) $Ca_2Fe_5Si_8O_{22}(OH)_2$, but in fact these two minerals constitute the end members of a continuous series of differing iron to magnesium ratios. Members of the series with more than 70 per cent of the actinolite molecule do not normally occur, the great majority of naturally occurring members of the series, including nephrites, having Mg>Fe.

Nephrite varies greatly in colour, though not as much as jadeite. It is, however, usually a darker green than jadeite. White is more frequent in nephrite, but pure white is rare; grey also is rare and yellow very rare. Most typical are shades of green variously described as olive green, seaweed green, golden green, emerald green, spinach green, light sage green, and dark green to greenish black. Many of the green colours are uniform through large blocks of the material. White nephrite, the so-called 'mutton-fat' jade, is a tremolite. It contains little or no iron, but with an increase in the iron content the colour changes to green. Finlayson (1909) has shown that for New Zealand nephrite an increase in the depth of green correlates with an increase in the content of FeO, as shown in Table 8.1. Some of the colours of nephrite are probably caused by the presence of trace amounts of elements such as chromium and manganese, but there seems to have been no scientific study of this. A brown colouration in some nephrites is attributable to weathering, usually forming streaks along cracks or a brown skin around pebbles and boulders which Chinese carvers sometimes incorporated into the design of their work.

A yellowish or greenish brown colour is characteristic of the so-called 'burial jade' from some Chinese archaeological sites. This colour is caused by long burial in the yellow loess of China. The patchy white chalkiness of some Chinese tomb jades, particularly those of the Shang to Han Dynasties

Table 8.1. Variation of ferrous iron with colour in New Zealand nephrites.

	deep green	medium green	olive green	pale green	greenish white
SiO_2	56.25	56.01	55.89	57.45	58.28
Al_2O_3	0.42	0.65	2.34	1.09	0.88
Fe_2O_3	1.67	1.88	2.39	0.24	0.29
FeO	5.61	5.02	2.34	1.35	0.35
MnO	0.33	0.29	0.41	0.28	trace
MgO	20.55	20.65	18.72	20.61	22.08
CaO	12.67	13.41	13.97	15.41	14.98
Na_2O	0.35	0.45	0.51	—	0.42
K_2O	—	0.28	—	0.51	0.38
H_2O	1.89	2.03	2.21	2.65	1.98
Total	99.74	100.67	98.78	99.59	99.64

Taken from Finlayson (1909).

(1766 BC–AD 220), has been shown to be due to alteration by contact with fluids of high pH released from decaying corpses (Gaines and Handy 1975).

Nephrite is very fine-grained and the texture, by definition, is compact, but there is often a distinct foliation or slatiness, which in some types is enhanced by thin folia of differing shades. This allows easier cutting in the direction of foliation. A further characteristic feature of some nephrites, particularly noticeable in boulders from Siberia, New Zealand, and British Columbia, is the presence of small fractures controlled by the foliation direction which cause small scale-like flakes to whiten. This feature, absent from jadeite, is apparent on some nephrite axes and other carved objects.

The hardness of nephrite is about 6½ on Mohs' scale, which is not particularly high; quartz, for instance, is 7 and feldspar 6 on the same scale. However, the fine grain size and interlocking texture endow nephrite with great tenacity so that it is extremely difficult to break. A thorough study of the mechanical properties and toughness of jade has been made by Bradt, Newham, and Biggers (1973), who showed that both nephrite and jadeite are more than ten times tougher than, for instance, quartzite. Freshly fractured surfaces have a dull and wax-like lustre whereas that of polished surfaces is somewhat greasy in appearance, particularly in the paler varieties. Thin slices are often slightly translucent.

The density of nephrite increases from 2.90 to about $3.09 \mathrm{g\ cm}^{-3}$ with increasing iron content; a histogram of 88 nephrite determinations is shown on Fig. 8.1. The spread of values is largely because nephrite, like jadeite, usually contains other minerals such as feldspar, quartz, chlorite, and talc, which are less dense than nephrite; or chromite, magnetite, and garnet, which are more dense. This problem is discussed below.

The upper and lower refractive indices of individual crystals range between 1.600–1.627 and 1.614–1.641, but the fine grain size and fibrous nature of the mineral makes such determinations difficult. If the refractive index of a polished surface is measured using a gemmological refractometer (e.g. Rayner), only a vague reading of about 1.62 can be obtained owing to the aggregate nature of the material.

Fig. 8.1. Histogram of densities of nephrite (88 measurements – lined ornament) and jadeite (173 measurements – dotted ornament) artefacts. The nephrite data are taken from Bauer (1914) and Bishop (1906), and the jadeite measurements from the same sources together with Foshag (1957) and over 100 determinations of British and continental European Neolithic axes from Smith (1963), Jones, Bishop, and Woolley (1977), and unpublished measurements made at the British Museum (Natural History) by D. T. Moore, mainly from axes in the collections of the British Museum and the University Museum of Archaeology and Ethnology, Cambridge. The graph on the left of the diagram is based on 491 density measurements on nephrite artefacts and boulders given in Bishop (1906). Note that the graph has a vertical scale 1/5th of that of the histogram.

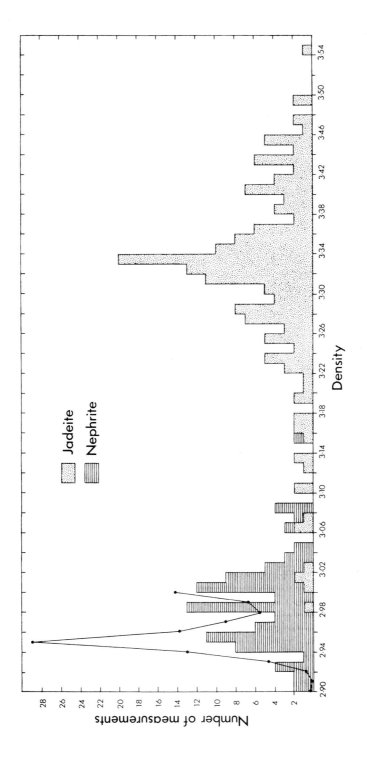

Nephrite is perhaps most easily identified by X-ray powder photography. Very small amounts are required (see p. 32 for details of the method), about the size of a grain of sand, and the X-ray photographs which result are characteristic of the tremolite–actinolite series. Although it is possible to distinguish pure tremolite from the other members of the series by this technique, it is not possible to estimate the proportions of the iron and magnesium end-members; for this a chemical analysis by electron microprobe or other method is necessary.

In summary, if X-ray facilities are not available, a density determination will usually suffice and will distinguish, in most cases, nephrite from jadeite, as illustrated by Fig. 8.1. In Fig. 8.2, after Smith (1963, Fig. 1), density is plotted against refractive index, and the distinction between nephrite and jadeite, and some other minerals which could be mistaken for nephrite, is clear.

Geological provenance of nephrite

The tremolite–actinolite amphiboles are essentially confined to regional and contact metamorphic areas and are characteristic of low to medium grade metamorphism of basic and ultrabasic igneous rocks, and of certain types of sediments including impure dolomitic limestones, from which tremolitic rocks in particular may be generated. There is commonly a close association with serpentinites and talc-bearing rocks.

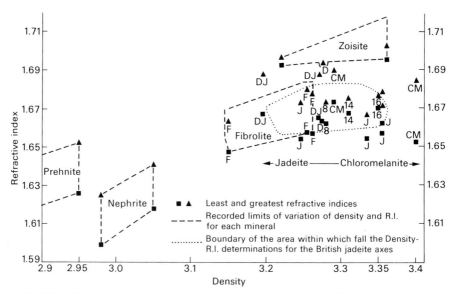

Fig. 8.2. Plot of density against refractive index for nephrite and jadeite, and a range of similar materials, taken from Smith (1963, Fig. 1); reproduced by permission of The Prehistoric Society.

The New Zealand nephrite occurrences, which are perhaps the most thoroughly described (Finlayson 1909; Turner 1935), are all associated with ultramafic igneous rocks including pyroxenites, peridotites, serpentinites, and hornblendites. The nephrite is probably produced by the alteration to actinolite during the metamorphism of pyroxene, olivine, and possibly hornblende. Dynamic metamorphism also seems to have been important in the New Zealand occurrences and it is noteworthy that most nephrite is found in geologically young mountain belts such as the Alps and those around the Pacific Ocean, including New Zealand, New South Wales in Australia, New Guinea, New Caledonia, Taiwan, Alaska, British Columbia, and the western USA.

The first reported occurrence of nephrite in Europe was given by Traube (1885) from a locality at Jordansmühl, now in Poland, but there is a number of potential, and more likely, sources in the Alps. An outline of the principal Swiss occurrences is given by von Dietrich and Quervain (1968), but there have been no attempts in recent years to establish the provenance of European nephrite artefacts using chemical techniques.

Because of its great toughness nephrite resists physical and chemical breakdown and so persists as river boulders, for example in Pakistan, often being transported hundreds of miles from its source. In a number of places boulders constitute the sole supply of nephrite, the *in situ* outcrops having never been found.

Petrological work on nephrite artefacts

During the second half of the nineteenth century and the first decade of the twentieth, considerable data were accumulated on the chemical and physical properties and, to a lesser extent, the petrography of nephrite artefacts and possible source material from most of the known localities. However, since the work funded by Bishop (1906) and the compilation of Bauer (1914) little chemical work has been carried out. Apart from a few determinations of nickel and chromium (Bishop 1906) there has been no trace element work and, as discussed later, this is clearly where advances are likely to be made.

Many density determinations of nephrite artefacts, objets d'art, and natural rocks are given by Bishop (1906), Hintze (1894), and Bauer (1914). Fig. 8.1 is based on these data and shows also a graph based on measurements of 491 nephrites (Bishop 1906), which has two distinct peaks. The histogram is more complex but also gives some indication that the measurements do not give a normal distribution curve. Density histograms for different areas are shown in Fig. 8.3 and it would appear that the abnormal distribution in Fig. 8.1 reflects similar distributions in the European and Chinese data, and the fact that Siberian, New Zealand, and British Columbian nephrites all tend to give higher values. It is clear that the provenance of a nephrite piece cannot be assigned from its density.

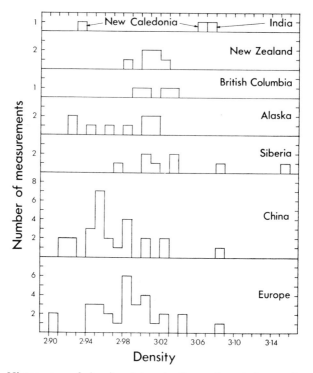

Fig. 8.3. Histograms of density determinations of nephrite artefacts plotted by region. Data sources as for Fig. 8.1.

Chemical analyses of nephrite artefacts, carved objects, boulders and samples from *in situ* outcrops are to be found in Fischer (1880); Hintze (1894); Bodmer-Beder (1903); Bishop (1906); Finlayson (1909); Bauer (1914); Niggli, Quervain, and Winterhalter (1930); and Dietrich and Quervain (1968); the last two references quoting earlier work. There are over 100 published analyses representing all the known types and provenances. Two analyses of supposed nephrite artefacts from Colombia and Brazil are quoted by Hintze (1894), but Foshag (1957) has shown that nephrite does not occur amongst Mesoamerican jades. In fact the Brazilian analysis gives a very high SiO_2 value and low MgO, and the analysis of a Colombian piece is remarkably high in FeO and MgO and very low in CaO. The latter is certainly not nephrite and the former is also probably spurious.

Unfortunately, many of the older analyses are incomplete and commonly do not distinguish between ferrous and ferric iron; also there are very few trace element data, the half dozen analyses for nickel and chromium given in Bishop (1906) apparently standing alone in this field. The quality of many of the analyses is also suspect, particularly the ferrous to ferric iron ratios. Plots of MgO against FeO using the 56 nephrite analyses quoted by Bauer (1914) and the 39 given in Bishop (1906) give quite different distributions because the ferric iron figures are consistently much lower in Bishop's analyses. In fact more than half of these show FeO as 0.5 per cent or less, with higher values for Fe_2O_3, and this is most unlikely to be correct. Of the 13 high quality tremolite–ferroactinolite analyses given in Deer, Howie, and Zussman (1963) not one shows $Fe_2O_3 > FeO$, and usually the $FeO:Fe_2O_3$ ratio is 10 or more.

Although simple plots using these data suggest that there may be groupings according to provenance, Siberian and New Zealand nephrites in particular showing restricted compositions, there is so much scatter, much of which is probably due to analytical error, that the available major element data prove of little use in attempts to correlate chemical composition and provenance. Because of the quality of the analyses it is felt that a selection of analyses of nephrite artefacts would not be helpful here.

Trace element work is sorely needed and, as work on jadeite is already proving, will undoubtedly be more fruitful in 'fingerprinting' localities. However, it is apparent from the available data that there is a moderate range of Mg:Fe ratios, even within one area, so that it will be necessary to distinguish trace elements which correlate with this ratio from those which are independent of it, and thus more likely to characterize a particular occurrence.

Petrographic descriptions and photomicrographs of central European nephrite artefacts are to be found in Bodmer-Beder (1903), of nephrites from British Columbia in Harrington (1890), and from Alaska in Clarke and Merrill (1889), the last reference also including photomicrographs of New Zealand and Siberian nephrite. A very detailed petrographic account, though unillustrated, of New Zealand nephrite artefacts based on over 100 pieces is given by Turner (1935), and an earlier account by Finlayson (1909) describes the different types of New Zealand nephrite. Petrographic descriptions and photomicrographs of very high quality, of both nephrite rock and artefacts from most of the major occurrences, are given in Bishop (1906).

Jadeite

Chemical and physical properties

Jadeite is one member of the large and important group of rock-forming minerals known as the pyroxenes. Pure jadeite has the chemical composition $NaAlSi_2O_6$ but the pyroxenes, like most silicates, form series of differing chemical composition and pure 'end-members' are exceptional. Jadeitic pyroxenes are best represented in terms of three end-members, jadeite ($NaAlSi_2O_6$), acmite ($NaFe^{3+}Si_2O_6$) and augite ($(Mg,Fe^{2+},Al)(Si,Al)_2O_6)$);

compositions intermediate between these end-members can be represented by the triangular diagram illustrated in Fig. 8.7(a). 'Jadeite' artefacts cover a wide range of composition and many of the pyroxenes are not jadeite *sensu stricto*, as defined in terms of Fig. 8.7(a); a nomenclature problem thus arises, which is discussed in Woolley, Bishop, Harrison, and Kinnes (1979).

Although green is the predominant and characteristic colour of jadeite, it displays an even wider colour range than nephrite, including black, white, pink, brown, red, orange, yellow, mauve, blue, and violet, as well as mottled green and white. The most highly prized is a rich emerald green. Like nephrite, it will weather to a brown colour and boulders of Burmese jadeite often have such a brown outer skin.

Jadeite takes a very good polish, but it commonly displays a dimpled appearance owing to the slightly uneven hardness of the surface. Also, the individual crystals are often several millimetres or more across and so can be clearly distinguished. Jadeite has an even, granular texture resulting from the equant shape of the grains, in contrast to the fibrous nature of nephrite.

Individual jadeite crystals have a Mohs' hardness of 6, that is they are a little softer than quartz, but massive material has a hardness of $6\frac{1}{2}-7$ and is extremely tough, giving a splintery fracture. The density ranges from 3.24 to $3.43g\,cm^{-3}$ for pure material, but the presence of other minerals in jadeite tends to reduce the density (Fig. 8.1). A subsidiary cluster of jadeite densities in Fig. 1 in the range 3.38–3.50 represents chloromelanite, a pyroxene intermediate in composition between jadeite and augite and well represented amongst European Neolithic axes; data from these were used in compiling the figure (Woolley *et al.* 1979). As can be seen from Fig. 8.1, a density measurement normally clearly distinguishes jadeite from nephrite.

The maximum and minimum refractive indices of jadeite range between 1.640 and 1.692, but if a polished surface is measured with a refractometer only a vague shadow edge will be seen at about 1.66. A plot of density against refractive index, after Smith (1963), is shown in Fig. 8.2 and normally gives an unambiguous determination of jadeite.

X-ray powder photography will give an unequivocal determination of jadeitic pyroxene. However, there are some variations in the powder patterns, presumably reflecting the presence of other pyroxene end-member molecules, but it is not possible at present to distinguish precisely between the pyroxene species in Fig. 8.7 from their X-ray patterns.

In summary, jadeitic pyroxene can be determined by X-ray powder photography, but this technique will not distinguish clearly the different sodium-bearing pyroxenes, which are best determined by electron microprobe or other chemical analysis. A density greater than 3.1 can be relied upon to differentiate jadeite from nephrite and most simulants (Fig. 8.2). If individual crystals are visible to the naked eye, the material is almost certainly jadeite and not nephrite.

Geological provenance of jadeite

Like nephrite, jadeite is restricted to metamorphic rocks and is thought to be characteristic of areas of the crust which have been subjected to very high pressures, probably of at least 7 kilobars (Newton and Fyfe 1976). Although jadeitic pyroxene is relatively common in some high-pressure rocks, pure jadeite rocks occur only rarely, and only some of these were exploited by man.

Probably the finest jadeite comes from Tawmaw in north Burma, and this material has been used almost exclusively by Chinese lapidaries since the eighteenth century: a full description of the geology, the mine workings, and the carving and trade in jade is given by Chhibber (1934), and the geological map (Fig. 8.4) is based on his work. Outcrops of jadeite rock are indicated by crosses, and are believed to represent four distinct dykes or sills of jadeite–albite rock trending NE–SW, which were intruded into a mass of serpentinized peridotite. However, the field relationships are not well known due to poor exposure and the general inaccessibility of the area. Although the jadeite rock was mined *in situ* for many years, most of the jadeite output came from boulders won from the Uru Boulder Conglomerate (no. 5 in Key of Fig. 8.4), a sedimentary formation occupying a large area to the south and south-east of Tawmaw and reaching a thickness in places of 305 m. Chhibber (1934, p. 42) states that it is believed locally that the jadeite boulders in the conglomerate are more 'mature' than the material mined *in situ*, presumably because the brown weathered skin has been removed by erosion during transport.

Jadeite occurs at several places in the Sanbagawa and Kamuikotan metamorphic belts in Japan, but only the occurrence in the Kotaki-Omi area of the Niigata Prefecture, central Japan, appears to have been exploited as a raw material (Chihara 1974). The jadeite occurs within serpentinites which occur along major fault boundaries; the jadeite association is typically zoned from an inner albite rock through white jadeite rock, green jadeite rock, to an amphibole layer and finally the host serpentinite.

Although the widespread use of jadeite in Mesoamerica has been known since the Spanish conquest, it was not until 1955 that Foshag and Leslie (1955) reported the finding of boulders in the alluvial terraces of the Montagu River near Manzanal, Guatemala. Three *in situ* outcrops, together with further boulder sources, have been described by Hammond, Aspinall, Feather, Hazelden, Gazard, and Agrell (1977), and further outcrops have since been located in both Guatemala and Costa Rica (G. Harbottle and E. V. Sayre, pers. comm. 1979). (See Fig. 4.13.)

In the southern part of Guatemala there is an east–west-trending fault zone, associated with which are many intrusions of basic and ultrabasic rocks including a number of serpentinite bodies (McBirney, Aoki, and Bass 1967).

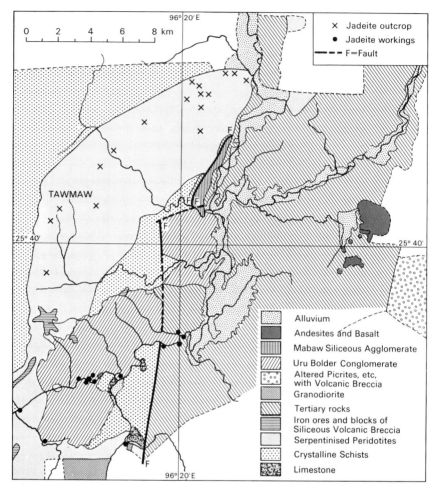

Fig. 8.4. Map showing the geology of the jadeite-bearing region of Burma (after Chhibber 1934, Fig. 1); reproduced by permission of Macmillan, London.

The jadeite apparently occurs within the serpentinites and is associated with albitites; sometimes relatively pure masses of jadeite rock have a selvedge of albitite.

Jadeite and other sodic pyroxenes occur in schists at many localities in the western Alps and these are summarized in Deer, Howie, and Zussman (1978). The Alpine localities include the Mount Mucrone area, the Ambin, and Monvisa massifs, and the Cottian Alps. So far none of these localities has been shown to be the source of the Neolithic axes which are widespread in western Eurpoe. As with other jadeite source areas the Alpine jadeite-bearing rocks are associated with ultrabasic igneous intrusions, including serpentinites, and seem to be spatially related to the zone of deep faulting, known as the Insubric Line, which effectively defines the southern limit of the western Alps.

Rocks containing jadeite pyroxenes are also known from many and widespread localities including Corsica, Greece, Sulawesi, California and elsewhere in the western United States, the Guajira Peninsula in Colombia, and the Polar Urals and Balkhash regions of the USSR, but for none of these is there any evidence that the jadeite was exploited by man as a natural resource.

Petrological work on jadeite artefacts

Early work on jadeite artefacts, like that on nephrite pieces, comprised density determinations, petrography, and some chemistry, the last for major elements only and on whole rock samples, as opposed to purified mineral separates. Reviews of this work will be found in Hintze (1894); Bodmer-Beder (1903), who included photomicrographs; Bishop (1906), who included a petrographic account together with photomicrographs of a high quality; and Bauer (1914). None of these data were analysed nor compared critically with material from outcrops in an attempt to establish provenance. Instead, they were compiled principally for purposes of identification, although in Europe the provenance problem was widely considered and possible localities identified.

Collected density measurements of jadeite artefacts are plotted by region in Fig. 8.5. As with nephrite (Fig. 8.3), density cannot be used to determine

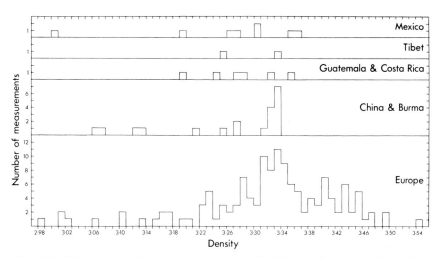

Fig. 8.5. Histogram of density determinations of jadeite artefacts plotted by region. Data sources as for Fig. 8.1.

locality, but the European data are of some interest because of the subsidiary peaks in the range 3.38–3.50; these, as discussed earlier, essentially represent chloromelanite. It was shown by Woolley *et al.* (1979) that amongst European axes there is a correlation of density with typology, as shown in Fig. 8.6, the large, triangular-shaped European axes having lower densities than the small 'hachettes'.

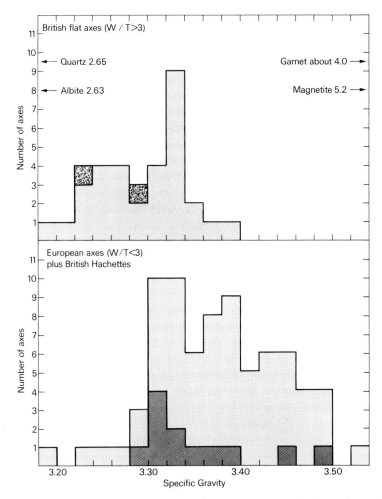

Fig. 8.6. Histograms of specific gravity (determined by the hydrostatic method) of British and continental European axes to show the correlation of sp. gr. with typology. The upper diagram is confined to the large, flat, triangular axes from Britain, defined as having a ratio of width to thickness greater than 3. The lower diagram is for British hachettes and continental European axes with a width/thickness ratio less than 3. It is clear that the triangular axes have an average sp. gr. lower than the others. Redrawn from Fig. 3 of Woolley *et al.* (1979).

Recent researches on European jadeite began with the work of Smith (1963, 1965) who, from the study of thin sections, described and illustrated a range of petrographic types and showed some correlation with typology, although this work was mostly on British axes since only a few sections of continental European axes were then available. He also critically assessed the proposed source rocks, but considered that none of these had so far produced material of the quality and purity characteristic of the large triangular jadeite axes found in northern Europe, including Britain. Smith also discussed the available chemical analyses of jadeite implements and pointed out the wide range of compositions. This can be illustrated by Fig. 8.7 (b), which is based on analyses of European artefacts in Bauer (1914) and Bishop (1906). Although many of these analyses are not reliable, they indicate the range of composition typically to be found. Schmidt and Štelcl (1971) described and illustrated the petrography of eight Neolithic axes from

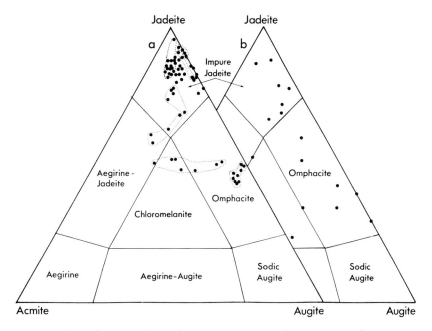

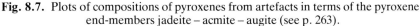

Fig. 8.7. Plots of compositions of pyroxenes from artefacts in terms of the pyroxene end-members jadeite – acmite – augite (see p. 263).

(a) Pyroxene compositions from 14 European Neolithic axes determined by electron microprobe. Dotted lines enclose plots obtained from individual implements to indicate the range of compositions that can occur. Composition fields of pyroxene types are defined and named. Redrawn from Fig. 4 of Woolley *et al.* (1979).

(b) A similar plot but using data for European artefacts from Bauer (1914) and Bishop (1906). Inspection of many of the analyses indicates clearly that they are of a low standard; nevertheless they do indicate a similar range to (a).

Moravia, together with physical and X-ray data, and summarized work on the Moravian jadeite finds.

Further work on European jadeite axes, described in Bishop, Woolley, Kinnes, and Harrison (1977) and Woolley *et al.* (1979), has utilized two relatively new techniques, the thin-wire saw and the electron microprobe. Because jadeite is essentially a rock, usually containing other minerals such as garnet, feldspar, sphene, magnetite, and quartz, besides pyroxene, comparative studies of major elements based on whole rock analyses are distorted by variations due to the other minerals present. For this reason exploration of major element variation is probably best based on pyroxene analyses, which are most easily obtained with the microprobe.

This approach was adopted by Woolley *et al.* (1979) using an initial sample of 14 European axes. Considerable variation in pyroxene composition was found, not only between axes, but also amongst pyroxenes within a single section, as shown in Fig. 8.7 (a). It was also shown that as well as jadeite *sensu stricto* the pyroxenes omphacite, chloromelanite, and rarely aegirine-jadeite (Fig. 8.7 (a)) also occur, posing a problem of nomenclature for this

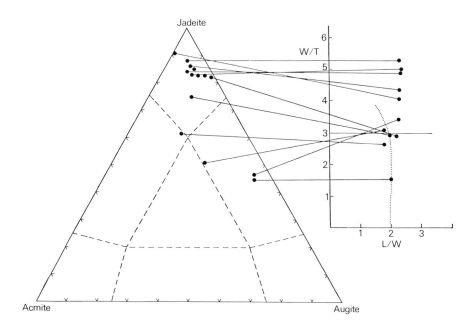

Fig. 8.8. Plot of same pyroxene data as in Fig. 8.7(a), but using average compositions for each artefact, tied to a plot of the width/thickness against length/width of the implements. The trends of the tie-lines indicate a good correlation of pyroxene type with axe typology. Redrawn from Fig. 6 of Woolley *et al.* (1979), in which a fuller discussion will be found.

group of artefacts as a whole. This work also demonstrates a close correlation between pyroxene composition and axe typology, expressed conveniently by a plot of the ratios width/thickness against length/width (Fig. 8.8), which correlates with the double grouping revealed by the density histogram (Fig. 8.6). This study is continuing with the analysis of pyroxenes from a much larger sample, with the analysis of trace elements, and with comparisons with potential source rocks. Indeed, first observations of the petrography of samples of pyroxene-bearing rocks from the Alpine area of north-west Italy indicate that some of these are very similar to some axe types. However, establishing the provenance of European jadeite axes is a difficult problem because of the wide variety of typologies and materials used, which certainly indicates a number of sources.

Guatemalan jadeite was first studied thoroughly by Foshag (1957), who outlined the physical and chemical nature of the material and its archaeological and historical context. On Fig. 8.9 (a) are plotted published compositions of Guatemalan jadeite artefacts (Foshag 1957; Bauer 1914) and pyroxenes analysed by microprobe on rock specimens (Hammond *et al.* 1977). Apart

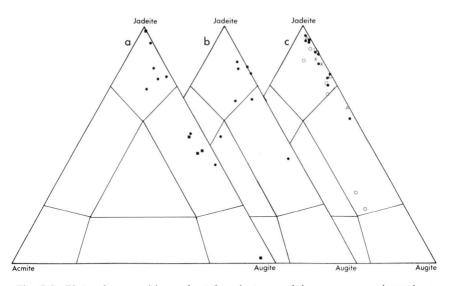

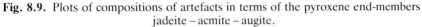

Fig. 8.9. Plots of compositions of artefacts in terms of the pyroxene end-members jadeite – acmite – augite.
(a) Guatemala. Circles, artefacts from Foshag (1957) and Bauer (1914); squares, pyroxenes in natural rocks determined by electron microprobe, from Hammond *et al.* (1977).
(b) Mexican artefacts from Bishop (1906), Bauer (1914), and Foshag (1957).
(c) Burma, natural rock (solid circles); China, artefacts (open circles); Tibet, artefacts (open triangles); and Japan, natural rock (crosses). Data from Bishop (1906), Bauer (1914), and Chihara (1974).

from the pyroxene plotting close to the augite corner of the diagram, it is clear that jadeite *sensu stricto* and omphacite groups occur. Hammond *et al.* (1977) report an extensive chemical study of Mesoamerican jadeite using neutron activation analysis and X-ray fluorescence techniques. Over 70 samples of jadeite materials, some collected from workshop sites, as well as artefacts, and including pieces from Guatemala, Belize, and Honduras, were investigated and the results subjected to detailed statistical analysis. It was shown that some of the sources could be characterized chemically and mineralogically, but it was considered that more data were required to characterize the jadeite sources unequivocally. This work is continuing (see Hammond *et al.* 1977), with further neutron activation analysis, and detailed results are awaited with great interest.

It will be particularly interesting to discover if, by the use of trace element analyses, Mexican jadeite objects can be linked with Guatemalan sources, or whether there is an independent Mexican source. The few available analyses of Mexican artefacts are plotted on Fig. 8.9 (b) and, apart from the point in the chloromelanite field, which is a very poor analysis, there is a double grouping similar to the Guatemalan data. This may suggest a common provenance.

Jadeite artefacts in Japan, mainly in the form of personal ornaments, are restricted to the mid-Jomon, Yayoi, and Kofun periods (Chihara 1974) and there was formerly considerable controversy as to whether the sources were located within Japan. However, a jadeite source was discovered in Japan in 1939 and other Japanese sources have been located since. An outline of the geology and archaeology of jadeite in Japan is given by Chihara (1974) and papers cited therein, and it appears that Japan was the source of the jadeite artefacts found in South Korea.

Analyses of green and white jadeite from Kotaki, Japan, are plotted on Fig. 8.9 (c) and prove to be relatively pure jadeite. However, there appear to be no available detailed analyses of artefacts by which the actual sources used might be defined, although preliminary trace element work on Japanese jadeite is reported by Osawa, Kiyota, Furuya, Fujikura, Suka-kibara, and Kasuya (1974).

It is known that from the eighteenth century onwards most of the jade worked in China was jadeite imported from Burma. A number of analyses of both Burmese jadeite and Chinese artefacts have been published, and they are plotted on Fig. 8.9 (c). Making allowance for the unreliability of the older analyses it is clear that Burmese jadeite is a relatively uniform, pure jadeite containing very little of the acmite molecule. Apart from the two old analyses which fall in the augite-rich part of the omphacite field, and for which there is at present no explanation, the double grouping characteristic of European and Guatemalan jadeite is absent. Also plotted on Fig. 8.9 (c) are two analyses of jadeite from Tibet (Bauer 1914; Bishop 1906), one of which is a very pure jadeite while the other is an omphacite. It is possible that Tibetan jadeite originated in Burma, and the omphacite analysis is in error, but a source of jadeite is known in Tibet.

Jade simulants

Simulants of jade are widespread in the jewellery and gem trades, and there are many references in the archaeological literature to pieces which have been erroneously identified as jade. It is perhaps worthwhile, therefore, to list some of the commoner simulants, and to stress that identification should be based on the physical and chemical properties discussed earlier in this chapter. A fuller account of jade simulants will be found in Webster (1975, 231).

A mineral easily mistaken for jade is bowenite, a variety of serpentine. Bowenite from Kashmir, Afghanistan, and China is passed off as 'new jade' and the same mineral from Korea as 'Korea jade'. Bowenite from Milford Sound, New Zealand, has long been mined and worked by the Maoris, who called it 'tangiwaite'.

Smaragdite, a variety of amphibole, can closely resemble jade as can the green variety of chalcedony, chrysoprase. Poorer simulants include the massive variety of idocrase, known as californite; green microcline feldspar, which has been passed off as 'Amazon jade'; green aventurine quartz, which has been given the pseudonym 'Indian jade'; and chlorite.

A number of rocks consisting principally of hydrogrossular or grossular garnet and idocrase, and known as rodingites, have been mistakenly called and passed off as jade. These include 'South African jade' or 'Transvaal jade', the green variety of which contains idocrase, and the pink variety hydrogrossular garnet. 'Lytton jade' from Canada is also a grossular-idocrase rock. Surprisingly the green 'Connemara marble', also known as *Verd-antique*, has been mistaken for jade, as shown by the unpublished work of W. Campbell Smith on a Neolithic axe from Ireland.

Some problem areas

There are several parts of the world for which there appear to have been no scientific descriptions of artefacts thought to be jade and for which provenance studies are needed. For instance, Bishop (1906) describes a number of nephrite pieces from India and points out that these are distinctive so that there is probably an Indian source.

It would be interesting to know the nature of the artefacts from the Bering Sea coast of Siberia, and how they compare with the material used for artefacts from Alaska and British Columbia. Similarly, apart from the well-known jadeite of Central America, jade artefacts are also reported from Peru, Colombia, Venezuela, Brazil, and Chile, while there is an axe blade in the British Museum collection from Tobago, West Indies, and two West Indian axes are referred to by Bishop (1906). All this material, assuming it proved to be jade, might have a Guatemalan or Costa Rican provenance – or it might not – and clearly the source of Mexican jadeite artefacts is of interest in this context.

The nephrite axes of New Caledonia are distinctive, but there appears to have been no petrological study of them. In the collection of the British Museum there is a greenstone axe from West Irian which could be jade, and Bishop (1906) refers to two pieces from New Guinea, so that there would appear to be a south-west Pacific province which might be investigated as a whole. Jade has also been reported from Java, the Marquesas, the New Hebrides, and elsewhere, but these identifications are likely to be in error.

The source of the jadeite on which Chinese carvers largely drew from the eighteenth century onwards is well known, but the provenance of the nephrite used in earlier times is not so well documented, although there is an extensive literature discussing some possible sources of Chinese nephrite (see, for example, Hansford 1968). However, the extraordinary range of colour and texture of this material, and the very long period over which it was used, suggest that this would be a daunting but probably very rewarding field of research.

Elaborately shaped battle-axes, variously referred to as jadeite (Piggott 1965) or nephrite (Gimbutas 1956), were found in the Borodino hoard, USSR, and similar forms have been found in other parts of the USSR (Gimbutas 1956). Also widespread over northern and central USSR and extending eastwards to China, are rings described by Gimbutas as white nephrite or serpentine, but considered here to be almost certainly nephrite, and it is perhaps noteworthy that white nephrite is a common material of some Chinese artefacts and so may have a common source. The author is unaware of any provenance studies of jades from the USSR, but jadeite is known from the Pay-Yer Mountain in the Polar Urals and elsewhere in the USSR, and there is also the potential source in Tibet (for references see Deer, *et al.* 1978, pp. 477–8).

References

Bauer, M. (1914). Nephrit und Jadeit. In: C. Doelter: *Handbuch der Mineralchemie*, Bd 2. Verlag von Theodor Steinkopff, Dresden und Leipzig, 649–704.
Bishop, A. C. and Woolley, A. R. (1973). A new technique for cutting archaeological material. *Antiquity* 47, 302–3.
Bishop, A. C., Woolley, A. R., Kinnes, I. A., and Harrison, R. J. (1977). Jadeite axes in Europe and the British Isles: an interim study. *Archaeologia Atlantica* 2, 1–8.
Bishop, H. R. (1906). *Investigations and studies in jade*. Privately printed, New York. [2 vols.]

Bodmer-Beder, A. (1903). Petrographische Untersuchungen von Steinwerkzeugen und ihrer Rohmaterialien aus schweizerischen Pfahlbaustätten. *Neues Jahrbuch für Mineralogie, Geologie und Paläontologie. Beilagabände* **16**, 166–98.

Bradt, R. C., Newnham, R. E., and Biggers, J. V. (1973). The toughness of jade. *American Mineralogist* **58**, 727–32.

Chapman, F. R. (1892). On the working of greenstone or nephrite by the Maoris. *Transactions and Proceedings of the New Zealand Institute* **24**, 479–539.

Chhibber, H. L. (1934). *The mineral resources of Burma*. Macmillan, London.

Chihara, K. (1974). Jadeite from the Kotaki-Omi area, Niigata Prefecture, Japan. *Journal of the Gemmological Society of Japan* **1**, 7–18. [In Japanese.]

Clarke, F. W. and Merrill, G. P. (1889). On nephrite and jadeite. *Proceedings of the United States National Museum* **11**, 115–30.

Deer, W. A., Howie, R. A., and Zussman, J. (1963). *Rock-forming minerals*. 2: *Chain silicates*. Longman, London.

——— ——— ——— (1978). *Rock-forming minerals*. 2A: *Single-chain silicates*. Longman, London.

Dietrich, V. von and Quervain, F. de. (1968). Die Nephrit-Talklagerstätte Scortaseo (Puschlav, Kanton Graubünden). *Beitrage zur Geologie der Schweiz* **46**, 1–78.

Finlayson, A. M. (1909). The nephrite and magnesian rocks of the South Island of New Zealand. *Quarterly Journal of the Geological Society of London* **65**, 351–81.

Fischer, H. (1880). *Nephrit und Jadeit nach ihren mineralogischen Eigenschaften sowie nach ihrer urge schichtlichen und ethnographischen Bedentung*. Schweizerbart'sche Verlag, Stuttgart.

Foshag, W. F. (1957). Mineralogical studies on Guatemalan jade. *Smithsonian Miscellaneous Collections* **135(5)**, 1–60.

——— Leslie, R. (1955). Jadeite from Manzanal, Guatemala. *American Antiquity* **21**, 81–2.

Gaines, A. M. and Handy, J. L. (1975). Mineralogical alteration of Chinese tomb jades. *Nature* **253**, 433–4.

Gimbutas, M. (1956). Borodino, Seima and their contemporaries: key sites for the Bronze Age chronology of Eastern Europe. *Proceedings of the Prehistoric Society* **22**, 143–72.

Hammond, N., Aspinall, A., Feather, S., Hazelden, J., Gazard, T., and Agrell, S. (1977). Maya jade: source location and analysis. In: T. K. Earle and J. E. Ericson (ed.): *Exchange systems in prehistory*. Academic Press, New York, 35–67.

Hansford, S. H. (1968). *Chinese carved jades*. Faber and Faber, London.

Harrington, B. J. (1890). Notes on specimens of nephrite from British Columbia. *Proceedings and Transactions of the Royal Society of Canada* **8**, 61–5.

Hintze, C. (1894). *Handbuch der Mineralogie*, Bd 2(2). Veit, Leipzig.

Jones, V., Bishop, A. C., and Woolley, A. R. (1977). Third supplement of the catalogue of jade axes from sites in the British Isles. *Proceedings of the Prehistoric Society* **43**, 287–93.

McBirney, A., Aoki, K., and Bass, M. N. (1967). Eclogites and jadeite from the Motagua fault zone, Guatemala. *American Mineralogist* **52**, 908–18.

Newton, R. C. and Fyfe, W. S. (1976). High pressure metamorphism. In: D. K. Bailey and R. Macdonald (ed.): *The evolution of the crystalline rocks*. Academic Press, London, 101–86.

Niggli, P., Quervain, F. de, and Winterhalter, R. U. (1930). Chemismus schweizerischer Gesteine. *Beiträge zur Geologie der Schweiz* **14**, 1–389.

Osawa, M., Kiyota, S., Furuya, K., Fujikura, M., Sukakibara, Y., and Kasuya, H.

(1974). Trace element abundances in obsidians and jadeites – a preliminary report on archaeological provenance studies. *Bulletin Tokyo Gakugei University* **26**, 188–208. [In Japanese with English abstract.]

Piggott, S. (1965). *Ancient Europe*. Edinburgh University Press.

Schmidt, J. and Štelcl, J. (1971). Jadeites from Moravian Neolithic Period. *Acta Universitatis Carolinae* **1–2**, 141–52.

Smith, W. Campbell. (1963). Jade axes from sites in the British Isles. *Proceedings of the Prehistoric Society* **29**, 133–72.

—— (1965). The distribution of jade axes in Europe. *Proceedings of the Prehistoric Society* **31**, 25–33.

Traube, H. (1885). Ueber den Nephrit von Jordansmühl in Schlesien. *Neues Jahrbuch für Mineralogie Geologie und Paläontologie. Beilagebände* **3**, 412–27.

Turner, F. J. (1935). Geological investigation of the nephrites, serpentines, and related 'greenstones' used by Maoris of Otago and South Canterbury. *Transactions of the Royal Society of New Zealand* **65**, 187–210.

Webster, R. (1975). *Gems, their sources, descriptions and identification*. 3rd edn. Butterworths, London.

Woolley, A. R., Bishop, A. C., Harrison, R. J., and Kinnes, I. A. (1979). European Neolithic jade implements: a preliminary mineralogical and typological study. *Council for British Archaeology Research Reports* **23**, 90–6.

9. Petrological aspects of some sharpening stones, touchstones, and milling stones

D. T. Moore

Introduction

Sharpening stones have been in use since the advent of metal blades. Shotton (1968 p. 489) reports that in the Bronze Age in Britain whetstones were rod-shaped pieces of stone, sometimes squared, and pierced at one end; also, that the choice of specific stones for whetting or honing was reached quite early on. He continues: 'Expediency dictated a careful choice of stone, and the most favoured [in the British Bronze Age] is a closely cemented fine sandstone, although fine quartzose schists were also used.' In this connection, Sanderson (1972) identified a silty greywacke from a Bronze Age barrow, near Beddingham, Sussex.

Others have also discussed the petrographic qualities of good sharpening stones (Tarr 1930; Ellis 1969; Moore 1978), the essential textural requirements being an angular hard mineral, usually quartz, magnetite, or garnet, set in a softer micaceous or calcareous matrix. The shape and usage of sharpening stones have also affected the nomenclature; thus whetstones and scythestones are usually rod-shaped, slipstones wedge-shaped, and batts rectangular. Hones are usually considered to be flatter sharpening stones, but in practice the terms whetstone and hone are freely interchanged. For example, Arkell and Tomkeieff (1953 p. 125) define a whetstone as 'any hard fine-grained rock of which whetstones are made: honestone,' and state that the term has been used in this way since the sixteenth century; before that its meaning was 'any shaped stone used for giving a smooth edge to cutting tools.' The same authors (1953 p. 60) define honestone as 'any fine-grained siliceous stone suitable for sharpening razors or knives.'

Honestones have been quarried since antiquity. Davies and Baines (1953) and Ellis (1969) drew attention to English place names such as Whetstone (Middlesex) and Honor End (Buckinghamshire), where sharpening stone was probably obtained in time past. Arkell and Tomkeieff (1953) suggest that Hanham near Bristol also has etymological connections with the procurement of sharpening stones. Again, the word Wetzstein in the Thüringer Wald of Germany suggests a similar origin, and the nearby Fichtelgebirge were also known as a hone producing area in the nineteenth century (Roth 1887; Lepsius 1903; Schuster 1924). Interestingly also, the Assyrian words for whetstone and corundum appear to be related (Thompson 1934).

It is clear from Pliny (book 36: 164 in Eichholz 1962 p. 131) that in classical times various whetstones were used for sharpening iron. Stones used with oil were obtained from Crete, and from Mt Taygetus, in Laconia, Greece. Sharpening stones used with water were obtained from Naxos, localities in Armenia, and Cilicia, modern Turkey. But these localities now appear to have been lost.

Hones were of some interest to early mineralogists; thus Kirwan (1794, vol. 1, p. 239) mentions novaculite and coarse sandstone as being used in sharpening, and draws attention to the calcareous nature of the 'Turkey Stone'. Sowerby (1811, vol. 4, p. 101–2) mentions novaculite, the 'Turkey Stone', and 'Charley Forest' honestone, which he wrongly said came from Lancashire. Novaculites are not considered further in this chapter as they are of limited archaeological importance. Unquestionably, however, the best nineteenth century reviews of sharpening stones in use, as opposed to excavated sharpening stones, are those of Farey (1811) and Grisewold (1892).

Amongst the first excavated hones to receive any petrographic mention in Britain were two (chlorite-bearing?) 'greenstone' hones excavated in Yorkshire in 1841 (Anon 1864), and Evans (1897) mentions them again, in addition to some other examples. However, it was not until the mid-twentieth century that any systematic honestone investigation was begun. In Britain systematic petrological investigation of stone artefacts began during the 1930s, but even then studies of sharpening stones lagged behind comparable studies of, for example, stone axes. Thus, hones are not mentioned in the compilations of stone implements according to petrographic type of Clough and Green (1972) and Evens, Smith, and Wallis (1972). The few available studies of sharpening stones have been concerned with the establishment of a provenance for the stone. In this connection a thorough petrographic examination of a thin section is essential.

It was Morey and Dunham (1953) who, in Britain, began the study of honestones and their provenance, and later the subject was considerably developed by Ellis (1969). The morphology and other archaeological aspects of Ellis's (1969) material were outlined by Evison (1975). Thin sections of hones had, however, been examined in Germany in the last century (Roth 1887), but were treated in their stratigraphic context, as geological specimens. Recent petrological studies of hones appear to be mainly confined to Britain and Scandinavia, but little has been published.

Ellis's (1969) classification of English hones suggested that some 67 rock types had been in use from Roman to recent times. A re-examination of the Anglo-Danish Thetford material reveals that some of Ellis's hone types are unlikely to have been hones at all, and Moore published a revision of Ellis's (1969) scheme in 1978. In this revised version, Moore suggested that the hone types in archaeological use in England from Roman to more recent times belong to two major groups – exotic material, and more local (and often makeshift) hones. It is this latter material that is such a problem to classify, for many stones will whet a blade after a fashion, but are not sharpening stones *sensu stricto*. For convenience, Ellis and Moore in the Winchester excavation report (in press) called hone material of this type (which in some cases is former masonry) secondary hones. Interestingly in this latter connection, even lapis lazuli appears to have been used as a hone (Hermann 1966, plate 21), and nephrite have been used as hones.

On a world-wide basis, the intrinsic association of sharpening stones with a metal-working culture excludes many geographical areas from this study. However, aboriginal North American whetstones from Alaska were described by Keithahn (1962) as being 'mudstone, siltstone, slate', and 'tuff', but no petrographic details are given.

There is reference in the literature to 'grinding benches', which can probably be considered as stationary whetstones or grinding stones, used for grinding artefacts including stone axes. Sarsen stones, which are silicified sands from the Eocene Reading Beds of southern England, are known to have been used as grinding benches. A grooved sarsen at Overton Down, in Wiltshire, was described in this connection by Lacaille (1963). Sarsens also occur in the Tertiary rocks of the Paris basin and the *polissoirs* of this material found south of Paris are considered by Lacaille (1963) to have been used similarly. Sarsens were also used as querns (Wheeler 1943; see under milling stones). Grooved polishing or grinding stones also occur in Africa; Fagg (1959), for example, mentions artificially grooved rocks at Apoje near Ijebu-Igbo in western Nigeria. Similarly, Kennedy (1962) describes grinding benches on the island of Fernando Po, and Grisewold (1892) mentions grooved rocks from Brazil. Hones or abrasive rubbing-stones were also used to shape bone or other material, according to Lacaille (1954).

Touchstones are far less varied, and are nearly always black fine-grained stones, often pierced for hanging up.

Sharpening stones of metamorphic rock

Schist hones

Attention was first drawn to the widespread occurrence of schist hones in English medieval archaeology by Dunning in 1938 and again in 1948, while Morey and Dunham (1953) and, later, Ellis (1969) undertook the only systematic petrological work on these hones. It was Ellis who first suggested

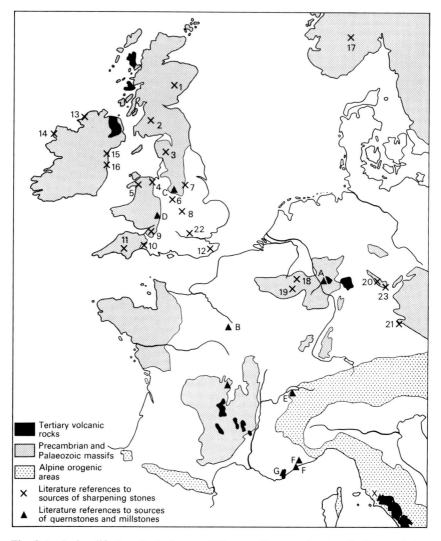

Fig. 9.1. A simplified geological map of Western Europe, showing the Precambrian and Palaeozoic massifs and the Alpine belts shaded. Sites 1–23 are believed to be associated with the procurement of some kind of sharpening stones in historical times. Sites A–W are believed to be associated with milling stones. Compiled from the data of Page (1874); Woodward (1887); Roth (1887); Grisewold (1892); Lepsius (1903); Barrow (1904); Goby (1906); Schuster (1924); Tarr (1930); Wallis (1963); Lacaille (1963); Ellis (1969); Tucker (1977); Bakels (1978); Peacock (1980); and Ellis and Moore (in press).

1. Honestone Series, Allt Bhronn, near Braemar, Aberdeenshire. A quartz-biotite schist.
2. Water-of-Ayr stone, or Snake Stone. A metamorphosed Coal Measures sandstone.
3. Upper Longsleddale, Cumbria. A quartz-mica-cordierite metasiltstone.
4. Flint Coal Measures sandstone.
5. Welsh oilstones from (a) Beddgelert and (b) the 'Crown Hone' from Corwen.
6. Uttoxeter sandstone hone.
7. Yorkshire Coal Measures sandstone.

a Norwegian provenance for a distinctive quartz-muscovite schist commonly used as a hone in medieval times. A schist hone of this material from an excavation in the City of London (Ellis 1969 p. 149) was dated by the K/Ar method, and gave a date of 950 ± 30 m.y., which suggested a provenance in the 'Gothic' metamorphic belt of southern Norway. Ellis (1969) classified this Norwegian Ragstone from Eidsborg as his type $IA_{(1)}$ on this and petrographic grounds.

The Eidsborg schist area of Telemark, Norway (Fig. 9.1), has a history of honestone production (Grisewold 1892; Falck-Muus 1920), and Falck-Muus described two facies of the Eidsborg quartz-muscovite schist, or Norwegian Ragstone: 'hardstein' and 'blautstein'. In Norway the rock was obtained from the top-most Bandak Group of the Telemark Suite (Dons 1960); it is a low grade regionally metamorphosed psammitic schist, within the greenschist facies. The hardstein is a fine-grained blue-grey schist, and the blautstein has a silver-grey colour due to its greater content of muscovite; however, the two types are probably gradational. They are illustrated in thin section in Fig. 9.2 (b) and Fig. 9.3, while modes and new chemical analyses are given in Table 9.1.

Ellis and Moore (in press) noted the occurrence of this Norwegian Ragstone in the medieval Winchester excavation, and Ellis (1969) remarked on

---

8. 'Charley Forest' hone from Charnwood Forest, Leicestershire.
9. Pennant Grit, from Hanham, Bristol. A quartz-muscovite grit.
10. Devonshire Batt. A quartz-muscovite-tourmaline grit from the Blackdown Hills.
11. Tavistock oilstone.
12. Kentish Ragstone. A quartz-glauconite fossiliferous limestone.
13. Killicreen, Donegal.
14. Clare Island.
15. Drogheda.
16. Howth, Dublin Bay.
17. Norwegian Ragstone. A quartz-muscovite-biotite-calcite-chlorite-zircon-ore-bearing schist from Eidsborg.
18. Recht-Stavelot area of the Ardennes, Belgium.
19. Hones from (a) Viel-Salm and (b) Ottré, Ardennes.
20. Wetzstein, Thüringer Wald, Germany.
21. Ratisbon razor hone, from Regensburg, Bavaria, Germany.
22. Sarsen stones from the Chalk downlands.
23. Fichtelgebirge, Germany.

A. The Rhineland Tertiary lavas.
B. French Burrstone from near Fontainebleau.
C. Derbyshire and Yorkshire Millstone Grit millstones.
D. 'Welsh' millstones, from Herefordshire.
E. Biot.
F. Villeneuve–Louvet.
G. Antibes.
H. Auvergne Tertiary lavas.
J. Draycott, Mendip Hills, Somerset.
K. Forest of Dean, Gloucestershire.
L. Winslow, Buckinghamshire.
M. Collier Law, Stanhope, Co. Durham.
N. Carr Crags, Nr Newbiggin-in-Teesdale, Co. Durham.
P. Gateshead, Co. Durham.
Q. Glenstocken, Kirkcudbright.
R. Kaim Hill, Ayrshire.
S. Craigmaddie Muir, and Abbey Craig, Stirling.
T. Spittal, Stirlingshire.
U. Penallt, Gwent.
V. Bridgend, Glamorgan.
W. Llanbedrgoch, Anglesey.
X. Orvieto, Italy.

Other less well documented sharpening stones, rubbing stones, and milling stones may reasonably be expected to occur in the Precambrian and Palaeozoic massifs and the Alps.

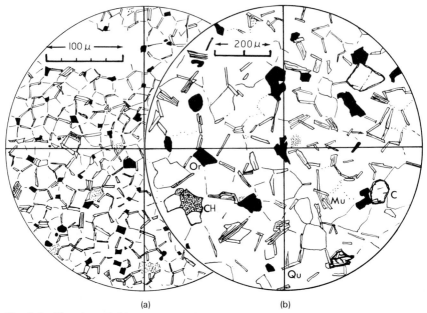

Fig. 9.2. Sketches of thin sections of (a) blue phyllite and (b) Eidsborg schist. Note the scale difference; see also Fig. 9.3. C = calcite, CH = chlorite, Or = ore, Qu = quartz, Mu = muscovite.

its medieval occurrence at York, Thetford, and elsewhere. Moore (1978) reported on its comparable occurrence at Bristol, Oxford, Northampton, Yarmouth, Hull, and in Haithabu (Hedeby) in West·Germany (Fig. 9.4).

The Eidsborg hones appeared in East Anglia at about the time of the first Danish invasion (Ellis 1969), and their use continued until recent times (Grisewold 1892; Moore 1978). It is known, too, from the Klastad ship (Christensen 1970; Moore 1978) that Norwegian Ragstone was carried on Norwegian ships in the medieval period, almost certainly for trading purposes.

Dunning (1948) described medieval hones of quartz-mica-calcite-chlorite granulite from Leicester. From the mineralogy it seems reasonable to classify these hones as probably Norwegian Ragstone. Also, Ellis (1971) and Sanderson (1975) described Norwegian Ragstone (Ellis's type IA(1)) from the deserted medieval village of Lyveden, Northamptonshire. Some recent finds of what are probably Norwegian Ragstone are illustrated in Fig. 9.4, based on the data of Ellis (1969), Sanderson (1975), and Moore (1978). Data from the earlier maps of Dunning (1938, 1948) are reproduced only as small dots, as it is felt that the use of the term 'mica-schist' (Dunning 1948 p. 231) does not necessarily suggest a Norwegian provenance.

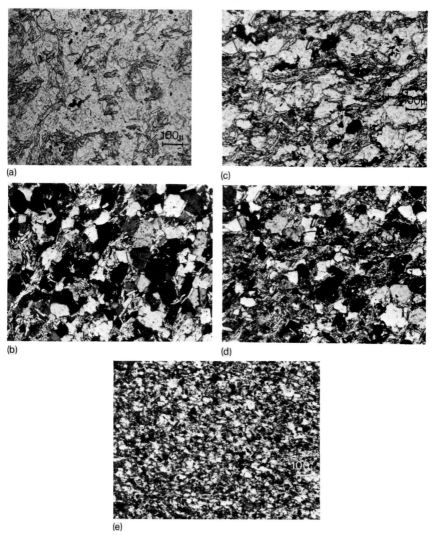

Fig. 9.3. Eidsborg schist; (a) and (b), hardstein [BM 1977, P3(1)]; (c) and (d), blautstein [BM 1977, P3(2)]. Plane polarized light above; crossed polars below. Also blue phyllite (e), plane polarized light. The bar is 100 μm.

Norwegian Ragstone was not the only schist hone in use in ancient times (Ellis 1969). Page (1874), in addition to Norwegian Ragstone, recognized 'Scotch' (Scottish) and Russian Ragstone, and the position could be still more complex. For example, Barrow (1904) gives some account of the schistose Scottish 'Honestone Series' of Allt Bhronn, Aberdeenshire, and

Table 9.1. Chemical analyses of the Eidsborg schist (Norwegian Ragstone).

	1	2
SiO_2	80.10	76.50
TiO_2	0.523	1.22
Al_2O_3	8.38	8.62
Fe_2O_3	1.19	3.39
FeO	1.45	1.44
MnO	0.032	0.031
MgO	1.00	1.33
CaO	1.23	0.93
Na_2O	0.98	0.70
K_2O	2.56	2.94
H_2O^+	1.11	1.47
H_2O^-	0.03	0.21
P_2O_5	0.079	0.118
CO_2	0.97	0.24
Other elements	0.30	0.54
Total	99.93	99.68

Other elements		
Cr_2O_3	0.031	0.067
V_2O_3	0.01	0.009
NiO	0.209	0.404
CoO	0.003	0.003
BaO	0.029	0.038
SrO	0.001	0.002
Li_2O	0.002	0.002
Rb_2O	0.006	0.007
BeO	0.001	0.001
CuO	0.001	0.001
ZnO	0.007	0.005
Total	0.30	0.54

Analyst: V. K. Din. Methods: XRF, AAS, CHN analyser, and gravimetric.

Modal analyses		
quartz	60.3	49.9
muscovite	32.8	45.2
biotite	0.8	1.8
chlorite	0.05	0.2
ore	2.8	4.6
calcite	2.6	nil
points counted	1857	1089

1. Hardstein [BM 1977, P3(1)] Eidsborg, Telemark, Norway.
2. Blautstein [BM 1977, P3(2)], Olsunstak, Eidsborg, Telemark, Norway.

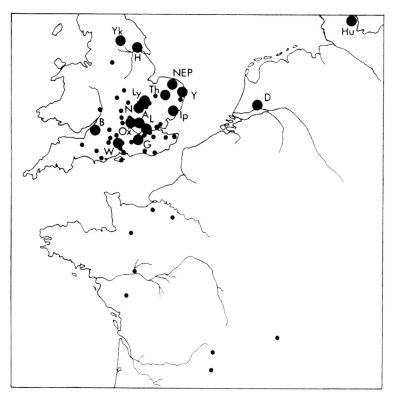

Fig. 9.4. Sites which have yielded medieval 'schist hones'. The small dots indicate sites mentioned by Dunning (1938, 1948). The large dots are occurrences of better accredited Norwegian schist hones (see text), of distinctive mineralogy, from the data of Ellis (1969, 1971), Sanderson (1975), and Moore (1978).

A	Aylesbury	Hu	Haithabu (Hedeby)	Ox	Oxford
B	Bristol	Ip	Ipswich	Th	Thetford
D	Dorestad	L	London	W	Winchester
G	Guildford	Ly	Lyveden	Y	Yarmouth
H	Hull	NEP	North Elmham Park (Norfolk)	Yk	York

Ellis (1969) points out that, in hand specimen alone, the Norwegian Rag-stone is indistinguishable from some Scottish schists. Sanderson (1975) describes a quartz-tremolite-epidote schist used as a hone from Lyveden which, although it could be Norwegian, is equally likely to have a Scottish provenance. Thus, a few Norwegian schist hones, obtained perhaps from glacial deposits, could well have been used in pre-Viking times.

Phyllite hones

Associated with the schist hones in many Viking and medieval sites, most notably Hedeby, York, and Thetford, is a dark, blue-purple, very fine-grained hone (Fig. 9.3 (e) and Fig. 9.2 (a)). In thin section this material is composed of very fine-grained quartz, of the order of 20 μm grain diameter, with muscovite and abundant ore. Ellis (1969) called this hone type IB$_{(1)}$; unfortunately, its provenance is unknown.

Petersen (1951) mentions a blue-violet slate from Norway, which was used as a hone in the main Viking period, but Ellis, who had examined some Norwegian 'bluish slate' hone material in thin section (Ellis 1969 p. 150), reported that Petersen's specimens were of two main types: the Eidsborg 'schist hone' mentioned above and what are called here the phyllite hones.

The relative abundance of the quartz-muscovite-ore phyllite hone at the important Viking site of Hedeby led Moore (1978) to consider whether this stone had a German or central European source. As was suggested earlier, the Wetzstein area of the Thüringer Wald, and also the Fichtelgebirge, have a history of hone production. Violet slates, however, also occur associated with the well known Ratisbon (Regensburg) hone (see Fig. 9.1). Again, violet slate hones are well known to have been obtained from the Viel-Salm and Recht areas in the Ardennes in the nineteenth century (Renard 1882; Roth 1887) and were said to contain quartz, spessartine, sericite, chlorite, rutile, tourmaline, and hematite. However, some other purple Ardennes hones from the Ottré area of Belgium contain the rather rare variety of chloritoid, ottrelite (Renard 1882).

Phyllites and Wetzschiefer (slates), however, occur in all the Precambrian and Palaeozoic massifs of north-west Europe (Fig. 9.1), and no doubt found some local use as hones in times past.

Sharpening stones of greywacke, grit, gannister, and sandstone

Greywackes and sandstones are defined here in the petrographic terms of Pettijohn (1975), and hones of these arenaceous rocks have some features in common, such as a content of sharp angular quartz grains in a very fine-grained clayey or micaceous matrix. Such rocks occur frequently in the Precambrian and Palaeozoic massifs of north-west Europe. Thus, the Wetzschiefer of the Fichtelgebirge (No. 23 in Fig. 9.1) are Upper Cambrian to Upper Devonian in age (Roth 1887), and the Viel-Salm and Recht hones of the Ardennes (Nos 18 and 19 in Fig. 9.1) are fashioned from Cambrian rocks (Renard 1882; Roth 1887). The use of greywacke from the British Palaeozoic, most notably Wales, the English Lake District, and southern Scotland, is discussed by Ellis (1969). The regions where these rocks are prevalent are shaded in Fig. 9.1. Hones of this type are documented as having been used in medieval times; a greywacke siltstone hone was mentioned by Sanderson (1975) from Lyveden, Northants. Sanderson (1972) also described a bronze age silty greywacke hone from Sussex. Ellis

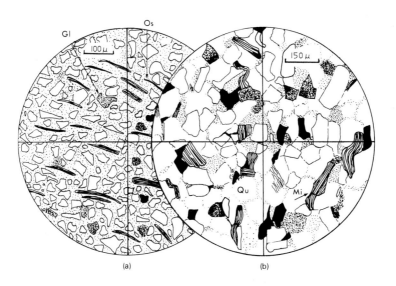

Fig. 9.5. Sketches on thin sections of (a) Kentish Ragstone and (b) Pennant Grit. Qu = quartz, Mi = mica, Os = ostracod fragments, Gl = glauconeite.

(1971) and Sanderson (1975) further describe greywacke hones of the Carboniferous Millstone Grit type excavated from Lyveden.

Certain hones are of gannister and other poorly-sorted and deltaic sandstones of Coal Measures age. A thin section of a rock of this type (Pennant Grit) is illustrated in Fig. 9.5 (b) and Fig. 9.6 (c) and (d).

The nineteenth century hones of Coal Measures sandstone type are important, because writers early in the last century described well-established quarries from which honestones had been extracted in earlier times. Thus Farey (1811) mentions the Coal Measures sandstone hones and grindstones of Yorkshire and Derbyshire at some length. Ellis and Moore (in press) matched in thin section hones from medieval Winchester with Pennant Grit from Hanham, near Bristol. The Pennant Grit is a variable Coal Measures sandstone, occurring only in the South Wales, Forest of Dean, and Bristol coalfields at the base of the Upper Coal Series. Earlier, Dunham (1948–9) had described a twelfth century hone from Oxfordshire as being of Coal Measures sandstone type. William Smith (1769–1839), the 'Father of English Geology', in his county geological map of Gloucestershire of 1819 annotated the Forest of Dean area with 'coal with . . . micaceous gritstone rocks which rising into high hills on the borders of the forest are wrought for paving stones, steps, cyder mills, grindstones & c'. There is

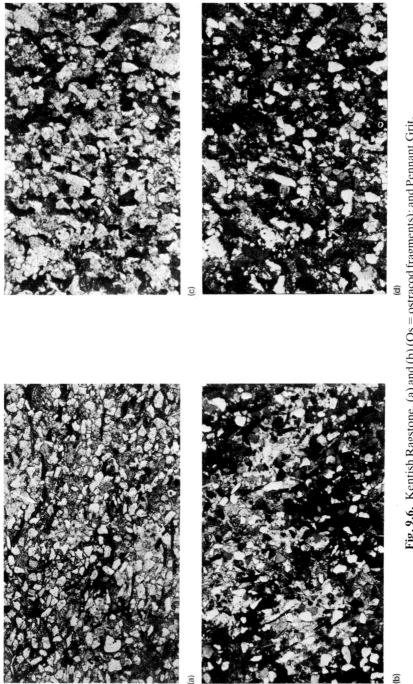

Fig. 9.6. Kentish Ragstone, (a) and (b) (Os = ostracod fragments); and Pennant Grit, (c) and (d). Plane polarized light above; crossed polars below.

reason for thinking, therefore, that Coal Measures sandstones in general, and the Pennant Grit in particular, have been associated with sharpening, grinding, and milling for some considerable time.

Vancouver (1808) mentions the Devonshire batts and gives a passing account of the honestone-producing areas of the Blackdown Hills on the Somerset–Devon border. Fitton (1836) also develops this account of the Devonshire batts; in petrographic terms, Moore (1978) noted that a Devonshire batt was a quartz-muscovite-tourmaline grit.

Sandstone hones are described from several archaeological sites in England. Atkinson (1942) mentions sandstone hones of the Roman period as being obtained from the neighbourhood of Stony Stratford, Buckinghamshire, but whether these are true sandstone and would be recognized as such by a petrologist looking at a thin section is not known. Powell (1974) also noted the occurrence of hones of this general type from Roman Longthorpe, near Peterborough. Oakley (1936) mentions a pink micaceous rock similar to some Carboniferous sandstones obtained from an excavation in Rutland.

Interestingly, two of the most abundant sandstones in central England, the Devonian Old Red Sandstone and the Permo-Triassic New Red Sandstone, are little used as hones; their rounded, aeolian, desert-type quartz grains make a less satisfactory hone than the sharper, angular grains of the grits. Old Red Sandstone is used in milling however, see below.

Sharpening stones of limestone type

Of greatest importance in this group of sharpening stones is the Lower Cretaceous Kentish Rag hone of Roman times and, to a lesser extent, some hones of Jurassic Purbeck Limestone. Morey and Dunham (1953) first matched hones from Canterbury with samples of the Kentish Rag (Lower Greensand) from Chilmington quarry, Ashford, Kent, and Ellis (1969) called this rock his type IVB. Ellis and Moore (in press), however, found another sandy limestone, perhaps Purbeck in age, to be of probable local importance at Winchester.

Ellis (1969) and Moore (1978) list some English archaeological sites where the Kentish Rag is known to have been found. The Rag is a characteristic rock, containing similarly sized grains of angular quartz, glauconite, and fossil debris (echinoid spines and ostracod tests) in a calcareous matrix, and hones made of this material frequently wear to a characteristic rounded cross-section; it is illustrated in Fig. 9.5 (a) and Fig. 9.6 (a) and (b). The 'calcareous siltstone', for example, used as a hone in Roman Leicester (Hebditch and Mellor 1973) is in all probability Kentish Rag, but this has not been confirmed by a thin section examination.

The calcareous 'Turkey Stone' is so badly defined and little mentioned in archaeological literature that it is not considered here.

Touchstones

Touchstones are used to estimate the proportion of gold in an alloy and in the hands of a skilled assayer, and over a certain alloy range, are known to be remarkably accurate (Oddy and Schweizer 1972). Thin sections show that touchstones contain angular hard minerals conferring abrasive qualities. This enables the stone to remove sufficient gold to leave a streak.

Theophrastus first mentions the use of touchstone for assaying in Lydia (Caley and Richards 1956) and gives the provenance of the touchstone material as the bed of the River Tmolos, but its precise location and geological formation is not clear: the River Tmolos is believed by Caley and Richards to be in the Boz Dagh massif of western Turkey, ancient Lydia. Pliny, using Theophrastus' data, also mentions the touchstone (book 33: 126 in Rackham 1961 p. 94) and likewise gives its source as the bed of the Tmolos, although he says that the touchstone is now found in various places – *nunc vero passim*. Consequently the names 'Lydian stone', basanite (see below), and touchstone have become synonymous. However, there is no petrological reason for believing that post-Classical touchstones from north-west Europe have any connection with Lydia whatsoever.

At the time of writing, only some six touchstones are known to have been examined in thin section in Britain: three from the Ludlam collection in the Geological Museum, Institute of Geological Sciences, by courtesy of E. A. Jobbins; one from medieval Winchester (Ellis and Moore, in press); and two present day touchstones from Czechoslovakia, by courtesy of W. A. Oddy of the British Museum Research Laboratory. In these six sectioned touch-stones some five rock types have so far been recognized (data of Moore and Oddy). These include: (i) a 'black matrix' type, containing quartz grains in an opaque ferruginous (or carbonaceous) matrix; (ii) a tuffaceous type, remarkably similar to Langdale axe Group VI, and conceivably from the Borrowdale Volcanics, Cumbria; (iii) a fine-grained and probably magnetite-bearing silicified siltstone; (iv) a cherty type; and (v) a greywacke type.

Domkář, Pelc, and Zoubek (1978) in Czechoslovakia, however, found that the best quality Czech touchstones in contemporary use were black quartz-bearing slates and 'silicites', known as lydite (probably for the reasons discussed above). Petrographic examination reveals these rocks to be contact metamorphosed siltstones and slates with a grain size less that 50 μm containing chlorite, biotite, quartz, and plagioclase. The authors suggested a provenance in the Barrandian area.

Grain size is apparently critical to the assaying properties of a touchstone, larger grains than those mentioned above, as well as cracks, veins, etc, tending to lower the quality. The coarser greywackes were therefore less desirable than the finer-grained types.

Johannsen (1938, vol. 4, p. 231) and Gary, McAfee, and Wolf (1974) outline the nomenclatural problem concerning touchstones. The word 'basanite' is used in different ways by Classical students and petrologists, and each group appears to be largely unaware of the other usage of the word.

The term βασανος was applied by the Greeks to touchstone (Lydian stone). Unfortunately, Brongniart used the word basanite as a rock name in 1813 and again in 1827. In modern petrological usage, Johanssen (1938, vol. 4, p. 232) and Gary *et al.* (1974) define basanite as a fine-grained basic alkaline rock made up of pyroxene, calcic plagioclase, nepheline or other feldspathoid, and olivine (without olivine, the rock would be tephrite). Also, perhaps due in part to their black colour, and in part to the derivation of the name basalt also from βασανος (Johanssen 1938, vol. 3, p. 246), the belief has grown up that touchstones are of basalt. However, of the touchstones that have so far been examined in thin section, none are basanite or basalt.

Milling stones

There appears to be considerable variety in the types of stone used in milling. However, there does appear to be some similarity between the textures of sharpening and milling stones, for both usually contain hard angular minerals.

Classical writers appear to have known something of the rock types used in milling. Thus Ovid (*Fasti* 6: 318 in Page, Capps, and Rouse 1931) mentions '*quae pamiceas versat asella molas*' (and the ass which turns the mill [stones] of pumice). Also, Pliny (book 36: 136 in Eichholz 1962, p. 111) refers vaguely to rotary querns from Volsinis.

Arkell and Tomkeieff (1953) quote English place names as suggesting sources for quernstones in bygone days. Quern is considered by them as being derived from the Old English *Cweorn* or *Cweornstan* (quernstone). Thus, for example, Querndon (Derbyshire), Quarrington (Durham), and Quarlton (Lancashire) were presumably places connected in Anglo-Saxon times with some kind of milling.

The Carboniferous Millstone Grit of England has long been associated with milling, as its name suggests (Whitehurst 1778; Arkell and Tomkeieff 1953; Tucker 1977), and Kenyon (1950) mentions a quern of 'porous sandstone' which is considered to be of Derbyshire Millstone Grit. Sanderson (1975) described Millstone Grit querns from the medieval site at Lyveden, Northants. Romano-British querns from Scole, Norfolk (Moore 1977), also included representatives of Millstone Grit. The mineralogy of these Millstone Grit querns consists of quartz, microcline, plagioclase, biotite, and muscovite. There are fragments of quartzite, and the grains are frequently cemented by ferruginous material. Beehive querns from north-east York-

Table 9.2. Some major millstone sources in the United Kingdom abbreviated from Tucker (1977, pp. 13–16). For other sources and bibliography see Tucker (1977); also Farey (1811); Smith, Rhys, and Eden (1967); Stevenson and Gaunt (1971); Ramsay (1881); and Greenly (1919). Geological annotations are by the present writer.

England

Dracott, Somerset. Dolomitic conglomerate. Millstone specimen from a tannery at Fairland, Cheddar. Quarries at ST 48 51. [Dolomitic conglomerate (Triassic) of the Geological Survey]. See letter J on Fig. 9.1.

Forest of Dean, Glos. Sandstone and sandstone-quartz conglomerate. Reputed Roman millstones and more recent millstone making. [Pennant Grit (Coal Measures) outcrops in the area, see text.] See letter K on Fig. 9.1.

Winslow, Bucks. Conglomerate millstones supposedly made in Middle Ages. [Jurassic, possibly Corallian. In this connection millstone grit is not the same rock as Millstone Grit (Carboniferous), known to British geologists.] See letter L on Fig. 9.1.

Peak District, Derbyshire–Yorkshire border. Source of the Millstone Grit (Carboniferous) millstones known to have been obtained from Stanage Edge, Hathersage, Burbage, and Padley. Also the Lower Kinderscout Grit (Carboniferous) from near Cluster Rocks, SK 074 878, the Ashover Grit (Carboniferous) at Robin Quarry near Ashover, SK 342 616, and the Crawshaw Sandstone (Coal Measures) at Stone Edge, SK 34, 67. See letter C on Fig. 9.1.

Collier Law, near Stanhope, Co. Durham. Millstone Grit quarry at Millstone Rigg, NZ 005 420. [Millstone Grit in the geological sense – see above.] See letter M on Fig. 9.1.

Carr Crags, near Newbiggin-in-Teesdale. A quarry at NY 918 316 still contains some half-finished millstones according to Tucker (1977). See letter N on Fig. 9.1.

Gateshead, Co. Durham. Several quarries in the neighbourhood. Windynook quarries centred at NZ 277 606, Eighton Banks quarries around NZ 277 583, and Gateshead Fell quarries around NZ 265 605. [Coal Measures sandstone]. See letter P on Fig. 9.1.

Scotland

Glenstocking, Kirkcudbright. A quarry at NX 864 527 [The quarry referred to by Tucker (1977) is close to the metamorphic aureole of the Criffel granite.] See letter Q on Fig. 9.1.

Kaim Hill, Ayrshire. Quarries SE of Fairlie at approx NS 22 53 in 'millstone grit'. [Conceivably the millstones were won from one of the bands of cornstone of the Upper Old Red Sandstone (Devonian), or possibly from the intermediate volcanic rocks of the neighbourhood.] See letter R on Fig. 9.1.

Craigmaddie Muir, Stirlingshire. Quarries along line NS 578 762–581 762 and at NS 587 765 with many abandoned unfinished millstones in lava. See letter S on Fig. 9.1.

Spittal, Stirlingshire. Minor millstone quarry in conglomerate at NS 507 973. [Possibly conglomerate or cornstone of the Lower Old Red Sandstone (Devonian), which occurs near the Highland Boundary fault.] See letter T on Fig. 9.1.

Abbey Craig, near Stirling. Basalt millstones possibly from NS 81 95. [The Midland Valley of Scotland; Upper Palaeozoic basalts occur in the area.] See letter S on Fig. 9.1.

Wales

Penallt, Gwent and neighbourhood. The main source of the 'Welsh Stones' in red sandstone-quartz conglomerate at SO 503 092 and area. [The Lower and Upper Old Red Sandstone (Devonian) outcrop in the area.] See letter U on Fig. 9.1.

Near Bridgend, Glamorgan. A silica burr used for millstones. See letter V on Fig. 9.1.

Near Llandbedrgoch, Anglesey. Quarry around SH 51 82 has old millstones lying around. Ynys nearby is also connected with millstones. See letter W on Fig. 9.1.

shire were also made from Millstone Grit, according to Heyes, Hemingway, and Spratt (1980).

Tucker (1977) gives a review of nineteenth century milling stones comparable with that of Farey (1811) concerning hones. Tucker's (1977) data, slightly modified, are given in Table 9.2. It should be remembered, however, that these were millstones used in the nineteenth century; the position a thousand years before is not so clear. Nevertheless, John Whitehurst (1713–88), writing in 1778, recorded the term Millstone Grit as being well established, and it seems reasonable to assume that some of the other milling stones in Table 9.2 may also be of some antiquity. A study of Yorkshire beehive querns by Heyes, Hemingway, and Spratt (1980) also locates factories and discusses the rock types used. The sources of sandstone and more calcareous rocks used for these querns are considered to be in the Jurassic Deltaic Series of Yorkshire.

In Roman and medieval times the Coal Measures sandstone, Pennant Grit, was used at Winchester (Ellis and Moore, in press) and other Coal Measures sandstones are also known in milling and grinding (Table 9.2). Pennant Grit (Fig. 9.6 and 9.7) was also identified as a fourteenth century quernstone at Penhallam in Cornwall, together with 'Sutton Stone' from near Bridgend, South Wales (Smith 1974).

Hertfordshire Puddingstone, a distinctive silicified conglomerate from the Eocene Reading Beds, was used in East Anglia in pre-Roman times (Curwen 1941; Moore 1977). The well-known sarsen stone of southern England, of similar age, was noted by Wheeler (1943) as having been used for quernstones in Iron Age and Roman times at Maiden Castle, Dorset.

In a study of quernstones by Bennett and Elton (1898) 'sandstone', 'grit', 'trachyte', 'trap', and 'granite' are quoted as rock types from which querns are known to have been made. However, no mention is made of petrographic characteristics, nor is provenance considered. Bennett and Elton (1898 p. 182) mention a Roman quern found at Ham, near Poole, as being made of a hard 'grit rock', considered to be from Ardenach on the Rhine. Wallis (1963) suggests that lava from the Auvergne of central France was also used as a quernstone, as was sandstone from the Old Red Sandstone (Devonian) of the English Mendips.

Goby (1906) considers that various milling stones were used in France, but Goby's account again contains little petrology. He quotes a red or purple-blue 'porphyry' from the mountains of Esterel as being used as a quern; also a 'pyroxene trachyte' occurring at Biot, Antibes, Villeneuve-Loubet, and elsewhere. Goby (1906) also quotes a 'lava' as being used in milling, as well as 'granite' and 'sandstone'. Probably the best known French milling stone, however, is the Burrstone ('Buhrstone' of Tarr 1930) which is a grey silicified sedimentary rock from the Oligocene of the Paris Basin, near Fontainebleau (Page 1874). According to Tucker (1977), this millstone

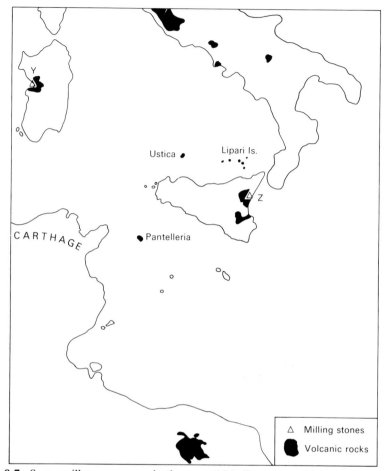

Fig. 9.7. Some millstone sources in the central Mediterranean. Volcanic areas are shown in black. Y: Molaria and Monte Ferru area of Sardinia; Z: Etna, Sicily. Modified after Peacock (1980).

came into use in England in the eighteenth century. Quartzite and quartz arenite grindstones and querns were used in southern Holland and Belgium in pre-Roman times (Bakels 1978), and are thought to have come from the Ardennes and Maas River areas. Much has been written on querns by Curwen (1937, 1941) but the petrography of the stones is not discussed.

Lavas of Tertiary age from the Rhineland (the Niedermendig or Mayen tephrite) have long been known to have been used as quernstones in Roman and medieval times (Hörter, Michels, and Röder 1950–1; Crawford 1955). The use of scoriaceous lava has the advantage that repeated wear continuously exposes new sharp cutting surfaces, thus removing the need for the periodic dressing of the stone. This rock was apparently used in Roman times as far away from the Rhineland as Edinburgh (Maxwell 1974) and it was also identified at the Romano-British site at Scole, Norfolk (Moore 1977).

Petrological aspects of this rock have been reviewed recently by Wimmenauer (1974): it is a vesicular pyroxene-alkali feldspar and frequently nepheline-bearing tephrite, the milling qualities of which are probably as much determined by its vesicular nature as its mineralogy. In practical terms, however, the presence of feldspathoid minerals in any lava used as a quernstone in north-west Europe probably suggests a Rhineland provenance.

In the Aegean area, a scoriaceous or cellular trachyte from Milos is also known to have been used in milling, but less seems to be known of millstones from the Aegean than from the Rhineland. The Kyrenia ship excavations revealed that part of the cargo of this early Greek vessel consisted of hand mills or querns. From Katzev (1969, 1970, 1972) it appears that querns are made of volcanic rock, conceivably from Milos, Thera (Santorini), Kos, or Nisyros; from published illustrations, the stone appears to be a scoriaceous lava. Curwen (1956) located a present-day quernstone quarry near Tangier in Morocco.

In a paper on the petrography and provenance of millstones, especially those from the central Mediterranean area, Peacock (1980) described five types of rock used as milling stones:

1. A leucite-aegirine-augite-ore-bearing leucitophyre from the Orvieto region of Italy. Millstones of this petrographic type were found at Pompeii, Herculaneum, and elsewhere (Fig. 9.7).

2. A reddish-brown persilicic lava from Sardinia, composed of glassy shards, with a groundmass of quartz, andesine, and augite. Millstones of this type were much associated with Roman Carthage.

3. Olivine basalts believed to be from the Etna area of Sicily.

4. A trachyandesite from Volvic in the Massif Central of France, composed of phenocrysts of hornblende and labradorite, in a groundmass of andesine, oligoclase, and K-feldspar, with olivine and augite.

5. The well-known nepheline tephrite from the Rhineland (mentioned above). Interestingly, Peacock (1980) considers that since millstones of this material have only rarely been thin-sectioned, archaeological identifications as Mayen or Niedermendig lava may often have been erroneous.

In Africa 'stone' querns from the Neolithic of Kenya are referred to by Leakey (1931) but without petrological data. Again, 'slabs of basalt or fine-grained quartzite' were used as the lower stone in what were probably primitive querns by the Stone Age Kafue of Zambia (Gabel 1965). In India, Sankalia (1959) described rotary querns made of 'basaltic trap' and 'gritty sandstone'.

In the Americas, prehistoric milling stones from southern California were described by Greenwood (1969) as being made of 'native sandstone'. Further south, in Mexico, pre-conquest metates from the Tehuacon Valley were described by MacNeish, Nelken-Terner, and Johnson (1967) as being made of 'volcanic tufa' [sic; but in fact 'tuff'] and 'sandstone'; metates of grey tuff are also known from Panama. In Venezuela pre-conquest grinding stones of banded gneiss were recorded by Wagner and Schubert (1972) as coming from the Mucuchiés area, Mérida State.

Conclusion

It is difficult to classify sharpening stones and milling stones in the same way as, for example, stone axes, because of the number of secondary rock types used. Further, so little petrographic work has been done that the reviewer is usually unable to recognize from excavation reports the definite rock types used. But of what we may call the primary hones, i.e. stones quarried and traded specifically for sharpening purposes, some types occur repeatedly. Thus, in Europe, Norwegian Ragstone, blue phyllite, and in England the various types of Coal Measures sandstones and the Kentish Rag turn up again and again. Millstone Grit, French Burrstone, Rhineland tephrite lava, and the Orvieto leucitophyre are similarly well documented as milling stones.

Acknowledgements

The author thanks his wife, Ruth H. Moore, for advice on classical matters and Dr A. R. Woolley for critically reading the manuscript.

References

Anonymous (1864). Antiquities and works of art exhibited [by the Archaeological Institute of Great Britain and Ireland]. *Archaeological Journal* 21, 101.
Arkell, W. J. and Tomkeieff, S. I. (1953). *English Rock terms, chiefly as used by miners and quarrymen*. Oxford University Press.
Atkinson, D. (1942). *Report on excavations at Wroxeter, 1923–1927*. Oxford University Press.
Bakels, C. C. (1978). *Four linear band keramik settlements and their environment: a palaeoecological study of Sittard, Stein, Elsloo, and Heinheim*. Leiden University Press.
Barrow, G. (1904). On the Moine gneiss of the east-central Highlands and their position in the Highland sequence. *Quarterly Journal of the Geological Society of London* 60, 400–49.
Bennett, R. and Elton, J. (1898). *History of corn milling*. Vol. 1. *Handstones, slave and cattle mills*. Simpkin Marshall, London.
Brongniart, A. (1813). Essai d'une classification minéralogique des roches mélangées. *Journal des Mines, Paris* 34 (199), 1–48.
—— (1827). *Classification et caractères minéralogiques des roches homogènes et heterogènes*. F. G. Levrault, Paris.

Caley, E. R. and Richards, J. F. C. (ed.) (1956). *Theophrastus on stones*. Ohio State University Press, Columbus.

Christensen, A. E. (Jnr). (1970). Klastadskipet. *Nicolay* **8**, 21–4.

Clough, T. McK. and Green, B. (1972). The petrological identification of stone implements from East Anglia. *Proceedings of the Prehistoric Society* **38**, 108–55.

Crawford, O. G. S. (1955). The quern-quarries of Mayen in the Eifel. *Antiquity* **29**, 68–76.

Curwen, E. C. (1937). Querns. *Antiquity* **11**, 133–51.

—— (1941). More about querns. *Antiquity* **15**, 15–32.

—— (1956). Tangier quern quarry. *Antiquity* **30**, 174.

Davies, A. M. and Baines, A. H. J. (1953). Preliminary survey of the sarsen and puddingstone blocks of the Chilterns. *Proceedings of the Geologists' Association* **64**, 1–9.

Domkář, F., Pelc, Z. and Zoubek, J. (1978). Prubířské kameny a jejich prospekce. [Properties and prospection of touchstones: translated by P. Jakes] *Casopis pro Mineralogiia Geologii* **23**, 395–400.

Dons, J. A. (1960). Telemark supracrustals and associated rocks. *Norges Geologiske Undersögelse* **208**, 49–58.

Dunham, K. C. (1948–9). Three late Saxon and Medieval sharpening-stones from Longworth, Sunningwell and Wallingford. *Berkshire Archaeological Journal* **51**, 68–70.

Dunning, G. C. (1938). Notes on schist hones. In: H. F. Poole and G. C. Dunning: Twelfth century middens in the Isle of Wight. *Proceedings of the Isle of Wight Natural History and Archaeological Society* **2**, 683–95.

—— (1948). [New petrographic identifications by K. C. Dunham.] In: K. M. Kenyan: Excavations at the Jewry Wall site, Leicester. *Reports of the Research Committee of the Society of Antiquaries of London* **15**, 230–2.

Eichholz, D. E. (ed.) (1962). *Pliny natural history, Books 36–7*. Volume 10. William Heinemann, London.

Ellis, S. E. (1969). The petrography and provenance of Anglo Saxon and medieval English honestones, with notes on some other hones. *Bulletin of the British Museum (Natural History)* Mineralology **2**, 135–87.

—— (1971). In: G. F. Bryant and J. M. Stearne: Excavations at the deserted medieval settlement at Lyveden. A third interim report. *Journal. Northampton County Borough Museums and Art Gallery* **9**, 3–93.

—— Moore, D. T. (in press). The medieval honestones. In: M. Biddle (ed.): The crafts and industries of medieval Winchester. Part II Crafts and industries other than ceramic. *Winchester Studies* **7**.

Evans, J. (1897). *The ancient stone implements, weapons and ornaments of Great Britain*. 2nd edn. Longmans, Green and Co., London.

Evens, E. D., Smith, I. F. and Wallis, F. S. (1972). The petrological identification of stone implements from southwestern England. Fifth report of the southwestern federation of museums and art galleries. *Proceedings of the Prehistoric Society* **38**, 235–75.

Evison, V. I. (1975). Pagan Saxon whetstones. *Antiquaries Journal* **55**, 70–85.

Fagg, W. (1959). Grooved rocks at Apoje near Kjebu-Igbo, Western Nigeria. *Man* **59**, 330.

Falck-Muus, R. (1920). Brynestensindustrien i Telemarken. *Norges Geologiske Undersögelse* **87**, 1–179.

Farey, J. (1811). *General view of the agriculture and minerals of Derbyshire*. The Board of Agriculture, London.

Fitton, W. H. (1836). Observations on some of the strata between the Chalk and the Oxford oolite in the south-east of England. *Transactions of the Geological Society of London* (2nd Series) **4**, 103–388.

Gabel, C. (1965). *Stone age hunters of the Kafue. The Gmisho A Site.* Boston University Press.

Gary, M., McAfee, R., Jr., and Wolf, C. L. (ed.) (1974). *Glossary of geology.* American Geological Institute, Washington D.C.

Goby, P. (1906). Contribution á l'étude des moulins primitifs. *Annales de la Société des Lettres, Sciences et Arts des Alpes-Maritimes* **19**, 93–120.

Greenly, E. (1919). *The geology of Anglesey.* H.M.S.O., London. *Memoir of the Geological Survey.*

Greenwood, R. S. (1969). The Browne site. Early milling stone horizon in southern California. *Memoir Society of American Archaeology* **23**.

Grisewold, L. S. (1892). Whetstones and the novaculites of Arkansas. *Annual Report of the Geological Survey of Arkansas* **1890**, vol. 3.

Hebditch, M. and Mellor, J. (1973). Objects of stone. In: The Forum and Basilica of Roman Leicester. *Britannia* **4**, 1–83.

Hermann, G. (1966). *Lapis lazuli in the ancient near East.* D. Phil. Thesis, University of Oxford.

Heyes, R. H., Hemingway, J. E. and Spratt, D.A. (1980). The distribution and lithology of beehive querns in northeast Yorkshire. *Journal of Archaeological Science* **7**, 297–324.

Hörter, F., Michels, F. X. and Röder, J. (1950–1). Die Geschichte der Basalt lavaindustrie von Mayen und Niedermendig. *Jahrbuch für Geschichte und Kultur des Mittelrheins und seine Nachbargebiete.*

Johannsen, A. (1938). *A descriptive petrography of the igneous rocks.* University of Chicago Press.

Katzev, M. L. (1969). The Kyrenia shipwreck. *Expedition* **11**, 55–9.

—— (1970). Kyrenia 1969: a Greek ship is raised. *Expedition* **12**, 6–14.

—— (1972). *The Kyrenia ship.* In: G. F. Bass, (ed.): *A history of seafaring based on underwater archaeology.* Thames and Hudson, London.

Keithahn, E. L. (1962). Stone artifacts of southeastern Alaska. *American Antiquity* **281**, 66–77.

Kennedy, R. A. (1962). Grinding benches and mortars on Fernando Po. *Man* **62**, 129–30.

Kenyon, K. M. (1950). Excavations at Breedon-on-the-Hill. *Transactions of the Leicester Archaeological Society* **26**, 17–82.

Kirwan, R. (1794). *Elements of mineralogy.* 2nd edn. P. Elmsly, London.

Lacaille, A. D. (1954). *The Stone Age in Scotland.* Oxford University Press.

—— (1963). Three grinding-stones. *Antiquaries Journal* **43**, 190–6.

Leakey, L. S. B. (1931). *The Stone Age cultures of Kenya Colony.* Cambridge University Press.

Lepsius, R. (1903). *Geologie von Deutschland.* 1. Wilhelm Engleman, Leipzig.

MacNeish, S. R., Nelken-Terner, A. and Johnson, I. W. (1967). In: D. S. Byers, (ed.): *The prehistory of the Tehuacan valley.* University of Texas Press, Austin. Volume 2. Nonceramic artifacts.

Maxwell, G. (1974). Objects of stone. In: A. Rea and V. Rea: The Roman fort at Cramond, Edinburgh. Excavations 1954–1966. *Britannia* **5**, 163–224.

Moore, D. T. (1977). Objects of stone. In: A. Rogerson: Excavations at Scole, 1973. *East Anglian Archaeological Report* **5**, 148–52.

—— (1978). The petrography and archaeology of English honestones. *Journal of Archaeological Science* **5**, 61–73.

Morey, J. E. and Dunham, K. C. (1953). A petrological study of medieval hones from Yorkshire. *Proceedings of the Yorkshire Geological Society* **29**, 141–8.

Oakley, K. P. (1936). In: G. C. Dunning: Alstoe Mount, Burley, Rutland. *Antiquaries Journal* **16**, 396–411.

Oddy, W. A. and Schweizer, F. (1972). A comparative analysis of some gold coins. In: E. T. Hall, and D. M. Metcalf (ed.): Methods of chemical and metallurgical investigation of ancient coinage. *Special Publication Royal Numismatic Society* **8**, 171–82.

Page, D. (1874). *Economic geology*. William Blackwood and Sons, Edinburgh.

Page, T. E., Capps, E. and Rouse, W. H. D. (ed.) (1931). *Ovid's Fasti with an English translation by Sir James George Frazer*. William Heinemann, London.

Peacock, D. P. S. (1980). The Roman millstone trade: a petrological sketch. *World Archaeology* **12**, 43–53.

Petersen, J. (1951). *Vikingetidens Redskaper*. Jacob Dybwad, Oslo.

Pettijohn, F. J. (1975). *Sedimentary rocks*. 3rd edn. Harper and Row, New York.

Powell, H. P. (1974). Objects of stone. In S. S. Frere and J. K. St. Joseph: The Roman fortress at Longthorpe. *Britannia* **5**, 1–129.

Rackham, H. (ed.) (1961). *Pliny: Natural history books 33–5*. (Volume 9). William Heinemann, London.

Ramsay, A. C. (1881). Geology of north Wales. 2nd edn. *Memoirs of the Geological Survey of Great Britain* **3**, 1–611.

Renard, A. (1882). Les roches grenatifères et amphiboliques de la région de Bastogne. *Bulletin du Musée Royale d'Histoire Naturelle de Belgique* **1**, 1–47.

Roth, J. (1887). *Allgemeine und Chemische Geologie*. 2. Wilhelm Hertz, Berlin.

Sanderson, R. W. (1972). In: E. W. Holden: A bronze age cemetery-barrow on Itford Hill, Beddingham, Sussex. *Sussex Archaeological Collections* **110**, 70–117.

—— (1975). In: J. W. Stearne and G. F. Bryant: Excavations at the deserted medieval settlement at Lyveden. Fourth Report. *Journal. Northampton Borough Council Museums and Art Gallery* **12**, 3–160.

Sankalia, H. D. (1959). Rotary querns from India. *Antiquity* **33**, 128–30.

Schuster, M. (1924). *Abriss der Geologie von Bayern r. d. Rh.* **5**, 1–76.

Shotton, F. W. (1968). Prehistoric man's use of stone in Britain. *Proceedings of the Geologists' Association* **79**, 477–91.

Smith, D. (1974). Appendix IX, Quernstones. In: G. Beresford: The manor of Penhallam, Jacobstow, Cornwall. *Medieval Archaeology* **18**, 90–145.

Smith, E. G., Rhys, G. H., and Eden, R. A. (1967). Geology of the country around Chesterfield, Matlock and Mansfield. Explanation of one-inch geological sheet 112, new series. H.M.S.O., London. *Memoirs of the Geological Survey of Great Britain, England and Wales*.

Sowerby, J. (1811). *British Mineralogy*. [Volume 4 published 1811]. R. Taylor (Printers), London.

Stevenson, I. P. and Gaunt, G. D. (1971). Geology of the country around Chapel en le Frith. Explanation of one-inch geological sheet 99, new series. H.M.S.O., London. *Memoirs of the Geological Survey of Great Britain, England and Wales*.

Tarr, W. A. (1930). *Introductory economic geology*. McGraw-Hill, New York.

Thompson, R. C. (1934). On the Assyrian words for 'whetstone' and 'corundum'. *Journal of the Royal Asiatic Society* **1934**, 343–6.

Tucker, D. G. (1977). Millstones, quarries, and millstone makers. *Post-medieval Archaeology* **11**, 1–21.

Vancouver, C. (1808). *General view of the agriculture of the county of Devon*. The Board of Agriculture, London.

Wagner, E. and Schubert, C. (1972). Pre-Hispanic workshop of serpentinite artifacts, Venezuelan Andes and possible raw material source. *Science* **175**, 888–90.

Wallis, F. S. (1963). In: E. Pyddoke, (ed.): *The Scientist and Archaeology*. Phoenix House, London.

Wheeler, R. E. M. (1943). Maiden Castle Dorset. *Report of the Research Committee of the Society of Antiquities* **12**, xx 1399.

Whitehurst, J. (1778). *An inquiry into the original state and formation of the earth.* J. Cooper, London.

Wimmenauer, W. (1974). The alkaline province of central Europe, and France. In: H. Sorensen: (ed.) *The alkaline rocks*. John Wiley, London.

Woodward, H. B. (1887). *Geology of England and Wales*. 2nd edn. George Philip and Sons, London.

10. Petrology of ceramics

D. F. Williams

Introduction

In recent years there has been an increasing interest in the study of ancient pottery by ceramic petrologists. Due to the work of such people as Josef Frechen in Germany, O. Yu Krug in the Soviet Union, David Peacock in England, Tiziano Mannoni in Italy, and the late Anna Shepard in America, the petrological analysis of pottery is approaching the stage where it will be regarded as a routine part of the post-excavation study of a pottery assemblage. It is perhaps easy to understand the growth of this method of pottery analysis, since the techniques involved, thin sectioning, heavy mineral separation, and electron microscopy, have much to recommend them to the archaeologist. On the majority of sites the archaeologist is faced with the problem of classifying a diverse group of pottery, usually the most ubiquitous and at the same time the most important of artefacts, given its undoubted value for establishing relative chronologies and indicating exchange mechanisms. In this connection, petrology can often provide a quick, relatively inexpensive means of establishing: origin; comparability with similar material of known origin; and the technology involved. Any one of these may provide invaluable information relative to both the dating and the movement of pottery. In addition, the ceramic petrologist will describe in detail the fabric of the pottery sampled, thus enabling the archaeologist to recognize in the hand specimen characteristic inclusions (where visible) for future identification of similar fabrics.

Petrological methods have an advantage over plain chemical analysis in that any compositional changes recorded in pottery during burial are usually evident. Post-depositional infiltration may well explain the differences in the origins suggested for Romano-British black-burnished ware from Mumrills fort on the Antonine Wall, following spectographic and heavy mineral analyses of the same samples (Richards 1960; Williams 1977a). Furthermore, the view that petrology is not really practicable with fine-textured pottery (Peacock 1970) needs some modification, since useful results have been obtained from thin-sectioning and heavy mineral separation of fine-grained Hellenistic glazed wares (Prag, Schweizer, and Williams 1974) and Roman arretine and samian pottery (Williams 1978a, 1979a).

In view of the advantages and limitations in ceramic studies of both petrology and chemical analysis, it is encouraging that in a number of cases both approaches have been applied to the same range of pottery in a multi-analytical programme, to see how far the results from one technique complement the other (Duma and Ravasz 1973; Kingery 1974; Prag *et al.* 1974; Williams, Jenkins and Livens 1974; Williams and Jenkins 1976; Williams and Ovenden 1978). In any programme of pottery analysis, there is much to be said for considering petrology as a first choice. A representative sample of sherds should initially be thin-sectioned in order to obtain information on the types of inclusion present in the clay body. If these results are inconclusive as regards origins, or if a greater refinement of grouping is required, chemical analysis can then be employed. Thin-section details of the range and relative proportions of inclusions present in the pottery can help to formulate the choice of chemical elements to be measured, and may well aid the interpretation of these results.

Methodology

Thin-sectioning and heavy mineral separation have both been borrowed and adapted from standard geological techniques used for many years in the study of rocks and soils. Indeed, to the ceramic petrologist a sherd of pottery can be regarded as a metamorphosed sedimentary rock, for the fabric of a sherd consists principally of clastic grains held in a clay matrix, both partially altered during firing. Petrological microscopy allows the examination and identification of the minerals and rock fragments which may be present in a sherd of pottery. However, the ceramic petrologist is often handicapped in predicting the source of the material because of the comparative smallness of the crushed rock fragments present in pottery, and by the fact that the potters tend to choose disintegrated weathered material that can often make precise identification difficult. Also, there is the possibility of alteration in certain minerals due to the effect of pottery firing temperatures which may be in excess of 1000 °C. For these reasons great emphasis is often placed on the availability of comparative samples of pottery or clay/sand from known origins, so that not only the content, but also the size, shape, condition, and arrangement of the inclusions can be compared, and the likelihood of an origin in the same area assessed.

In recent years considerable use has been made of thermoluminescence (see Chapter 2) as a dating technique for ceramic materials. Chemical analysis, and SEM, have also become far more widespread with the use of the electron microprobe (see Chapter 2); analysis of the minerals contained in pottery fragments, especially their trace elements, can be of considerable value in establishing common origin and provenance (cf. Tite, Freestone, Meeks, and Bimson 1981; Freestone and Rigby 1981; Freestone 1983).

Thin-sectioning

The technique of thin-sectioning provides an objective method for classifying pottery pastes. Classification is based on the wide variety of minerals, rock fragments, and other non-plastic inclusions that normally occur in pottery. A study of a thin slice of pottery will reveal the size, shape, and arrangement of the mineral grains in a sherd. The various optical properties of the transparent minerals can be used, as in rocks, to assist in their identification. Unfortunately, thin-sectioning suffers from the limitation that it does not fully allow the determination of the mineralogical composition of the clay. In the majority of studies this handicap is minimized by the variety of the temper constituents, whereby each category of inclusions defines a particular paste type.

The minimum sample of pottery required for a thin section can be comparatively small, of the order of 10mm × 10mm. However, a great deal of pottery is in a friable condition when recovered from the earth, and will not stand up to the rigours of grinding and polishing without previous treatment. Impregnating such sherds in a thermoplastic cement medium such as Cosmonoid 80 or Lakeside 70 will usually stabilize all but the most stubborn of sherds.

The most striking results achieved by the thin-sectioning of ancient pottery have usually been in studies concerned with fairly coarse wares containing exotic minerals or rock fragments, which can be shown to have a limited geological distribution. Allowing for glacial drift, where applicable, or the possibility of transportation of materials by the potters themselves, the source of the inclusions present in pottery will usually indicate the area of manufacture of the vessels. Thus Shepard (1942), in a study of Pueblo glazed and painted pottery from New Mexico, was able not only to identify several groups of wares with distinct inclusions, such as andesite, basalt, and sandstone, but also to isolate separate areas of production based on the local availability of these materials. Similarly, an examination by Peacock (1969*a*, *b*) of certain Neolithic and Iron Age wares from south-western Britain showed that the pottery was made from gabbroic clay, probably originating from a restricted area of the Lizard peninsula.

An interesting situation involving the long-distance transportation of pottery, as revealed by petrological study, can be seen in the examination of early Bronze Age II pottery from Arad in Canaan and two possible industrial sites in southern Sinai, Nabi Salah, and Sheikh Muhsein (Amiran, Arieth, and Glass 1973). Thin-sectioning showed that certain coarse cooking ware from Arad contained non-local inclusions of arkosic sand geologically similar to material in the Precambrian area around Nabi Salah and Sheikh Muhsein, while the fabric of fine-textured pottery from the latter two sites indicated a sedimentary terrain similar to that around Arad. The implication is of a two way exchange of wares between the two areas, some 300–400 km apart: fine pottery from Arad to the south and coarse ware from Sinai to Arad.

Often, however, such precision is not possible due to the more common nature of the non-plastic inclusions present in pottery. Much contains little else but quartz sand, occurring either naturally in the clay or present as a deliberate additive on the part of the potter to form a tempering agent. When dealing with such ubiquitous materials in thin section, it is difficult to predict sources. However, useful information can still be obtained from a textural analysis of the section: that is an examination of features such as size, shape, and frequency of the component quartz grains, all of which may help to group homogeneous sherds or, alternatively, suggest that several different centres were responsible for the manufacture of the pottery. This approach, which is effectively the equivalent of the archaeologist's 'feel' when comparing the fabric of sherds, can be expressed by isolating and measuring standard geological particle size parameters. The method is based on the premise that pottery made in a restricted geological area, and hence probably from the same formation, should contain sand grains of approximately the same size, all subject to similar degrees of sorting and weathering.

In the method testing study of a selection of Roman coarse pottery from Fishbourne, Peacock (1971a) chose four textural parameters to characterize the quartz inclusions in the sherds. These were: percentage inclusions; roundness; sphericity; and mean size, sorting, skewness, and kurtosis. The results indicated that the sandy grey wares tested were likely to have been made at the same centre, despite a degree of typological variation within the group, while different sources were suggested for the mica-dusted and glazed ware pottery also examined during the same programme.

The granulometric techniques illustrated by Peacock were adapted and simplified by Hodder (1974), in an investigation of the distribution of two distinct types of Romano-British ware in the west Sussex region. In this study, the average size of the quartz inclusions were plotted against the ratio of inclusions to clay matrix, and the results presented in graphical form. More recently, Streeten (1979) has refined Peacock's original approach on particle size measurements, by concentrating on a graphical representation of grain size plotted against frequency. These results, based to a large extent on differentiation between material from known medieval kilns, have proved highly successful, and this work suggests the possibility of further speeding up the method.

Thin-sectioning can also help to answer certain questions concerned with the technological aspects of pottery making. Slips can be readily identified under the microscope – not always easy macroscopically – as a distinct line of demarcation from the body. Frierman (1970) has demonstrated how mineralogical study of early glazes, in particular those of Palestinian Crusader pottery, can provide information on the techniques involved in the glazing process.

In certain circumstances, it is also possible to give some idea of the firing temperature of a pot by the presence or absence of specific minerals, or in the change in colour of certain minerals. Sabine (1958) has attempted to assess the firing temperature of thirteenth century sherds from Beere, Devon, on the basis of the structure and optics of black mica, which is known to change its properties on heating. Grimanis, Filippakis, Perdikatsis, Vassilaki-Grimani, Bosana-Bouron, and Yalouris (1980) have estimated that certain Greek late geometric pottery was fired at temperatures higher than 900 °C, based on the absence of clay minerals and lack of primary calcite. Wheel-thrown pottery can be identified in thin section, providing that the section is cut horizontally from the sample vessel. This is due to the fact that in wheel-thrown pottery, particles and voids in the clay tend to lie parallel to the plane of the wheelhead, and this flow pattern can be recognized in polarized light.

Heavy mineral separation

This method allows the study of the wide range of detrital heavy minerals (specific gravity greater than 2.9) which are found in sedimentry environments, sands in particular, as well as those pure samples of essential and accessory minerals from crushed igneous and metamorphic rocks. Since much pottery contains sand, it follows that sandy pottery also contains heavy minerals. The range of heavy minerals varies according to the geological formation from which the sand derived, and so a particular combination of heavy minerals may indicate a restricted geological source. In Britain, a large body of geological literature exists on the source areas for heavy minerals, and this information can be readily utilized to suggest likely production areas for pottery which contains distinctive heavy minerals. In this respect the lighter fraction of minerals, mainly quartz and feldspar, is not normally useful, as both of these mineral types are extremely common and therefore do not provide the necessary degree of uniqueness needed to characterize a particular geological system.

Heavy mineral separation thus provides a very valuable supplement to thin-sectioning where the latter method is restricted in suggesting possible source areas, due to the common nature of the quartz inclusions. For the thin-sectioning of sandy pottery fabrics tends to reveal little else but quartz grains set in a baked clay matrix. The main drawback of heavy mineral separation is that a relatively large sample is necessary to obtain a representative number of heavy minerals: normally a minimum of 250–500 grains are required for counting. In the case of very sandy wares the sample required is about 17–25g; more may be needed for less sandy pottery. No doubt due partly to the factor of sample size, the most rewarding results achieved by this method have usually been carried out on coarse fabrics, heavily tempered with sand (Peacock and Thomas 1967; Loughlin 1977; Williams 1977b). Indeed, given a limited amount of pot as a sample, especially for finer-textured wares, large numbers of heavy minerals are not always forthcoming. However, recent work by Williams (1979a) on a number of finer-textured wares has suggested that centifruging the sample of crushed pottery greatly increases the chances of obtaining an adequate number of heavy minerals when compared with the more traditional settling technique (Cornwall 1958; Peacock 1967a). If this is supported by more extensive applications, then the potential of heavy mineral separation is greatly enhanced, for it means that a finer range of pottery can be analysed usefully by the method.

The process of separating out the heavy minerals from a sample of pottery is a fairly long and laborious task (see Chapter 2). After crushing, the grains are passed through a sieve of an appropriate size. A 500 μm aperture size is suitable for very sandy wares, while an aperture size in the range of 200–60μm is recommended for finer-textured pottery. The powdered sample is then treated in the manner described in Chapter 2.

The individual heavy mineral grains are identified, counted, and the average percentages calculated for each type present. These figures can usefully be set out in the form of histograms for easy recognition of the frequencies of the main types of mineral. Alternatively, to emphasize the underlying mineralogical differences between groups of heavy mineral suites, three-coordinate graphs can be constructed based on selected minerals. The minerals chosen for this are not necessarily those which have recorded the highest totals in an assemblage – for example, zircon is usually omitted because of its ubiquity – but rather those minerals which normally occur in much smaller amounts, and where an increase or decrease in their frequency is more apparent and therefore possibly more significant.

In some cases the presence, or absence, of particular species of heavy minerals can provide valuable information as to whether pottery is likely to have been made from materials available in the general area of the original site of discovery or some distance away. Thus the heavy mineral residue from a hand-made jar from the Romano-British site at Thundersbarrow Hill, Sussex, did not match that obtained from the local Tertiary clays, suggesting that the pot was not made on the site (Reynolds 1933). On the other hand, heavy mineral assemblages obtained from a selection of Dark Age pottery from Pant-y-Saer, Anglesey, proved to be identical to those present in the local drifts and Triassic boulders, suggesting that local boulder clays were used for the pottery (Wallis and Evens 1934).

Recently, heavy mineral analysis has been applied to Bronze Age pottery from two important Cycladic sites, Phylakopi on Melos and Akrotiri on Thera (Santorini). Both these islands belong to the calc-alkaline Cycladian volcanic arc and are composed predominantly of volcanic rocks which range in composition from andesites to rhyodacites. The volcanic formations of both islands often makes it possible through thin-sectioning to distinguish those vessels which are likely to be locally made and those which can be considered as imports (Williams 1978b). There are occasions, however, when the precise identification of the inclusions of crushed volcanic fragments is difficult, due to their comparative smallness and the fact that potters tend to choose disintegrated weathered material. A small programme of heavy mineral separation has shown that it is possible to differentiate between locally made pottery from both sites, despite the thin-section difficulties (Williams 1980a).

The classification of heavy mineral suites is not solely based on determining which particular types are present in the sample. Of equal importance are their quantitative proportions and individual characteristics. The percentages of the various minerals present, and also their size, shape, and colour, can all be diagnostic of the geological origins of an assemblage. A good illustration of this is afforded by the Romano-British black-burnished category 1 ware (BB1), where the heavy mineral assemblage was dominated by a high percentage of tourmaline, a fairly common mineral but one which is rarely to be found in excess of zircon (Peacock 1967a, 1973; Williams 1977b). This suite resembled in some measure that of the Upper Greensand of Devon, but archaeologically was more likely to come from an area further east. Attention was drawn to suspected BB1 factory sites situated around the shores of Poole Harbour, Dorset, and in turn to the Tertiary sands of the region as a source for the tourmaline-rich heavy mineral suite. The heavy mineral composition from sand and 'waster' samples from this area, both in proportions and characterization of the grains, closely matched BB1 wares over much of the country. There now seems little doubt that throughout the Roman period the Wareham-Poole Harbour area was the main production centre for BB1.

In some cases, the heavy minerals recorded in pottery are common types, when it is not possible to predict a likely source. The method can still prove useful, however, for an examination of the proportions of the different minerals present, allied to a consideration of their size, shape, and condition, should be able to indicate whether or not a group of sandy pottery is likely to have been made in the same area, or at a number of widely scattered production sites. Barclay (Biddle and Barclay 1974) was able to show that medieval Winchester ware was made at two different centres, based on the proportions of the tourmaline present in the sample sherds.

Electron microscopy

The advantages of the high magnifications available through transmission and, especially, scanning electron microscopy have been usefully applied to pottery studies; SEM has the advantage of enabling the morphology of mineral grains to be examined directly. This technique has been concerned mainly with problems centred on the composition of slips, atmospheric conditions during firing, and an estimation of the firing temperatures; also, to a lesser extent, with the study of grain surface features.

Hedge (1966) was able to confirm that the black colour of the slip of Northern Black Polished ware of India was due to the presence of magnetite, by clearly identifying euhedral crystals of this iron oxide at an enlargement of 10 000 ×. Similarly, Hofmann's (1962) electron microscope study of Attic black and red figured pottery enabled the composition of the slip to be identified as a refined illitic clay, and also gave information on the manufacturing techniques involved. High magnification showed that the surface of the red paint was thin, rough, and remained porous on firing, while the black paint was thicker, fine-grained, and had sintered to form a more impervious layer. This suggested that the black areas were coated with a thick illitic clay which remained reduced during the oxidizing final stages of firing, when the rest of the vessel turned red.

The firing temperatures of pottery have been successfully estimated by observing at high magnification the microstructural changes which occur in clays during advanced heating. The internal morphology of clays reflects structural changes at certain key temperatures up to total vitrification. By reheating an appropriate sample of pottery, or similar clay sample, and noting the changes at different temperatures, it is possible to estimate accurately the firing temperature. Taking into account the changes in internal morphology of a sherd of Karanova pottery baked at a pre-set scale of temperatures, Kingery and Frierman (1974) were able to demonstrate that the pot was unlikely to have been fired at a temperature in excess of 800 °C, and that the true temperature was more likely to have been around 700 °C. This was considerably less than the visually estimated firing temperature of between 1000 °C and 1105 °C. Further work along these lines has been carried out by Tite and Maniatis (1975) and Maniatis and Tite (1979), who have conducted a major programme of analysis on the technology of prehistoric pottery, much of it from Greece and the Near East. In this work, use of the scanning electron microscope, with X-ray fluorescence spectrometer attachment, has allowed a detailed study to be made of the approximate firing temperatures of different types of clay used for pottery manufacture.

The interpretation of the surface features of highly magnified quartz grains present in pottery can be a useful index of origin, giving information on the environmental history of the deposit from which the grain has come.

Using the scanning electron microscope, Shackley (1975) was able to show that quartz grains from the distinctive 'carrot-shaped' amphorae, found on many British sites during the first century AD, contain features typical of a hot sandy climate, possibly Palestine.

Applications

In this section, some of the results of petrological research into pottery of the Prehistoric, Roman, and Medieval periods are reviewed.

Prehistoric pottery

It is, perhaps, not too much of an exaggeration to claim that during the last decade the application of petrological analysis has revolutionized the traditional approach to prehistoric pottery studies. Although, previous to this, pioneering work in Germany (Buttler 1935; Obenauer 1936; Schmitt 1939) and North America (Shepard 1942) had shown that prehistoric pottery was capable of being carried great distances, and in certain circumstances might be regarded as a 'traded' product, the implications of these results were not fully appreciated at the time. Instead, most prehistoric archaeologists still tended to look upon pottery as essentially the product of each separate community. Typological nuances were generally regarded as providing a means for formulating cultural zones, and for yielding evidence for the introduction of fresh settlers (Hawkes 1959). However, in the light of Peacock's (1968, 1969a, b) petrological work on Neolithic and Iron Age pottery of the west Midlands and south-west Britain, this view has had to be somewhat altered.

Earlier work on British Neolithic pottery from Windmill Hill by Cornwall and Hodges (1964) had shown the value of thin-sectioning prehistoric pottery when used in conjunction with a knowledge of the geology of the area in which the find took place. Most of the pottery examined proved likely to have been made from locally derived raw materials, but there were a number of notable exceptions. Petrologically, the most distinctive group of sherds were those which contained large angular grains of altered feldspar and fibrous aggregates of pale green amphibole. These inclusions were clearly not local to the Windmill Hill area, though the suggestion that they were derived from the 'border of the Dartmoor granite mass' was soon refuted. Instead, Peacock (1969a) traced the source of this, and similar pottery, to the gabbroic clay outcrop on the Lizard peninsula.

A concurrent study of the distinctive curvilinear decorated Iron Age Glastonbury ware of the south-west revealed that the largest petrological group was also made of gabbroic clay from the Lizard (Peacock 1969b). In addition, Iron Age 'duck-stamped' wares from Wales and the west Midlands were found to contain predominantly a range of igneous and metamorphic rock fragments which could only have outcropped in a restricted area of the Malvern Hills (Peacock 1968). The seemingly large operating scale of both of these industries precludes the explanation of a casual movement of pottery with itinerant peoples. Continuity of style and distribution across suggested tribal boundaries also weighs against the shipment in bulk of the raw materials to individual centres for local manufacture. The inference to be drawn from all three sets of petrological results clearly points to the existence during the prehistoric period of groups of professional or, perhaps more likely, semi-professional potters, obtaining their raw materials from restricted geological areas, and distributing their finished products over a wide region.

There may be some evidence for a movement of gabbroic clay in the Bronze Age, where in a number of cases additional inclusions appear to have been added to this type of clay (pers. comm. M. Parker-Pearson). The raw materials from both areas, the Lizard and the Malvern Hills, appear to have been utilized for some time, for further work has since shown that these were also used during the Roman and medieval periods (Peacock 1967b; 1975; Williams 1976; Vince 1977). With regard to the properties of the Lizard gabbroic clay, it is interesting to note that in his technological study of medieval Ligurian pottery, Mannoni (1974) showed that locally made gabbroic dishes have good heat-storing qualities and provide high resistance to thermal shock. This suggested a possible reason for their popularity and longevity. If these attributes are true also of the Lizard gabbroic clay, they may go some way to explain the latter's undoubted popularity for use in making pottery over many hundreds of years.

In view of these thin-section results on certain types of British prehistoric pottery, the earlier petrological suggestions of imported pottery on continental sites, for instance at Köln-Lindenthal (Obenauer 1936), might usefully be re-examined. These vessels might conceivably be items of trade, rather than merely reflecting movements of peoples. There are as yet no indications of a prehistoric continental equivalent to the large British 'gabbroic' pottery centre. Indeed, it remains to be shown that the majority of prehistoric pottery from Britain, as well as the continent, was not made from locally obtained raw materials. This in itself can be useful information for the ceramic petrologist to present to the archaeologist, as it provides the basis for a quantitative fabric classification; there should be little difficulty in recognizing those sherds unlikely to have been made locally.

The use of petrology to isolate likely foreign ceramic material in a given area can be of the utmost value in establishing contacts between different cultural groups. Connections between the stroke-ornamented ware culture of Bohemia and that of the Lengyel culture of Moravia had been postulated for some time, but was only confirmed when thin-sectioning of a possible Lengyel vessel from a stroke-ornamented grave from Prague-Dejvice proved to be identical with clay samples from Moravia (Bares and Licka 1976). The other pottery from the grave site was shown to be homogeneous in fabric and compared well with local clay samples. Petrological analysis by Hays and Hassan (1974) of Sudanese Neolithic pottery showed that the decorative 'Khartoum horizon style', which was common to a large part of that country, was in fact produced separately by several groups, thereby indicating a degree of cultural tradition over a wide area.

Surprisingly little petrological work has been done on ancient traded pottery from the Aegean in view of the useful results achieved by Felts (1942) on early Bronze Age pottery from Troy and by Farnsworth on classical pottery from Athens (1964) and Corinth (1970). However, recent

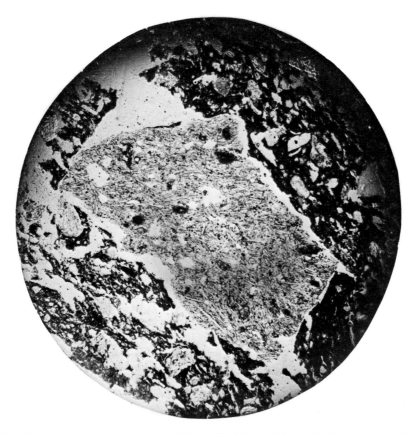

Fig. 10.1. Late Bronze Age vessel from Phylakopi, Melos. In the centre of the picture is a large fragment of fine-grained volcanic rock consisting for the most part of feldspar microlites, with a small number of grains of pyroxene scattered throughout. This type of inclusion in the clay suggests that the pot was made locally on Melos. Plane polarized light ($\times$ 36).

work by Williams (1978*b*, 1980*a*) and Riley, Peacock, and Renfrew (1980) has shown the potential of a petrological approach to pottery distribution when applied on a wide scale to Aegean Bronze Age pottery.

Another way of recognizing cultural connections by way of pottery is in the study of similar technological methods. In fact, the choice and preparation of materials in prehistoric pottery are probably a stronger reflection of tradition and culture than are form and decoration. A study of the temper constituents of early Scandinavian pottery has shown that once established, manufacturing methods tend to remain fairly stable over long periods, and that the introduction of new techniques are usually associated with the

Fig. 10.2. Iron Age vessel from Danebury hillfort, Hampshire. The principal inclusions are large oolitic grains, with a concentric structure. The presence of ooliths in the pot points to the Jurassic Oolite ridge as a likely source for the temper. The nearest outcrop to Danebury lies some 20 miles to the south-west, thereby suggesting that the vessel was brought to the site from some distance away. Plane polarized light (× 36).

movement of fresh cultures into the area (Hulthen 1976). A similar situation is that regarding the problems of continuity between Neolithic and Bronze Age pottery in Britain. On the whole, much late Neolithic ware contains inclusions such as quartz, flint, and shell. In contrast, Peacock (1970) has drawn attention to the presence in the primary series of Bronze Age collard urns of large quantities of grog (crushed pottery). This form of tempering is commonly found in the intrusive Bronze Age beaker pottery, and it is clear that it was being copied by the Collard Urn potters, implying a degree of technological change at this time. Thus it now appears that the Beaker influence during the early Bronze Age was probably more important than first thought, since Beaker decorative details were rarely copied on collard urns. This information could only have been forthcoming by a consideration of the fabrics involved.

In the later Russian Cherniakov culture of the second to fourth centuries AD, Krug (1965) has noted what seems to have been a common recipe for preparing clay for fine wares that existed over a wide area of the Ukraine, irrespective of the type of clay used (Peacock 1970). A similar example may also occur to some extent with the Neolithic grooved ware pottery of the Orkneys, where the writer has noted what may be a tradition of making pottery in a particular way by adding crushed dyke rock (mainly camptonite, also monchiquite, bostonite, and alkali basalt), possibly because of its hardness during firing.

Roman pottery

With a high standard of communications by sea, river, and road, and the demand for material goods stimulated by the frequency of large urban centres and the presence in the frontier provinces of the army, the Roman Empire affords a unique opportunity to study in some detail early economics and commerce. At the height of its territorial expansion under Trajan (AD 98–117), the Roman Empire formed a vast economic unit stretching from the River Euphrates in the east to Britain in the west, and from the Rivers Rhine and Danube in the north to the Sahara Desert in the south. Allowing for local variations in most provinces, a fairly uniform degree of material culture could be found throughout this whole area. It followed, therefore, that within the boundaries of the Empire (and to some extent without) there was a demand for a particular range of goods and materials, including certain types of pottery, to supplement local products. The opportunities afforded for the study of widely distributed pottery types during this period have been realized for some time (Hayes 1972; Lloris 1978). However, it is true to say that with the application of scientific techniques to pottery studies, this work has been given a degree of precision rarely possible in the past, apart from samian-ware studies.

Given the comparatively large amount of pottery that was traded over considerable distances throughout the Roman world, it is not surprising that petrological analysis on Roman pottery has tended to be concerned with identifying widely-traded wares. This has involved pin-pointing as far as possible source areas, using this information to suggest the most likely routes by which the vessels in question arrived at their find sites, and speculating on the economic questions raised by such importations.

Foremost in this work have been those scholars concerned with the study of Roman amphorae. These large two-handled container jars were used primarily for transporting a variety of merchandise over long distances. The limitations of a strictly typological approach to the problems involved with the source areas of amphorae, and by implication with the goods carried in them, can be seen in Callender's (1965) study of these vessels. Although work of this nature can be of great value in the standardization of types and identification of *tituli picti* and stamps, many questions regarding the individual origins of amphorae, and hence their economic significance, often remain unanswered.

In a study of amphorae in British pre-Roman Iron Age contexts, based on both typology and petrological analysis, Peacock (1971b) drew attention to the variety of sources from which these vessels originated. He was able to show that the important first century BC Dressel form 1 wine amphora was made principally in Campania and Latium. Moreover, Dressel form 1A and turned out to be petrologically similar, both containing characteristic inclusions of green augite and volcanic rock fragments, and therefore did not represent the products of two different centres as previously suggested (Ettlinger 1960). The distribution pattern of both amphora types is revealing (Peacock 1971b, Fig. 36). The earlier, Dressel 1A form (first half of first century BC), is present in some numbers at Hengistbury Head, in the south of England, while finds of the later Dressel 1B form are concentrated in eastern Britain. Both distribution patterns seem to reflect historically known events: the uprising of the Veneti in 56 BC disrupting Roman trade with Hengistbury Head, and the friendship of Rome with the Trinovantes in the east of Britain during the second half of the first century BC. Both of these events coincided roughly with the typological change in amphora form from Dressel 1A to 1B. The lack of finds of both sub-divisions of this type of amphora in northern Gaul indicates direct exportation to Britain from the Mediterranean.

The distribution pattern of another distinctive amphora type, Dressel form 30, is also instructive, though in this case more from an economic than a political point of view. Kilns producing this amphora form are known from southern France, though close parallels were also made in Portugal, Spain, and north Africa (Peacock 1978b). The petrology of the southern French type shows a degree of textural variety, implying several centres of production. The range of inclusions present in the pottery – metamorphic rocks, limestone, quartz, and mica – can all be found in the area of the mouth of the Rhone or around the Gulf of Lyons. The distribution of this amphora fabric is concentrated along the Rhone–Rhine river system, which suggests that the British Dressel 30 finds came via this waterway rather than by the easier Narbonne–Bordeaux route. As Peacock points out, this situation is probably to be explained in terms of the Rhineland being the primary commercial market for southern Gaulish wine, with Britain receiving shipments by way of that region.

Through work of this kind, it is becoming increasingly possible to recognize petrologically the more common amphorae products of a number of different centres. This is important, for similar types of amphorae were produced in different regions, with only slight typological variations. The Koan (Dressel form 2–4) type, for example, was made in both Italy and Spain (Tchernia and Zevi 1972), while the Rhodian (Callender form 7) form, although most probably made predominantly on the Island of Rhodes, appears in a number of different fabrics, not all of them consistent with a Rhodian origin (Peacock 1977a). In view of this 'duplication of types', petrological characterization of the wasters from amphorae kilns which were producing common forms takes on an added significance (Peacock 1974, 1978a).

Another form of pottery which was widely traded was the fine quality red-slipped arretine and samian wares. The typological study of this pottery has reached a very high standard of scholarship, due to a combination of known kilns, name stamps, extant moulds, and a careful appreciation of the style of decoration of individual potters. However, there is still scope for a scientific approach as many sherds, particularly small undecorated examples, remain difficult to allocate to specific centres on visual appearance alone. Due to the fine texture of the pottery, scientific analysis has tended to be concerned with determining the chemical composition of the clay, and the results have gone some way in characterizing the products from the known manufacturing centres (Picon, Vichy, and Meille 1971; Picon, Carre, Cordoliani, Vichy, Hernandez, and Mignard 1975; Widemann, Picon, Asaro, Michel, and Perlman 1975). Recent work by Williams (1978a) on a small method-testing programme of thin-sectioning has also demonstrated differences in fabric (reproduced in photomicrograph form) of Italian arretine from Arezzo and Puteoli, as well as early samian ware from La Graufesenque, Montans, Lyon, and Lezoux. The differences in fabric between Arezzo and Puteoli were particularly revealing: an extremely fine clay matrix was used for Arezzo, while the single sample attributed on name stamp evidence to Puteoli appeared much coarser than this, and contained grains of clinopyroxene, entirely in keeping with the volcanic rocks around the Bay of Naples.

It will be interesting to see if the apparent visual differences in fabric of the arretine series from Britain (Dannell 1971) match the petrological groupings worked out for the known manufacturing centres. In dealing with the comparatively small number of arretine vessels in Britain, it should be possible to work out the proportions of vessels from each production centre, plot the distribution of these, and see how the find sites reflect the chronology of the continental evidence (Williams 1978a).

The problems involved in correctly identifying source areas, where a number of production centres are involved in making typologically similar forms, are not uncommon in ceramic studies. Pompeian red ware, for example, appears in a narrow range of bowls and dishes with only slight typological variations and has a wide distribution. However, Peacock (1977b) has shown that there are at least seven different petrological fabrics involved, all representing separate production centres. The most common fabric is distinguished by black sand in the hand specimen, and is petrologically similar to certain of the Dressel amphora form 1, shown to have been largely made in the Campania region of Italy (Peacock 1971b, Group 2).

This is a good example of the petrological evidence from one study providing information for locating the origin of a quite different type of vessel, and demonstrates one of the major advantages of ceramic petrology: that petrological slides, whether thin sections or of heavy mineral assemblages, can be kept indefinitely for future comparative studies. This will involve not only a consideration of the types of rock fragments and minerals present, but also their qualitative features. Another example which may be quoted in this context is the Romano-British gabbroic pottery of south-west Britain. This is petrologically indistinguishable from similar prehistoric fabrics (Williams 1976) and therefore also undoubtedly originates from the Lizard.

Some types of coarse utility wares were also carried quite extensively during the Roman period. An interesting case of the long distance movement of coarse pottery has recently been noted in a preliminary study of the locally made late Roman wares of the island of Pantelleria, situated halfway between Sicily and north Africa (Peacock in press). The petrology of these vessels is particularly distinctive, as they contain minerals characteristic of peralkaline volcanic rocks, the main formation of Pantelleria and comparatively rare elsewhere in the Mediterranean. Despite the fact that Pantellerian pottery appears in a limited range of crude hand-made types, examples have been recognized from a number of sites along the north African coast, as well as on mainland Italy, indicating a wide distribution. These vessels seem to have been traded for their own sake rather than used as containers for other goods since, as far as is known, the island produced no natural commodities for export at this time. The main period during which this pottery was exported, the fifth and sixth centuries AD, seems to coincide with a time of local impoverishment, leading Peacock to believe that the export of pottery may have been a part-time activity during times of economic hardship.

An excellent example of the bulk movement of coarse pottery is that of Romano-British black-burnished ware. This type of pottery occurs in a variety of forms, and is present in some quantity in a majority of military and civil sites over much of Roman Britain from the early second century AD to the end of the fourth century. As this pottery is predominantly sand-tempered, heavy mineral examination was used (Peacock 1967a) and confirmed the division of the ware into two distinct types, BB1 and BB2, each with its own separate forms. The majority of analysed samples of BB1 show a distinctive tourmaline-rich assemblage of heavy minerals, suggesting large factory scale production, identified with a source in the Wareham–Poole Harbour area of Dorset (Peacock 1967a, 1973; Williams 1977b). Previous to this, a source area in the Midlands had been tentatively suggested, due to the presence in that region of large numbers of BB1 vessels (Frere 1967, p. 292; Hartley 1972, p. 47), while spectrographic tests of pottery from Mumrills fort on the Antonine Wall had indicated the Hertfordshire–Middlesex area as a possible source (Richards 1960). The other category of black-burnished ware, BB2, appears to have been made mostly in the east of the country, at Colchester and at a number of smaller production sites in northern Kent (Williams 1977a, b).

The distinctive heavy mineral suites obtained from the majority of black-burnished ware fabrics have not only made it possible for source areas to be identified in most cases, but have also allowed similar fabric types from a number of widely scattered sites to be directly attributed to these centres. It seems probable, for instance, that most of the BB1 and BB2 vessels recovered from the large northern military market were shipped in bulk up the western and eastern coastlines from the production centres at Wareham–Poole Harbour and Colchester–northern Kent, respectively.

Heavy mineral separation has been used to good effect on another Romano-British coarse pottery, Dales ware. This pottery appears as shell-tempered cooking pots, with a distinctive outspringing rim and internal ledging. It is common in the north-east of England during the late third and early fourth centuries AD, although present to a lesser extent both before and after these dates. Previous to Loughlin's (1977) study of this pottery, several possible centres of manufacture had been put forward in the absence of known kilns. A small programme of heavy mineral analysis confirmed the visual separation between true Dales ware, with its characteristic shell-gritting, and the numerous sandy 'Dales ware type' imitations, as well as suggesting that one large scale centre was probably responsible for the production of true Dales ware.

The resultant narrowing down of a suitable geological source which could have provided the raw materials used in the making of Dales ware is an excellent demonstration of the potential in ceramic studies of both heavy mineral separation and thin-sectioning. The heavy mineral suite in this case was distinctive, consisting overwhelmingly of anhydrite, which at first suggested derivation from Permian Magnesian Limestone and marls of the vale of York, one of the source areas previously put forward. However, thin-sectioning and study of the shell content of the pottery showed it to be fossiliferous, and as comparatively few fossils are present in these Permian deposits, this effectively ruled out that area. Anhydrite also occurs in the Trias of south Yorkshire, Nottinghamshire, and Lincolnshire, more particularly in the Keuper Marls, though the latter is devoid of fossil shells. In view of this, Loughlin advocated an origin in north Lincolnshire, at the junction of the Keuper Marls and Rhaetic beds, the latter containing fossil shells comparable with those in the Dales ware pottery. The petrological characterization of Dales ware has allowed a detailed distribution analysis for different classes of site to be evaluated, taking into account settlement patterns, transportation, and competition from other potteries.

Besides pottery, Roman bricks and stamped tiles also have been studied with some success by petrological methods. The bricks and tiles of the Classis Britannica, the Roman fleet operating on both sides of the English Channel, have been systematically examined by Peacock (1977c). Once again, thin-sectioning was able to add little about origins for these sandy fabrics. Instead, a laborious heavy mineral analysis, concentrating on the siltstone content of one of the two major fabrics recognized, yielded a wide range of heavy minerals, the most distinctive element of which was a high percentage of leucoxene. By obtaining samples of sand and modern bricks from the suspected production area – the southern central Weald – Peacock was able to show that the Fabric 2 bricks most closely resembled the local Wealden Fairlight Clay. Moreover, perhaps the most interesting feature to emerge from this study was the huge numbers of bricks of this fabric that occurred at Boulogne, indicating shipment in some bulk from one side of the English Channel to the other.

Medieval pottery

To a large extent the study of medieval pottery, particularly in the earlier period, is a study of regional variation. True, there are a number of medieval wares that were exported over some distance, but none that can be compared to the vast Roman samian and north African red-slipped ware products. In view of this, petrological analysis has tended to be concentrated on detailed regional studies of medieval pottery fabrics, though a number of imported pottery types have also received attention, as well as pottery technology.

Foremost in the field of regional studies have been those continental scholars whose work has involved large programmes of thin-section analysis of pottery from the Rhineland and adjoining areas. Frechen's (1948) work on Frankish 'Mayen' ware from the middle Rhineland showed that it contained inclusions of a distinctive volcanic nature, undoubtedly derived from the Eifel region, which allows this pottery to be easily distinguished from imitations. Some form of continuity between this ware and similar fabrics of the late Roman period seems probable (Fulford and Bird 1975). Petrological characterization has also proved invaluable in showing that Tating ware, a tinfoil decorated pottery type of the eighth and ninth centuries AD, was made at a number of places, rather than being the specialized product of just one centre (Peacock in press). Detailed petrological work of this kind has made it possible to differentiate clearly between early medieval pottery from such centres as Cologne (Lung 1956, 1959), Frankfurt (Frechen 1962), Munich, and Strasbourg (Frechen 1969). However, the answers to questions of source areas are not always forthcoming. It has, for example, proved difficult to establish the source of certain early medieval granitic or gneissic tempered pottery common to the lower Rhineland, due to the large tracts of glacial clay which cover this area (Frechen 1950).

A systematic thin-sectioning programme of later medieval pottery, mainly from the west Mediterranean region, has been carried out for a number of years by Mannoni, at the Institute of Mineralogy, University of Genoa. He has shown that north African Islamic pottery found in Spain and Italy can in general be identified by the presence of well-rounded aeolian (wind-blown) sand, a feature lacking in European pottery (1972). One aspect of Mannoni's work has been concerned with a study of the large Spanish centres which produced tin-glazed maiolica from the thirteenth to fifteenth centuries AD. In particular, he has been able to distinguish petrologically between the important production centres of Malaga and Valencia, as well as suggesting that lustreware forms closely allied to the products of these two centres were made elsewhere, possibly at Granada or Barcelona, or further afield in Sardinia or north-west Sicily.

Work by Williams (1979b) on Spanish 'Merida ware' pottery from the Armada wrecks, and elsewhere in Britain, has raised doubts that this type of coarse red micaceous ware, usually in the form of costrels, can be characterized by the presence of volcanic glass as stated by Mannoni (1972, Tabella I and II, nos. 136–7). The area around Merida is unlikely to contain volcanic glass; it comprises granites and porphyries, with some sandstone, limestone, and shales. Petrological analysis of imported 'Merida ware' vessels in Britain reveals a variety of different fabrics, suggesting that several production centres were involved in the manufacture of this pottery, and that it was not made exclusively at Merida. From these results it would appear that red micaceous pottery was made at a number of different sites in the Iberian Peninsula, and that the term 'Merida ware' should be used in a generic sense, rather than as implying the source of the pottery.

In Britain, the petrological identification of foreign imported medieval pottery is not an easy task, due to the common range of inclusions which seem to characterize many fabric types. A notable exception to this is the range of imported amphorae which occurred in western Britain during the late fifth and sixth centuries AD (Thomas 1959; Alcock 1971, map 6). As yet the actual source areas remain unknown, although as close parallels to each of the British 'B' sub-classes are to be found in some number in the eastern Mediterranean and around the Black Sea, it is likely that they originated in this region. The lack of finds in northern Spain and France suggests a direct sea-borne trade through the Straits of Gibraltar to Britain. Thin-sectioning by Peacock (1971c) of Bi and Bii amphorae from Glastonbury Tor showed

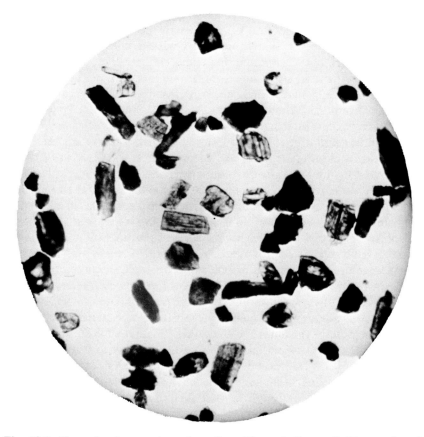

Fig. 10.3. Byzantine imported amphora from Tintagel, Cornwall. Heavy mineral residue showing large grains of pyroxene (diopside and enstatite; some masked by staining). The distribution and fabric of this type of amphora (Bii type) suggest a source in the eastern Mediterranean, possibly northern Syria. Plane polarized light (× 65). (Photomicrographs by N. Bradford.)

that the fabrics from both forms were different, and unlikely to have come from the same area, as previously thought (Thomas 1959). Bi is characterized by limestone and mica, indicating a source area of sedimentary rocks, while Bii contains pyroxene and limestone, indicating a source area of both basic igneous and sedimentary rocks. As these rocks are fairly common in the probable source areas mentioned above, it was not possible for Peacock to be specific about origins.

Recently, petrological analysis by Williams (1982) on both of these types of amphorae has considerably restricted the likely geological areas involved, thus reducing to manageable proportions the detailed search for the actual production centres. Further thin-sectioning of Bi amphora fabrics has shown that a number contain fragments of volcanic glass, though typologically and in hand specimen these samples appear identical to those from Glastonbury Tor. This additional information indicates an origin for the Bi amphorae in an area which includes both volcanic and sedimentary formations. Furthermore, an origin near the coast for both types of amphorae is to be expected, for there appears to have been a sea-borne trade in these vessels (Thomas 1959; Hayes 1973). The coastal volcanic regions of the Aegean which would qualify as potential source areas include many of the Greek Islands, as well as north-west Asia Minor.

The fabric of the Bii amphora is considerably more sandy than that of the Bi, and so heavy mineral analysis was used. This revealed an assemblage dominated by diopside and enstatite, which, taking into acount the comparative lack of other minerals, especially zircon, suggested derivation from peridotite, an ultrabasic rock. This type of rock has a fairly restricted distribution in the eastern Mediterranean, and hardly appears at all around the Black Sea coast. Small outcrops occur on Cyprus, Lesbos, and Euboea, while larger tracts are to be found in south-west Asia Minor and northern Syria. If olive oil was carried in the British series of 'B' amphorae (Thomas 1957; Alcock 1963), a source in north Africa, the traditional suppliers of olive oil to the west, seems unlikely given the petrology of the Bi and Bii types. It is tempting, therefore, to see the Bi amphora primarily as a container for wine (from the Greek Islands?), and the Bii for carrying olive oil (from the north-eastern area of the Mediterranean?).

Another type of early medieval imported sandy ware whose precise source is as yet unknown, but which has been narrowed down to certain likely areas through the application of heavy mineral analysis, is Class 'E' ware, found on a number of sites in western Britain and Ireland (Peacock and Thomas 1967). Petrological analysis of this pottery is important, for it indicated possible source areas not previously considered. The heavy mineral suite included kyanite, which is found principally in post-Triassic sediments, and andalusite, which is commonest in the Tertiary, and which effectively discounted the previously suggested Rhineland origin for this pottery, since that region consists mainly of Triassic and earlier rocks. Instead, on geological grounds, this pottery was thought likely to have been made in the area of the Paris Basin or Aquitaine, with the latter region appearing archaeologically the more probable of the two.

More recently, the heavy mineral assemblage of a fine-textured sherd of Roman '*à l'éponge* ware' from London recalled that of Peacock's results on Class 'E' ware, and also suggested an origin in Aquitaine rather than the Rhineland or Moselle regions, which are other possible source areas for 'marbled ware' imports to Roman Britain (Williams 1980*b*).

In Britain, much indigeneous medieval pottery contains common inclusions such as sand, shell, and organic matter, which makes the problems involved in characterizing such fabrics and identifying source areas particularly difficult. There are, however, a number of exceptions which allow the origins of certain wares to be quite closely defined. Vince (1977) has drawn attention to the presence in certain west Midland pottery of the twelfth to seventeenth centuries AD of inclusions derived from the Precambrian of the Malvern Hills. This follows on from Peacock's work on Iron Age (1968) and Roman (1967*b*) pottery from the same region, while his analysis of a twelfth century grass-marked sherd from Southampton indicates the use of Lizard gabbroic clays at this time.

When dealing with distinctive igneous rock fragments in pottery, the petrological evidence is not always as clear cut as the above examples suggest. Work by Williams (1977*c*) and Walker (1978) on early–middle Saxon pottery from east Midlands sites has shown that fragments of granitic inclusions, made up of large grains of plagioclase feldspar and brown hornblende, are present in some types. The nearest suitable igneous formations to the find sites are the Charnwood Forest Precambrian rocks (including the Mountsorrel diorite) to the south-west of Leicester, and the post-Tremadoc 'diorites' around Nuneaton. It is possible, therefore, that this petrologically distinctive pottery could be regarded as a traded ware from a single production centre. In this connection it might also be worth while noting that similar granitic inclusions have been recognized by Frechen (1950) in Saxon pottery from north Germany. The situation is complicated by the fact that the majority of British find sites are situated close to boulder clay glacial deposits which contain a number of igneous erratics. The widespread distribution of find sites in the east Midlands makes a local source in each case less likely than some form of centralized production, as the frequency of the glacial igneous erratics seems rather limited.

Much medieval pottery contains a range of common inclusions, principally quartz sand, when thin-section analysis can often lead to inconclusive results (Knight 1970; Barton 1973). Heavy mineral separation is not always a viable alternative, if only because the amount of pottery required for this method is not available in many cases. In these circumstances, the best approach may lie in a detailed textural analysis of the quartz content. Granulometric analysis has been applied to medieval Polish pottery by Kociszewski and Kruppé (1964) to differentiate between natural and deliberately added inclusions, by Debska-Lutowa and Grezegorczyk (1969) in suggesting a non-local source for the pottery from Castle Lad, and by Janssen and De Paepe (1976) to help characterize later medieval pottery from a wide geographical range of kiln sites.

Thin-section analysis has been used extensively to help answer questions concerning certain aspects of medieval pottery technology. The method has been successfully employed to provide information on the selection of clay and temper used for pottery made at the later medieval factory site at Siegburg (Beckmann, Strunk-Lichtenburg, and Heide 1971). This showed that twelfth century earthenware fabrics contained a particular size grade additive of Pleistocene sand from the Rhine, recalling that of tenth century Pingsdorf ware, from which the technique seems to have been adopted. In contrast, the Sieburg stoneware fabrics of the fifteenth century contain no deliberate additions of sand. The fine-grained quartz which is present in the latter vessels occurs naturally in the local Tertiary clays that were utilized. In In a similar way, Mannoni (Mannoni and Magi 1974) was able to show in his extensive work on Ligurian pottery that different local clays were chosen for glazed and non-glazed pottery. In addition, due to the limitations imposed by the generally coarse local clays, more refined clays were imported for use in the area in response to competition from the better quality Antibes ware.

Conclusions

In addition to petrography there are, of course, many other scientific techniques which are being successfully applied to characterize pottery and help establish likely source areas. There is no one single method of analysis which is suitable for every kind of pottery fabric. The method of examination should always be chosen after taking into account the type of fabric involved and the kinds of question that need to be answered to shed light on characterization, origins, or technology. For example, petrography is severely limited in characterizing certain kinds of pottery fabric, i.e. when common inclusions such as flint, shell, or organic temper are present, and chemical analysis may have much more to offer in these cases. Thin-sectioning is really at its most useful when dealing with exotic inclusions, and where a prediction of a source may be possible even on a single sample. Heavy mineral separation can often provide invaluable evidence of origins for sandy pottery, even fairly fine-grained wares, though distinctive heavy mineral suites are not always forthcoming. As sandy wares are one of the commonest fabric types, increasing use will undoubtedly be made of textural analysis in thin-sectioning, involving a consideration of the size, shape, and frequency of the quartz grains.

For practical purposes, only a very small proportion of the total ceramic assemblage from an excavation can be subjected to petrological analysis. In these circumstances, it is essential that petrological details should go hand-in-hand with macroscopic descriptions of the sherds examined, in order that fabric types can be more easily identified in the hand specimens.

Acknowledgements

I am gratful to M. Parker-Pearson for information on the petrology of certain Bronze Age pottery of south-west Britain, and above all to my wife for her assistance in the preparation of this chapter. Dr David Peacock very kindly read a first draft and made many constructive comments.

References

Alcock, L. (1963). *Dinas Powys*. University of Wales Press, Cardiff.
—— (1971). *Arthur's Britain*. Allen Lane, London.
Amiran, R. B., Arieth, Y., and Glass, J. (1973). The interrelationship between Arad and sites in southern Sinai in the early Bronze Age II. *Israel Exploration Journal* **23**, 193–7.
Bares, M. and Licka, M. (1976). K exaktnimu studiu staré keramidy. *Acta Musei Nationalis Prague* **30**, 137–244.
Barton, M. (1973). Report on thin sectioning. In: N. P. Thompson and H. Ross: Excavation at the Saxon Church, Alton Barnes. *Wiltshire Archaeological Magazine* **68**, 78.
Beckmann, B., Strunk-Lichtenburg, G., and Heide, H. (1971). Die frühe sieburger kerami, und ihre Entwicklung zum Steinzeug. *Keramische Zeitschrift* **23**, 1–4.
Biddle, M. and Barclay, K. (1974). Winchester ware. In: V. I. Evison, H. Hedges, and H. Hurst (ed.): *Medieval pottery from excavations*. John Baker, London, 137–81.
Buttler, W. (1935). Ein Hinkelsteingefass aus Köln-Lindentral und seine Bedeutung fur die chronologie der rheinischen Bandkeramik. *Germania* **19**, 193–200.
Callender, M. H. (1965). *Roman amphorae*. Oxford University Press.
Cornwall, I. W. (1958). *Soils for the archaeologist*. Phoenix House, London.
—— Hodges, H. W. M. (1964). Thin sections of British Neolithic pottery: Windmill Hill – a test site. *Bulletin of the Institute of Archaeology. University of London* **4**, 29–33.
Dannell, G. B. (1971). The samian pottery. In: B. Cuncliffe: Excavations at Fishbourne 1961–1969. *Research Report of the Society of Antiquaries* **27**, 260–316.
Debska-Lutowa, K. and Grezegorczyk, M. (1969). Badania petrograficzne naczynia wczesnośredniowiecznego z grodziska w Ladzie, pow slupca. *Fentes Archaeologici Poswandiensis* **20**, 232–46.
Duma, C. and Ravasz, C. (1973). Mineralogical-petrographical and chemical investigation on archaeological ceramic gravegoods. *Acta Mineralogica-Petrographica* **21**, 41–7.
Ettlinger, E. (1960). Review of Uenze, 1958, Frührömische Ampheren als Zeitmarken im Spätlatene. *Germania* **38**, 440.
Felts, W. M. (1942). A petrographic examination of potsherds from ancient Troy. *American Journal of Archaeology* **46**, 237–44.

Farnsworth, M. (1964). Greek pottery: a mineralogical study. *American Journal of Archaeology* **68**, 221–8.

—— (1970). Corinthian pottery: technical studies. *American Journal of Archaeology* **74**, 9–20.

Frechen, J. (1948). Ergebnisse der mineralegischen Untersuchung. In: A. Steeger: Der frankische Friedhof in Rill bei Xanten. *Bonner Jahrbucher* **148**, 296–8.

—— (1950). Das Ergebnis der mineralogischen Untersuchung. In: K. Bohner, P. J. Tholen, and R. Vslar: Augrabungen in den Kirchen von Breberen und Deveren. *Bonner Jahrbucher* **150**, 219–20.

—— (1962). Mineralogisch-petrographisches Untersuchungsergebnis. In: O. Stamm: *Spatromische und fruhmittelaterliche Keramik der Alten Stadt Frankfurt am Main.* Frankfurt.

—— (1969). Mineralogische Gutachten. In: W. Hubener: Absatzgebiete frugesehichtlicher Topfereien in der Zone nordlich der Alpen. *Beitrage zur Keramik der Merowingerzeit* 301–8.

Freestone, I. C. (1983). Applications and potential of electron probe micro-analysis in technological and provenance investigations of ancient ceramics. *Archaeometry* **25** (1).

—— Rigby, V. (1982) Class B cordoned and other imported wares from Hengistbury Head, Dorset. In: I. C. Freestone, C. John, and T. Potter (ed.): Current research in ceramics: thin section studies. *British Museum Occasional Paper* **32**, 29–42.

Frere, S. S. (1967). *Britannia: a history of Roman Britain.* Routledge and Kegan Paul, London.

Frierman, J. (1970). Physical and chemical properties of some Medieval Near Eastern glazed ceramics. In: R. Berger (ed.): *Scientific methods in medieval archaeology.* University of California Press, 379–88.

Fulford, M. and Bird, J. (1975). Imported pottery from Germany in late Roman Britain. *Britannia* **6**, 171–81.

Grimanis, A. P., Filippakis, S. E., Perdikatsis, B., Vassilaki-Grimani, M., Bosana-Bouron, N., and Yalouris, N. (1980). Neutron activation and X-ray analysis of 'Thrapsos Class' vases. An attempt to identify their origin. *Journal of Archaeological Science* **7**, 227–39.

Hartley, B. R. (1972). The Roman occupation of Scotland: the evidence of samian ware. *Britannia* **3**, 1–55.

Hawkes, C. F. C. (1959). The ABC of British Iron Age. *Antiquity* **33**, 170–82.

Hayes, J. W. (1972). *Late Roman pottery.* British School at Rome, London.

—— (1973). The Roman deposits. In: J. Boardman and J. Hayes: *Excavations at Tocra 1963–1965: The Archaic Deposits II and Later Deposits.* The British School of Archaeology at Athens, London, 107–19.

Hays, T. R. and Hassan, F. A. (1974). Mineralogical analysis of Sudanese Neolithic ceramics. *Archaeometry* **16**, 71–9.

Hedge, K. T. M. (1966). Electron microscope study on the Northern black polished (N.B.P.) ware of India. *Current Science* **35**, 623.

Hodder, I. (1974). The distribution of two types of Romano-British coarse pottery in the west Sussex region. *Sussex Archaeological Collections* **112**, 86–96.

Hofmann, V. (1962). The chemical basis of ancient Greek vase painting. *Angewandte Chemie* **1**, 341–50.

Hulthen, B. (1976). Technological investigations for evidence of continuity or discontinuity of ancient ceramic traditions. In: S. J. DeLaet (ed.): *Acculturation and continuity in Atlantic Europe.* Brugge.

Janssen, H. L. and De Paepe, P. A. (1976). Petrological examination of Medieval pottery from South Limburg and the Rhineland. R O B **26**, 217–27.

Kingery, W. D. (1974). A technological characterization of two Cypriot ceramics. In: *Recent advances in science and technology of materials.* Second Solid State Conference, Cairo, 169–86.

—— Frierman, J. D. (1974). The firing temperature of a Karanova sherd and inferences about south-east European Chalcolithic refractory technology. *Proceedings of the Prehistoric Society* **40**, 204–5.

Knight, J. K. (1970). Some late medieval pottery from St. Dogmael's Abbey, Pembrokeshire. *Archaeologia Cambrensis* **119**, 125–30.

Kociszewski, L. and Kruppé, J. (1964). A method of physico-chemical investigation prompting the study of technology in the history of pottery production. *Archaeologia Polona* **6**, 161–84.

Krug, O. Y. (1965). Primeneniye petrografii v arkeologii. In: B. A. Kolchina (ed.): *Arkheologiva i Yestestvennye nauki.* Moscow, 146–52.

Lloris, M. B. (1978). *Ceramic Romana: Tipologia y Classificacion.* Zaragoza.

Loughlin, N. (1977). Dales ware: a contribution to the study of Roman coarse pottery. In: D. P. S. Peacock (ed.): *Pottery and early commerce,* Academic Press, London, 85–146.

Lung, W. (1956). Die Ausgrabung nachkarelingischer Topferofen in Paffrath, Gemeinde Bergisch Gladbach, Rheinisch-Bergischer Kreis. *Bonner Jahrbucher* **156**, 355–71.

—— (1959). Zur ver-und fruhgeschichtlichen Keramic im Kolner Raum. *Kolner Jahrbuch fur Ver-und Fruhgeschichte* **4**, 45–65.

Maniatis, Y. and Tite, M. S. (1979). Ceramic technology in the Aegean world during the Bronze Age. In: C. Doumas (ed.): *Thera and the Aegean World* I. Thera and the Aegean World, London, 483–92.

Mannoni, T. (1972). Analisi mineralogiche e technologiche della ceramiche medievali – Neta II. *Atti v Cenvegno Internazionale della Ceramica,* 107–128.

—— (1974). Mineralogical analysis of medieval pottery. *Records of the VII International Ceramics Congress.*

—— Magi, M. G. (1974). Some technological characteristics of everyday Ligurian pottery. *Records of the VII International Ceramics Congress.*

Obenauer, K. (1936). Petrographische Untersuchung der Keramik. In: W. Buttler and W. Haberey: *Die bandkeramische Ansiedlung bei Köln-Lindenthal,* Leipzig, 123–9.

Peacock, D. P. S. (1967a). The heavy mineral analysis of pottery: a preliminary report. *Archaeometry* **10**, 97–100.

—— (1967b). Romano-British pottery production in the Malvern district of Worcestershire. *Transactions of the Worcestershire Archaeological Society* **1**, 15–28.

—— (1968). A petrological study of certain Iron Age pottery from western England. *Proceedings of the Prehistoric Society* **34**, 414–27.

—— (1969a). Neolithic pottery production in Cornwall. *Antiquity* **43**, 145–9.

—— (1969b). A contribution to the study of Glastonbury ware from south-western England. *Antiquaries Journal* **49**, 41–61.

—— (1970). The scientific analysis of ancient ceramics: a review. *World Archaeology* **1**, 375–89.

—— (1971a). Petrography of certain coarse pottery. In: B. Cuncliffe: Excavations at Fishbourne. Vol. II. *Research Report of the Society of Antiquaries* **27**, 255–9.

—— (1971b). Roman amprhorae in pre-Roman Britain. In: M. Jesson and D. Hill (ed.), *The Iron Age and its Hill forts.* University of Southampton, 169–88.

—— (1971c). Imported pottery. In: P. Rahtz: Excavations on Glastonbury Tor, Somerset, 1964–6. *Archaeological Journal* **127**, 65–7.

—— (1973). The black-burnished pottery industry in Dorset. In: A. P. Detsicas (ed.): Current research in Romano-British coarse pottery. *Research Reports Council for British Archaeology* **10**, 63–5.

—— (1974). Amphorae and the Baetican fish industry. *Antiquaries Journal* **54**, 232–43.

—— (1975). The grass-marked sherd. In: C. Platt and R. Coleman-Smith: *Excavations in Medieval Southampton, 1953–1969.* Leicester University Press, 47.

—— (1977a). Roman amphorae: typology, fabric and origins. *Ecole Francaise de Rome* **32**, 261–78.

—— (1977b). Pompeian red ware. In: D. P. S. Peacock (ed.): *Pottery and early commerce*, Academic Press, London, 147–62.

—— (1977c). Bricks and tiles of the Classis Britannica: petrology and origins. *Britannia* **8**, 235–47.

—— (1978a). Recent discoveries of Roman amphorae kilns in Italy. *Antiquaries Journal* **58**, 262–9.

—— (1978b). The Rhine and the problem of Gaulish wine in Roman Britain. In: J. Taylor and H. Cleere, (ed.): Roman shipping and trade: Britain and the Rhine Provinces. *Research Reports Council for British Archaeology* **24**, 49–51.

—— (in press). Archaeological investigations on the Island of Pantelleria, Italy. *National Geographical Society Research Report.*

—— (in press). Petrology and the study of medieval ceramics; a review.

—— and Thomas, A. C. (1967). Class 'E' imported post-Roman pottery: a suggested origin. *Cornish Archaeology* **6**, 35–46.

Picon, M., Vichy, M., and Meille, E. (1971). Composition of the Lezoux Lyon and Arezzo samian ware. *Archaeometry* **13**, 191–208.

—— Carre, C., Cordoliani, M. L., Vichy, M., Hernandez, J. A., and Mignard, J. L. (1975). Composition of the La Graufesenque, Banassac and Montans Terra Sigillata. *Archaeometry* **17**, 191–9.

Prag, A. J. N. W., Schweizer, F., and Williams, J. L. W. (1974). Hellenistic glazed wares from Athens and southern Italy: analytical techniques and implications. *Archaeometry* **16**, 153–87.

Reynolds, D. L. (1933). Appendix. In: K. P. Oakley: The pottery from the Romano-British site on Thundersbarrow Hill. *Antiquaries Journal* **13**, 151.

Richards, E. E. (1960). Report on black-burnished ware from Mumrills. In: K. A. Steer: Excavations at Mumrills Roman fort, 1958–60. *Proceedings of the Society of Antiquaries of Scotland* **94**, 129–30.

Riley, J., Peacock, D. P. S., and Renfrew, A. C. (1980). The petrological characterization of ceramics from the eastern Mediterranean. *Revue d'Archeometrie* **3**, 245–9.

Sabine, P. A. (1958). Black mica in the pottery fabric. In: E. M. Jepe and R. I. Threlfall: Excavation of a medieval settlement at Beere, North Tawton, Devon. *Medieval Archaeology* **2**, 140.

Schmitt, R. R. (1939). Moglichkeiten und Grenzen des Einsatzes der Petrographie bei der Untersuchung van Verzeitfunden. *Nachrichtenblatt fur deutsche vorzeit* **15**, 47–51.

Shackley, M. (1975). *Archaeological sediments: a survey of analytical methods*, Butterworths, London.

Shepard, A. C. (1942). *Rio Grande glazed paint ware, a study illustrating the place of ceramic technological analysis in archaeological research.* Carnegie Institute, Washington.

Streeten, A. D. F. (1979). Fabric analysis and distribution. In: D. J. Fieke: The excavation of a sixteenth century pottery kiln at Lower Parrock, Hartfield, East Sussex, 1977. *Post-Medieval Archaeology* **13**, 114–20.

Tchernia, A. and Zevi, F. (1972). Amphores vinaires de Campanie et de Tarraconaise á Ostiè. *Collection de L'Ecole Francaise de Rome* **10**, 35–67.

Thomas, A. C. (1957). Some imported post-Roman sherds in Cornwall and their origin. *Proceedings of the West Cornwall Field Club* **2**, 15–22.

—— (1959). Imported pottery in Dark-Age western Britain. *Medieval Archaeology* **3**, 89–111.

Tite, M. S. and Maniatis, Y. (1975). Examination of ancient pottery using the scanning electron microscope. *Nature*, **257**, 122–3.

—— Freestone, I. C., Meeks, N. D., and Bimson, M. (1981). The use of scanning electron microscopy in the technological examination of ancient ceramics. In: *Ceramics as archaeological material*. Smithsonian Institution, Washington.

Vince, A. (1977). The medieval and post-medieval ceramic industry of the Malvern region: the study of a ware and its distribution. In: D. P. S. Peacock (ed.): *Pottery and early commerce*. Academic Press, London, 257–305.

Walker, J. (1978). Appendix: Anglo-Saxon traded pottery. In: D. F. Mackreth: Orton Hall Farm, Peterborough: a Roman and Saxon settlement. In: M. Tedd (ed.): *Studies in the Romano-British villa*. Leicester University Press, 224–8.

Wallis, F. S. and Evens, E. D. (1934). Report on the heavy minerals contained in the coarse Pant-y-Saer pottery. In: C. W. Phillips: The excavation of a hut group at Pant-y-Saer in the parish of Wanfair-Mathafarn-Eithaf, Anglesey. *Archaeologia Cambrensis* **89**, 29–32.

Widemann, F., Picon, M., Asaro, F., Michel, H. V., and Perlman, I. (1975). A Lyons branch of the pottery-making firm of Ateius of Arezzo. *Archaeometry* **17**, 45–59.

Williams, D. F. (1976) Petrology of the pottery. In: J. Schwieso: Excavations at Threemilestone Round, Kenwyn, Truro. *Cornish Archaeology* **15**, 63–4.

—— (1977*a*). Black-burnished ware from Mumrills: a reappraisal of sources by heavy mineral analysis. In: J. Dore, and K. Greene (ed.): Roman pottery studies in Britain and beyond. *British Archaeological Report* **30**, 177–87.

—— (1977*b*). The Romano-British black-burnished industry: an essay on characterization by heavy mineral analysis. In: D. P. S. Peacock (ed.): *Pottery and early commerce*. Academic Press, London, 163–220.

—— (1977*c*). Petrological analysis of Saxon pottery from Brixworth. In: P. Everson: Excavations in the Vicarage Garden at Brixworth. *Journal of the British Archaeological Association* **130**, 84–5.

—— (1978*a*). Petrological analysis of arretine and early samian: a preliminary report. In: P. Arthur and G. Marsh (ed.): Early fine wares in Roman Britain. *British Archaeological Report* **57**, 5–12.

—— (1978*b*). A petrological examination of pottery·from Thera. *Thera and the Aegean World* I. Thera and the Aegean World, London, 508–14.

—— (1979*a*). The heavy mineral separation of ancient ceramics by centrifugation: a preliminary report. *Archaeometry* **21**, 177–82.

—— (1979*b*). Petrological analysis. In: C. J. M. Martin: Spanish Armada pottery. *International Journal of Nautical Archaeology* **8**, 298–9.

—— (1980*a*). Heavy mineral analysis of Bronze Age pottery from Melos and Thera: a preliminary report. *Revue d'Archeometrie* **3**, 321–3.

—— (1980*b*) Un tesson de céramique [á l'éponge] provenant du New Fresh Wharf á Londres. In: P. Gailliou, M. Fulford, and M. Clement: *La diffusion de la ceramique [á l'éponge] dans le nord-ouest de l'empire Romain. Gallia* **38**, 277–8.

—— (1982). The petrology of certain Byzantine amphorae: some suggestions as to origins. *C E D A C Dossier* **1**, 99–110.

—— Ovenden, P. J. (1978). Medieval pottery from Rome: petrographical and chemical analysis. In: H. M. Blake, T. W. Potter, and D. B. Whitehouse (ed.): Papers in Italian archaeology I: the Lancaster seminar. *British Archaeological Report* **41** (Supplement), 507–19.

Williams, J. L. W. and Jenkins, D. A. (1976). The use of petrographic, heavy mineral and arc spectrographic techniques in assessing the provenance of sediments used in ceramics. In: D. A. Davidson and M. L. Shackley (ed.): *Geoarchaeology*. Duckworth, London, 115–35.

—— Jenkins, D. A., and Livens, B. G. (1974). An analytical study of the composition of Roman coarse wares from the fort of Bryn-y-Gefeiliau (Caer Llugwy) in Snowdonia. *Journal of Archaeological Science* **1**, 47–67.

11. Native metals and minerals

M. P. Jones

The native metals

Many metal artefacts have survived from early times and some of them clearly pre-date the time when any metals could have been produced by primitive smelting processes. These artefacts must, therefore, have been made from naturally occurring metals.

It is well known by geologists that small amounts of some metals, such as copper, gold, silver, and iron, occur naturally in the elemental state. Some of these naturally formed metals react only very slowly with atmospheric oxygen and with natural aqueous solutions and so they remain essentially unaltered at, or near, the Earth's surface where they were occasionally found by man.

Such metallic materials are readily distinguished from other natural materials because they are relatively heavy, feel cold to the touch, have distinctive 'lustres', and they are deformed, but not broken, when hammered.

Naturally occurring (or native) metals are very similar to smelted metals but the two groups can often be distinguished by differences of microscopic texture, by the presence of mineralogical impurities or slaggy inclusions, and by the amount and distribution of alloying or trace elements. These features can also occasionally be used to indicate the geographical source of a fragment of native metal.

Even with copper (the most abundant of the native metals) the total quantity available was always small and the native metals would, therefore, have been used only to make small artefacts: articles of personal adornment such as rings, armlets, and brooches; weapons such as spear heads; tools such as scrapers and knives; small utensils; and coins.

Only with the availability of much larger quantities of smelted material would metal have been used as load-carrying beams; as armour for the protection of the person; as cladding for the protection of ships from attack by marine organisms; or as roofing materials.

Native copper

This native metal exists in larger quantities than any other metal and it also occurs as the largest fragments. It is widely distributed over the Earth's surface since small copper-rich deposits occur in very many parts of the world and most of these contain (or, at one time, did contain) traces of metallic copper, e.g. Erzegeberge, the Carpathians, Lake Superior, Cornwall (a piece from Cornwall weighing 56 kg is on display in the Geological Museum, London), Hungary, South America; but not, apparently, Egypt (Dayton 1978).

Native copper commonly occurs as small dendritic or wiry aggregates that weigh a few grammes but large lumps weighing up to many tonnes have been, and occasionally still are, found. It has a density of about 8940 kg m^{-3}; its hardness ranges from 2½ to 3 on Mohs' scale of hardness, and it melts at 1083 °C. When the metal is hammered or bent its hardness increases markedly and values ranging from 59 to 108 on the Vickers hardness scale have been reported for artefacts that are thought to have been fabricated from native copper. A freshly-broken surface of the metal is 'copper'-red in colour but this quickly tarnishes. A freshly-polished surface is rose-white when examined under vertical, reflected light and its reflectivity in white light is 81.5 per cent. Lumps of native copper are often partly, or almost completely, altered and can then be difficult to distinguish from the naturally occurring 'oxide' copper minerals such as cuprite, malachite, or azurite. Because native copper is readily attacked by oxygenated water and is also very soft and readily abraded it is seldom found as a constituent of alluvial deposits.

It would be of great assistance to the archaeologist if native copper could be unequivocally distinguished from smelted copper but this is not always possible. In general, however, native copper tends to be much purer than the copper produced by the earliest smelters, but this is not invariably the case and native copper can contain up to 0.6 per cent silver with traces of gold, and small amounts of iron, arsenic, and lead (Table 11.1). Furthermore, skilfully smelted copper produced from especially pure copper-bearing minerals can itself be comparatively pure. Consequently, the overall composition of the metal cannot, by itself, be used to distinguish unambiguously between artefacts made from native copper and those made from smelted metal (Maddin *et al.* 1980). Moreover, the composition of a piece of native copper is often non-uniform, and the result of an analysis depends on the fragment chosen for analysis. Thus, the silver content has been shown by electronmicroprobe analysis to vary from 0.024 to 0.116 per cent in different grains within a single specimen; because of these small compositional differences, some grains react differently to others when a polished section of the metal is etched and this can produce a distinctive textural effect. Smelted metal, on the other hand, tends to be more uniform in composition.

The metallographic grain size distribution of unworked native copper is very variable. The metal sometimes shows dendritic crystals many centimetres in size: other specimens consist of aggregates of much smaller grains. The natural grain size of the native metal can, however, be changed

Table 11.1. Range of
trace element com-
position of comparatively
impure native copper
specimens

element	compositional range %
Ag	0.004–0.6
Au	trace only
As	0.002–«1.0*
Sb	up to 0.4
Pb	0.0001–0.3
Ni	0.0003–0.5
Co	up to 0.1
Fe	0.005–2.1
Sn	up to 0.27
S	up to 0.49

* (See Maddin, Stechwheeler, and Muhly 1980).
After Tylecote (1976).

by working or by heat treatment below its melting temperature. Smelted copper tends to be uniform in texture and comparatively finer-grained. Therefore, native copper can only be reliably identified if it is unworked and shows very large crystal grains.

Unworked, native copper frequently shows large, twinned grains and it has been claimed (Maddin *et al.* 1980) that the metal can usually be identified by an experienced observer by the general appearance of these twins. The twins can survive when the metal is lightly annealed but extensive working (e.g. hammering) or high-temperature annealing tends to obscure them. The hardness of copper is a function of both its composition and its treatment history and, consequently, hardness cannot provide an unambiguous guide to the identification of native metal.

Native copper often contains small inclusions that consist of minerals derived from the enclosing rock mass. Some of these minerals, such as calcite, would decompose during high-temperature annealing or during a smelting operation. Consequently, such inclusions, where they are clearly of primary origin and have not been incorporated into the metal by, for example, subsequent burial, serve to differentiate unheated native metal from other kinds of copper. Other mineral inclusions, such as iron sulphide or copper sulphide grains, can be found in both native and smelted copper and do not provide reliable guides to the origin or to the history of the surrounding metal.

Although no single feature among those given can be used to provide an unambiguous identification of native copper, the combined use of: overall chemical composition; detailed compositional variations; grain size distributions; type of grain twinning; hardness; nature of inclusions; and also the age and archaeological provenance of an artefact, often make it possible to establish the kind of metal used in making it. However, as with all metals, native copper may have been repeatedly re-used and copper from different sources may have been mixed to make an artefact and in these instances recognition of metal type and origin is almost impossible.

Archaeologists have claimed that native copper was used in Iran and Anatolia to make beads, pins, and awls in the period between the ninth and seventh millenia BC (Tylecote 1976). Furthermore, large amounts of copper from the Lake Superior area of northern USA are known to have been used by local people to make similar articles from the third or fourth millenium BC onwards: for example, spearheads of native copper made by the Old Copper Culture (3000 to 1500 BC) were work-hardened by hammering to give Vickers hardness values between 59 and 108 (Mellink 1965; Patterson 1971). It has been estimated that, on average, the Lake Superior Indians mined about 1 tonne of native copper per year in the 6000 years between 4200 BC and recent times. Therefore, a total of about 6000 tonnes of native metal was produced from a single large geological occurrence. In view of the ready availability of such quantities of copper, it is not surprising that there is no evidence that the Lake Superior Indians ever learnt either to melt the native copper or to smelt the associated copper ores (Dayton 1978).

Native gold

Native gold was the only form of the metal that was known to primitive man and, until quite recent times, no gold compounds were ever treated in order to produce the pure metal.

The primary geological sources of gold are narrow rock veins that consist largely of quartz and/or sulphide minerals. When these veins are broken down by natural weathering processes the gold is released and finds its way into the local drainage system where, because of its high density and resistance to chemical attack, it collects in the river gravels.

The gold-bearing source veins seldom contain more than a few hundred parts per million of gold. However, this gold is distributed non-uniformly and comparatively rich fragments that contain 1 per cent or more of gold can be picked out by hand sorting. These richer fragments were finely ground to release the gold which was then concentrated and recovered by simple washing operations. The early Egyptians practised these methods in the Eastern Desert of Upper Egypt and in Nubia, and the Romans used similar processes in their gold mining operations at Dolau Cothi, South Wales.

The greater amount of ancient gold (and also, in all probability, the earliest gold) was, however, obtained from river gravels. In these gravels the gold was, on rare occasions, found as large nuggets that weighed up to a few kilogrammes. Much more commonly, the gold was found as minute, irregularly-shaped scales less than a millimetre in size. However, because of their extremely high density when compared with most of the other minerals found in the gravels, the gold scales could be readily concentrated by simple washing or 'panning' procedures.

Alluvial (i.e. river gravel) gold often occurs with small amounts of other heavy minerals that are of considerable archaeological interest. These include cassiterite (SnO_2), the source of all smelted tin, and the naturally-occcurring platinoid alloys (Ogden 1977; see below). These additional heavy minerals would tend to collect along with gold during any washing operation and some of them have been accidentally incorporated into gold artefacts. These minute inclusions can remain, virtually unchanged, in the gold arte-facts; for example, small greyish-white inclusions of the platinoid alloys, especially those containing osmium and iridium, have been found in gold artefacts from Ecuador, Colombia, and Greece (Ogden 1977). Detailed studies of such inclusions are now possible using electronmicroprobe analysis.

Gold was, and still is, highly prized for its colour, its ease of working, and its resistance to corrosion. Larger fragments of the metal were fashioned by hammering into decorative or ornamental artefacts such as wires, sheets, and beads. However, if fine-grained gold flakes are hammered together at ambient temperatures they will not consolidate into larger fragments. This is due to the presence of thin films of oxidation products and other impurities. Consequently, in earliest times the small gold flakes may only have been used as 'dust' for decorative purposes. Later, when it became possible to melt the gold, the flakes were melted in crucibles and then cast or hammered into usable shapes.

Pure gold is a soft and extremely malleable metal; its hardness is $2\frac{1}{2}$ to 3 on Mohs' scale; it has a density of 19 300 kg m^{-3}, and melts at 1063 °C. Its colour is 'golden'-yellow but, in polished section under vertical, white illumination, the colour is brilliant yellow and its reflectivity is 70 per cent. Native gold, however, generally contains significant amounts of alloying elements and these can greatly modify its properties: for example, the colour of a polished section can be changed to pale yellow and the reflectivity can be increased to 85 per cent by the presence of significant amounts of silver; similarly, the presence of other alloying elements can reduce the density to 15 000 kg m^{-3}.

The purity of gold is expressed in a number of ways: by the percentage of gold that it contains; by 'fineness', i.e. the number of parts per 1000; and by 'carats', where 24 carats is pure gold.

Tables 11.2 and 11.3 give the ranges of composition of alluvial and of vein

Table 11.2. Variation in composition of alluvial gold from different localities

locality	composition (per cent)		
	silver	copper	iron
Ural mountains	0.16	0.35	0.05
Finland	1.79	≯0.21	
	9.61	≯0.89	
	21.90	≯1.0	
Colombia	9.3		
(Colombia mine*)	(16.9)		
Italy	4.69		
	6.40		
Ireland	6.17	≯0.73	0.78
	8.85	nil	
	8.1	trace	2.1
Cornwall, England	9.05	nil	

* It is not known whether the Colombian alluvial material was derived from the same source as this Colombian mined gold.
After Tylecote (1976).

Table 11.3. Variation in composition of vein gold from different localities

locality	composition (per cent)		
	silver	copper	iron
Altai	38.38	>0.31	0.033
Czechoslovakia	14.68	0.04	0.13
Clogau, Wales	9.26	trace	

After Tylecote (1976).

gold, respectively, from a number of localities. Some native gold contains up to 40 per cent silver, about 1 per cent copper, and 0.5 per cent iron. Some of these natural alloys have been given distinctive mineralogical names: for instance, gold that contains more than about 20 per cent of silver is whitish in colour and is called electrum; palladium-rich gold, called porpezite, is straw-yellow in colour and is found at Korbulag, USSR. (Timofeeva, Mansurov, Goloshchukov, Stashkov, Bogdanova, and Bragin 1978). Other native gold alloys of unusual composition have not been given separate mineralogical names; thus at Primorye, USSR, a variety of native gold that contains 5 per cent antimony has recently been found (Kazachenko, Chubarov, Romanenko, Vialsov, and Basova 1979).

It is an interesting fact that silver-bearing gold fragments from primary geological sources such as quartz veins tend to contain more silver than similar fragments found in the associated secondary alluvial deposits. This is because the silver tends to be leached from the surface of the fragment whilst it is in the alluvial environment.

There is, of course, no problem in distinguishing natural gold from smelted gold since none of the latter existed in antiquity. However, it is difficult to differentiate between unmelted native gold and the melted native metal except (as with native copper) by using a combination of textural and compositional features.

Similarly, it is seldom possible to deduce the provenance of a gold artefact from its composition. However, the broad compositional differences that exist between certain groups of artefacts are often useful in establishing their source locations; for example, a specimen of alluvial gold from Bohemia contains 0.1 per cent tin, 1 per cent lead, 0.01 per cent silver, and traces of zinc, bismuth, and mercury; gold of this distinctive composition, and especially this tin/lead ratio is restricted, as far as is known, to Bohemia (Dayton 1978). Native gold obtained from the Prestea gold mine, Ghana, has been shown by electronmicroprobe analysis to contain silver, copper, lead, zinc, and, more usefully, occasionally to contain mercury and tellurium. Sutton, Havens, and Sainsbury (1973) describe a spectrochemical method for determining the composition of small fragments of native gold. This method was used to analyse about 100 small nuggets that had been obtained from a single small placer (i.e. alluvial) deposit in the Seward Peninsula of Alaska. All the nuggets were assumed to have been derived from a single, but unknown, primary source by natural weathering. Many were coated with iron and titanium oxides and some had inclusions of both silicates and sulphides; the coatings were carefully removed and each of the nuggets was then analysed. Their silver contents ranged from 3.8 to 17.8 per cent and copper from 56 p.p.m. to 8254 p.p.m. In addition, about 20 per cent of all the nuggets contained lead and the proportion of this element ranged from 38 p.p.m. to 178 p.p.m.; 4 per cent of the nuggets contained small amounts of chromium and a further 2 per cent contained both chromium and nickel. Mercury was detected in small amounts in most of the nuggets but the proportions could not be determined by the analytical technique used. These variations in composition cannot be accounted for by variations in the mineralogy of the specimens since only two out of the 188 nuggets that were examined by the petrographic microscope showed inclusions of other minerals. However, the composition of native gold is known to change when it is transferred to an alluvial environment. Consequently, the variation in the compositions of the nuggets from this single small alluvial source does not, necessarily, show that the gold in the primary location was of variable composition. It may, instead, show only that primary gold nuggets of essentially uniform composition have been in the alluvial environment for varying lengths of time and have suffered different degrees of chemical leaching.

Sutton *et al.* (1973) claim that the gold nuggets they analysed were of relatively uniform composition when compared with nuggets obtained from much larger placer deposits – deposits that could readily contain gold from more than one primary source.

Results such as those given above show clearly that great care is needed when attempting to attribute gold artefacts to specific deposits, or even to broad areas, on the basis of composition alone.

Meeks and Tite (1980) show that platinum group elements frequently occur as inclusions up to 200 μm in size in gold antiquities (Fig. 11.1). These elements occur as natural alloys of ruthenium, osmium, and iridium; they do not consist of platinum–iridium, as suggested by Whitmore and Young (1973).

The presence of these distinctive inclusions (see Platinum-group metals, below) is additional evidence that can be useful in establishing the provenance of gold. The platinum-group elements rarely occur with gold in primary (hard rock) deposits but gold is often found with platinum-group alloys in alluvial (placer) deposits. Consequently, the presence of platinoid inclusions in gold artefacts is a strong indication that the gold was originally

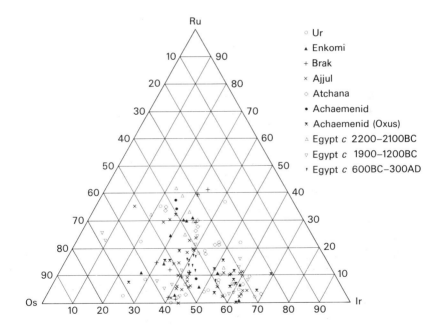

Fig. 11.1. Ternary diagram showing composition (weight per cent) of osmium–indium–ruthenium alloy inclusions in gold jewellery from the Near East and eastern Mediterranean (from Meeks and Tite 1980, Fig. 3).

obtained from an alluvial source. Unfortunately, gold placer deposits that contain platinoid fragments are quite common and source correlation can, therefore, still be extremely difficult (Ogden 1977).

The probability that an inclusion will occur on the *surface* of an artefact is small. Thus, virtually all the inclusions in a thin gold strip will be seen, whilst most of the platinoid inclusions in coins or jewellery may occur beneath the surface (Table 11.4).

Meeks and Tite (1980) used a scanning electron microscope to analyse a number of inclusions from Near East and eastern Mediterranean jewellery and coins that range in age from 3200 BC to 300 AD (Table 11.4 and Fig. 11.1). All the inclusions were alloys of Ir–Os–Ru; there were none of Pt–Ir. Inclusions found in a single object often show a wide range of composition. This is more likely to be due to the wide compositional variations that can occur in a single placer deposit rather than be an indication that the gold was derived from a number of such deposits. The composition of an isolated inclusion, therefore, need not always provide unambiguous evidence of the provenance of the enclosing gold matrix.

A statistical evaluation of the composition of a number of such inclusions can, however, provide a basis for a characterizing procedure: thus, Egyptian jewellery from the VIth Dynasty to the 1st Intermediate period contained inclusions that contained between 25 and 40 per cent of ruthenium, whilst from the XIIth Dynasty onwards the inclusions contain less than 25 per cent ruthenium. This change of composition may reflect a change from the exploitation of gold sources in the Eastern Desert to those in the Nile Region (Meeks and Tite 1980). Unfortunately, much more work is needed on the characterization of the extremely small amounts of platinoid alloys that occur in very widely scattered placer deposits.

Despite the widespread geographical occurrence of native gold, the ease with which it can be collected from alluvial sources, and its great resistance to corrosion, no gold artefacts have been found that are earlier than the end of the fifth millenium BC (Tylecote 1976). This is probably due to the virtually complete recycling of all early gold artefacts. Such recycling, and the possible mixing of gold from different localities, further complicates the problems of relating a gold artefact to its original geological source.

Native silver

Native silver occurs much less frequently and in much smaller quantities than native gold. For these reasons silver was twice as valuable as gold in the middle of the second millenium BC, that is in the period before it could be produced by the smelting of silver ores or could be obtained from the refining of lead. It is widely distributed in small amounts in the upper oxidized zones of sulphidic veins and is derived from the silver-bearing minerals acanthite (Ag_2S), proustite (Ag_3AsS_3), and pyrargyrite (Ag_3SbS_3).

Table 11.4. Data on the number of PGE inclusions found and analysed in gold jewellery and coins

provenance	period	type of object	no. of objects examined	no. of objects with inclusions	total no. of inclusions analysed	no. of inclusions with Pt
Egypt	c. 3200–2100 BC	Jewellery	6	2	6	1
Egypt	c. 1900–1200 BC	Jewellery	16	7	25	3
Egypt	c. 600 BC–AD 300	Jewellery	8	3	18	1
Ur (Tomb 1–PG 804)	c. 2500 BC	Strips	105 cm[a]	—	49	3
Ur (Tomb 2)	c. 2500 BC	Strips	55 cm[a]	—	51	2
Ur	c. 2500–1800 BC	Jewellery	14	9	27	2
Brak. Syria	c. 2200–2100 BC	Jewellery	7	6	10	—
Ajjul, Palestine	c. 1700–1500 BC	Jewellery	8	1	2	—
Atchana, Syria	c. 1500–1400 BC	Jewellery	5	2	12	—
Hittite	c. 1350 BC	Jewellery	1	0	—	—
Crete	c. 1700–1600 BC	Jewellery	3	0	—	—
Enkomi, Cyprus	c. 1400–1100 BC	Jewellery	12	2	14	1
Ialysus, Rhodes	c. 1400–1300 BC	Jewellery	3	0	—	—
Carchemish, Syria	c. 1100–600 BC	Jewellery	6	0	—	—
Archaemenid (Oxus)	c. 600–400 BC	Jewellery	6	4	43	3
Achaemenid	c. 500 BC	Jewellery	12	1	5	—
Lydia and Ionia	c. 650–550 BC	Coins (electrum)	35	12[b]	12	3
Lydia	c. 560–510 BC	Coins (gold)	7	6	34	3

After Meeks and Tite (1980).
[a] Overall length of strip examined.
[b] Inclusions in only five of these 12 coins were analysed by X-ray fluorescence.

It is usually found as wiry aggregates or small slabs, although lumps weighing up to 800 kg have been found in recent times in Canada (Kostov 1968). In AD 1477 a mass of native silver (with argentite, Ag_2S) weighing 20 tonnes was found in a mine near Freiberg (Dayton 1978). Smaller, but potentially significant, amounts of native silver have also been found in Norway, Bolivia, Mexico, and Germany. Small amounts of native silver are found in association with native copper (see above) in Michigan, USA. The metal tends to tarnish easily in the atmosphere and it rapidly loses its original, characteristic metallic lustre; it is then more difficult to identify.

The pure metal has a density of $10\ 500\ kg\ m^{-3}$ and a Mohs' hardness of $2\frac{1}{2}$ to 3; its melting temperature is 960 °C. Clean native silver is 'silver'–white in colour but tarnishes to dark grey or even black. In polished section it is brilliant white and has the highest reflectivity of any metal (94 per cent).

Native silver is generally very pure but it can contain small amounts of gold: when the gold content becomes significant the alloy is called küstelite. Native silver from Köngsberg, Norway, contains up to 10 per cent copper and the metal can also contain small amounts of mercury, lead, arsenic, antimony, and bismuth. A native silver that is rich in bismuth is found occasionally and this alloy is called chilenite.

Because of its range of possible compositions it is not always easy to differentiate native from smelted silver. It is true, however, that if the smelted silver was produced by the cupellation of silver-bearing lead metal then it usually contains much more lead than native silver. Furthermore, melted or cupelled silver is unlikely to contain much arsenic since this element volatilizes at modest temperatures.

Platinum-group metals

The platinoid metals (platinum, iridium, osmium, palladium, rhodium, and ruthenium) have similar atomic radii and readily form a wide range of native alloys with each other. They also form alloys with iron, mercury, tin, copper, and nickel. Iridium and osmium are invariably found together, either as iridosmine (with osmium ranging from 35 to 80 per cent) or as osmiridium (with osmium less than 35 per cent). The wide compositional range of these alloys is indicated by the fact that ferroplatinum contains 10 to 30 per cent iron and is magnetic; cuproplatinum contains up to 14 per cent copper; stannopalladinite has the composition Pd_3Sn_2; and nickel-platinum contains 3 per cent of nickel.

These alloys generally occur in stream gravels as small grains less than 1 mm in size but much larger fragments are occasionally found. The main locations for the platinum-group alloys are the Urals, California, South Africa, Canada, and especially Colombia where, in 1750, the 'white gold' found in the Pinto River was called plata (i.e. silver) del Pinto (and, later, platinum). Small fragments of platinum have also been found in Egypt.

All the platinum group alloys are very dense and their specific gravities range from 22.6 for platiniridium to about 14.6 for the lighter alloys. For this reason it is very easy to recover the platinoid minerals by simple washing methods and any small proportions of platinoids that occur in a gold-bearing gravel would be concentrated along with the gold flakes during gold recovery operations.

The melting temperatures of the platinoid alloys are invariably very high, ranging from about 1700 °C to 2350 °C and only rarely were primitive people able to melt them.

Alloys that contain 50 to 80 per cent platinum are steel-grey to silver-white in colour and often show a yellowish tinge. In polished section they are white, generally isotropic, and have reflectivities ranging from 65 to 72 per cent. Their hardness depends on the alloy composition but ranges from 4 to 7 on Mohs' scale (unusually high for metals).

A rare native alloy of palladium and mercury (potarite) is known only from Guyana (Schouten 1962). An alloy of platinum with tin, niggliite (Pt_2Sn_3), is found in heavy mineral concentrates from Insizwa, South Africa; polished sections of this alloy appear pinkish-cream to pale blue in reflected light.

Platinum alloys of various compositions have recently been found in meteorites (El Goresy, Nagel, and Ramdohr 1978) as nuggets or small beads but these are unlikely to have found their way into alluvial deposits (see Gold section).

Much work remains to be done to characterize fragments of the native platinoid alloys and, as yet, only broad indications of provenance can be obtained from their chemical compositions. Platinum alloy from the Pinto River was widely used in Ecuador and Colombia to make artefacts that contain from 26 to 72 per cent of the metal. However, the people of this area also seem to have been able to make artificial alloys of the platinoid metals with gold and silver (Tylecote 1976) and it does not follow that all their artefacts were necessarily made from native alloys. Since the platinoid-group alloys are sometimes found in the same alluvial deposits as native gold it is not surprising that artefacts of native gold (whether melted or not) occasionally show small inclusions of the platinoid alloys; see Gold section (Whitmore and Young 1973; Ogden 1977). Thus, Lydian coins contain small, rounded, or angular silver-white inclusions measuring 80 to 150 μm in diameter. These inclusions have been shown by electron microprobe analysis, to contain approximately 60 per cent platinum, 40 per cent iridium, and small amounts of osmium. They also contain trace amounts of tin, ruthenium, rhodium, and nickel. The inclusions were, therefore, the rare alloy platiniridium, generally found only in gold placer deposits in the Urals, Brazil, and Burma. Identical platiniridium inclusions have also been found in an Achaemenian earring and in a stamp seal dating from the fifth century

BC. A fluted gold beaker, large earrings, a necklace, gold beads, and a bracelet from the grave of Queen Shub-ad at Ur (about 3000–2500 BC) contain similar platiniridium inclusions. In fact, Ogden (1977) claims that in many categories of gold artefact platinoid inclusions are extremely common, especially in Egyptian goldwork from the twelfth Dynasty onwards and the general frequency of these platinoid inclusions indicates the extent to which the gold was obtained from alluvial sources.

Native iron

There are two distinct primary sources of native iron – meteoric and terrestrial. The ancient name for iron has been interpreted as 'celestial metal' or 'metal from heaven'; whether this is true or not, it is a fact that meteoric iron is found scattered in small quantities over the Earth's surface. All this meteoric iron occurs in the form of alloys with nickel. It has been calculated by Zimmer (1916, p. 335) that approximately 250 tonnes of meteoric iron were known to exist in museums and other collections; see for example, Rickard (1941). (This compares with the 6000 tonnes of native copper thought to have been used in a similar time span in a single area of North America p. 333.) Natural iron–nickel alloys occur in two forms: kamacite, containing 6–9 per cent of nickel, and taenite, with about 48 per cent nickel. These two phases generally occur together and give rise to distinctive eutectic structures (Fig. 11.2). Various proportions of these two phases (along with non-metallic impurities) result in the overall nickel contents of meteoric iron varying from about 4 to 26 per cent.

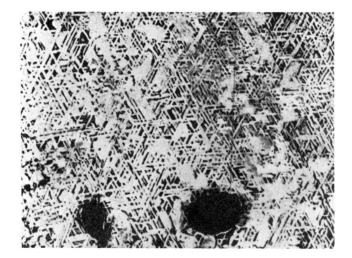

Fig. 11.2. Meteoritic iron showing Widmanstatten structure (from Kostov 1968, Fig. 69).

The distinctive texture of much of the meteoric iron alloys, coupled with the unusual chemical composition (which is not approached by any known ancient smelted iron) generally serve to distinguish meteoric native iron from smelted iron. Furthermore, specimens of meteoric iron occasionally contain distinctive small inclusions of troilite (FeS) and cohenite (Fe, Ni-carbide) that are not found in other forms of iron or in smelted iron. Meteoric iron alloys are hard (about 230 Vickers hardness) and very difficult to work with primitive tools. Small flakes were broken off the larger natural fragments with stone hammers and were then set in bone or walrus ivory (Tylecote 1976), and used as cutting tools by the lithic peoples of north and west Greenland. These flakes of alloy retain their distinctive eutectic structure. The density of iron ranges from 7300 to 7900 kg m^{-3}, depending on its composition, and its colour varies from steel grey to black. Table 11.5 gives the range of composition of iron–nickel artefacts that were found in pre-Iron Age contexts and presumably, therefore, made from meteoric iron alloys. Other iron artefacts found in pre-Iron Age contexts do not contain nickel and must, therefore, either be wrongly dated, made from iron formed accidentally during copper smelting, or made from native iron of terrestrial origin.

Native iron of terrestrial origin is found in only a few places. It usually occurs (Kostov 1968) where igneous intrusions have cut coal seams, providing the temperature and the reducing environment needed to convert some of the original iron-bearing minerals into globules of metallic iron. Since it is very difficult to differentiate between terrestrially-formed native iron and the iron formed by primitive smelting operations, there is no clear evidence that terrestrial iron was ever used by ancient peoples.

Fragments of early iron artefacts have occasionally been found incorporated into later iron objects (Piakowski 1960) and these inclusions may well have been of meteoritic origin. For example, an iron axehead that consisted of 4 per cent nickel, overall, was found to contain inclusions that themselves contained 8 to 10 per cent of nickel.

Table 11.5. Range of composition of meteoritic iron artefacts

element	per cent
Fe	88.0–92.5
Ni	7.5–11.8
Co	Trace–0.5
Cu	Trace–0.02

After Tylecote (1976).

Other native metals

Other native metals have been found by mineralogists. None of these is known to have been used intentionally by primitive peoples but they may have been accidentally incorporated into ancient artefacts made of smelted metal.

Native nickel has been found in small amounts in the nickel-bearing laterite of New Caledonia. Further, a nickel–iron alloy (awaruite) that contains up to 67 per cent nickel has been found in Oregon, USA, where it is thought to occur as an alteration product from a peridotite rock.

Very small amounts of native zinc and native tin have been found by geologists but are of no known archaeological significance. The zinc is a rare product of volcanic activity whilst much of the tin is thought to have formed by the reduction of cassiterite (SnO_2) by forest fires, for example in the tin fields of Nigeria and south-east Asia. Very small amounts of native tin (with lead and iron) have also been found in Greenland in pegmatites and hydrothermal veins (Karup-Møller 1978).

Native, liquid mercury was known to the ancient peoples of Spain and China, where it was called 'liquid silver'. It also occurs as a native amalgam and can combine with up to 40 per cent of gold (gold amalgam), 35 per cent palladium (potarite), or with silver (köngsbergite). Mercury, both native and prepared metal, was used in BC 210 by the Chinese to depict oceans and rivers on maps (Tylecote 1976).

Native lead is extremely rare. However, it has been found – principally at Långban, Sweden – where crystalline masses weighing up to 50 kg have been located. There are no known instances of its use. Small amounts of lead do, however, occur incorporated in some of the other native metals.

The natural change in the $^{207}Pb/^{206}Pb$ ratio over a period of a few thousand years is negligible: furthermore, the chemical properties of the lead isotopes are nearly identical and, consequently, these isotope ratios are not affected by chemical processes such as smelting nor by physical processes such as melting, casting, or hammering. The lead isotope ratios also tend to be specific to one geological occurrence and these ratios can provide valuable information regarding the sources of native metals.

Unfortunately, metal (whether native or smelted) was re-used many times by ancient people and, during re-use, metals from various sources – native and smelted, or metal from different geographical or geological occurrences – have often been mixed. Coinage metal was especially liable to be mixed in this way.

Some artefact minerals

Turquoise

The term 'turquoise' is used by mineralogists to describe a blue, bluish-green, or light green mineral having the general composition $(Cu, Zn)(Al, Fe)_6 (PO_4)_4(OH)_8.5H_2O$. The name is used in a more restricted sense for the copper-aluminium end-member of that series which has the composition $Cu Al_6(PO_4)_4(OH)_8.4H_2O$. A copper-iron end-member of the series, having the composition $CuFe_6(PO_4)_4(OH)_8.5H_2O$, is called chalcosiderite, and the zinc-aluminium end-member is called faustite. The mineral series occurs as dense masses or concretionary aggregates and is formed by the action of surface waters on some aluminium-rich rocks. The hardness of the minerals in the series ranges from about 4.5 to 6 on Mohs' scale and their densities range from 2920 to 3220 kg m^{-3}.

The archaeologist, on the other hand, uses the term turquoise for a whole range of blue and blue-green minerals that include the true turquoise of the mineralogist as well as malachite, azurite, chrysocolla, other green copper-bearing minerals, and green garnet.

The name turquoise means 'turkish', i.e. obtained from Turkey, but the finest turquoise in the ancient world was the sky-blue variety obtained from the Nishapur district of Persia. The early Egyptians obtained 'turquoise' from Sinai but this material was of poor quality and quickly lost its colour. In North America turquoise was used extensively in the Classic Period (AD 100–900) and formed an important part of the trade in luxury mineral products (Weigand, Harbottle, and Sayre 1977; see also Gettens 1962). It has also been used widely in Zanskar, Ladakh.

As with other minerals there are, almost invariably, significant differences in the trace element compositions of turquoise specimens derived from different geological localities. If it can be shown that the differences between specimens from different locations exceed the differences between specimens from the same source, it may then be possible to use the trace element compositions to trace a turquoise artefact to its source.

Weigand *et al.* (1977) and Sigleo (1975) have tried to correlate North American turquoise artefacts with probable source localities by using the results of detailed, multi-element neutron activation analyses. In addition, they used X-ray diffraction techniques to identify the minerals that are included under the archaeological term 'turquoise'. Almost 1000 specimens, including rock fragments, beads, amulets, mosaic blanks, and the 'waste' material found in workshops where turquoise artefacts were produced have been analysed by these methods (Weigand *et al.* 1977). Some turquoise specimens temporarily changed colour after bombardment by neutrons and a few of the specimens were reduced to a black powder.

The copper oxide content of pure, stoichiometric turquoise is 9.8 per cent but values ranging from 3 to 10 per cent were measured by Weigand and co-workers in various 'turquoise' specimens. The concentrations of other elements such as arsenic, scandium, manganese, thorium, lanthanum, iron, cobalt, europium, antimony, zinc, sodium, potassium, rubidium, cerium, and phosphorus were also determined (Weigand *et al.* 1977). The results obtained from the different specimens were compared by means of a cluster-analysis procedure in which similar specimens are grouped together. This work showed that the analytical procedure has a high degree of reproducibility since repeated analyses of a single specimen gave closely similar results. Furthermore, results from different specimens derived from a single mine tended to cluster together. Specimens from different mines in the same general locality, however, varied significantly in chemical composition and specimens from widely separated areas tended to differ even more markedly from each other. The analytical results obtained from turquoise artefacts found in specific hoards tended to form clusters that matched those obtained from rock specimens obtained from single sources. However, the results are far from being conclusive and the authors warn that many more analyses of both geological specimens and of artefacts are needed before it will be possible to draw firm conclusions about the provenance of turquoise artefacts.

Sigleo (1975) reported the results obtained from the analysis by INAA of 24 turquoise specimens from various 'mines' in south-western USA and also the results from 13 disc-shaped beads from a Gila Butte Phase (AD 500–700) site at Snaketown, Arizona (Table 11.6). The analyses of both mine and artefact samples fell into two groups (A and B) and Sigleo concluded, on the basis of a multivariate statistical analysis, that the Snaketown artefacts all came from the Himalaya 'mine' – a series of saucer-shaped sites 10 m wide by 2 m deep – in California. The Crescent mine sample is clearly unrelated. This conclusion was unexpected since there are many nearer sources of

Table 11.6. Trace element data on the Arizona turquoise bead source

element (p.p.m.)	Snaketown group A	Snaketown group B	unclassi-fied	Himalaya group A	Himalaya group B	Crescent
Co	1.67	1.78	1.95	1.30	1.78	1003.0
Cr	1.66	1.44	1.20	1.54	2.30	67.3
Eu	0.26	0.32	0.28	0.27	0.63	n.d.
Sb	2.10	2.90	1.43	1.76	2.10	4.66
Sc	35.1	101.5	15.1	36.2	106.4	65.3
Ta	n.d.	n.d.	n.d.	n.d.	n.d.	326.0

n.d. = not detected.
After Sigleo (1975).

turquoise; the results, therefore, are useful in determining aboriginal procurement systems and exchange patterns.

Hypersthene

This is an orthopyroxene ($Fe_2Si_2O_6$) that generally occurs as massive, granular fragments in basic or ultrabasic rocks. Hypersthene seldom exists in its pure, end-member form since gradual replacement of Fe^{2+} by Mg^{2+} ions gives rise to bronzite (with 10 to 30 per cent of the $FeSiO_3$ molecule), and enstatite ($Mg_2Si_2O_6$). It is distinctly pleochroic in shades of green and red. Its hardness ranges from 5 to 6 on Mohs' scale and its density from about 3200 kg m^{-3} to 4000 kg m^{-3}.

A number of commemorative scarabs of Amenophis III have been examined by Overweel (1964). Some of these were made from high quality, natural hypersthene; some were made from enstatite or bronzite; and others from an impure hypersthene containing talc and other minerals. The scarabs were examined by X-ray powder diffraction methods and under the microscope. Some scarabs were covered with a glazing material and were difficult to examine, others were coated with a thin alteration layer of low refractive index (1.57). The overall chemical compositions of the scarabs are confused because of the presence of original impurities such as talc and plagioclase feldspar and of secondary impurities such as sand grains and halite (common salt).

Overweel (1964) claimed that the hypersthene of the scarabs probably originated from a hypersthene-steatite rock, since a small magic stele, which is much younger than the scarabs, was carved from a rock that consisted partly of steatite and partly of hypersthene.

Lapis lazuli

This is an opaque stone that consists of a mixture of several minerals: the principal component is lazurite, essentially (Na, Ca)$_4$ (SO$_4$, S, Cl) (AlSiO$_4$)$_3$. Lapis lazuli often contains speckled grains of yellow pyrite and veins of white calcite in addition to lazurite, and its density ranges from 2700 to 2900 kg m^{-3}. Other components include pyroxenes, amphiboles, and and micas. The intense purple-blue or azure-blue colour of lazurite is modified in lapis lazuli by the presence of the other minerals.

The mineral occurs in only a relatively small number of geological locations (Herrmann 1966), and is almost invariably found associated with marble deposits. The ancient mines at Firgamu in Badakshan, north-east Afghanistan, the most important locality, are still productive (Sinkankas 1966; Sariandi 1971). Other occurrences are known as Slyudyanka, near Lake Baikal, and Uzbekistan, USSR; at Ovalle in Chile; and at various localities in the USA, Burma, Pakistan, Nubia, and possibly Egypt (Herrmann 1966).

Objects carved from lapis lazuli are not uncommon among archaeological finds; the stone seems to have been used initially for cylinder and stamp seals. Later, it was used for jewellery, amulets, small vessels, and dagger handles, and as an inlay material on mosaics, plaques, and tablets. Later still, powdered lapis lazuli was used as the vivid blue pigment, ultramarine. Well known examples of lapis lazuli objects include a Roman spread eagle found near Naples and the lapis and gold 'ram in a thicket' found at Ur.

Some other minerals

The gemstones – diamond, ruby, sapphire, emerald, alexandrite (green chrysoberyl) – and the many semi-precious stones form a subject on their own and cannot be treated here. They have been used for ornamental purposes since earliest times, their colour, clarity, sparkle, and extreme hardness and resistance to corrosion making them particularly attractive. Alluvial diamonds have been mined in India for millenia; the Saxons used garnet in brooches, as demonstrated by the Sutton Hoo, Suffolk, burial ship, while the Moghul emperors used every available ornamental stone to decorate their palaces and mosques (Bimson, La Neice, and Leese 1982).

Perhaps the largest group in the semi-precious category consists of the silica minerals. Quartz occurs in several varieties: rock crystal (clear), amethyst (purplish), citrine (yellow), and cairngorm (smoky). The chalcedonies include banded agate, chrysoprase, carnelian, onyx, sardonyx, bloodstone or heliotrope, jasper, and others, and the amorphous opal is a highly valued cloudy stone.

Artefacts have also been made of augite, crocidolite, and fluorite, especially the purplish blue-john variety used for a multitude of vessels and small figures. Malachite (green copper carbonate) has been used for jewellery and small ornaments, as has the blue copper carbonate azurite; mica was used for small 'windows'; and massive graphite in Ceylon has been carved into bowls and ladles. Magnetite was used as a lodestone, and even galena (lead sulphide) was utilized in North America. Artefacts of this material of Middle Woodland Hopewellian Copena age, associated with obsidian and copper objects, were analysed by atomic absorption for their trace elements Sb, Cu, and Ag by Walthall, Stow, and Karson (1980), who regard the Upper Mississippi Valley as their most likely source.

References

Bimson, M., La Neice, S., and Leese, M. (1982). The characterisation of mounted garnets. *Archaeometry* **24**, 51–8.
Dayton, I. (1978). *Minerals, metals, glazing and man.* Harrap, London.

El Goresy, A., Nagel, K., and Ramdohr, P. (1978). Fremdlinge and their noble relatives. *Geochimica et Cosmochimica Acta* (Supplement) **10**, 1279–1303.

Gettens, R. J. (1962). Minerals in art and archaeology. *Report of the Board of Regents of the Smithsonian Institution* **1961**, 551–68.

Herrmann, G. (1966). *The source, distribution, history and use of lapis lazuli in Western Asia from the earliest times to the end of the Seleucid era.* D. Phil. thesis Oxford University.

Karup-Møller, S. (1978). The ore minerals of the Ilimaussaq intrusion: their mode of occurrence and their conditions of formation. *Bulletin Geological Survey of Greenland* **127**, 1–51.

Kazachenko, V. T., Chubarov, V. M., Romanenko, I. M., Vialsov, L. N., and Basova, G. V. (1979). Ore minerals in a polymetallic deposit of Primorye, USSR. *American Mineralogist* **64**, 432–5.

Kostov, I. (1968). *Mineralogy.* Oliver and Boyd, London.

Maddin, R., Stechwheeler, T., and Muhly, J. D. (1980). Distinguishing artefacts made of native copper. *Journal of Archaeological Science* **7**, 211–25.

Meeks, N. D. and Tite, M. S. (1980). The analysis of platinum-group element inclusions in gold antiquities. *Journal of Archaeological Science* **7**, 267–75.

Mellink, M. J. (1965). Archaeology in Asia Minor. *American Journal of Archaeology* **69**, 133–49.

Ogden, J. M. (1977). Platinum-group metal inclusions in ancient gold artefacts. *Journal. History of Metallurgical Society* **11**, 53–72.

Overweel, C. J. (1964). A petrography of twenty-three commemorative scarabs of Amenophis III. *Oudbeidkundige Mededeflingen van het Rijksmuseum van Oudbeiden te Leiden.* **45**.

Patterson, C. C. (1971). Native copper, silver, and gold accessible to early metallurgists. *American Antiquity* **36**, 286–321.

Piakowski, J. (1960). An interesting example of early technology: a socketed axe from Wietrzno-Bobrka in the Carpathians. *Journal of the Iron and Steel Institute* **194**, 336–40.

Rickard, T. A. (1941). The use of meteoric iron. *Journal of the Royal Anthropological Institute* **71**, 55–65.

Sariandi, V. I. (1971). The lapis lazuli route in the Ancient East. *Archaeology* **24**, 12–15.

Schouten, C. (1962). *Determination tables for ore microscopy.* Elsevier, Amsterdam.

Sigleo, A. C. (1975). Turquoise mine and artefact correlation for Snaketown Site, Arizona. *Science* **189**, 459–60.

Sinkankas, J. (1966). *Mineralogy.* Van Nostrand Reinhold, New York.

Sutton, A. L., Havens, R. G., and Sainsbury, C. L. (1973). A spectrochemical method for determining the composition of native gold. *Journal of Research United States Geological Survey* **1**, 301–7.

Timofeeva, T. S., Mansurov, M.-M., Goloshchukov, M. M., Stashkov, G. M., Bogdanova, L. A., and Bragin, I. K. (1978). Palladous gold from Kochbulag. *Uzbekskii Geologicheskii Zhurnal* 1978(5), 40–2.

Tylecote, R. F. (1976). *A history of metallurgy.* The Metals Society, London.

Walthall, J. A., Stow, S. H., and Karson, M. J. (1980). Copena galena: source identification and analysis. *American Antiquity* **45**, 21–42.

Weigand, P. C., Harbottle, G., and Sayre, E. V. (1977). Turquoise sources and source analysis: Mesoamerica and the south-western USA. In: T. K. Earle and J. E. Ericson (ed.): *Exchange systems in prehistory.* Academic Press, London. 15–34.

Whitmore, F. E. and Young, W. J. (1973). Application of the laser microprobe and electron microprobe in the analysis of platiniridium inclusions in gold. In: W. J. Young (ed.): *Application of science in examination of works of art.* Boston Museum of Fine Arts, 88–95.

Zimmer, G. F. (1916). The use of meteoritic iron by primitive man. *Journal of the Iron and Steel Institute* **94**, 306–56.

Author index

Subject and geographical index